WITHDRAWN
HARVARD LIBRARY
WITHDRAWN

The Rhetoric of Sir Garfield Todd

Studies in Rhetoric and Religion 2

EDITORIAL BOARD

MARTIN J. MEDHURST
Editorial Board Chair
Baylor University

VANESSA B. BEASLEY
University of Georgia

RANDELL L. BYTWERK
Calvin College

MICHAEL W. CASEY
Pepperdine University

JAMES M. FARRELL
University of New Hampshire

JAMES A. HERRICK
Hope College

MICHAEL J. HYDE
Wake Forest University

THOMAS M. LESSL
University of Georgia

The Rhetoric of Sir Garfield Todd

Christian Imagination and the Dream of an African Democracy

MICHAEL W. CASEY

BAYLOR UNIVERSITY PRESS

© 2007 by Baylor University Press
Waco, Texas 76798
All Rights Reserved. No part of this publication may be reproduced, stored in a retrieval system, or transmitted, in any form or by any means, electronic, mechanical, photocopying, recording or otherwise, without the prior permission in writing of Baylor University Press.

Scripture quotations are from the *New Revised Standard Version Bible*, copyright 1989, Division of Christian Education of the National Council of the Churches of Christ in the United States of America. Used by permission. All rights reserved.

Cover design by Pam Poll
Cover illustration of Garfield Todd was used by permission of Judith Todd.
Book design by Diane Smith

All photos supplied by and used by permission of Judith Todd, Disciples of Christ Historical Society, and Rhodes House Oxford University.

Library of Congress Cataloging-in-Publication Data

Casey, Michael W.
  The rhetoric of Sir Garfield Todd : Christian imagination and the dream of an African democracy / Michael W. Casey.
       p. cm. -- (Studies in rhetoric and religion ; 2)
  Includes a selection of Sir Garfield Todd's sermons and speeches.
  Includes bibliographical references and index.
  ISBN 978-1-932792-86-7 (cloth/hardcover : alk. paper)
  1. Todd, Garfield, 1908---Language. 2. Todd, Garfield, 1908---Oratory. 3. Rhetoric--Political aspects--Zimbabwe--History--20th century. 4. Christianity and politics--Zimbabwe--History--20th century. 5. Democracy--Zimbabwe--History--20th century. 6. Zimbabwe--Politics and government--1890-1965. 7. Zimbabwe--Politics and government--1965-1979. 8. Speeches, addresses, etc. I. Todd, Garfield, 1908- Selections. II. Title.

DT2979.T63C37 2007
968.9'03092--dc22
                              2006034403

Printed in the United States of America on acid-free paper with a minimum of 30% pcw content.

For Judy and Allan

CONTENTS

Acknowledgments		xi
Introduction	Sir Garfield Todd, Rhetoric, and Zimbabwe's Struggle for Democracy	1
1	Democratic Disciples	15
2	The Democratic Missionary	25
3	Moving toward Democracy: Todd as the Limited Democratic Politician	39
4	Todd the Prophetic: The Radical Democrat	69
5	The "Horrible Speech": Todd's Effort to End White Supremacy	91
6	Todd's Narrative Rhetoric: The Preacher of Democratic Virtues	101
Conclusion: Fighting the Good Fight		117

Sermon Texts

Conference Sermon	127
The Unfinished Task of Christian Missions in Southern Africa	136
Christian Unity, Christ's Prayer	145
Our Timeless Missionary Mandate	156
The Church Knows No Boundaries	165
My World and Its Need	171

CONTENTS

Political Speeches

First Campaign Speech	181
Maiden Speech—June 3 and 4, 1946	186
Speech on Federation—June 23, 1952	198
1956 Congress Address by the Prime Minister	208
Franchise Speech	217
Immorality Debate Speech	227
Reply to the Toast "Southern Rhodesia" by the Prime Minister of Southern Rhodesia at the St. Andrew's Night Banquet at Bulawayo—Saturday, November 30, 1957	238

Prophetic Speeches

Statement against the "Colour Bar"—March 10, 1959	245
After Independence, What? Political Imperatives	247
Letter Delivered to Secretary of State for Commonwealth Relations—July 26, 1960	260
United Nations Speech 1962	262
Can Christianity Survive In Africa?	282
Danger! Men Thinking!—The First Feetham Lecture	286
1977 UN Speech	293
International Center of Indianapolis Luncheon on Basic Issues	305
University of Otago Graduation Speech	312
"The Speech that Says it All—in Silence"—The Second Feetham Lecture	318
The Tübingen Festival Address	324
Keynote Speech at the Celebration of Joshua Nkomo's 72nd Birthday and 40th Wedding Anniversary	336

Concluding Sermon

Reflections on Fifty-four Years of Service	343
Notes	347
Bibliography	371
Index	381

ACKNOWLEDGMENTS

Many people made this book possible. First I would like to thank the late Sir Garfield Todd for answering innumerable questions about his life, career, and his speaking. Sir Garfield also supplied many of the speech texts used in the book. Judith Todd's support has been indispensable, especially her willingness to convey messages to her parents via e-mail. Allan Todd, Garfield's nephew and his wife Majorie Todd, were gracious hosts while I visited Wellington, New Zealand, and Allan supplied indispensable information and background materials on Garfield and Grace. Susan Paul, who is writing Sir Garfield's official biography, also supplied copies of several important speech texts. I owe a special thanks to Pepperdine's Seaver Research Council and to Lee Kats, Associate Provost of Research, for granting me release time, which helped me find the time to complete the book and for granting me the Manchester-Harris College, Oxford University Fellowship, which enabled me to research at the Rhodes House Library, a part of Oxford's Bodleian Library. Lucy McCann, the archivist at Bodleian Library of Commonwealth and African Studies at Rhodes House was extremely helpful in locating relevant materials on Todd. Sue Killorian, librarian at Harris-Manchester College, Oxford University, was gracious in helping me plan my research at Oxford and at the British Library. I also owe a special thanks to Terrance Ranger for giving me permission to use his papers located at Rhodes House and telling me about the Roy Welensky papers, which are indispensable to anyone researching topics on Colonial Rhodesia. Janet Horncy and the librarians at the Alexander Turnbull Library, Wellington, were helpful beyond what any researcher would expect. Clinton Holloway and Lynn Morgan found relevant sources, speech texts, and photographs at the Disciples of Christ Historical Society, Nashville, Tennessee. Also Don Haymes, theological librarian at Christian Theological

Seminary alerted me to some key sources. Melinda Raine, librarian at Pepperdine University, and Laurie Kram, librarian at UCLA, located transcripts of Todd's UN speeches. Melissa Nichols helped innumerable times with my many interlibrary loan requests. Travis Wesley, a reference specialist at the Library of Congress, helped me locate copies of the *African Daily News* and other Zimbabwean newspapers held there. The staff at the British Library also helped me locate copies of Zimbabwean newspapers held at the Colindale facility. John and Susan Sweetman, Ron O'Grady and Roger Russ helped in finding resources in Auckland. The Institute for Faith and Learning at Baylor University provided a fellowship that enabled me to complete a large portion of the manuscript. I also would like to thank the undergraduate Crane Scholars at Baylor University for their reactions to earlier versions of the introduction. I also presented some of the ideas in the book at Lipscomb University through the school's Center for International Peace and Justice. I would like to thank Don Cole, Richard Goode, and Craig Bledsoe for that opportunity. In addition, I presented an early version of some of the ideas at the Christianity and Human Rights: The Fourth Annual Lilly Fellows Program National Research Conference, in Birmingham, Alabama, November 13, 2004. I owe a special debt of thanks to my former student Nicola Kaiwai and her parents Helen and Peter Kaiwai for being gracious hosts during my stay in Wellington. Finally I also owe a special debt to Marty Medhurst, the editor of the Rhetoric and Religion series, and Carey Newman, the editor of Baylor University Press, who helped bring the book to fruition as I faced some difficult health problems near the completion of the book. The book would not have appeared except for their essential help and belief in the project.

>*Conference Sermon*. Reprinted with the permission of the *New Zealand Christian*.

>*Our Timeless Missionary Mandate*. Used by permission of the Disciples of Christ Historical Society.

>*After Independence, What? Political Imperatives*. Used by permission of the Disciples of Christ Historical Society.

>*Speech at the International Center of Indianapolis Luncheon on Basic Issues*. Used by permission of the Disciples of Christ Historical Society.

The Church Knows No Boundaries. Copyright *Christian Standard* and reprinted with permission.

Reflections on Fifty-four Years of Service. Copyright *Christian Standard* and reprinted with permission.

1956 Congress Address by the Prime Minister. Used by permission of Rhodes House, Bodleian Library, Oxford University.

Letter Delivered to Secretary of State for Commonwealth Relations July 26 1960. Used by permission of Rhodes House, Bodleian Library, Oxford University.

Keynote Speech at the Celebration of Joshua Nkomo's 72nd Birthday and 40th Wedding Anniversary. Used by permission of Terrance Ranger and Rhodes House, Bodleian Library, Oxford University.

Introduction

SIR GARFIELD TODD, RHETORIC, AND ZIMBABWE'S STRUGGLE FOR DEMOCRACY

"Rise Sir Garfield—'protect the poor and punish the wicked,'" so stated Queen Elizabeth II. The motto of the Degree of Knight Bachelor, the oldest order of chivalry, is an appropriate description for the life of Reginald Stephen Garfield Todd. Sir Garfield Todd (1908–2002) led a remarkable and significant life: missionary to Africa starting in 1934, the first missionary to become a head of state (prime minister of Southern Rhodesia in 1953), imprisoned by Ian Smith for his outspoken criticism of racist policies in the 1960s and 1970s, awarded a papal medal by Pope Paul VI in 1973, and knighted by Queen Elizabeth II in 1986 for his lifelong support of African rights, freedom, and democracy.

Despite numerous resources of people and goods, Zimbabwe, and Africa in general, has had difficulties developing democratic traditions and entering into its rightful place on the world stage in this postcolonial age. Surprisingly, there are resources and traditions in its history upon which Zimbabwe can draw to develop a real democratic state. Garfield Todd's long career (1934–2002) spanned the most significant changes in modern Zimbabwe. He brought a democratic sensibility that was transformed from paternalism to a prophetic stance. His example, thought, and rhetoric provided ways to conceive a democratic state that welcomed people from all backgrounds and affirmed basic human rights. This unique preacher-politician used his power of persuasion through key speeches to articulate, spread, and convert others to this democratic sensibility. He gave speeches in important and obscure venues all over the world as he spread his gospel of democracy. Unlike many politicians, however, he ever remained a preacher of the gospel as well as democracy. And because of the religious tradition from which he came, he saw both gospels spreading good news and the hope of the good life for all people.

Previous scholarship on Todd, while noting his Christian background, has incorrectly attributed his support for human rights to British political liberalism.[1] Todd, a native of New Zealand, came from a politically conservative family and never lived in Britain. Dickson Mungazi mistakenly claims Todd embraced the "Asquith-Lloyd George [liberal] philosophy."[2] Ruth Weiss rightly notes that Todd "represented the true values of that western Christian civilisation, which racist whites mistakenly thought they defended,"[3] but she does not explore how his religious heritage played a key role in his rhetoric and understanding of human rights. Todd, while considered liberal, drew from his Christian perspective, especially from his lifelong denominational tradition, the New Zealand Churches of Christ. Historically connected to the American Stone-Campbell tradition (Disciples of Christ, conservative Christian Churches, and a cappella Churches of Christ), the New Zealand Churches of Christ were an ecumenically minded group interested in reasonable Christianity and education. Throughout his entire career, Todd tried to build coalitions with like-minded people and appeal to the best interests of others—even his enemies—believing that reason could win over prejudiced and skeptical racist whites and build a multiracial society. Furthermore, Todd's rhetoric and oratory were firmly grounded in his Christian stance and nurtured in his "Campbellite" heritage in the New Zealand Churches of Christ. If it were not for his particular religious heritage and its distinctive theology, style, and ways of thinking, Todd would never have been the speaker he was or made his mark in history.

Todd's outstanding skill at oratory cut across and enabled his entire public career and his support for human rights. Both friends and foes of Sir Garfield Todd testified to his public speaking ability. Historian Miles Hudson observed that Todd "was a brilliant speaker in public (one of the comparatively few orators in recent Rhodesian history)."[4] Chester Woodhall, a British missionary to Africa, praised Todd's preaching in the 1970s. Woodhall offered that Todd "was an electrifying speaker and really made the pages of the Bible come alive as he preached on the oneness of all people—black, brown, and white—in Jesus Christ. In segregationist Rhodesia this was a revolutionary message."[5] Todd's fellow liberal politician and friend Hardwicke Holderness described Todd's political campaign oratory during his tenure as prime minister of Southern Rhodesia:

He had a commanding platform presence—tall, clean-cut, powerful build; shock of dark hair—and a command of the English language and delivery which no doubt owed a lot to his training as a preacher but, adapted to dealing with the whole range of national affairs . . . [his demeanor] seemed to be sufficiently down to earth and appropriate for politics; and heckling and hostile questions usually provided fuel for the best part of the performance—highly intelligent, instantaneous and humorous. It was a delight to listen to.[6]

The *Sunday Mail*, a local Rhodesian paper, commented on the 1946 Legislative Assembly: "Of the new speakers, Mr. R. S. G. Todd takes the palm. He has a sure, broad, well-informed humanitarian outlook and his way of address is attractive."[7] Emory Ross, a Disciples of Christ preacher, missionary to the Congo, and lifelong friend of Albert Schweitzer, said in 1954, "I have known Mr. Todd for 15 years. He has great ability. He has a fine mind and a cultured heart . . . and [I] would say without any hesitation that he is a really great preacher."[8]

Todd, as we shall see, transformed the role of the Rhodesian prime minister into a rhetorical presidency. He used his speaking ability and the opportunities the position afforded (the bully pulpit) to press his political agenda. He tried to transform Rhodesian society into a multiracial state in which white prejudice ended and blacks became a fully engaged democratic citizenry. Todd participated in the same phenomenon identified by political scientists as the rhetorical presidency and by rhetoricians as "presidential rhetoric." Todd seized the opportunities that the media gave to persons with rhetorical capabilities, and he ended up using his rhetoric in ways he did not anticipate as he became a prophetic voice against racism.

The New Zealand-born Todd and his wife Jean Grace Isobel Wilson Todd (1911–2001) were sent as missionaries to the Dadaya Mission in Southern Rhodesia by the New Zealand Churches of Christ in 1934.[9] Following his Disciples namesake, American president James A. Garfield, the preacher became a politician. Like Garfield, Todd became a head of state when he became prime minister of Southern Rhodesia in 1953, after Sir Godfrey Huggins vacated the position to become the prime minister of the newly created Central African Federation made up by the British colonies Northern Rhodesia, Southern Rhodesia, and Nyasaland.

Educated at Glen Leith Theological College in Dunedin, Todd adopted the view of Glen Leith's principal, A. L. Haddon, that life was a unity from God and should not be divided into the secular and the sacred. Todd saw his political career as an extension of Christianity. First elected to parliament in 1946, Todd became an advocate for modest improvements for black Africans in education, jobs, and voting rights and was known for his eloquence as a speaker. While prime minister, Todd made the first of several international trips during which he met important American and Canadian politicians: U. S. Secretary of State John Foster Dulles, Canadian prime minister John Diefenbaker, and others. Such contacts became critical as Todd lobbied for support of African nationalism in the 1960s and 1970s.

After Todd was removed as prime minister in 1958 for moving too quickly for African rights, he began to speak out against the racist white establishment and to argue for black majority rule. In 1962, 1964, and 1977, Todd delivered important speeches before the United Nations on behalf of the African nationalist cause. Fearing Todd's eloquence, in 1965, just before Rhodesia's Unilateral Declaration of Independence from Britain, Ian Smith put Todd under house arrest for a year. In January 1972, after Todd and his daughter Judith had successfully campaigned against an agreement Smith made with Britain that would have kept Smith in power, Todd was arrested, imprisoned for thirty-six days, and then restricted to his ranch until June 1976. Todd was not allowed to communicate with anyone directly, so Grace wrote all letters to the outside world. During both detentions, international outcry especially by British, Kiwi (the New Zealand prime minister), and American leaders (Senator Edward Kennedy and others) was instrumental in obtaining his freedom. All through the 1970s, and at considerable risk, the Todds supported the Africans in their civil war against Smith by supplying food and clothing. Todd also gave information to the British Intelligence Service about South Africa's illegal economic support of Smith's regime by observing the train shipments that came by his ranch. Both actions were capital offenses.

In 1976, Todd joined Joshua Nkomo's delegation at the Geneva talks on Rhodesia/Zimbabwe. In 1978, Todd chaired an Amnesty International Conference in Stockholm.[10] Shortly before the declaration of independence, Todd was arrested and accused of treason for helping the guerrillas. If the white-backed candidate had won the election, Todd probably would have been hanged.[11] After Zimbabwe's independence in 1980, Todd was a senator in Mugabe's elected government, but he retired in 1985, as he grew critical of Mugabe's repressive tactics. Todd received honorary doctorates from Butler University, Eureka College, Minnesota Bible College, and Otago University.

Todd remained active in mission work during his entire political career. He was the Superintendent of the Dadaya Mission from 1934 until 1953. He remained on the Dadaya governing board after 1953, and from 1963 to 1985 he was the board chair.[12] Todd, true to his religious heritage, was active in many ecumenical efforts. For example, in 1967, during the struggle for African independence, Todd brought the Dadaya Mission and the Churches of Christ into the Zimbabwe Christian Council (ZCC), an ecumenical organization that supported human rights during and after the civil war. Todd soon became an active member of the executive committee when he was not in detention. Todd wrote various ZCC official positions that criticized settlement proposals that were not equitable for blacks, urged reconciliation between the warring parties, and pleaded for the elimination of the death penalty for prisoners of war. With his relationship with Nkomo, Mugabe, and other nationalist leaders, Todd's influence carried weight with other religious leaders and helped the churches have a voice in the political process.[13]

Supporting Todd throughout his mission and political work was his wife, Grace. Trained as a teacher in New Zealand, Grace developed an educational curriculum for Dadaya that was adopted by secular and mission schools across Rhodesia, enabling Zimbabwe to have one of the highest literacy rates of all Africa. The Dadaya Mission became a place where many twentieth-century African leaders of Zimbabwe either studied or taught.

The Deep Democratic Tradition, Cornel West, and Garfield Todd

Todd's life and rhetoric exemplified the same democratic ideals that Cornel West calls a "deep democratic tradition," which can inform the future of Zimbabwe and serve as a representative anecdote to both budding and stable democracies all over the world.

West states that "the fight for democracy has ever been one against the oppressive and racist corruptions of empire."[14] While Todd worked in Africa and Zimbabwe rather than the United States, he clearly battled both oppression and racism. Todd's story evolved gradually into a fierce battle against these corruptions, and by the end of his career, he was standing as a deep democrat against all oppression and racism. Todd's political and prophetic stance for black Africans against racist white colonialists is a model in the ongoing fight for democracy.

West argues that there are three crucial traditions that fuel deep democratic practices: the Greek practice of Socratic questioning, the Jewish prophetic commitment to justice, and the tragicomic commitment to hope.[15] The antidemocratic oppression faced in America parallels the oppressive and racist practices found in Africa, allowing West's three traditions, especially as exemplified by Todd, to fuel democratic possibilities for Zimbabwe and Africa.

West believes the Greek tradition of Socratic questioning will cut through the lies and manipulation perpetrated by oppressive elites. For West, fearless speech or *parrhesia* exemplifies the best of the Greek tradition as it "unsettles, unnerves, and unhouses people from their critical sleepwalking." Siding with Socrates and Plato against the sophists, West says Socrates' "courageous opposition to the seductive yet nihilistic sophists of his day—Greek teachers who employed clever but fallacious arguments—exposed the specious reasoning that legitimated their quest for power and might." Such questioning, West argues, will cut through the "rampant sophistry" of current politicians and "media pundits."[16] Todd exemplified this Greek tradition that West hopes will bring "intellectual integrity and moral integrity."

West says that democrats "in the face of callous indifference to the suffering wrought by . . . imperialism . . . must draw on the prophetic." The Jewish prophets called on all nations and people "to be just and righteous." West points out that "there is nothing tribalistic or nationalistic about prophetic witness. Xenophobic prejudices and imperialistic practices are unequivocally condemned."[17] Todd, at great personal risk and at the cost of his political career, called for the immediate enfranchisement for all black Africans. Todd the politician became Todd the prophet.

In his study of how prophetic rhetoric informed American radical causes, James Darsey offers a further theoretical exploration of the prophetic speech outlined by West. Darsey correctly says that the best evidence for a prophet's radicalism "is his opposition to the regnant power structure."[18] After 1960, Todd was unbending in his opposition first to white gradualism and then to extreme white racism and Ian Smith. Like the prophets of old, Todd was excoriated in his home but lionized everywhere else. He was not without honor except in his own country. Like the ancient Hebrew prophets, however, the powerless of Zimbabwe honored Todd in the face of powerful elites who despised him. Blacks sensed that Todd was supportive of their cause even when he was still a gradualist; as he changed to radicalism, blacks openly and warmly called Todd a prophet.

Todd's character and *ethos* became a critical part of his rhetoric. As West says about prophetic *ethos*, "the legacies of prophetic Christianity put a premium on the kind of human being one chooses to be rather than the amount of commodities one possesses."[19] While Todd did not die a poor man, he also did not amass great wealth on the backs of the people he served. He donated land and money for missions, schools, and displaced freedom fighters from the Zimbabwean civil war. He supported black soldiers with food and supplies during the fighting. Eventually, Todd sold his ranch and created a scholarship fund for Zimbabweans with the proceeds.

Third, West calls for tragicomic hope, "a profound attitude toward life," that retains a critical optimism despite the most daunting and dire circumstances. For example, in blues music "a black interpretation of tragicomic hope open to people of all colors—expresses righteous indignation with a smile and deep inner pain without bitterness or revenge."[20] This spirit characterized Todd for his entire life, especially at the end of his career and in retirement when tragedy descended on his beloved Zimbabwe during the Mugabe era. In addition, West says that both the blues and jazz heritage "created and enacted a profound *paideia*—a cultivation of critical citizenry—in the midst of the darkness of America." As will be developed later, Darsey ties the idea of tragicomic hope to the prophetic tradition.[21] In a far different context than America and in a very different way, Todd cultivated a critical citizenry for Zimbabwe through his tragicomic spirit. Through his prophetic optimism, his religious heritage that saw the African people as a reasonable people, and his interest in cultivating a *paideia*, Todd remained a tough-minded and critical optimist, cultivating hope in the face of daunting evil.

Democracy Matters and Rhetoric

While West correctly turns to the Greek tradition as an important resource for deep democracy, he unfortunately turns to the antidemocratic and authoritarian figure of Plato. Toward the end of his book West recognizes this problem: Plato's "fierce Socratic questioning led to aristocratic conclusions." In the republic, only the enlightened elite philosopher-king "equipped with the knowledge of the good-life could control the unruly passions of the demos."[22] Plato's philosophy inexorably leads to totalitarianism. West overlooks the deep democratic resources found in Plato's enemies: the sophists and other Greeks and Romans who preferred democracy to Plato's authoritarian elitism. In addition to philosophy, Greek culture produced rhetoric—that most democratic practice in which the free and engaged citizen argues for the best (*arête*) and most expedient practices for society. While some sophists may deserve the criticism that West and other philosophers bring to the despised discipline of rhetoric, not all of them do. West clearly is concerned with what rhetorician Wayne Booth calls rhetrickery—by both politicians and the media.[23] Booth's concerns are almost identical to West's, but unlike West, he turns to the rhetorical tradition for the antidote to sophistry and rhetrickery. The venerable Greco-Roman tradition of rhetoric that originated with the Sophists has supplied essential resources for deep democracy.

While innumerable quotes can be found on the link between rhetoric and democracy, rhetorician Jim Kuypers's is elegant: "Rhetoric sustains democratic culture. Rhetoric uses accepted beliefs to produce new beliefs and in so doing builds the stock of communal wisdom. It safeguards the stable beliefs that provide communal identity yet allows the community to manage change in ways that do not rent it apart and leave its people adrift."[24] Furthermore, rhetoric seeks to build the civic and democratic society for which West calls. Martin J. Medhurst gracefully states: "One of the central roles of rhetoric is—and has been for 2500 years—to hold forth a vision of a better life, a better way; to make arguments about how to improve civic life; to expose those who would seek to shrink the public sphere or to limit debate therein; and to utilize various discursive practices to maintain contact between and among the many social actors in the drama."[25] According to Thomas Conley, the sophist Isocrates "was famous in his own day, and for many centuries to come, for his program of education (*paideia*), which stressed above all the teaching of eloquence. His own works . . . were the vehicles for his notion of true 'philosophy,' for him a wisdom in civic affairs emphasizing moral responsibility and equated with mastery of rhetorical technique."[26]

Isocrates, the originator of the civic tradition of rhetoric, saw rhetoric as the cornerstone of civilization: "there has been implanted in us the power to persuade each other and to make clear whatever we desire, not only have we escaped the life of wild beasts, but we have come together and founded cities and made laws and invented arts; and generally speaking, there is no institution devised by [hu]man[s] which the power of speech has not helped us to establish."[27] Recognizing the power of rhetoric and its attendant responsibilities (along with Plato's ethical critique), Isocrates emphasized the high moral character of the rhetor who led the demos.

Cicero, who continued the civic tradition in Rome, repeated Isocrates' beliefs that rhetoric created human civilization in *De oratore*. He emphasized the link between the democratic impulse and rhetoric: "in every free nation . . . has this one art flourished above the rest and ever reigned supreme." In a passage on rhetoric that West could easily affirm, Cicero said: "What function again is so kingly, so worthy of the free, so generous, as to bring help to the supplicant, to rise up those who are cast down, to bestow security, to set free from peril, to maintain men in their civil rights?"[28]

While Aristotle's rhetoric differs from the civic tradition, he also developed the civic dimension in his *Rhetoric*, in which he emphasized the importance of deliberative rhetoric. Aristotle articulated the resources the political orator needed in advocating the most expedient and best course of action for the state. Aristotle was also very aware of Plato's attacks on the sophists and rhetoric. He developed a science (*techne*) of rhetoric to counter Plato's charge that rhetoric was merely a knack that made the bad appear to be good and the good appear to be bad.[29]

Some might ask if there is no role for *parrhesia* as West defines it. I think there is, and in many instances truthful speech is a characteristic of what West calls prophetic speech. Certainly Darsey sees this as a part of the prophetic rhetorical tradition, and we will see this characteristic in Todd's rhetoric. In addition, this type of truthful speech is a part of contemporary extensions of classical rhetoric, especially in the work of the master rhetorician Kenneth Burke.

To West's credit, he is not completely unaware of the civic tradition of rhetoric. West's comments on the powerful example of Ralph Waldo Emerson, who crafted a democratic rhetoric, are worth quoting at length:

> He crafted a soaring and emotionally powerful rhetoric that made him the most popular speaker of this time. He believed deeply in the need for democratic intellectuals to exercise powers of persuasion, to take back the public's attention from superficial and unfulfilling diversions, and to hold our public officials to a higher standard. To do just that, he trained his artistic voice to sing in order to spark courage, confidence, and comfort in our perennial struggles to become who we are and what America can be. His inspirations in this regard were the Roman public figures Quintilian and Cicero, who put forth seminal arguments about the powers and the mandates of public rhetorics in terms of keeping a government and society honest and inspiring the public to be engaged.[30]

West agrees with George Lakoff that progressive democrats need to construct an "inspiring rhetoric that speaks to the democratic issues of equality of opportunity, service to the poor, and a focus on public interest."[31] Significantly, West sees the Ciceronian tradition of civic rhetoric as supplying truthful speech or *parrhesia*, and Emerson is his exemplar: "Emerson took that rhetorical mission seriously, writing prose songs that were meant to unsettle the public, to jolt us out of our sleepwalking and inspire us to stay the democratic course."[32]

In this spirit, then, Garfield Todd's rhetoric will be explored using contemporary rhetorical theory and criticism to illuminate the deep democratic resources in Todd's religious and political speeches. Rhetoric may also be described as persuading and speaking through "street-smarts."[33] Contemporary rhetorical theorists are developing understandings of how humans can resist oppression, sophistries, and authoritarianism, and advance democratic causes in an effort not only to survive but to thrive—in other words, how to live "smartly" in a tough and dangerous world. These various rhetorical theorists and their critical insights are important and badly needed resources for deep democracy. Todd survived a long time in difficult social worlds. The critical understanding these rhetorical critics bring to Todd's democratic speeches and sermons hopefully will heighten the awareness of the important contribution that the broad rhetorical tradition can make to democratic and religious sensibilities in our world.

Todd's own democratic *ethos* and essential practice of rhetoric was forged in one of the most democratic Christian traditions: the Churches of Christ or Disciples of Christ. Todd's life and rhetoric cannot be understood apart from his religious tradition. The politician was always the preacher, and his preaching is a key to understanding his eloquence. The next chapter explores how the democratic *ethos* of the Disciples of Christ fueled four democratic themes in religion and society: the priesthood of all believers, the right of an individual to think for oneself, the importance of education and reason, and the impulse to reform society by spreading liberty and liberation. In the Churches of Christ, a reasonable rhetoric was seen as a means of furthering these goals in church and society.[34]

Todd's career had three stages, all of which were critical in the development of his democratic rhetoric and *ethos*. "The Democratic Missionary" explores the first stage of his rhetorical development. He was a missionary of the New Zealand Churches of Christ to Southern Rhodesia. His background, training, and exposure to democratic practices in the Churches of Christ shaped his rhetoric and overall outlook. Todd brought to Africa the considerable democratic sensibilities of the Campbellite tradition, which had its beginning in the American democratic experiment. Todd sought to educate black Africans: he built an educational system that led to high literacy rates for all Zimbabweans and helped develop the leadership of black African nationalist political leaders. He was a paternalistic but democratic missionary.

The next chapter, "Moving toward Democracy: Todd as the Limited Democratic Politician," traces his critical transition into politics and the world stage. Racist but progressive-minded whites recognized his rhetorical talents, and so Todd was brought into the political system of white colonial Rhodesia. Todd worked within the political system, first as a backbencher, then as prime minister, and finally as an outsider. He worked cautiously but relentlessly to expand the opportunities for black Africans in education and politics in the hopes of building a multiracial society. Todd was a gradualist, democratic, "liberal" politician. His progressive views on race, however, created a trajectory through the rhetorical and ideological choices that inexorably led him out of gradualism into radicalism.

"Todd the Prophetic: The Radical Democrat" explores Todd's prophetic rhetoric. After realizing that he could no longer work within the limiting and racist colonial system, Todd began a long prophetic journey, seeking universal suffrage for all Africans. He first fought for black African rights, and later he opposed the oppression he found in black politicians who attempted to oppress Zimbabweans different from themselves. Todd became the radical democrat in the prophetic tradition that remained hopeful even in the bleakest circumstances. Todd's life and rhetoric is one of the best examples of the deep democratic tradition.

"The 'Horrible Speech': Todd's Effort to End White Supremacy" is a close reading of Todd's most important speech, which he delivered before a key United Nations Committee on Colonialism in 1962. Todd exemplified Kenneth Burke's impious evangelist who used perspective by incongruity to try to end white racist power in Rhodesia and get Britain to intervene to make sure that whites gave up power. The speech shows prophetic rhetoric at work with a devastatingly effective effort defending democracy against the wily and devious efforts of oppression. In a stunning combination of traditional refutation learned in his religious tradition with perspective by incongruity, Todd the impious evangelist for democracy persuaded most of the free world and third world to reject white proposals that were cleverly and falsely clothed as democratic. Todd's speech is a perfect example of what West calls prophetic speech. Burke's rhetorical theory illuminates how some prophetic speech functions rhetorically to defend democracy and fight oppression.

The final chapter looks at Todd's later prophetic speeches after Zimbabwe achieved independence. Todd became a preacher for the democratic virtues for which Zimbabwe's metanarrative of liberation called. His rhetoric turned toward preserving and remembering the story of Zimbabwe's struggle for democracy. Todd correctly feared that the great promise of Zimbabwe would be forgotten and the democratic virtues the story of Zimbabwe stood for would be rejected. Furthermore, Todd's own story was an enactment of those very democratic virtues. He lived by those values and his own actions were a key part of Zimbabwe's story. His own presence before an audience along with his own narration of his own story reminded everyone of the democratic virtues for which he had suffered. Building on Walter Fisher's narrative paradigm, I show that Todd called all deep democrats to practice *phronesis* or practical wisdom as he had tried to do across his entire career.

Todd's life and rhetoric exhibits true practical wisdom. The preacher turned politician turned prophet remained a preacher at heart his entire life. As one who did not see any division between the sacred and secular his rhetoric is an excellent example of religious sources for political rhetoric. The importance of rhetoric for this democratic Disciple of Christ shows the critical and central resource that rhetoric can be for deep democracy in advocating and preserving democracy and refuting its enemies: racism and oppression. His deep democratic belief grounded in his religious heritage and lived out on the world stage also provides an excellent resource for building a democratic heritage in Zimbabwe, Africa, and for the entire world.

CHAPTER 1

DEMOCRATIC DISCIPLES

In his 1955 tour of North America, Garfield Todd met another head of state, a committed Christian who later introduced the first Canadian Bill of Rights in 1960, John Diefenbaker, a Canadian Baptist. They both shared a believer's church background where one deliberatively chooses to be a member rather than being automatically added as an infant. The two prime ministers shared their faith in democratic religious traditions and were quickly drawn to their common faith. "I think you are a member of the Church of Christ?" Diefenbaker also asked: "Like us, you baptize by immersion?" The door opened and in walked Donald Fleming, the Canadian minister of finance. Diefenbaker without missing a beat added, "Not like Donald here, a dry-cleaning Presbyterian!"[1] The right of choosing one's religious beliefs, so emphasized in the various believers churches, was clearly a part of Todd's rhetoric and democratic *ethos*. One American Disciples of Christ leader was probably correct that among the Disciples tradition Todd made the most effective Christian witness in politics.[2]

Reginald Stephen Garfield Todd was born July 13, 1908, in Waikiwi, New Zealand, to Thomas and Edith Todd. Todd's parents were so devoted to the Churches of Christ that they named their son Garfield after James A. Garfield, the assassinated president of the United States, who at that time was the most prominent political leader who had been a member of the Campbellian religious heritage.[3] Todd received as a prize in primary school a biography of Garfield, *From Log Cabin to the White House*, so for a while he aspired to become the president of the United States until he realized one had to be an American citizen![4]

The Todds, steeped in the *ethos* of their religious tradition, were highly aware of its democratic culture. For example, Grace Todd wrote that they were close friends with Anglican bishop Hugh Prosser even though he was English and a High Churchman while they were "two colonials from a 'low' and democratic church."[5] Todd's tradition, the Churches of Christ, is steeped in a democratic culture.[6]

Alexis de Tocqueville pointed to the "principle of the sovereignty of the people" as one of the greatest triumphs of American society: "The people reign over the American political world as God rules over the universe. It is the cause and end of all things; everything rises out of it and is absorbed back into it."[7] The democratic tradition ran deep in Garfield Todd's religious heritage. A key founder of the Disciples of Christ, Alexander Campbell (1788–1866) drank deeply from the democratic *ethos* of Jacksonian America and Campbell clearly set the stage for Garfield Todd's remarkable democratic outlook. In this chapter I will trace this democratization in four major themes of the Disciples as exemplified by Campbell: the priesthood of all believers, the right of an individual to think for oneself, the importance of education and reason, and the impulse to reform society or the spreading of liberty and liberation across all society. Finally I will return to the practice of rhetoric as a key means to accomplish these tasks.

Many scholars, from Arthur Schlesinger Jr. to Nathan Hatch, develop the importance of democratization in Alexander Campbell and the Disciples of Christ.[8] Schlesinger says about the democratic spirit in America: "Perhaps most basic was the new estimate, emerging over the last two centuries, of worth and possibility of the ordinary individual, not only as a soul to be saved, but equally as a being deserving happiness during his passage on earth. From this new focus much else followed. A heightened faith in individual dignity was leading to the assertion of man's right to acquire and judge for himself."[9] Schlesinger points out that the democratic spirit led to a simplification and humanization of theology. Instead of Christianity being complex and creedal it was simple, intelligible, and noncreedal. Instead of a severe, arbitrary God seeking justice, God was viewed as gracious, merciful, and willing to collaborate with humans. Thomas and Alexander Campbell, notes Schlesinger, "expressed this democratic spirit with great fidelity."[10]

The Irish-born Alexander Campbell moved to the United States in 1809 and quickly began imbibing the democratic spirit. In 1815 he wrote to his uncle in Scotland that America "was delivered from a proud and lordly aristocracy." In contrast, Europe was oppressed by the evils "of civil and religious tyranny." Campbell proudly proclaimed: "I have had my horse shod by a legislator, my horse saddled, my boots cleaned, my stirrups held by a senator. Here is no nobility but virtue and knowledge. The farmer is lord of the soil, and the most independent man on earth." Campbell "would not exchange the honor and privilege of being an American citizen for the position of your King."[11]

Priesthood of All Believers

Fundamental for Campbell was the priesthood of all believers. Campbell believed that Christianity had become corrupted over the years by various theological systems and he called for a return to the pure stream of Christianity found in the original source, the New Testament. Ordinary people could read, interpret, and understand the Bible for themselves; so the people, if empowered with liberty, could restore original apostolic Christianity and overthrow the polluted systems (the denominations) and the polluters (the clergy). Campbell called for the restoration of the church as found in primitive Christianity, and he believed that all of Christendom could be reunited through this restoration. For Campbell and other leaders in the Restoration Movement, "the 'restoration of New Testament Christianity' would entail a liberation of individual consciences."[12] Within Christ one found true freedom and democratic religion. According to Campbell, Christ "establishes the doctrine of personal liberty, of freedom of choice, and of personal responsibility, by commanding every man to judge reason and act for himself." In addition, Campbell said, "the Christian church is the only perfect cradle of human liberty, as it is the only school of equal rights and immunities on earth. It commands every man to think, speak, and act for himself."[13] Schlesinger, Hatch, and West all show that Campbell attacked the clergy on democratic grounds. "As a body of men," Campbell wrote, "they have taken away the key of knowledge from the people." Schlesinger states, "Alexander Campbell's own mission—it was 'to take the New Testament out of the abuses of the clergy and put them into the hands of the people.'"[14]

The Right to Think for Oneself

Intimately connected to the priesthood of all believers was Campbell's belief that every person had the right to think for oneself. Democratic primitive Christianity and political democracy were the best places for this to happen. Campbell argued incessantly for "the inalienable right of all laymen to examine the sacred writings for themselves" and believed that individuals should not simply accept what the church said on its authority "but to judge and act for, and from themselves."[15]

Campbell served as a member of the 1829 Virginia Constitutional Convention, agreeing to do so primarily because he wanted to play a role in the abolition of slavery.[16] In his speeches and arguments at the convention he extended his democratic ideals of individual judgment into the political realm. Campbell advocated universal suffrage believing that the right to vote was a natural right by God extended to humans:

> It is not a right derived from or conferred by society, for it is a right which belongs to him as a man. Society may divest him of it, but it cannot confer it. But what is the right? It is that of thinking, willing and expressing his will, and no man ever did, as a free agent, enter into any society without willing it. And we may add, no man could enter into a social compact without first exercising what we may call the right of suffrage. It is a right *natural* and *underived*, to the exercise of which every man has by nature as good a reason as another.[17]

Suffrage was simply an expression of the right of the ordinary person to think for oneself. Furthermore Campbell centered his democratic political philosophy on the Bill of Rights declaring: "I am more attached to the Bill of Rights, than I was before the late discussion commenced. I have seen that this instrument has been our palladium, and the only bulwark against the demolition of our republican citadel."[18] Like the democratic primitive church Campbell thought that ordinary citizens who thought for themselves could form the best government possible and rule wisely:

> King Numbers, Mr. Chairman, is the legitimate sovereign of all this country. General Jackson, the President of these United States, is only the representative, the *lawful representative* of King Numbers. And, whither, Sir can that gentleman fly from the government of this King? . . . Except that he cross the ocean, he can put himself under no King. And whenever he may please to expatriate himself, he will find beyond the dominions of King Numbers, there is no other monarch, save King Cypher, King Blood, King Sword, or King Purse. And . . . there is none of those august as our King. I love King Numbers, I wish to live, and I hope to die, under the government of this majestic personage. He is, Sir, a wise,

benevolent, patriotic and powerful prince—the most dignified personage under the canopy of Heaven.[19]

Campbell, representing the antislavery interests of western Virginia, failed in his efforts to limit slavery. He and the other like-minded representatives were outvoted by the eastern Virginians. Most of his proposals were eventually adopted at the 1850 Virginia Constitutional convention, and the anti-slave points of views eventually led to the breakaway of West Virginia during the Civil War. However, Campbell retreated from active politics and focused the rest of his career directly on his religious movement or on social reform.

Educated Citizenry

Campbell also focused his democratic spirit on universal education, recognizing that an educated citizenry and educated Christians were essential for true democracy and true Christianity to flourish. As Lunger notes, "apart from his work as a churchman, Alexander Campbell's chief contribution to American democracy was undoubtedly in the field of public education."[20] Campbell thought that if a person could read the Bible for oneself then he or she could discern God's will without the aid of clergy or creed.[21] Teaching people to read and write was fundamental then to being a true primitive Christian. As Campbell said in the Baccalaureate Address of 1853, education was "one of the chief bulwarks of religion, morality, and representative government."[22] The right to vote, Campbell stated, "can be exercised with safety to all interests only by an intelligent, moral and virtuous people." This made essential "schools, Bibles and teachers," without which "such a population cannot be created."[23] Campbell became a leading advocate for free public education in America.[24] He regularly participated in the meetings of the Western Literary Institute and College of Professional Teachers, an effective lobby group for public education in the American west.

In one address to an education convention Campbell laid out the seven essential subjects or "arts" that students needed to learn in the common or public schools: thinking, speaking, reading, singing, writing, calculating, and bookkeeping.[25] Such an education was "perfect" for students for they prepared one for life as well as for further education. Unsurprisingly, thinking was fundamental and the first art that a child learned "naturally" because it facilitated the mastering of the other arts.[26]

Campbell did not stop with basic public education; in 1840 he established Bethany College, a liberal arts college modeled in many ways after Thomas Jefferson's University of Virginia.[27] Bethany was one of the first of several colleges that have been established by the Restoration tradition. A familiar pattern within the tradition was for preachers, missionaries, and other leaders to establish schools at all educational levels. The belief that education can lead humans to embrace religious and political truth as well as to improve themselves and the greater society is a strong democratic impulse of the heritage.

Campbell studied at Glasgow University where he was schooled in Scottish Common Sense Philosophy, the intellectual basis of the Scottish Enlightenment which became the leading perspective of education, philosophical, religious, and scientific thinking in antebellum America. Campbell, like so many others in America, adapted Scottish Enlightenment thinking for the American democratic *ethos*. Campbell believed that all knowledge, including Christianity, could be faithfully recast on an inductive scientific basis. This idea called Baconianism thought that all "facts" could be inductively built into certain knowledge structures that all reasonable people, including the common people, would readily understand and accept. Campbell thought that the "facts" of the Bible could be inductively structured into clear and compelling doctrines and practices that would be faithful to the primitive church and thereby usher in a united Christianity and a postmillennial utopia. His reasonable approach to Christianity brings us full circle. Any ordinary person (who could read) could inductively see these "obvious" teachings of the Bible without the aid of clergy or creed or any supernatural intervention of the Holy Spirit. There was no need of the emotional revivals; instead, individuals in the privacy of their own study engaging their critical faculties could convert to true Christianity. Christianity was within reach of anyone who could read.[28]

Reforming Society

Through all his democratic efforts Campbell believed that he was reforming society and he supported various social reforms when he could. His postmillennial views fit in with the many social reforms of the nineteenth century.[29] Whether it was education, temperance, peace, abolition, women's rights, capital punishment, or the rights of native Americans, Campbell and other leaders in the Disciples often spoke out on these subjects. Believing that the world was gradually getting better and eventually would be converted to Christianity, Campbell kept most of his focus on religion rather than on any particular reform. Campbell noted "in this partisan and political age it is expected that every man must join in some of the popular crusades against some one of the hundreds of evils that afflict society." Campbell preferred to focus on "the root of the tree" while the reformers "who can handle the axe better . . . delight in loping off the branches." He even praised reformers: "the violent partisan may often be a useful man—more useful occasionally than the moderate one." For himself he thought the gospel "in its genuine catholicity aims a mortal blow at the root of every political, every mortal, every antichristian error and defect in society."[30]

Many in the tradition though went far beyond Campbell in their participation in reform movements. As I have argued elsewhere, the tradition spawned a diverse set of reformers: socialists, communists, pacifists, civil rights advocates, abolitionists, environmentalists, anticommunists, and others.[31] The optimistic and pragmatic outlook of the tradition contributed to the viewpoint of many reformers that society should and could be changed for the better. In Campbell's day many within the Disciples of Christ became ardent abolitionists, even supporting the Garrisonian movement.[32] For example, James A. Garfield shed his apolitical and pacifist views inherited from Campbell, ended his preaching career, and signed up as an officer in the Ohio volunteer army. His military exploits launched his political career which eventually led him to the American presidency. Despite Garfield's tragic assassination, his prominence became a point of pride reaching mythic proportions for most within the Campbellian tradition. Todd's parents naming him in honor of Garfield is one indication of this.

Other international leaders from the tradition who espoused democratic ideals also indicate that the democratization of the tradition was not restricted to the American Disciples. British Prime Minister David Lloyd George, raised in the British Churches of Christ in Wales, said that he learned all his "democracy from Alexander Campbell and Abraham Lincoln."[33] The British Churches of Christ looked mostly to the writing of Alexander Campbell for the inspiration for their British brand of the Churches of Christ. The British Churches spawned a democratic *ethos* of lay leaders—preachers and elders from working-class society. These men often became labor union activists and spread their democratic egalitarian notions into pacifist, socialist, and Labor Party efforts in the twentieth century.[34] The New Zealand Churches of Christ were mostly derived from immigrants from the British Churches of Christ.

Rhetoric: The Means of Preserving and Spreading Democracy

Whether in America, Britain, or New Zealand, rhetoric played a pivotal role in the Disciples democratic tradition. Preaching has always been central; in educational circles, training in public speaking and preaching is considered essential. Again, this is a flowering of the Scottish Enlightenment mediated through Campbell, who studied rhetoric under George Jardine, Professor of Logic and Belles-Lettres at Glasgow. Here he was exposed to the rhetorical theory of George Campbell, who adapted the Common Sense philosophy of Thomas Reid to rhetoric. George Campbell argued that rhetoric was limited to the management of the "facts" discovered through inductive means. As Lloyd F. Bitzer comments, "In human nature [George] Campbell and others found the natural logic of induction. Thinking that human nature supplied rhetoric's deep principles and methods, theorists resisted searching for principles elsewhere. . . . As well, human nature was considered the authoritative criterion. Induction is right because human nature supplies it—we reason inductively by nature."[35] A speaker expressed the management of "facts" for one of four purposes: to inform, to delight, to move, or to persuade. These four purposes were based on the four human faculties developed by faculty psychology: the understanding, the imagination, the passions, and the will.[36]

Following George Campbell's new rhetoric, Alexander Campbell said that preachers should

> first address themselves to the understanding, by a declaration or narrative of the wonderful works of God. They state, illustrate, and prove the great facts of the gospel; they lay the whole record before their hearers; and when they have testified what God has done, what he has promised,

and threatened, they exhort their hearers on these premises, and persuade them to obey the gospel, to surrender themselves to the guidance and direction of the Son of God. They address themselves to the whole man, his understanding, will and affections, and approach the heart by taking the citadel of the understanding.[37]

Campbell forged a rational alternative to both the emotional excesses of the American revivalists and to staid classical rhetorical practices found in the elite intellectual centers of the American eastern seaboard. As I have written elsewhere:

> Alexander Campbell lived at a strategic point in American history when Jacksonian ideals of democratic populism swept the American frontier placing aristocratic ideals in religion and politics on the defensive. Campbell was able not only to accommodate religion to the democratic spirit of the times, he also was able to accommodate Baconian rhetoric to the democratic spirit of the times. . . . The new social context of the American frontier demanded the new use of Baconian rhetoric, with its philosophy of humanity based on a new science and faculty psychology. Baconian rhetoric emphasized the "natural" over the "artificial" and "common sense" over the "irrational." In the American frontier the rhetorical tradition that trained the "gentleman" of Scotland was found to be flexible enough to further the freedom of the individual and the democratic impulses of society. What was considered "natural" in the American frontier was very different from polite society in Scotland. Campbell and others on the frontier attacked elitism and defended the rights of the "common man" in both political and religious contexts. The "common sense" of the ordinary person was preferred to the "artificial" and "out of touch" "speculations" of the elite. For rhetoric a truncated Ciceronianism was relegated to increasingly isolate social contexts on the American scene. In its place astute rhetors adapted Scottish rhetoric to the American context to further democratic causes in politics and religion. American and European reformers who came to America in the 19th century forged an American democratic rhetoric out of Scottish rhetoric and through that rhetoric built American religious and political institutions.[38]

Campbell and others from this heritage sought to create a *paideia* through their democratic rhetoric and the four democratic practices of the priesthood of all believers, the right for one to think for oneself, the development of an educated literate citizenry, and the reformation of society. This *paideia* produced what Cornel West calls a "critical citizenry" who were willing to battle against all forms of oppression political and religious.[39] As Peter Verkruyse points out, Campbell's rhetorical leadership "reached international proportions" as readers of Campbell's writings "acknowledged its role in the development of fraternal efforts in Great Britain, New Zealand, Australia and Canada."[40] Perry Gresham, a Campbell scholar and friend of Garfield Todd called Alexander Campbell "a hero to Garfield Todd." As Gresham further notes: for Todd, "Liberty under God and liberty before the law were one in his teaching and ministry."[41] Garfield Todd emerged out of the deep democratic rhetorical tradition of the Disciples of Christ and carried that tradition to a surprisingly new and different context: Africa.

CHAPTER 2

THE DEMOCRATIC MISSIONARY

When Garfield Todd came to Africa in 1934 he found a rural and tribal society that rejected both Christianity and education because it did not trust white missionaries. A patriarchal society existed where males lived a carefree life with women bearing the "brunt of the work load, tilling the fields, maintaining the homes, and caring for children."[1] The development of mines brought the first significant social change to the old ways, forcing males into the workforce. In the 1930s, the Todds began to build bridges to suspicious Africans. He brought in an egalitarian and Christian *ethos* where he would help anyone in need no matter how helpless or marginalized they were. "Garfield performed burials even for Catholics, was a builder, an arbitrator in community disputes, and—most dramatically—a doctor."[2] Soon after Todd arrived at Dadaya a priest called him and asked Todd to help Jonah Mantjontjo, who had suffered severe burns from an accident and was in a hospital in Bulawayo. Todd was appalled at what he found. Mantjontjo "was covered in filthy bandages, smelled to high heaven and could not move." Two of Todd's "staff members fainted at the sight of the poor man."[3] Hearing that engine oil was a good disinfectant for burn victims, Todd put oil soaked bandages in the infected burns. The next day the infection was gone, so Todd remarked, "we always used engine oil for burns." After Mantjontjo recovered Todd took him home, but his family and friends were shocked: "they thought he was dead and seeing him actually standing there and talking they concluded that the white missionary had raised him from the dead."[4]

Todd and the New Zealand Churches of Christ

Garfield Todd grew up in the New Zealand Churches of Christ where he learned his democratic *ethos*. New Zealand became a British crown colony when the Treaty of Waitangi was signed by the Maori people and the British in 1840. On March 2, 1844, Thomas Jackson founded the first Church of Christ in the Southern hemisphere in New Zealand at Nelson. Soon congregations followed in Auckland on the north island and in Dunedin on the south island. The Churches of Christ grew at a slow but steady rate as British immigrants came from the British Churches of Christ or similar restorationist groups. Jackson and other Kiwi leaders kept in touch with Alexander Campbell in the United States and with James Wallis, a key leader of the British Churches of Christ.[5] The New Zealand Churches maintained a democratic *ethos* through lay leadership (mutual ministry by male congregational members) and congregational autonomy. Ackers points out the democratic nature of the British Churches of Christ: "The chapel trained the ambitious individual in the skills of reading, writing and speaking, and administration, so necessary to leadership positions, while tying this to a solidaristic *ethos* of brotherhood and social responsibility."[6] From Britain they brought their democratic practices to New Zealand.

Starting in the 1880s with the arrival of American, Australian, and British preachers, the New Zealand Churches began to shift away from the sectarian radical democratic *ethos* to a more denominational and less egalitarian culture. The new preachers paved the way for acceptance of geographically located professional ministers for congregations. District conferences were set up and starting in 1901 a national conference met in Wellington. In 1920 the congregations associated in a national conference that met annually and the first national denominational paper, the *New Zealand Christian*, was published. Completing the march to respectability in 1927, the Glen Leith Theological College was established in Dunedin to train ministers; Todd entered the first class.[7] The New Zealand Churches remained small with fifty churches and 2,463 members in 1905. In 1938 the Churches reached their highest point with 4,962 members.[8] Government statistics, which included all adherents (unimmersed children of adults), indicated there were 11,197 people attending the New Zealand Churches in 1936.[9] Like their British Churches of Christ counterparts, the New Zealand Churches went into decline and published their official statistics for the final time in 1979 (forty-three churches and 2,926 members). In 1972 some congregations from the New Zealand Churches of Christ united with other declining mainline protestant churches (Congregational, Methodist, and Presbyterian) into "union parishes" or "cooperative ventures," following a similar path of the British Churches of Christ who merged with the United Reformed Church. Now the Churches have about eighteen hundred members.[10]

Todd lived to see the radical democratic *ethos* disappear from the New Zealand Churches of Christ, however his family's history and his entire life can be understood through the transition from sectarianism to denominationalism. Todd was well aware of the transition and had family members on both sides of the divide. His father, an elder in the Invercargill Church of Christ was a second-generation member of the Stone-Campbell tradition.[11] Garfield Todd's grandparents, Cameronian Presbyterians and Scottish immigrants to New Zealand, decided to convert to the Churches of Christ "after much deep thought and prayer" soon after arriving in Dunedin in 1865.[12] They decided that the Church of Christ rather than the particular Presbyterian church to which they previously belonged was the true primitive church found in the New Testament. Todd's parents lived in the time of transition to denominationalism in the New Zealand Churches of Christ. Naming their son after American President James A. Garfield is a telltale sign that the Todd family was moving toward sociological denominational pride and away from radical sectarianism. Still, it was a movement in transition, and like the British Churches of Christ democratic sectarianism remained. Todd, the son of a devout elder, went to church, Sunday school, and the various activities designed for developing faith in children. He read and learned, as all good children in the Churches of Christ, the content of the Bible. He gave his first public speeches at the Invercargill church and Sunday school where his grandfather served as the superintendent for twenty-five years.[13] Todd was a democratic-leader-in-training in his church.

Alexander Campbell was a key founder of Todd's religious heritage. Another aspect of Campbell's Scottish Common Sense philosophy was that he approached the Bible with a Baconian scientific, empirical, and rational lens, stating, "the inductive style of inquiring and reasoning is to be carried out in reading and teaching Bible facts and documents, as in the analysis and synthesis of physical nature."[14] Christianity consisted of historical facts that needed to be studied the same way that a scientist studied the empirical facts of physical reality. Campbell stated in *The Christian System*:

> All revealed religion is based upon facts. Testimony has respect to facts only; and that testimony may be credible, it must be confirmed. These points are of so much importance as to deserve some illustration, and much consideration. By facts we always mean something said or done. The works of God and the words of God, or the things done or spoken by God, are those facts which are laid down and exhibited in the Bible as the foundation of all faith, hope, love, piety, and humanity. All true and useful knowledge is an acquaintance with facts; and all true science is acquired from the observation and comparison of facts.[15]

Just as any scientist removed all personal prejudices to reach certain irrefutable conclusions about the physical world, all persons who studied scripture with this method would supposedly reach the same conclusions about Christianity. The lost ecclesiastical forms and practices of the primitive church could be restored through a rational scientific investigation of the pages of the New Testament. Unity of all Christians was possible through a rational process of restoration. This Baconian lens produced a reasonable and rational rhetoric for Campbell and inspired many others from the tradition who practiced a reasonable rhetoric.[16]

Todd was clearly a child of his religious heritage. In his sermon *Christian Unity* he stated in Campbellian terms:

> In Christianity we don't have a set of abstract truths, or arguable philosophy. What we do have is a set of historical facts, a record of happenings which can be examined and checked, which must be accepted or rejected. A person lived and that person was Jesus Christ. He lived a life, a record of which we have. He died and was raised from the dead. This is something very different from speculative theologies which are the explanations of these facts in the thought forms of a particular age. Here we have a body of facts which are of major importance and which are binding upon all Christians.[17]

Often in his rhetoric Todd appealed to "facts" or saw "facts" as the foundation or warrant of the arguments that he made.

In many ways Todd's Christian philosophy emanated from his experience at Glen Leith and tutelage under A. L. Haddon, the principal of Glen Leith. Todd recalled in 1962, "A. L. Haddon taught me that life is a unity given whole from the hand of God and not to be divided into sacred and secular. Preaching, teaching, healing, governing, farming, building, but in all things serving: this I learned in theory at Glen Leith and practise as best I can in Africa."[18] Glen Leith and Haddon reinforced the rational dimensions of the Churches of Christ. Haddon's biographer said Haddon had a "precise, logical and step-by-step approach to any subject he dealt with" as a preacher.[19] The content of the Bible and its rational interpretation was stressed in the curricula of Glen Leith.

Todd at Glen Leith, in addition to the usual course in biblical and theological content, had courses that stressed public speaking: two courses in homiletics and one course in elocution. In addition, the college had two courses that accented the rational dimension present in the Churches of Christ: deductive logic and inductive logic. Haddon reports that one of William Stanley Jevons's books on logic was a standard text for the logic courses.[20] E. P. Aderman taught the homiletics courses until he left as a New Zealand MP for the conservative National Party in 1938. S. H. Osborn taught elocution for one hour a week, giving "effective instruction in voice production."[21]

Training in homiletics and elocution in America, Britain, and New Zealand was dominated by the Scottish/British empirical tradition or Scottish Common Sense philosophy—the same philosophical outlook that profoundly influenced the Churches of Christ and Alexander Campbell in Britain and America. Elocutionary theory grounded its approach to delivery in eighteenth- and nineteenth-century views of science. Elocutionists thought they could scientifically and atomistically categorize delivery into single specific gestures and voice modulations that would fit specific speaking moments. While Todd does not remember the specific content of his elocution training, there is a continuity of elocutionary thought that stretched from the seventeenth century to the early twentieth century. Todd's teacher taught at Otago University, and the university library carries a copy of the leading elocution text used at that time in New Zealand: John Rigg, *Elocution and Public Speaking (lessons in)*. Rigg by 1921 had taught elocution and been in politics (including the New Zealand Legislative Council) for thirty years.[22]

Rigg's book, in addition to the outdated ideas on delivery, has some interesting aspects that illumine Todd's public speaking. Consistent with the Baconian orientation of the Churches of Christ, Rigg advised: "Words are the means by which we present our arguments to an audience, but the arguments themselves, to be sound, must be based on facts."[23] Rigg further emphasized the rational role for speaking in parliamentary debate especially by "back benchers" who wanted to have influence; "it is the accomplished debater who occupies the stage, moves in the limelight, and, by his sound knowledge and logical reasoning, influences the decisions of the assembly."[24] He further advised: "An efficient debater must have a thorough knowledge of the subject in debate; his mind must be stored with facts which he can use to support his arguments; he must be able to speak on some occasions without previous preparation of his subject; he must never make mistakes as to facts and figures; and his reasoning must be expressed in a logical manner."[25] Todd's political speeches in parliament had all these qualities about them—a thorough preparation, mastery of facts and figures, and incisive and precise reasoning. Rigg also said the debater in parliament "must always be prepared to receive the severest criticism from his opponents and reply to it."[26] Todd clearly relished the give and take and sometimes rude style of the Southern Rhodesia parliament. Rigg further emphasized reasoning logically in debate: "It consists in the ability of a person to put facts together and draw from them a sound conclusion, and, like the gift of common-sense, it is most uncommon."[27] With the emphasis of the Churches of Christ on reason and mastery of the "supernatural facts" of Scripture, it is no surprise that Todd received rhetorical training at Glen Leith that emphasized reason and command of facts, and that he exhibited good argumentation skills in his speaking, and saw its importance for education.

Todd graduated from Glen Leith in 1932 and became the minister of the congregation in Oamaru. He also married Grace Wilson who had completed her teaching credentials at Dunedin's Teacher's Training College.[28] Todd preached at Oamaru for two years but became restless. The church was settled into denominational respectability—"they had arrived" according to Todd and he wanted a greater challenge.[29] The African mission sponsored by the New Zealand Churches needed a new mission team and the Todds applied and were selected.

Todd and the New Zealand Mission in Southern Rhodesia

The New Zealand Churches of Christ, like the entire movement, were interested in missions and evangelism. In 1897 John Sherriff (1864–1935), a native New Zealander, moved to Bulawayo, Southern Rhodesia, where he established a church and then a school to train native boys in English and Christianity. Sherriff's mission work continued with other missionaries joining his efforts. In 1901 Sherriff visited New Zealand and asked for help from the annual conference. John Inglis Wright, Garfield Todd's father's cousin supported Sherriff's call and the New Zealand Churches agreed to sponsor a missionary.[30] F. L. Hadfield went in 1906 as the first missionary and in 1912 he established the Dadaya Mission. Over the years, despite the health problems of missionaries and other obstacles, the mission flourished with many baptisms and a growing school for the Africans. The New Zealand Churches of Christ with its steady growth and denominational economic prosperity was able to support the mission effort. In addition the Southern Rhodesian government was interested in the education of Africans and so gave "grants in aid" to missions. They also began to regulate the education and insisted that mission teachers have the necessary training and credentials. Grace Todd's training as a teacher made the Todds the choice despite their young ages (Garfield was twenty-five and Grace was twenty-four).[31]

Todd's initial years were spent totally immersed in African society running the Dadaya Mission of the New Zealand Churches of Christ and in almost complete isolation from whites. Most of the other Kiwi missionaries had to leave because of the growing worldwide depression, leaving Todd and his family alone to construct their own attitudes toward Africans. For thirteen years the Todds had minimal contact with white Rhodesians. Colonial Southern Rhodesia was dominated by British and South Africa immigrants who believed in white supremacy and who had little or no contact with the African population. While Todd's early views were very paternalistic toward the Africans, his ideas were far ahead of the typical prejudiced white Rhodesian. All along Todd believed that Africans as a whole were as capable as whites if given educational opportunity and training. Going completely against white Rhodesian customs, the Dadaya Mission held worship services attended and conducted by the entire staff—black and white.[32]

Todd brought his reasonable approach to Africa. Evangelism was at the heart of his efforts, baptizing hundreds of converts each year—405 were baptized in his first year. Secondly, typical to his religious tradition, education was emphasized. Murray Savage stated that the mission effort was pleased to help educate the Africans "as Christianity is then founded on an intelligent appreciation and not on unsound emotionalism."[33] Consistent with his philosophy that the sacred and secular could not be divided, Todd said that separation of education and the church was a "common fallacy." His aim was "that Christ may crown education and His spirit and outlook pervade it."[34] Displaying his democratic philosophy, Todd held that the rational approach to Christianity and the need for education went hand in hand: "As Churches of Christ pleading for the authority of God's word, we are surely united in our appreciation of the need for such a standard of education as will allow African boys and girls the privilege of proving all things for themselves."[35] Thirdly, consistent with his philosophy, Dadaya established a medical clinic where Todd with his limited medical knowledge helped sick and injured Africans as best he could.[36] The success of the Dadaya clinic along with the great need for medical treatment among the Africans is one reason Todd always pushed for better medical facilities, health care, and medical training for Africans in all of Southern Rhodesia.

The Dadaya school took off when the Todds arrived. The boarding school enrollment increased from 21 to 80 students the first year to 222 in three years along with 89 day students. In 1937 there were 1574 church members along with 1000 scholars in the village or kraal schools in the Lundi Reserve, the area where Dadaya was located. The village schools taught beginning reading, math skills, and devoted thirty minutes a day to Bible study while the boarding school students were mostly in the lower elementary grades.[37] However, in 1937, Dadaya began a Standard 5 (upper grade) class and started a debating society which was "a valuable factor in leadership training." Grace pulled together all her lesson plans into a series of small books which the government inspectors recommended for the other mission schools. Soon seventeen mission schools across Southern Rhodesia adopted her curriculum plans. In 1938 Standard 6 was achieved by Dadaya and two students were admitted to Southern Rhodesia's African Teacher Training College.[38]

In addition to introducing new methods of agriculture, educating students, and teaching various trades, Todd established a Christian Endeavor youth group where African students learned how to debate and speak in public. Also in the Sunday school at Dadaya, Todd reported that the "improvement society," where Sunday school teachers were trained, "reached a high standard of attainment and debates and speeches" that were "well worth hearing."[39] Todd believed that Africans were a rational and reasonable people who could accomplish anything if properly trained.[40] Todd put this into practice at the Dadaya school. Within a few years the school system was primarily run by African teachers. Todd reported in 1941 that the central primary school was the only one in the country "with so large an African staff in proportion to its European staff."[41]

Todd saw many lives, especially in his teaching staff, transformed by the gospel. One of his teachers, Zeko Sumbwanyame, who originally came from Zambia, was baptized in 1935, attended village schools, and eventually finished Training College in 1938. He returned to Dadaya to teach in 1939 and married an uneducated woman before becoming a Christian. His wife and family waited in Zambia until he completed his education, obtained a job, and found a place for them to live. Hearing that his wife was trying to divorce him, he left Dadaya to return to Zambia. Five months later Zeko returned to Dadaya with his wife and family and soon his wife decided to become a Christian. Todd commented about Zeko's situation:

> There are Europeans in this land who hold that God created the African people to be for them hewers of wood and drawers of water. There are many African peoples whose lives appear anything but beautiful, but here is just one instance of an African with a purpose in his life, with ideals great enough to make him persevere in the face of overwhelming difficulty—just another instance of a life changed and fortified by Christ.[42]

Once again the story can be seen as paternalistic, but at the same time the seeds of radical democratic *ethos* were sown in Todd's thinking and in the life of one African family. Such ideas were certainly beyond the pale for most white Rhodesians of the 1940s.

In November 1943 Todd was proud that a new oversight committee of church leaders was appointed for Dadaya with Africans holding all the leadership positions. Todd admitted that in 1935 he did not foresee "the day" when he would turn over "the conduct of the meetings to African brethren."[43] The Todds believed that they were building an indigenous church "with African elders, evangelists, teachers and a Churches committee of Africans" which shared "full responsibility for the oversight and administration of the mission."[44] This was completely consistent with the Churches of Christ democratic belief in the priesthood of all believers. Todd believed in developing lay leadership in the entire church. Todd told the Southern Rhodesian

Missionary Conference in 1944 at Salisbury: "More dependence must be placed upon a priesthood of all believers, rather than leaving the activities of the Church entirely in the hands of a trained priesthood specially set apart from others. The rank and file of the Church members must share in the Church's tasks."[45] In 1945 Todd reported that in most mission schools whites taught the upper grades but at Dadaya all classes through Standard 6 had qualified Africans as teachers. He had "no hesitation in saying that Dadaya had "the best staff in the country."[46] By 1949 Dadaya's schools had a staff of 116 workers and an enrollment of three thousand children in primary and secondary departments.[47]

Todd wanted to see African development even though it was paternalistic in his early days. For example, he proudly told a white visitor that he had not built the beautiful fireplace in the sitting room nor did any car maintenance, nor managed food supplies: "The care of gardens, of brickmaking and pressing, of woodwork, of the giving out of supplies of food, and a dozen other activities which used to be our personal responsibility, have gradually passed to the hands of Africans who, by taking these responsibilities, are making possible the rapid progress of the work, on the right basis—that of African cooperation."[48]

While clearly paternalistic, Todd himself had apprenticed in his own family's brick-making business, doing hard manual labor. Seen in this context, his training of Africans also fits into the working-class model of skilled apprenticeships for unskilled labor. Whites could see this as menial training meant to keep Africans in their place while Todd could see the same training as a means for progress. The African, gaining both the labor and educational skills of the Dadaya system, eventually thought of this as a stepping-stone to liberation and full democratic rights. Eventually Todd would think the same.

In their mission work the Todds realized that they were creating potentially greater problems for Africans as they faced racial prejudice from whites. Grace Todd wrote: "Africans are beginning to see visions and dream dreams, and at Dadaya we have some who will become leaders of their people. . . . [T]hey find themselves in a world where so much is against them because they are black. The colour-bar is the curse of Africa."[49]

Todd's effort to see the work of church and school as one was successfully communicated to the Africans. Todd reported: "In the minds of the African people themselves there is no hard and fast distinction between Church and School. The Church and School are both held in the one building, the teacher is usually a leader in each, and at School the Bible is read and expounded, it well could be termed a 'Church-School,' and most of the teachers 'Preachers-Teachers.' "[50] He gave a concrete example, telling how a deacon spoke up at church to complain about how a school was run; however, "no one felt he was 'out of order,' or that the business in no way affected the 'Church.' "[51] Todd modeled the union of sacred and secular himself when he entered politics, which was probably another reason why Africans liked him. He led them as the missionary and educator; they also saw him as the same kind of leader in the political arena. With the union of the sacred and secular made seamless in the minds of many Africans, it came as no surprise that the efforts of the missionaries laid the groundwork for African leaders to shift from religion to politics or more accurately for many African leaders to be active in both arenas at the same time. Many of the twentieth-century educational and political leaders of Zimbabwe came through the Dadaya school system.

In particular Ndabiningi Sithole (1920–2000) emerged directly from the Dadaya system. In 1935 Sithole came to the Todds as "a raw native boy," but he progressed through the education system at Dadaya. After Dadaya he completed his teacher training at Wesleyan Methodist Waddilove Training Institution and started a Bachelor of Arts degree from the University of South Africa via correspondence, as he taught at Dadaya.[52] Todd considered Sithole "outstanding" and "in the vanguard of progress in this country."[53] Sithole clearly was a rising star for the Todds. Grace Todd proudly reported that Sithole was selected to give a speech before four thousand people and the Chief Native Commissioner at a Show Day in the Lundi Reserve. She claimed Sithole's speech was "something of a sensation" and "without a doubt the best of the day." The sixty or so Europeans who heard Sithole "were amazed," meaning that they did not think an African capable of delivering such an excellent speech.[54]

Sithole was learning well his lessons in democratic *ethos* under Todd. While he faithfully taught at Dadaya and amazed Africans and Europeans alike with his rhetoric, he also began to speak out for African rights. In March 1944 he wrote:

> We need high education, but high education needs high posts. To educate the African well and then close to him all doors of responsible

positions is to turn him into a useless agitator. Doors of commerce, industry and other advanced trades should be opened to those Africans capable of doing the work efficiently. We need schools of superintendents and principals, postmasters in Native Areas and many officers for public services. Should provision be made for this [sic], then the New World Order is meaningful to the African. . . . Let the government provide us with this education and with responsible posts, and the African has a place in the New World Order.[55]

The Atlantic Charter issued jointly by Franklin Roosevelt and Winston Churchill in August 1941 and World War II played no small role in awakening African nationalism. The Atlantic Charter called for the right of peoples to select their own government and the rhetoric of the war called for the elimination of theories of white racial superiority. Dadayan students fought with the British during the war and young students at Dadaya pointed to those older students and to Ndabiningi Sithole with pride.[56] Sithole also picked up the democratic *ethos* that he should think for himself. In 1947 Sithole demanded back pay for teachers given salary increases by government grants which Todd had not passed along immediately. Also in 1947 a student strike occurred when many female students, angered at being spanked, walked out of class in protest. Sithole apparently supported the strikers. He and four other teachers were fired by Todd after thirty students were arrested and convicted for "riotous assembly" and 170 others were expelled. Despite the bitterness over the strike and firing, Todd and Sithole later reconciled. Sithole left the Churches of Christ and joined the African Methodist Church, an African-run "Ethiopian" church. In 1953, he joined the mainstream Methodist church. Sithole studied in the United States from 1955 to 1958 and was ordained as a Methodist minister in 1958. He published *African Nationalism* in June 1959, which West states was "the first English-language book to be written by an African indigenous to Southern Rhodesia." The book quickly became "the 'bible' of African nationalism" in Southern Rhodesia and thrust Sithole into a leadership role in the nationalist movement.[57] Garfield Todd wrote the foreword to the book. In 1963 Sithole became the president of the Zimbabwe African National Union until a split occurred in the group mostly along tribal lines. Sithole formed a more moderate group ZANU (Ndonga) in 1975. He was imprisoned by Ian Smith for ten years (1964–1975). He joined the transition government of whites and blacks in 1979 led by Abel Muzorewa but lost political power when his political party won only one seat in the 1980 election. He went into exile in 1983, as did Joshua Nkomo and other Matabele leaders, but then returned in 1992 to oppose Mugabe. He was elected to Parliament in 1995 but then in 1997 was convicted for conspiring to kill Mugabe and denied his seat in Parliament. His health deteriorated and he died in 2000.[58]

Isolated from racist British whites, Todd with his Christian and Kiwi sensibilities saw Africans as individuals with self-worth, the ability to be educated, and the potential to become leaders on the world stage. The Disciples democratic *ethos* bore fruit in a place far away from Alexander Campbell's beloved United States. Todd was planting the seeds for African nationalism.

Chapter 3

MOVING TOWARD DEMOCRACY:
TODD AS THE LIMITED DEMOCRATIC POLITICIAN

Soon after Todd became prime minister in 1953 he took a taxi from the airport to his home. The African driver and friend in the front seat began to talk about the new prime minister who "seemed determined to bring about improvements in the lives of Africans." Todd asked them if they knew the prime minister and what he looked like. They replied, "No we really do not know him. But we hear that he was a teacher at a Mission school near Shabani Mine." Todd replied, "Well, you are driving that man just now, I am the prime minister of Southern Rhodesia." The astounded men did not want to charge Todd for the ride, but he paid them a lot more than what the meter stated.[1]

Todd was often a gracious person, especially to those who were marginalized. Solomon Nkiwane, a member of the Movement for Democratic Change, the opposition party to Robert Mugabe and ZANU (PF) wrote,

> I never tire of marveling at the positive images, and hope, that Todd's premiership evoked in the African population. For me, at that formative stage of my life, the name of Garfield Todd was mysterious. How could a white man, decide to be on the side of Africans in a country where all white people were ONE in ensuring that Africans were always at the BOTTOM of things, *in everything?* . . . [G]enerations of Africans in Zimbabwe will be forever grateful to him for sowing the seeds of their eventual emancipation.[2]

His premiership laid the groundwork for his eventual prophetic avocation of complete democracy. His rhetoric is a key to understanding this shift.

Rhetoric played a central role in Todd's political career. His preaching ability prepared him for politics and opened the door to public service. His speaking ability showcased in parliamentary debate and in his election campaigns was one factor that demonstrated his leadership potential and led to his surprising selection as prime minister in 1953. In a number of different means rhetoric was a way of being for Todd.[3] He also was ahead of his time in rhetorical practices as he attempted to use the media as an opportunity to be the prime minister of all the people.[4] He quickly mastered the use of the media through press conferences, newspaper reports on his speeches, and his international tours. In nine short years he went from an obscure missionary and backbencher to a national political leader who commanded international press scrutiny. In their entire colonial history Rhodesians never experienced a prime minister like Todd. Secondly, he constructed a number of different roles though in ways he did not anticipate. He constructed his role as a missionary through his preaching. Then he became the eloquent backbencher. He took his speaking ability and constructed the persona of the prime minister in new and different ways. His rhetoric allowed him to maintain a popular government for his first four years as prime minister, but then his speeches led to his troubles and eventual removal as his liberal policies on Africans alarmed white politicians. His speeches reveal the democratic impulses that eventually led him to radical democracy and full support for African rights. He wanted to construct a multiracial society where whites gave up on racial prejudice and Africans entered into modern industrial society as fully educated and engaged citizens. His rhetorical trajectory and new use of the media pulled Todd away from limited democracy toward full radical democracy. The trajectory naturally led him away from paternalism as Africans saw him both as a Moses and a Savior who was crucified by whites on a cross of racism. The new prophetic persona and *ethos* of Todd was born out of his political rhetoric.

Early Political Interest as Missionary

Even though fellow Church of Christ missionary F. L. Hadfield was a member of the first Southern Rhodesian parliament and had championed African rights throughout his legislative career, Todd had no political ambitions when he arrived in Southern Rhodesia.[5] Todd eventually shifted to politics to bring to fruition his beliefs about African potential.

Todd was forced to pay attention to politics almost as soon as he arrived in Africa. The government set standards for teachers at the mission schools and increasingly provided grants to improve the quality of education at those schools. While the amount of money was small, the deepening Great Depression and the resulting cutback in support from the New Zealand Churches of Christ made the government a critical source of income for all mission education. Todd monitored parliamentary debate on the "native question." In 1935 he noted that some MPs wanted the mission stations "cleared out" but he was relieved that "the vote for the Native Development was carried out without cutting any items."[6]

Todd's success with African education caught the attention of the Southern Rhodesian government. He took full advantage of this attention by lobbying for African education. His school won numerous government grants for teacher salaries and positions. Dadaya increasingly filled those positions with African teachers. As the education improved, Dadaya students won scholarships to attend teacher colleges and other professional training schools. Grace Todd's books on curriculum were approved by the government and other mission schools adopted her lesson plans. In addition to visits from government education inspectors, the Director of Native Education sometimes visited the school and stayed for several days.[7] Max Danziger, an MP from Gwelo who was a liberal in Prime Minister Godfrey Huggins's party, took an interest in the Dadaya mission. Danziger, a Jewish lawyer from Capetown, was liberal on African issues.[8] In 1939 he stayed at Dadaya for a weekend. Todd's sister Edith worked for Danziger. In 1941 Danziger and Harry H. Davies, the Minister of Internal Affairs, visited Dadaya so Todd could show them the needs of the Africans. Davies, onetime Labor Party chair, joined Huggins's cabinet as the Internal Affairs Minister in 1939 and was known for his support of African laborers and for African political expression.[9] Todd was pleased after the visit when Danziger gave a "long and most vigorous" speech in Parliament "on the needs of the people in the Reserves."[10] In 1942 Todd announced that Danziger was the new Minister of Finance in Huggins's cabinet and that "the vote for Native Education had been granted in full for the first time in years."[11] In 1944 Glenn Stark, the Director of Native Education, came to dedicate a new hospital building at Dadaya. He and several others in the department visited Dadaya for four days. Todd gushed in his report to New Zealand that "every member of the Native Education Dept. is an enthusiast" and added that in "many hours" of the visit they discussed "the future of education in this land."[12]

Todd emerged as a leader for missions in all of Southern Rhodesia. In 1939, because of his growing relationship with the government, Todd became a member of the joint conference of Inspectors and Missionaries that would meet in Salisbury. In 1939 they discussed secondary education for Africans, which Todd hoped would begin in 1941.[13] In 1938 Todd attended the Southern Rhodesian Missionary Conference in Bulawayo, representing the New Zealand Churches of Christ mission effort.[14] At the 1943 meeting of the Southern Rhodesian Missionary Conference, Todd became a part of the Executive Council and was appointed to two important committees: the first, a group of four missionaries to meet with government representatives to "guide" African education; and the second, a research group to explore the "future relations" between the government and missions regarding church work with the African people.[15] The next year at the Executive Council Meeting Todd was asked to convene a meeting between Europeans and Africans "to consider the whole field of cooperation between Missions and the Government and related matters."[16] Todd touted his growing political influence to his supporters in the New Zealand Churches of Christ:

> As a member of the Executive Council of the S. Rhodesia Conference, and a member of the joint conference of Inspectors and Missionaries, and also convener of a Committee on Government Relations, I have a great deal to do with considering the whole field of relations between the Government and Missions, and have helped prepare new proposals and financial regulations concerned with Native Education.[17]

Todd's political interests were awakening.

In addition to his various lobbying efforts for government support for African education by the missions, three events propelled Todd toward the political arena. World War II and the horrific ideals of Nazism put racism on the center stage. In 1944 Todd wrote friends, "The colour bar is an evil here as the race conscious theory of Hitler is in Europe. Africans are not in concentration camps, they are not often flogged or murdered, they are just trodden down. People mistake the tragedies of undernourishment, disease and the colour bar in general for the marks of a race which is sub-human, instead of realising things for what they are."[18]

Also in 1944 Todd decided to enroll in the medical school of the University of the Witwatersrand in Johannesburg, South Africa, as his medical skills were badly needed on the mission. At the very first day of school, Todd attended a debate over a proposed strike by the medical students. Fearing his opportunity for training would evaporate; Todd spoke out against the strike. Impressed by his speaking ability, a group of Jewish medical students approached Todd to help save the position of a black lab assistant that white South African students wanted removed. Todd helped and the assistant was kept. His fellow medical students proceeded to elect Todd as their class representative in student government for the academic year.

In 1945, after the year at Wits, Todd plunged directly into Rhodesian politics on an issue outside of African education. Following communal African practice, Chief Shumba and his people had lived on an area of land known as the Ghoko block for generations. However, the colonial government, without the knowledge or permission of the Africans, declared the area white-owned land and sold it to European farmers. The Africans were given less than a year to move to a new location one hundred miles away.

Some of the African children at Ghoko attended school at Dadaya—some sixty miles away. In 1942 one of these students established a Church of Christ at Ghoko. After many baptisms in 1943 and 1944, Todd went and occasionally preached for the church. Todd unsuccessfully lobbied the government for the Africans, arguing that they should be able stay on their land. Besides meeting with all the principal white parties and local government officials, Todd wrote a letter of protest to Prime Minister Godfrey Huggins and his Minister of Native Affairs, dated April 15, 1945. The government upheld its ruling that the land was European.[19]

Later Todd clashed with Huggins over some comments the prime minister made about New Zealand during a local political meeting in 1946. The United Party under Huggins controlled the Rhodesian parliament but they did not hold the seat in Todd's district. Huggins faced a difficult election. The war created a lot of economic difficulties: men left to fight in the war, draining the civil service; raw materials were taken away for the war effort and the country had to produce more goods locally with fewer resources and less skilled labor.

Huggins needed to compete in all districts.[20] Recognizing Todd's ability, he approached Todd about running for the seat. Todd reported to the New Zealand Churches of Christ that a "strong delegation of local residents gave a pressing invitation which was backed up by a letter from the Prime Minister and a member of the Cabinet [probably Danziger]." Todd said that his supporters felt "I would be able to give a major contribution to the solving of the greatest problem before this country, which is the relationship between African and European."[21]

Todd had major reservations about running. Godfrey Huggins became prime minister of Southern Rhodesia in 1933 and early in his leadership advocated segregationist views which were popular at the time.[22] Todd admitted that he did not like Huggins's early policies and that he "used to look askance at some of the things he said and did."[23] After 1936 Huggins began to revise his views and adopted a paternalistic ideal of eventual integration as Africans became civilized and educated and entered into a Europeanized Africa.[24] In 1941 under pressure from the British Colonial Office and growing liberal ideals, Huggins issued a white paper about African affairs stating that separate development of whites and Africans "would and should meet earlier than at infinity" and that land segregation and white preference for the best jobs "should not be permanent features of Rhodesian society."[25] Todd liked the new policies and so he later said in parliament: "I knew that [Huggins] had the true interests of the African people fully at heart, and unless I had been 100 percent satisfied on that particular point I would not be in this House today."[26] Todd studied the political parties "native policies" and while he "did not completely agree with any of them" he nevertheless thought Huggins's United Party came the closest to his own. Todd further disagreed with the United Party motto "that the Government of the people should be by white people for the people." Todd believed "that the Government of the people should be by the civilized people for the people."[27] While the substitution of "civilized" for "white" might not seem very important, rhetorically and politically it eventually made all the difference. Todd the paternalist was not racist, truly believing that one day Africans would be equals while most of his white colleagues suffered no illusions on that score.

Todd believed he would lose the election because his views on race were too radical and the opposition party held the seat. However, he concluded he would have "the privilege of stating the case for the African people ... and that is a contribution which has been worth while."[28] Todd told whites in Shabani that "intelligent, thinking Africans" did not want economic standards lowered for whites. He also thought that whites did not truly oppose segregation because two hundred thousand African workers were hired by sixty-five hundred whites to work on farms and mines in European land areas. Furthermore twenty-eight thousand white wage earners employed twenty-five thousand African domestic servants. Todd remarked, "This does not sound like segregation." He introduced a prominent theme of his political career: "It is in the best interests of the country that the Native standard should rise."[29] To his surprise, Todd won with 330 votes to 195 for second place and 190 for third. He reported to New Zealand that his main campaign speech "was published extensively" and he believed "that in such ways we have the opportunity of working for better relationships between black and white, and that our truest interest is to work for the progress of the country as a whole in the name of Christ."[30] The *Rhodesia Herald* editorialized that Todd's campaign speeches had the "most balanced survey" on the question of race relations with his idea that "the carefully guided advancement of the native was as much in European as in native interests," and cited the conclusion of Todd's campaign speech:

> On the question of native affairs, there will always be great differences of opinion. Almost everyone here has a feeling that he or she has some fairly sound ideas on what should be done. Let us respect each other's opinions on how things should be done, but let us be as united as possible in our determination to face the situation honestly, to be just in our judgments, to seek the true welfare of this land in which we are finding life very pleasant, and putting aside any master-race theories, for the abolition of which so many people of ours have died; let us strive for the good of all.[31]

Todd won despite the reservations settlers had about his liberal race views. Huggins barely won despite receiving a minority of the votes and holding a minority of seats. His opposition was split between the Labor and Liberal Parties so he retained power "walking a dangerous political tightrope" until the 1948 election when he won a clear majority.[32]

Todd Enters Parliament: His Maiden Speech

Todd's speaking ability, polished through many years of preaching, made him perfectly suited for the rough-and-tumble British style of debate found in the Rhodesian parliament. As Weiss stated, "Garfield had everything needed to make him a public person: good presence, good voice, good sense, and good ideas."[33] Reflecting the Churches of Christ rationality and penchant for facts, Weiss reported that in the parliament "Todd spoke often and to the point," especially about "subjects on which he was an expert: education, health and native policy."[34] He was seen "as a forthright speaker who greatly contributed to the quality of debate." Weiss said that Todd was "good-humoured, witty, and quick at repartee" and so he "became popular with MPs and the media."[35] Blake noted that Todd had "good looks and spellbinding oratory."[36] Friends and foes often noted his oratory as "impressive" and when he left parliament a newspaper remarked, "there goes the phrasemaker."[37] Todd's preaching background also made him unusual in the era of the rhetorical "presidency": being accustomed to writing his own sermons, he eschewed the use of ghostwriters by preparing and delivering his own political speeches.[38]

Todd was installed as a member of parliament on May 28, 1946, and then delivered his maiden speech June 3 and 4, 1946.[39] (Todd's speech started toward the end of the session on June 3, so they allowed him to finish the speech at the beginning of the next day's session, a fairly common practice for speeches in the Southern Rhodesian parliament.) In the British political tradition followed by New Zealand and by Southern Rhodesia, a politician's first speech or maiden speech is an important event. Tradition dictates that this speech should not be delivered in the heat of a parliamentary debate becoming "an artificial calm before the storm of parliamentary debate commences."[40] Three New Zealand political scientists further say that maiden speeches "are traditionally uninterrupted, and are between 3 and 45 minutes in length. The maiden speeches represent a source of data offering information about MP's aspirations, goals, motivations, issue concerns and philosophical orientations at the outset of their parliamentary careers."[41] Todd's speech, while given during a debate over the 1947 budget, otherwise generally follows the British tradition. Unlike the American *Congressional Record* with its heavily edited and phantom speeches, the *Southern Rhodesia Debates of the Legislative Assembly* were verbatim reports of speeches with audience reactions and comments interspersed throughout, so Todd's reasoning and speaking abilities were accurately reported.[42]

In his maiden speech Todd showed himself to be a loyal backbencher praising the "broad outlook" of Huggins and his "principle of humanitarianism."[43] Todd offered some criticisms of the proposed budget which he realized were not expected but he acknowledged, "because I believe that the hope of this country is placed in the Government of the day that I am determined to say anything that I think should be said for its welfare."[44] Todd's fellow MPs applauded what indicated his own selfless outlook derived from his Christian beliefs. Todd mainly pressed for more services and better use of resources. He wanted the government to provide free hospitals because it could afford to. Todd's concern for Africans is found throughout the speech as he ranged over several topics. Todd wanted more land to be provided for Africans so they could be encouraged to grow more crops which could be sold to urban Africans and thus reduce the amount of food imported from overseas. He also wanted the government to help make affordable housing available. He also suggested that legislation that mandated that major housing be built by white labor kept needed African hospitals, schools, and houses from being built. "Are we going to see these built with European labour while Europeans are waiting for homes to live in?" He believed such restrictions hurt Rhodesia's welfare. "It is time," he said, "that we awakened to the fact that the maximum skill and service of every member of the community is required if we are going to ensure the maximum development of the country." He also wanted more money for African education.

> I would suggest that the whole question of the development of natives and the native labour of this country comes right back to something which most people do not recognise, right down to a basis of native education. Unless you open the minds of the people and make it possible for them to receive the tuition which they will need as they take their place in industry and on the mines and in the many avenues which will be opened to the native people, they will not be able to satisfy their employers.[45]

Todd showed command of facts and figures—a common signature of his political speeches while MP and later prime minister. This was used by Todd to drive home his basic point that what is good for black

Africans is good for all Rhodesians and would benefit Southern Rhodesia's development as a nation. Todd's careful reasoning, command of the facts, and general philosophical support of his party made the speech appreciated by his fellow party members despite his mild criticism. His thesis, stated in his concluding line, drew applause: "I am quite convinced that if this House is willing to see that all the potentialities of the country are used to the full, then the future of Rhodesia is assured."[46] His conclusion captured his overall political philosophy which eventually became too liberal for most white Rhodesians.

While there is nothing revolutionary in Todd's maiden speech, his emphasis on African development and the need to include everyone in the community started Todd down the path to full democracy for all people regardless of their race, creed, or color. Edwin Black makes the salient point about the influence of discourse on a speaker: "The future commitments it makes for him, rhetorically and ideologically; the public image it portrays to which he must adjust."[47] Much controversy exists in the scholarly and popular literature on how liberal Todd actually was while in parliament and as prime minister.[48] While he clearly was not as radical as he was in the 1960s, his different background as a missionary rather than a settler, as a New Zealander and not British, South African, or Afrikaner made all the difference. His rhetoric charted a path and ideology that eventually moved him to democracy rather than paternalism or racism. His democratic rhetoric eventually trumped his paternalistic outlook. His ideas, influenced by changing social circumstances, led him to radical democracy. His discourse created democratic commitments that made him out-of-step with most of his fellow white Rhodesians.

There were early signs that Todd would move toward a more progressive position on democracy and race. The African press took quick notice of Todd and gave his speaking extensive coverage across his entire political career. First the *African Weekly* took notice of his campaign speech calling for more help for Africans even though Todd's district was in the southern part of the colony and a long way from Salisbury where the paper was published.[49] The paper then made his maiden speech and his plea for better African education the lead article on its front page.[50] The paper was also pleased that Todd indicted Huggins's government for merely "playing with African education."[51] Through the African media and speaking engagements with key African organizations Todd spread his reasonable rhetoric of African advancement. In July 1946 Todd spoke before the African Teachers' Association of Southern Rhodesia annual conference. Winning their goodwill, Todd told the association that Huggins promised higher pay for African teachers. He said that African leaders needed to understand the colony's economy "and the part that each race must play." And he encouraged "straight speaking" African leaders so long as their rhetoric was "founded on fact."[52]

A small group of liberal whites also saw potential progressivism in Todd. Hardwicke Holderness and other liberals formed The Rhodesia National Affairs Association in 1946 after the election. They organized a series of lectures and debates on principles for Rhodesian policy. Todd was scheduled to speak on "The Native as Human Being" on February 7, 1947. Prime Minister Huggins asked Todd not to give the speech because Todd would say some things that were too radical and not "in the public interest at that stage."[53] Todd was eventually allowed to give the address.

As an MP Todd remained a limited democrat. Despite the accolades he received from white liberals and Africans, he did not want a universal franchise in the 1940s and 1950s, believing that it would lead to "universal chaos."[54] However, he did believe that some Africans deserved the right to vote and more importantly he believed that eventually all Africans would get suffrage. For example, he thought the African people had "very great power" and in a classic liberal view proclaimed there was "more difference between individuals in any one race than there is between one race and another." He wanted franchise laws at a "fully civilized level" so that "we would take no note of race or colour."[55] He worried that African frustration would erupt unless something was done: "the degree of frustration would be nothing in comparison with a decision by ourselves to make it impossible for all African people to ever have the vote in this country."[56] During his political career he thought this would come in the distant future. He said it would "take a generation or two . . . before we can think of opening the Voters' Roll to all the people of this country."[57] While prime minister he also kept any target date vague and off in the distant future. While this sounds paternalistic by today's standards, Todd was far ahead of most white Rhodesians and while hopeful for progress he was very aware that others were still stuck in racist thinking: "Unfortunately, in this House there are some hon. members who are prepared to say that all black people are uncivilized and unworthy of the vote."

Todd reluctantly admitted that at this time "most black people" did not measure up and should not vote. However, if "even one or two" were worthy, "then the greatest measure of frustration" would be created by denying them, "because of their colour, the right to vote and have a say in the Government of this country."[58]

Todd's Christian Political Philosophy as an MP

Todd exhibited a consistent political philosophy in his seven years as a backbencher in parliament. Christianity, British tradition, civilization, a robust economy, and education were reliably articulated in his speeches from 1946 to 1952. As an MP Todd pressed for expanded African rights in education and voting rights. Todd recognized early that civil war would be inevitable unless whites gave Africans a voice in their own political affairs. He hoped for a multiracial society that would allow for opportunities for all individuals regardless of their racial background. In many speeches Todd made it clear that his Christian views informed his political views. In 1955, in a sermon delivered to the Park Avenue Christian Church in New York City, the *New York Times* reported that Todd argued that "the Christian spirit . . . must be instilled in the [African] people so they can surmount their problems." Christianity was the key to "both spiritual and physical happiness for Africa's masses."[59] Todd, grounded in his Churches of Christ heritage, believed that Christianity provided practical wisdom for political problems. While in parliament Todd argued "that one or two commonsense ideas" would help whites "understand the natives to a greater extent if we were to realise that we should do unto others as we would like others to do unto us."[60] The seeds of his radicalism can also be seen in an undated article from a South African newspaper about Todd during his waning days as prime minister. The article stated: "Mr. Todd has always been notable for his courage—both physical and moral. As a backbencher in the Huggins regime, he was a never-failing champion of the little man and the underdog, even though his outbursts sometimes were at variance with the Huggins party policy."[61] His interest in the marginalized eventually flowered into full-blown deep democracy.

Todd believed that his overall approach was reasonable, and he assumed that the parliament members were reasonable men. Typical of his religious heritage, he thought if the parliament would study the problems of Africans that they would respond to the facts or evidence. In 1948 he said, "I think the time has come for a complete investigation of native life and conditions. It is necessary for us to make changes in our own outlook and those changes of outlook will lead to big changes in our native policy. Until we are willing to face facts to concern ourselves with the life of the native people, we will find no satisfactory solution to the problem facing our land."[62] Just like Alexander Campbell, Todd was willing to think for himself and change his mind if he was presented with new compelling evidence. While Todd was appealing to the parliament, his rhetoric committed him to the same principles he articulated. When circumstances changed in the 1960s Todd made those same types of changes that he demanded of his colleagues.

The British Tradition of Democracy

Todd knew his parliamentary audience and he appealed to what they all had in common: British tradition and belief in the British democratic system: "Although in this House we are all British subjects we are of different races and of various religious beliefs, and I believe the House is fully determined and united in its determination to see that the democratic way of life is maintained."[63] He further pleaded "that one of the things particularly dear to the British people and one which they are determined to maintain, is that racialism shall not become part of the British way of thought."[64] Later, Todd said: "We are a young country, and we are a loyal country. Most of us are of British descent. Even if we did not come from Britain ourselves, our fathers or grandfathers came from that country. We are imbued with the British tradition and we are endeavoring to set up in this country to the best of our ability the British way of life."[65] Everyone in parliament agreed with this sentiment but Todd took it in an uncomfortable direction for many: "I believe that, generally speaking, the people of this country are endeavoring to fulfill their obligations to the native population. In some ways I qualify that quite considerably, but on the whole they are."[66] Unlike most of his white Rhodesian colleagues, Todd believed that all Rhodesians would eventually participate in the democratic process, and he wanted to help them attain the skills needed to become engaged citizens.

CHAPTER THREE

Civilization for All

In reaching for this goal Todd rehabilitated an old political term long used by Europeans in Rhodesia: civilization. Carol Summers shows that the idea developed early in colonial Southern Rhodesia, and it served key constituencies in different ways. The early use of civilization had three critical components. First, it focused on individualism, replacing an assumed African "primitive" communalism. Second, it meant assimilation to English culture by developing skill in the English language and sometimes a thorough knowledge of Christianity. Third, there was integration of Africans into capitalism as individuals, both as laborers and as consumers of goods. As Summers states: "Civilization, even in Southern Rhodesia, was a classically liberal ideology, emphasizing the individual's cultural and economic decision-making ability."[67] Missionaries often believed that Africans were children who could be trained to one day become full-fledged adults and assimilated into European culture. A potential "racial convergence" loomed. Many missionaries realized that white prejudice was a barrier and would become a source of considerable African frustration if Africans were trained but then denied access to jobs and better places to live. The government and politicians saw the concept as a basis to create a subdued and obedient African and thereby manage African social and economic conditions. Settlers, in contrast, rarely use the term civilization. They believed they were civilization's representatives and that Africans were "barbarians" who should be subjugated. The settlers sought to maintain and control their power and lifestyle and had no interest in changing the conditions of Africans.[68] Eventually, Summers argues, segregation replaced civilization as the ideology of the Southern Rhodesians.[69] If true, then Todd was swimming against the tide because civilization was a crucial idea in his political rhetoric, and its ultimate meaning pointed his path into radical democracy.

Todd clearly drew from the missionary concept of civilization. The concept usually came out in his discourse on voting rights and what kind of franchise should be made available to Africans. Todd was a limited democrat, one who believed that Africans were not ready for full voting rights. However, a complete franchise for all should be the goal of the colony regardless of how long it might take. In 1951 Todd articulated a view that he held his entire political career: "I do not want to see universal suffrage. I do not want to see the Europeans outnumbered or outvoted by the African people."[70] Todd, though, did not want the issue to be placed on a racial basis. Todd believed Europeans were "privileged" because of greater ability, greater knowledge, and because greater capital was at their "disposal." However, "the thought that for all time the interests of one race must be paramount" was "anathema" to Todd.[71] This is where he turned to the old concept of civilization: "The difference between my view and the view which has been expressed by some hon. members of this House is not a difference between black and white, but a difference between cultured or civilized and uncultured and uncivilized."[72] When challenged by another MP to define the civilized person, Todd replied: "We all know some of the marks of the civilised man. We expect of course, that he will be educated to a reasonable degree. We expect that he will live in reasonably good surroundings. We expect he will be a good workman. We expect that he will have a good character. In addition, there are other spiritual qualities which one cannot define."[73] Todd spelled out precisely the qualities that Dadaya and other mission schools were instilling in their African students. Literacy, speaking, math skills, vocational training, and improvement in health and character development were central to their efforts. Todd saw Rhodesia entering into the modern industrial world, and he believed all Africans had to face that reality. Ultimately civilization meant becoming a part of the global industrial society.

Todd also included a Christian dimension to civilization that can be easily overlooked. When he returned to New Zealand he worried that it only had a "veneer" of civilization because it was a wealthy, "self-satisfied" country with pleasure as "her goal." Without Christianity and its character development, New Zealand was "spiritually poverty-stricken" and "doomed to an era of civilized paganism."[74] While speaking to an audience in New Zealand, Todd identified the same issue with citizens in all countries. Civilization without the Christian aspect was an empty concept for Todd. In Southern Rhodesia it was the basis for his liberal political policies. He was, for example, opposed to polygamy because it discriminated against women, making their lives more difficult. Todd stated that a "distinguishing mark" of Christianity was the "higher standing" of women. He directly tied this to support for giving civilized Africans the vote by testing "whether they are going to give their women folk, their wives a decent standard, a decent position, or whether she is going to be one of a string of wives in a village."[75] Civilization meant developing the Christian, ethical and spiritual dimension in all Rhodesians, black and white. Persons of good character, Todd believed, would not have racial prejudice or discriminate against persons of lesser power.

A Good Economy for Rhodesia

While Christianity formed the basis of Todd's ideology and rhetoric and was central to his ceremonial speeches and sermons, it rarely emerged explicitly in his political speeches. Instead, knowing his settler audience both locally and in parliament, Todd usually put the question of African development into economic terms and appealed to the interests of a good economy for the entire country: everyone could enjoy the good life; in fact, eventually it would be impossible for the few (whites) unless all (the Africans) were brought into the system. Through economic interests Todd believed that consubstantiality could be achieved between blacks and whites. Just as Todd's Disciples heritage pursued unity among Christians, Todd wanted to pursue political and racial unity in Southern Rhodesia. In 1947 Todd stated: "When we realize how necessary it is to consider the unity of the resources of the country, it strikes us forcibly that the fortunes of black and white are very much bound up together, and national development must be vital for all."[76] He continued to hammer home the economic benefits of fully developing the Africans. In 1949, for example, Todd said:

> It is imperative that this House should from time to time consider the nutritional needs of the African population, the ravages of disease and their implications on our national economy. When the day comes that we are ready to provide the material, the men, and the money to really get ahead and usher in a new day for the African people, we will in fact be ushering in a new day for this land, and while we may think we are acting just for the welfare of the native people we will be acting in our own best interests.[77]

In 1952 Todd reminded the parliament that overseas investors and lenders were concerned about the progress of "good race relations" in Rhodesia. He wanted more money devoted to education and health services for Africans so that those "satisfactory race relations" would continue.[78]

The Centrality of Education

True to his heritage and belief in democracy, Todd placed much emphasis on education, saying: "there is also no quarrel between religion and education. . . . Christianity is an historical religion. There is a great deal concerned with it which can be taught. Religion and education go hand in hand."[79] Christian instruction had a positive impact on the curriculum because "there is much about it which is common to all churches; there is much about it which has the approval of the scholarship of all the churches. In religious education you bring together literature, history and geography, and it is a useful subject in a school."[80] Besides factual content Todd also believed Christianity had a role in the character formation and relationships between teachers and students, for "in a community such as a school, the Christian virtues can be developed by the relationships which exist between child and child, between teacher and child, and these relationships should show Christian grace."[81] Todd developed a long track record of support for education in Rhodesia. He frequently pressed for more money for African education.[82] He supported the development of a University for Rhodesia which eventually led to the present-day University of Zimbabwe.[83] He supported the continuation of government grants for mission schools.[84] He tied in the importance of education in developing a trained labor force for Rhodesia.[85] He also urged more support for education for Europeans.[86] For Todd education was the centerpiece to his Christian approach to politics and critical component to developing a democratic state for all Rhodesians.

An Unexpected Prime Minister

In 1953 when the Central African Federation was created by allying Southern and Northern Rhodesia and Nyasaland, Huggins became prime minister of the Federation. Most of the Southern Rhodesian leaders decided to take Federation positions. Todd, partially because of his speaking ability, was the backbencher selected as prime minister of Southern Rhodesia. The next year, taking the lead by effective speaking in the national campaign, Todd and his party (the United Rhodesia Party) took twenty-six out of thirty seats in the February elections and won 56.6 percent of the popular vote. The opposition party, the Confederate Party, did not win any seats, so Todd's only opposition was four independents.[87] Consistent with his speeches as a backbencher, Todd stated early in his term as prime minister that for social services and for general economic standards he wanted his government to look out for the welfare of all Southern Rhodesians: "This party and this Government is committed to maintain, for the very soundest of reasons, the standards of the European while at the same time we shall continue to help Africans and all others to rise as rapidly as possible to those standards which we employ."[88]

The Rhetorical Prime Minister

His speaking engagements quickly multiplied as organizations wanted to hear an excellent speaker. Todd took full advantage of the office's rhetorical possibilities that these speeches offered. Unlike his predecessors, he quickly made his leadership rhetorical and used the "bully pulpit" to press for his political agenda. He was trying to build what rhetoric scholar Thomas W. Benson calls "a universally available public sphere built upon the context of an actively civic society, implying citizens who recognize and enact their public obligations both locally and nationally, and discursive practices that are by some measure rational, accessible and reciprocal."[89] Todd's rhetorical leadership worked for four years but the racial attitudes of whites were too entrenched to be altered through political speeches, interviews, press conferences, international tours, and the media. One of his cabinet members who revolted "got worried over the prime minister talking at every street corner on racial matters."[90] Many party members did not like the transformation Todd made in the leadership role, claiming he spent too much time traveling and going to insignificant functions. Todd showed his MPs that for a one-year period in 1956–57 he attended 115 meetings and opening ceremonies and gave fifty-one speeches. Todd then laid out his schedule for the next few weeks, giving a revealing look at his rhetorical leadership:

> Soon I am opening a Congress of Journalists in Bulawayo. I am to address in Salisbury an African service concerned with the jubilee of the Methodist Church there. I am going to open a Municipal Conference in Victoria Falls. I am going to attend a Scout Parade in Bulawayo. . . . I will open a Careers Exhibition in Salisbury. I am going down to Fort Victoria

soon to open the Ray Stockil bridge. I am going to Bulawayo to address a large Scout gathering; am booked to speak at the St. Joseph's Home in Salisbury; am going to open an Art Exhibition in Bulawayo; am going to address the Youth Council in Salisbury. I am going to address a college in Johannesburg.[91]

He listed five more functions where he probably delivered a few thoughts and seven more full speaking engagements. Todd also knew that all of these events were covered by the media—both newspaper and the radio and if significant enough even BBC television might cover a speech.

True to the best in the democratic tradition, Todd welcomed debate and criticism of his policies. He saw the diversity of political views as "a virility greatly needed in a young country" like Southern Rhodesia. He did not want a parliament of "yes men."[92] Having been a backbencher, he even said, "There is . . . a great deal of criticism from some back benchers of this House, and perhaps sometimes Governments would like more praise; but I suggest that the criticism that comes from the back benches is constructive, because the aim of our back bench members is not to score politically but to see that the Government does its work to the very best of its ability. Along these lines we welcome criticism."[93] In turn Todd used key speaking events for criticizing those he disagreed with, especially the federal government. Twice he criticized federal policies and the federal prime minister to urge a change more favorable to Southern Rhodesia. In both cases the Southern Rhodesians, his own political party, and the cabinet agreed with Todd so the efforts won him political capital.[94]

Todd took the rhetorical premiership to another unprecedented level for Southern Rhodesia. As journalist Ruth Weiss notes, "Todd enjoyed a good press outside Rhodesia; numerous trips and his fluency as a speaker had seen to that."[95] The Disciples of Christ discovered that one of their own was now a prime minister, so in 1955 they invited Todd to speak at the World Convention of Churches of Christ meeting in Toronto.[96] The World Convention was a meeting of churches from the Campbell tradition from all over the world that convened every three to four years.[97] Todd decided to take advantage of the thirty-five-day trip to meet with politicians, journalists, academics, church leaders, and business executives to promote Southern Rhodesia. Filled with speaking engagements, interviews, and meetings with influential people, Todd's trip caught the attention of many important people and made a positive impression for himself and his political agenda. The Rhodesian press gave his tour, speeches, interviews, and meetings wide coverage as did the press in the United States and Canada.[98]

In his international speeches Todd's rhetoric against racism was prominent. At the World Convention in Toronto, Todd said: "In the love of God all men stand equal. However, there is not equality of opportunity and to whom much is given, from him much is expected—that means much from you and much from me. In the vision which confronts the Christian Church, there can be no racial differences, no national boundaries for the love of God is as wide as his creation and includes all his children."[99] The American religious press reported his progressive statements on race.[100] The Rhodesian press reported that Todd had told audiences that the Africans were moving toward "complete emancipation" politically.[101] While Todd did not state his ideas quite that way he still spoke out in a bold manner that won him international support but potentially at the cost of support at home. At the forum at Georgetown University broadcast over radio and television, what Todd actually said was not completely prudent for a Rhodesian audience: "I believe that we are laying the foundations of cooperation, and I'm not concerned so much whether it is a black man or a white man who is in control as that it is civilized Christian people, who have got the right motives and who will run the country well." Then in a telling statement he added: "There are at least 30 percent of our people in Southern Rhodesia, who would violently disagree with me on that statement, so that this is not the sort of statement which is a good one to make politically. . . . But those are my honest opinions."[102] He told the *New York Times* he thought racial troubles would be avoided in Rhodesia, however, he warned: "We have much to do and we have to move fast." If whites "are unable to produce" then Africans would conclude whites were "insincere."[103] So while his rhetorical activities overseas won over his international office, they did not play well at home. One opponent accused Todd of being the "archpriest of racial integration."[104] In later years when Todd stirred things up, his opponents sometimes sarcastically complained that Todd should go on another world tour.[105]

Todd also met with important political figures during his tour, including Canadian Prime Minister John Diefenbaker and U.S. Secretary of State John Foster Dulles.[106] Many of the contacts he made during this tour supported Todd as he shifted to a more radically democratic stance. Just as important, he became a recognized political figure. After this tour Todd's political activities were covered in the American media from 1955 through Zimbabwean independence in 1980. If Todd had not made this tour nor made full rhetorical use of his political office, it is doubtful that he would have commanded the media scrutiny and the notoriety that he did in the 1960s and 1970s. Such media coverage was one of the reasons Ian Smith confined Todd to his ranch on two prolonged occasions.

The Initial Limited Liberalism

Soon after winning the 1954 elections, Todd created a separate Ministry of Native Education removing it from the Native Affairs department and ran it as its minister. Todd immediately implemented an infusion of money into African education believing that £500,000 a year was inadequate.[107] Todd admitted in 1954 that the education bill was large at £1,300,000, that the increase in expenditure was "almost staggering," and to some MPs the program's cost assumed "alarming proportions."[108] In 1956 he went even further and developed an ambitious five-year plan for African education that would cost an estimated $45,000,000. Todd argued that education "was the key to the future of African progress."[109] Todd also tried to implement reforms in housing and in land appointment for Africans. The urban housing reform in 1954 angered the white electorate who thought Todd was placing black interests over the whites.[110] Land reform incited African nationalists because they saw it as unfair, inadequate for the growing African population, and insensitive to African culture. (The law called for Africans to cull their cattle herds with which they were emotionally attached.)[111]

Todd's limited liberalism continued into 1956 despite the earlier progressive-sounding rhetoric of his 1955 overseas tour. He still saw democratic rights as something that would happen sometime in the future. For example, speaking about the right to strike as prime minister, Todd said in 1956: "We in this country recognize that just as we are not prepared to have a universal franchise, so we are not prepared to give full rights in other realms as well, but the Government, and the great majority of the people of this country, are determined to assist the African people to come as quickly as possible to that state where no civilized rights will be denied them."[112] The contrast between Todd's liberal views and what happened under Ian Smith in the 1960s could not be greater. Despite this contrast in 1957 things began to change and Todd started to alter his views as circumstances overtook him.

The Perceived Shift to Support for Africans—1957

Despite his considerable skills, Todd's Christian perspective on race and politics was out-of-step with the views of white Rhodesians. Bengt Sundkler and Christopher Steed state: "This was a time of an emerging African nationalism, stimulated not least by the co-operation of the White prime minister, ex-missionary Garfield Todd, but rejected by the powerful White establishment."[113] Todd battled his own Parliament by going directly to the people through speeches over the new franchise bill designed to liberalize the vote for educated Africans. In particular he made a controversial and apparently extemporaneous speech to the Interracial Association on June 15, 1957. This liberal interracial organization had progressive whites and moderate educated Africans as members. Todd addressed the organization and scolded whites: "We are in danger of becoming a race of fear-ridden neurotics."[114] Shockingly he said, "We must work for the day when it will not be significant to a child whether he is born black or white or coloured for all will be offered equal opportunity in Southern Rhodesia."[115] He appealed to the ideals of Cecil Rhodes: "In southern Rhodesia, the spirit of Rhodes will pass from the land unless racialism is banished." Rhodes supported the "liberal dictum of equal rights for civilized men, regardless of colour." If legislation was introduced to keep six thousand Africans who had ten years of education and good white collar jobs as teachers, medical orderlies, and the like from voting "we would be betraying the spirit of Rhodes" and Todd "would not continue to lead his party."[116] The ploy worked as the right-wing in Todd's party decided to support his modest compromise to allow a few Africans the vote. The *Rhodesia Herald* hailed his speech as "courageous."[117] Moderate African Stanlake Samkange supported Todd calling it a "gigantic step in the right direction."[118] The *African Daily News* called Todd's speech a "brave stand" and the legislation "one of the last chances in establishing an integrated society."[119] The right-wing Dominion Party did not like Todd's "bullying," expressing an old view of rhetorical leadership that "it was not in keeping with his position as the party leader."[120] African nationalist leaders in the ANC did not like Todd's proposal because the qualifications for franchise were "too high" and it moved too slowly toward full African franchise.[121] Todd won his legislation, but the conservatives in the United Rhodesia Party "never forgave him for the substance of his speech or for his choice of where to deliver it."[122]

As Todd devoted more of the budget to African education and housing, and eventually a modest liberalization of the franchise, he faced increased criticism. The opposition within his own party criticized Todd for "bringing forward the African people at an untoward rate." Expressing a view congruent with his religious heritage, Todd believed that his government "was fully responsible" and "endeavored to face the facts." He cited the various progressive social services and legislation for all Rhodesians and the efforts at "native education." Todd argued that the change in the country from 1946 to 1956 was "as great as that between white and black." He would not flinch from the daunting challenge: "To take a whole population of hundreds of thousands from a rural peasant existence, and bring them into a developing, industrial economy is a very big undertaking." Everyone had to share responsibility since they agreed "to create a modern, progressive state in Southern Rhodesia." Todd hoped that Southern Rhodesia would carry "on in this reasonable and quiet happy way, so that everyone may benefit from the development which is taking place."[123] This appeal received applause from the parliament and one MP immediately congratulated Todd "on one of the best speeches I have heard him make."[124]

Todd's views were out-of-step with those of most white Rhodesians. His liberalism was different. Todd stated in the parliamentary debate on the franchise bill:

> It is not enough in a democracy to have power in the hands of those best qualified. It is dangerous to be governed by an oligarchy, even if it is an aristocracy, even in a homogenous community but I believe it is even more dangerous where the top group to whom you are going to give the franchise, to whom you are suggesting the franchise is to be restricted, is mostly from the race which is a minority, and in this small country a small minority.[125]

Todd tried to placate parliament and Rhodesian whites by adding that the government had to be kept "in the hands of responsible people." However, to the alarm of most MPs, Todd also argued that if voter qualifications were kept so high Rhodesia would "no longer" be a democracy and a revolution would overthrow the government.[126] Todd realized that the African people had changed and that Southern Rhodesia could be "overwhelmed by a tide of black nationalism or world Communism." The government needed the "imagination and courage to grasp our present problems," which meant that more than just token African representation was required.[127] But this was not to be. Todd and his cabinet had two versions of liberalism. Hardwicke Holderness reflected on these contrasting versions soon after Todd was removed as prime minister. He stated: "The former ministers consider that, as far as the African population is concerned, everything in the garden will be lovely as long as economic development is maintained, any manifestations of activities hostile to the established government are dealt with 'firmly' and European leaders remain apart and in a position of authority."[128] In contrast, Holderness said, "Mr. Todd's approach is based on the assumption that the leadership of the country must carry with it the confidence of at any rate a substantial part of the African population, and this necessarily involves making statements which command such confidence from them."[129]

Todd's ministers considered these statements along with meetings he had held with Nkomo, Sithole, and other African leaders as ill-advised and dangerous. Again Todd's missionary background came into play. Todd was at ease and very used to meeting and talking with African leaders. He spent his missionary years cultivating African leadership. In contrast, settlers and urban MPs had little or no contact with Africans, so the very idea of having high-level conversations with Africans was incomprehensible, even to the paternalistic liberals in Todd's party. As Holderness said: "a personal interview between a member of the Government and any of the 'naughty boys' on the African side of the fence is quite abhorrent."[130]

After a modest compromise franchise bill was passed, much to the consternation of many racist whites, that allowed some educated Africans voting rights, and with rising tensions between Southern Rhodesia and the Federation, and with white anger coming to a boil over Todd's secret meetings with black nationalist leaders, his cabinet and leading party members decided that it was time for Todd to go.

As he realized that he was getting into hot water with some whites, Todd again turned to political rhetoric to mollify his critics. Tradition held that the prime minister would give an important speech at the Caledonian Society's celebration of St. Andrew's Night on November 30, 1957, because so many white Rhodesians were of Scottish descent. The African National Congress (ANC), organized under the leadership of Joshua Nkomo and George Nyandoro, was the main organization pushing African nationalism. As the ANC became increasingly militant, Todd was caught in the growing tensions between white extremism and African nationalism. Todd had a long track record of criticizing the "extremists" in the nationalist movement who demanded universal franchise. In 1951 he called it a "misguided nationalism."[131] As prime minister he even used stronger language to condemn the ANC when he claimed that "the boycott, the strike, intimidation and witchcraft" gave it "prestige and power" among Africans. He warned: "How then can we tolerate in our Federation responsible people . . . whose actions and philosophy threaten the very foundation of the democracy upon which our Federation is supposed to be developing?"[132] Because Todd met with nationalist leaders, Africans, sensing Todd's pro-African stance, pressed for more and faster liberalization or a real partnership. Todd recalled about the St. Andrew's speech, "I felt that I must put a brake on the Nationalist demands so as to give the white electorate some assurance that the Government was in control of the situation."[133] The speech contained the same type of attacks on African nationalist agendas found in the earlier Todd speeches. Todd recalled later, "At the time, and increasingly since, I was unhappy and eventually ashamed of that speech, especially the tone of it."[134] Three days after the St. Andrew's speech he gave another paradoxical speech in Bulawayo where he denied he was in favor of integrating schools or that he would propose to integrate schools. However, he added: "I have continually worked and will continue to work, for justice and fair play for all sections of our community—for justice is indivisible—either it is extended to all people or it will pass from the land."[135] While it is hard to know how much regret he had in giving the St Andrew's speech in 1957, Todd was rhetorically dancing with a polarized constituency and paradoxical policies. And it was too little, too late for whites.

CHAPTER THREE

The End

Todd tried to use his rhetoric to save his premiership, but it failed despite his best effort. Trying to derail the ouster, Todd even announced, "I am not a liberal." He defiantly added, "I believe in the welfare of all people of all races and will not pander to any one section to get votes."[136] At the party congress where the leadership issue was decided, Todd gave one of his best speeches. Unfortunately the press was barred from the session, forcing reporters to find places outside the building to listen in on the proceedings. With no prepared speech Todd had to reply to various accusations of his cabinet: that he was dictatorial, that he had taken all the credit for legislation, that security reports had been withheld from the cabinet, and that he regularly visited ANC headquarters in Bulawayo. Julian Greenfield, a Todd detractor, reported, "Todd made a brilliant speech in reply." A reporter of a paper opposed to Todd observed that Todd "moved from point to point with superb skill, answering his accusers in detail."[137] His Campbellian background came to the fore as he presented evidence and arguments to refute his critics. A friendly reporter described part of Todd's speech as he overheard thirty minutes of the ninety-minute oration:

> He was answering each and every accusation in the minutest detail, citing exact chapter and verse for every action. The complete master of his material, he employed it with astonishing fluency, compelling conviction, and an unerring sense of both time and humour. Brick by brick, the incriminating edifice of his opponent's cause was demolished. Explosions of applause mounted in volume and frequency, and he closed to something like a demonstration.[138]

Another report said that Todd's speech was the best of the day, with a two-minute standing ovation after it was finished.[139] One delegate said, "I don't care on whose side anyone is that was a magnificent speech."[140] One of Todd's opponents even congratulated him for the speech—but still voted against him!

Two votes were taken. In the first ballot Todd led with 129 votes; Edgar Whitehead, a surprise compromise candidate, had 122; and Sir Patrick Fletcher, Todd's renegade minister, received 73 votes. Todd did not have a majority, so in the second ballot Whitehead won 193 to 129. The speech was so effective that even in defeat and against party rules and practice the taped speech was never transcribed or circulated, with the tapes mysteriously disappearing. Ian Smith recalled a comment by one of Todd's cabinet members at a break during the congress, "In the final analysis, if we have to choose between Todd and a donkey, then it's the donkey!"[141] This was not to be the last time that Todd was to be silenced through devious means.

While his *ethos* declined with whites, he had far more success with Africans. British historian Robert Blake perceptively wrote about African support for Todd:

> The roots of this confidence stemmed not only from his achievements in the direction of African advancement, although these were substantial and greater than his later critics allow. They stemmed above all from the way he spoke and the genuine impression which he gave of having African interests at heart. It was his oratory, his manner, his general political "style" which, in the disapproving words of some of his colleagues "give rise to a feeling in the country [and they meant the Africans] that he is a sort of 'Saviour.'"[142]

Todd apparently used his appearances before Africans to stress the need to end racism. For example, as prime minister he spoke before a racially mixed group of three hundred Boy Scouts and Girl Guides and cited the biblical ideal that there was a "great need for people to do unto others as they would have them do unto them." He told them that Rhodesia was divided along racial lines; however, "you can't tell by the color of a man's skin whether he is a devil or a saint, neither can you tell by the color of his skin whether he is educated or uneducated." He hoped the scouts and guides could "help destroy the ... prejudices, fears and anxieties" of whites and blacks in Rhodesia.[143] While it overstates the case, the *African Parade* claimed in late 1956 that 99 percent of Africans in Southern Rhodesia had "an unbounded confidence" in Todd. This goodwill and trust Todd earned was "undoubted and unique." Todd was "a sincere man" who had "never given Africans cause to think" he wanted "to catch votes at the expense of the Africans."[144]

African reaction to Todd's removal was uniformly negative. The *African Weekly* editorialized that Todd's purging "dealt ... a severe blow" to African-European cooperation. Todd "was a symbol of honesty of purpose, sincerity of intentions," and African "welfare on all fronts as full citizens of this country." Todd's "imagination, ability, capacity for work and grasp of political facts was so apparent that even his opposing candidates were compelled to acknowledge it publicly," the *African Daily News* editorialized.[145] K. T. T. Maripe, president of the prominent Southern Rhodesia Trade Union Congress, also thought Todd's ouster was a "severe blow to the African community." He correctly feared that racial tensions would grow.[146] Nathan Shamuyarira wrote in 1965 that the time "for peaceful cooperation and swift progress toward racial equality—or better, a non-racial state—were over." He recalled that an African composed a song that became a bestselling record that said, "Todd has left us / Go well, old man."[147]

Appropriately, biblical metaphors were applied to the situation as a prophetic persona and *ethos* emerged for Todd. The *African Weekly* said "Todd is the Moses of our age."[148] Most significant was the reaction by Joshua Nkomo and the ANC. Nkomo said the "African people are now horrified and distressed that Mr. Todd has been crucified by his colleagues, caucus, and the U.F.P. Congress which assumes to represent moderate opinion."[149] Todd was increasingly seen as a Moses figure and a Christ figure by Africans. He soon lived up to that persona as he began to practice prophetic rhetoric as a radical democrat. Yet that did not happen immediately; Todd continued to use his reasonable limited democratic approach for a time in an effort to bring around those who still held political power.

Similarly, the international community, especially in Britain, did not welcome Todd's ouster. F. S. Joelson, editor of the London-based *East Africa and Rhodesia*, believed that Todd's removal was a blow to race relations and potentially detrimental to the economic development of Southern Rhodesia and the entire Central Federation.[150] The London *Times* argued that the attempt to remove Todd was "a panic measure which would surely shake confidence abroad in the Central African Federation."[151] The *Manchester Guardian* warned that the defeat for Todd would be seen in Britain as "a shift away from racial liberalism in Central Africa" and have negative "political repercussions" for Southern Rhodesia.[152] The Commonwealth correspondent of the *Daily Telegraph* also agreed that if liberalism was rejected then British opinion would turn against Rhodesian whites. Similar statements were made by the *Spectator* and the *New Statesman*.[153]

After he was forced out as prime minister, Todd organized his own political party and ran a slate of candidates in the June 1958 election. Todd and his party, as Ian Hancock states "tried to reason with the electorate, appeal to its intelligence and conscience and when confronted with ignorance and prejudice, engage in . . . an exercise in adult education."[154] Todd's reasonable approach to politics, in the face of white fears, failed. He lost his seat in parliament and his party failed to gain a single seat.

For twelve years Todd worked within the political system, using the speaking opportunities and rhetorical forms available for persons holding power within the system. While having some success in adapting to his audience through classical forms of rhetoric, Todd suddenly found himself out of power. The old rhetorical forms were not necessarily effective for persons operating from outside standard power structures. Thus Todd's speaking and his views on human rights underwent a transformation.

CHAPTER 4

TODD THE PROPHETIC:
THE RADICAL DEMOCRAT

Truths must be supported and vindicated for their own sakes. . . . Truth is Truth, right is right, duty is duty and the end is God's not mine. —*Garfield Todd, 1967*

The free peoples of the world must work to ensure that freedom, liberty and opportunity be made the heritage of all men. We, who believe in democracy, cannot evade our responsibility, for liberty is threatened in America when it is denied in Africa; peace is in jeopardy when the minds of men are at war. —*Garfield Todd, 1960*

In 1977, "Taffy," the leader and chief assassin of Ian Smith's Central Intelligence Organization, noticed that Garfield Todd was on his flight to Lukasa, Zambia. He recalled "although *persona-non-grata* in the eyes of most white Rhodesians," Todd "remained a man of considerable influence with the dissidents as well as in the eyes of the world, principally because he had formerly held office as Rhodesia's premier."[1] Taffy and his partner tracked Todd's activities for more than thirty hours. He seriously considered assassinating Todd contrary to his orders from Smith's government. He said, "I thought of using an old trick popular with the various government security services throughout the world. I would knock on his door. When he answered I would club him, sweep him bodily to the window and throw him out head first. The inquest verdicts in such cases are invariably 'accidental death' or 'suicide while of unsound mind.'"[2] Fortunately for Todd the assassin simply followed Todd to Joshua Nkomo's house-in-exile next to the President of Zambia's official residence.[3]

The history of prophets is filled with martyrs.[4] While Todd escaped martyrdom he built his prophetic *ethos* from the African perceptions that he had suffered or been crucified by whites when he was removed as prime minister. The images of Moses leading the Africans and being a prophet ahead of his time stuck and Todd lived up to those images, creating a powerful prophetic persona that in combination with being a former prime minister made Todd a unique and formidable figure in the fight for human rights and democracy in Africa.

Todd believed his own ambitions had to be subsumed to the greater good of the self-evident, sacred truth. Furthermore he would be irresponsible if he did not speak out for that truth. James Darsey, in his theory of prophetic rhetoric, argues that prophets and reformers felt responsible for the consequences of their message only when they failed to speak their God-given, self-evident message.[5] Darsey shows the similarities between the pronouncements of the Hebrew prophets and the rhetoric of radical reform: "Both have in common a sense of mission, a desire to bring the practice of the people into accord with a sacred principle, and an uncompromising, often excoriating stance toward a reluctant audience."[6] Todd's rhetoric after 1960 turned radical and in so doing became an excellent exemplar of prophetic rhetoric. Todd's rhetoric followed prophetic *logos*, *pathos*, and *ethos*. In his *logos* he called for full democracy, which he believed was self-evident to all people. His *pathos* first emerged out of the crises of his failed premiership and the 1959 riots and in its full development warned of a stark moral choice: democracy or bloodshed. Finally his *ethos* emerged when he answered the call of Africans in 1960. He embraced the nationalist position and effectively ended his political career when he demanded that Britain intervene in Southern Rhodesia and force whites out of power by installing a truly democratic government.

Todd's Prophetic Rhetoric

Chris Laidlaw, former ambassador of New Zealand to Zimbabwe, called Todd the conscience of the country.[7] Todd's rhetoric after 1960 fits comfortably into the prophetic tradition as he opposed the oppressive political practices of the white Rhodesian governments. Darsey states: "The most accessible evidence of the prophet's radicalism is his opposition to the regnant power structure."[8] After Todd's sacking, the new prime minister, Edgar Whitehead, continued many of the same liberal and gradualist policies. Todd, however, believed "the time for liberalism was over,"[9] so he opposed many of the same policies that he had supported as prime minister. With prophetic *logos*, compromise is not possible; instead, the prophet proclaims what is true in such a way that "the people must come to God; He cannot come to them."[10] The truth for the reformer is self-evident and the people must be converted to the truth or the proposed reform. Todd proclaimed the truth of African freedom and the evil of racism no matter how unpopular it was with Rhodesian whites. Later in life, when he faced the reverse racism and oppressive political practices of Mugabe, Todd remained outspoken in his opposition to antidemocratic practices.

The prophetic voice is found in its fullest when there is "a time of crisis" or "a sense of overwhelming threat . . . a threat to the self-definition of a people."[11] Southern Rhodesia and later Zimbabwe with little exception have been in this state of crisis since Todd was removed as prime minister in 1958. The crisis over race propelled Todd to give speeches for African rights and make visits with leaders all over the world to lobby for the same cause. The world Todd faced in 1960 was far different than in 1958. Specifically the rise of African nationalism propelled him to a radical prophetic position in support of African enfranchisement. While appeals to reasonableness did not disappear from Todd's rhetoric, he shifted to *pathos* and became an accuser and a judge of Rhodesia's racist society. As Darsey states, "in a world where political and religious leaders fail to offer clear direction . . . prophetic rhetoric posits a clear dramatic opposition of protagonist and antagonist. It clarifies moral identities and structures desires for denouement."[12] Todd made attempts for compromise but unlike his earlier gradualist position the grounds shifted as he framed those compromises by the demands that black majority rule needed to rapidly emerge. It became a clear choice between the evil of racism or the good of true democracy. Here prophetic *pathos* and *ethos* merge and Todd as the judge of white racism was burdened by his opposition to bigotry as whites rejected his message. White Rhodesians in turn reinforced Todd's prophetic persona, especially when Smith decided to supply the ultimate *ethos* for Todd by restricting him to his ranch in 1965.

The period of crisis unfolded in Southern Rhodesia over time, but it took on urgency with Todd's removal as prime minister in 1958. While Todd remained in politics for a few more years, the deepening crisis propelled him to the prophetic stance, culminating in his withdrawal from party politics in 1961. He was exiled to the political wilderness and there his prophetic *pathos* took root. Bold images and metaphors, unlike his previous reasonable rhetoric, emerged becoming more striking as he fully entered into his prophetic phase.

In March 1959 the first major crisis since his removal propelled Todd toward full radical democracy for Africans. Just as Todd had feared, whites turned to force in a futile attempt to keep African nationalism at bay. Dr. Hastings Banda returned to Nyasaland after a forty-year exile, thus stirring nationalist aspirations. Demonstrations and riots broke out in early 1959 in Nyasaland. Whitehead claimed that similar riots were about to break out in Southern Rhodesia and so declared a State of Emergency on February 26, 1959. The Unlawful Organisations and Preventative Detention Acts were passed and all the leading African nationalist organizations, including the African National Congress (ANC), were banned. ANC offices were raided and five hundred Africans were jailed. Many ANC leaders were thrown into detention and others fled into exile. Detentions without trial and search and seizure by police without warrants were permitted. Todd returned from a tour of the Commonwealth and was horrified by the turn of events.[13]

He issued a statement on March 10 that set the stage for his important speeches on March 16. In an attempt to mollify whites, Todd called for full support of the government so that the state of emergency could end quickly, then he turned to his controversial proposal that there was only one thing that "would guarantee the safety of all our citizens."[14] Unless the color bar was "broken massively and immediately," within five years Africans would use it against whites and partnership would become "an impossible deal."[15] Whites were the only ones with the power to make the change. Over the next few days he spelled out some specifics which angered whites and galvanized the hopes and support of Africans. Todd wanted "Europeans Only" signs to be taken down. Hotels, restaurants, and cinemas should be immediately opened to "well dressed and well behaved Rhodesians of any race." He wanted African railways completely opened to all races and he wanted the Land Apportionment Act revised to open up business centers in towns to all races.[16] Setting the stage for his major speech on March 16, nine United Federal Party members of the federal parliament attacked Todd's proposals as an effort "to introduce confusion and doubts in the minds of the people."[17]

When Todd came to deliver a speech on March 16, 1959, at Athenaeum Hall in a white area of Salisbury, seven thousand Africans came to hear him speak, which at that time was the largest audience ever to hear a public speaker in Southern Rhodesia. Todd quickly arranged with the police to allow all the people to hear him in three successive hour-long sessions where he repeated his speech. Todd criticized the Federation as "a great bus which is taking us all to a happy place and higher standard of living but the unfortunate thing was that there were certain people who believed the bus was clearly marked 'Europeans Only.'"[18] Todd argued that true partnership needed to happen in a few months rather than years. He had faith in Africans because he and Grace "had lived in African areas as missionaries for 20 years."[19] Todd attacked the proposed Unlawful Organisations Bill because it rejected the principle of British law that an individual was innocent until proven guilty so it was "utterly unworthy of a British country." The law would bring Rhodesia "into the contempt of the whole Commonwealth" and it "could be a major cause to a break up of peace, order and tranquility" in Southern Rhodesia. Todd proved to be correct in his assessment of the law. It was renewed by the Rhodesian Front when it came to power and all of its draconian provisions remained in place until 1980.[20] Todd ended with a warning that Southern Africa was the only place in the British Commonwealth "that a person was judged on the color of his skin." He hoped that his European friends would "make the greatest contribution to the progress of the country," but they could only do it with the help "of all the other races." He urged his African friends to "eschew violence." He hoped that if all races worked together then the Federation would be made "great." And if they could do this, he concluded, "We must indeed deserve to be great."[21]

The first session went smoothly with an audience of mostly Africans who repeatedly cheered and applauded. In the second and third sessions heckling by whites repeatedly interrupted him. A woman who belonged to the League of European Loyalists objected to Todd's statement that the racial policy of South Africa was contrary to the British way of life, so she went within a few inches of Todd to heckle him.[22] A male jumped onto the stage and while the audience booed and jeered him he said, "I am standing here as a representative of the white race." Another heckler yelled, "You are a sell-out, Mr. Todd. You are selling our country to the munts."[23] Despite these extreme difficulties Todd never lost his composure. In this campaign-like setting, Todd interjected his wit. The hall was so hot Todd took off his jacket, rolled up his sleeves and said, "While I may be prepared to talk for three hours I am definitely not prepared to sweat for that length of time."[24] Todd and his political party, the Central African Party (C.A.P.), had been frequently accused of stirring up African emotions despite his reasonable rhetoric. Todd quipped that "that if stirring up people's emotions was an offence, he was not sure that the C.A.P. would not be proscribed." This brought laughter from the crowd.[25] The *Rhodesia Herald* nicely summed up the event, reporting that Todd's "control of the meeting was masterly, a lively and eye-opening meeting marred only by the bad behavior on the part of some of the Europeans present."[26]

The speech represents a key moment in Todd's career as he moved ever closer to a complete prophetic stance. His paternalism was melting away although he still was in transition. On March 11, 1959, he stated that some leaders of the ANC were "reasonable men, while others were adamant nationalists."[27] There was less effort to control the political discourse of the African Nationalists and a clearer adopting of their position. The *Rhodesia Herald* editorialized on the significance of Todd's meeting: "He has come back into prominence—joyfully welcomed albeit mainly by the voteless—by stepping into the void created when the Government swooped on the leaders of the African National Congress." They also correctly noted "Todd has become the symbol of black aspirations." And they concluded, "Todd is a force to be reckoned with . . . and the implications of his campaigning have not yet been clearly assessed."[28] While Todd still saw himself as a politician and a person who wanted to control the political policies and discourse of all Rhodesians, the editorial correctly pointed out that his future lay with the powerless (Africans) and not with the regnant power structure. Todd continued his attacks on a "pretence of partnership" that created dangers through "luke-warm policies" which lulled "the Europeans of Central Africa in the comfortable belief that all will be well."[29] He used more prophetic *pathos* when in November 1959 he called partnership a car that "failed to get us to the desired heaven."[30] The Africans were calling Todd to be a prophet but he did not completely answer the call until 1960.

As with most prophets, Todd's *ethos* stands squarely at the heart of his rhetoric. Darsey reminds us of I. A. Richards's thought that a person is sincere when one's actions, feelings, and thoughts are in harmony with "one's true nature." Darsey comments "The prophet's sincerity derives from the abolition of personal motive, from abnegation, so that 'one's true nature' becomes synonymous with the divine message and one's *pathos* with the divine *pathos*."[31] West also says that prophetic Christianity places "A premium on the kind of human being one chooses to be rather than on the amount of commodities that one possesses."[32] While Todd failed as a politician and his efforts to help black Africans were often frustrated as power elites in Africa and Britain ignored him, there was no question that Todd's *ethos* was a powerful dimension of his speaking. Todd lived up to the suffering implicit in the Christlike prophetic persona that Africans attributed to Todd after his removal as prime minister.

Important for a prophet's *ethos* is his call—in Todd's case by the people—to proclaim the truth in the face of powerful opposition and with the threat of loss of prestige, status, wealth, and even one's life. Todd's call came on July 26, 1960, in the aftermath of the Bulawayo riots. Whitehead, despite continuing a gradualist policy, became more repressive in dealing with the growing African nationalist movement. On January 1, 1960, the National Democratic Party (NDP) formed to replace the outlawed ANC. Now educated Africans joined the new party. With the older ANC leaders out of the picture, Sketchley Samkange and other younger men assumed leadership positions. Samkange and the NDP launched a nonviolent campaign for change, but Whitehead responded with arrests of key NDP leaders. This prompted a series of peaceful protest meetings starting in Harare on July 20, 1960. It degenerated into a riot when the police fired tear gas into the crowd of thirty thousand people. A few days later, on July 24 and 25 in Bulawayo a similar story unfolded when the NDP lost control of the situation and a riot ensued when police fired tear gas into the marchers. One died in Harare and eleven in Bulawayo—the first deaths from police action since the 1896 uprisings.[33]

Todd was in London when the Bulawayo riots happened. Whereas in 1959 Todd tried to mollify whites, in 1960 he felt that the time for placating whites was over and that the British government needed to intervene to push through a peaceful change to African leadership and control of Rhodesia. Todd admitted a few days later that this was his turning point: "I was not prepared to face the situation squarely until the inevitable riots occurred; until men were killed." He knew the Africans "were not prepared to submit any longer," so Britain had to either "face her responsibilities or abdicate and leave the struggle for freedom, for advancement, for dignity, to the two and a half million African people themselves."[34]

Todd drew up a statement calling for British intervention that he presented to Lord Home on July 26, 1960. Knowing that Nkomo and other NDP leaders were in London, he met with them and they read his memo. Nkomo, while agreeing with it, thought it did not go far enough, suggesting that Britain needed to suspend Southern Rhodesia's constitution. Todd agreed. He and the NDP leaders signed the memo which was given to Home. Todd and Nkomo held a press conference later that day as they released the statement to the public.[35]

Todd and Nkomo condemned the minority holding on to power through the use of force and asked Britain to peacefully intervene and bring democracy to Central Africa. They wanted Britain to set aside Southern Rhodesia's Constitution and bring in British troops to ensure a peaceful exchange of power. They called for self-government for all three territories of the Central Federation within five years, with universal franchise for adults.[36] At the press conference Todd lamented that Africans wanted a say in the government and "what we got was bullets." Africans were bitter "and it was only a matter of time before things blew up."[37] Todd had now completely abandoned paternalism and was endorsing the nationalist cause. Todd's position proved to be too radical for his liberal, multiracial Central African Party. Some whites left even though Todd resigned. Moderate Black Africans knew the game was up so they left for the NDP.

The NDP, recognizing that Todd had essentially moved to support African Nationalism, invited Todd to join. Many nationalists thought Todd was the only white to realize the need for "a revolutionary rethinking," and they appreciated what Todd had done.[38] William Takavarasha, the chair of the NDP at Gwelo, admired Todd for his foresightedness and called Todd "a political prophet" who was thinking five years ahead of all other European politicians."[39] Other African leaders called him a prophet because he "saw the signs of the coming storm in Africa more realistically than any other politician, newsman, or busybody." They also believed that Todd's loyalty to Nkomo's NDP, finally called ZAPU, and to Nkomo's leadership "was an act of supreme courage."[40]

Even whites inadvertently evoked his Christlike persona by despising and rejecting him. Whites were unwilling to hear Todd's message with some calling it "treason" and many calling for his deportation. One MP demanded that Todd's citizenship be nullified.[41] Fearing that he would be killed or injured because of white outrage, Todd secretly slipped back into the country after the London press conference.[42] Whitehead called Todd's statement "utterly irresponsible," and other MPs said it was "utterly disloyal" to Southern Rhodesia.[43] He defended himself while still in London: "I believe some people would call me a traitor, but I believe that I am a patriot. I believe somebody has got to say these things now."[44] However, Todd knew that he had committed political suicide. Todd resigned from his party and on September 2 retired from politics.[45] He made one more brief but abortive attempt to reenter politics in 1961 with the creation of the New Africa Party, but within six months that effort was dead.[46] Todd had become a prophet standing outside the political system. His despised status continued with whites for much of his life. A paper from the Australian Churches of Christ said that "Rhodesia's prickly whites" called him a "traitor, commie, Kaffir lover, and scab."[47] "White Rhodesia's most rejected white man" was the epigram for Todd.[48]

Todd's prophetic rhetoric can be traced back to his rationality and epistemology that was fundamentally grounded in the New Zealand Churches of Christ. James Darsey points to the Whigs of the American Revolution as exemplars of the prophetic tradition in America with their focus on "prophecy as sacred truth." He explains that Thomas Jefferson, the Whigs, and many of the American colonists shared the common epistemology of the British Empiricists and the Scottish Common Sense philosophy. This outlook provided the language or terms of the truths they believed. "Self-evidence," "moral sense," or "common sense" were axiomatic truths for the Americans.[49] Darsey says, "Whigs and Old Testament prophets had in common that they knew an absolute truth and to paraphrase William James, that they knew that they knew; it was by all appearance self-evident."[50] Grounded in the same epistemological outlook by his Churches of Christ heritage, self-evidence flowed from Todd's Christian and democratic beliefs. He stated this self-evident egalitarianism in Washington, D.C., in 1960, "the Bible teaches us we are all sons of God and therefore brothers."[51] Todd even recognized his common outlook with the American Revolution, as he often quoted Jefferson's words from the Declaration of Independence: "We hold these truths to be self-evident, that all men are created equal, that they are endowed by their Creator with certain unalienable rights that amongst these are life, liberty and the pursuit of happiness."[52] Todd further believed that the overwhelming majority black population made African enfranchisement self-evident—an idea he frequently cited in his speeches.

In his 1960 speech at Wellesley College in the United States, Todd recognized that the Christian message, along with democracy, was opposed to the racism of the white Europeans. As West says: "There is nothing tribalistic or nationalistic about prophetic witness. Xenophobic prejudices and imperialistic practices are unequivocally condemned."[53] Todd pressed this view in many of his speeches. At Wellesley Todd combined Paul's message that the gospel is for all from the sermon on Mars Hill with Jeffersonian Republicanism: "We are all members of the great family of men, of one blood, and within us we have the divine spark that lights the hearts of all men. It was no more remarkable for Jefferson to say that men had the right to 'life, liberty, and the pursuit of happiness' than it is for men in Africa to band themselves together to express this compelling belief in demands and actions."[54] In his American setting, Todd knew that these prophetic words were applicable to both the United States and Africa as the Civil Rights movement was gaining momentum.

In this early prophetic speech, Todd was concerned about developing democracy among African nationalists after they won independence. He knew that the hardest work was going to be developing democratic traditions when the white government was gone. He said in the middle of the nationalist effort:

> It is relatively easy to lead an awakening people against an antagonist who can be seen—who stands out clearly white against a background of colonialism. But when that battle has been concluded, must there be another enemy—must it be the Chiefs, or the Opposition, or a neighbouring state; or will the new leaders be able then to turn to the great challenge of meeting the needs of their people? Will they be able to turn from fiery speeches to hard work, to careful planning, to wise statesmanship?[55]

Franchise was merely the first step in democracy; the real strength was to develop a stable minority and allow free speech and a peaceful transfer of power: "It is the other side which gives democracy its strength and makes it the finest known system of government. The other side is the security of the minority; the right of these people to state their views, to exert their influence, and to work openly and freely to take over the government at a later date, by changing the opinions of the people and gaining a majority of votes."[56] Todd worried that autocratic colonialism worked against the future of Africa.

Todd accurately forecast the major problem of developing democratic government for Zimbabwe and for all of Africa. He believed that "security, liberty and opportunity are based upon the rights of each individual." However this was "the most difficult concept to get across to the people of the new nations. The upholding of such rights requires real stature and maturity within a community." Unfortunately, "the Governors and District Commissioners leaned towards autocracy and the experience of the peoples whom they governed was not always one which taught them the sweet reasonableness of democracy in action." Todd feared that the new governments would follow the colonial policies "to believe that they will also have to be very firm, because they too will work for the good of all and therefore any opposition is an unwarranted hindrance to the sound development of this country, and should not be tolerated."[57]

Knowing both the power and fickleness of the United States, Todd turned to his American audience and pleaded with them to help nurture democracy in Africa: "The free peoples of the world must work to ensure that freedom, liberty and opportunity be made the heritage of all men. We, who believe in democracy, cannot evade our responsibility, for liberty is threatened in America when it is denied in Africa; peace is in jeopardy when the minds of men are at war."[58] Todd the prophet often called on the West to help Zimbabwe and other African countries to achieve true democracy.

By 1961 Africans knew they had Todd's full support. Todd readily and bravely accepted African trust. A year after his call, Todd reaffirmed it in December 1961. The Whitehead government banned the NDP and once again called out troops. Todd had promised full cooperation with the NDP two weeks before. He wrote Emory Ross, a longtime Disciples of Christ missionary and head of the Albert Schweitzer society "the N.D.P. leaders and I have full confidence in each other . . . therefore we must act now." Accepting the Christlike persona of the prophet, he poignantly added, "Grace realizes that my time for action has come but neither of us is under any illusions as to what the cost might be." He ended his letter saying, "I am on my way to the first meeting with Africans in this new chapter of our experience."[59]

Africans not only admired Todd but they realized his *ethos* was important for the nationalist movement outside of Rhodesia. They readily took advantage of what Todd had to offer, including invitations to speak twice at the UN along with numerous speeches he gave on behalf of Nkomo and the movement. When Nkomo was accused of being a terrorist and Communist, Africans evoked Todd's *ethos*: "Would a man of fine repute willingly and knowingly associate himself with a terrorist organization and with a terrorist leader?"[60] The effective blunting of white attacks on Nkomo and the nationalist movement angered racist white Rhodesians.

When Todd completely turned to prophetic radicalism, the *pathos* of his message was turned up as he saw the terrible implications of the Rhodesian crisis. In his 1962 UN speech he warned that if Britain did not intervene in Rhodesia the prime minister would be "thrown out" or there would be "riots, bloodshed and economic attrition."[61] The speech was very effective in blunting the white Rhodesian message that they were gradually bringing democracy to Africans. Whites were even more infuriated with Todd.[62]

Todd openly continued his effort to end white supremacy in Rhodesia. In July 1962, in an ecumenical religious service in Salisbury with blacks and whites in attendance, Todd called the Rhodesian situation "intolerable" and "outrageous." He said the church needed to "support social justice for all people by its prayers and by the participation of individual members." He also thought the church was "silent" in the face of injustice and that missionaries feared "to tell the truth."[63]

While Todd's rhetoric clearly created separation rather than identification with white European audiences as good prophetic rhetoric does, there is another side to the story. Todd, like a good prophet, sided with the powerless who suffer injustice. The same rhetoric that created separation from the power elites also created identification with the powerless. After Todd defended African nationalism before the UN in 1962, he became more open in his associations with the nationalist movement. In a speech sponsored by the African Trades Union Congress in September 1962, Todd donned a traditional African fur hat following the practice of Joshua Nkomo and other nationalist leaders. In a clear break from his practice as prime minister, Todd said that trade unions "were based on the principles of democracy and consultation." He accused the white government of being a small group who ruled "with the backing of police and military forces." He praised the leaders of the nationalist movements in Northern and Southern Rhodesia, Kenneth Kaunda and Joshua Nkomo, because "they advocated democracy and equal rights for all."[64] Todd's statements along with his dress simultaneously created separation from the Europeans but identification with the African nationalists. Similarly, Todd noted that since Nkomo had rejected the proposed new Rhodesian constitution, Nkomo was "the one and only majority leader in this land."[65]

Todd's prophetic stance remained firmly grounded in his Christian outlook. As West states, "It has been the prophetic Christian tradition . . . that has so often pushed for social justice."[66] Todd forcibly restated his democratic *ethos* grounded in his religious heritage: "The Christian doctrine of the priesthood of all believers has about it a flavor of democracy and suggests that Christian men and women, like truth, can flourish best in a free and open society, a society where questions may be freely asked, where questions may be given without fear."[67] Todd continued to press for Christians and the church to remain outspoken against injustice. In 1963 on the government-sponsored Federal Broadcasting Corporation radio network, he said: "The Church must never evade her responsibility to choose the right, to protest not only against the violence but also against the use of repressive laws backed by force." He argued that the church needed to support African nationalism: "The nationalist cause is not in itself anti-Christian; in fact in so far as it presses for freedom of the individual, for social justice for all, without distinction of race, its principles are Christian." The overall mission for the Church in political action in Africa was "to achieve an atonement between black and white."[68]

Todd was using the premises of his white Rhodesian opponents against them. Darsey notes that this shows that the prophet shares the same world as his audience and yet they will still find his discourse too extreme.[69] White Rhodesians, and Todd himself, had long used the ideal of "Christian civilization" to justify their political control. Larry Bowman gives a nice summary of those premises justifying white rule:

> There was little need to justify white rule except on the commonly accepted ground that the whites were civilized and the Africans were not and therefore the whites had the right, even the obligation to rule. In the period of federation and after, the Europeans brought considerable new sophistication to their arguments. Civilized standards, advancement on merit, parity, partnership, and defense of Western civilization against communism are but a few of the slogans around which the Europeans have rallied in the past generation.[70]

Todd, though, turned the premises on their head by really believing that Africans would sooner rather than later (or never) attain the standards of civilization. Todd used insider rhetoric for an outsider position. The priesthood of all believers trumped any racist aspect of Christian civilization.

Todd continued to press whites about their racism in 1963. Before a white audience, he called the forthcoming Federal election "a sputnik which has been ever out of control since it left the launching pad." Segregation would not bring safety for Europeans but would bring "ultimate violence."[71] Todd continued to warn whites: "We are living in terrible days and we don't realize the depths to which we are sinking." Todd believed that as international boycotts began against Rhodesia's racist practices that there would be "bloodshed" if the boycotts did not bring about full democracy for all.[72]

In 1964 Todd gave two important international speeches: his second appearance before the United Nations Committee on Colonialism and his first Feetham Lecture at Witwatersrand University, South Africa. In 1964 Todd was worried that the Rhodesian Front, a right-wing government led by Winston Field and Ian Smith, would declare independence without Britain's approval and plunge Southern Rhodesia into civil war. This theme was an important part of his message to the UN. Todd prophetically warned in his 1964 UN speech: "It's either Britain or bloodshed." As with the 1962 UN speech, *Time* reported that the UN Committee on Colonialism voted overwhelmingly (19 to 0 with three abstentions) to support Todd's proposal "to give majority rule to Southern Rhodesian Africans and to restrain the white extremists."[73]

His prophetic *ethos* made his UN speech particularly compelling. Todd's past as a preacher and prime minister gave him incredible prophetic *ethos*, especially to blacks in Africa and to international audiences. Even his enemies had to begrudgingly admit his life and principles were beyond reproach. *Time* magazine reported about Todd's UN speech of 1964 that the colonialism committee had

> heard many an eloquent speech dedicated to the proposition that black men, rather than white men, should have the ruling voice in African nations. But seldom has the committee listened to this argument so intently as it did last week when a visitor from Africa roundly proclaimed that the Europeans of his country had "clung to power too long." What stirred the committee was the fact that the speaker—R. S. Garfield

Todd—was both a white man and a former Prime Minister of segregationist Southern Rhodesia.[74]

After Todd's 1964 UN speech Dr. Kenneth Kaunda, the prime minister of Zambia, said that Todd was the "Saviour" for white Rhodesians as he urged them to dump Ian Smith and back Todd, who would lead them to a peaceful transition to black power with Nkomo as the eventual leader of Zimbabwe.[75]

Todd also took his prophetic *logos* to South Africa in his Feetham lecture of August 6, 1964. Directly challenging apartheid grounded in the Afrikaners racist theological belief that they were chosen by God, Todd believed that true Christianity lined up with "minorities" or the oppressed as they could see truth while elites remained blind. Todd said:

> World opinion is a very real power today. It is a frightening power, not only to those who disagree with it but also to those who are inclined to look to minorities for sensitive understanding of the truth. Many of us believe that the most critical moment of history was posed over a minority of one, and Him crucified. At that moment the world held no hope—"What is truth?" Pilate had asked. The promise given to men is that we shall yet know the truth and that it shall set us free. I believe that truth alone can set us free so that he who finds freedom for himself and for his fellows must seek truth with clear eyes, an open mind, and a resolute heart.[76]

While sharing Christian premises with his European white audiences Todd gave those premises a different reading to encourage them to support black majority rule. Todd also shared their belief in democracy but he attempted to argue that true democracy could be found in supporting the nationalist causes. The whites had a false notion of democracy that was out-of-step with the British tradition and world opinion. Similarly, Todd challenged South Africans to embrace true democracy and reject racism: "What is to be our future? What is your thinking? The official policies of both our countries on race are unacceptable both to the world and to the vast majority of our own fellow-countrymen. And even if they were true could they stand before the onslaught of the spiritual force of the democratic urge which has been the vital phenomenon of the last three centuries?"[77] Todd argued that democracy was the best form of government and could transform all of southern Africa:

> The power of the democratic idea is at least partly explained by its results. Democracy, the right to participate equally in the government of one's country, has brought higher standards of living, better educational and medical facilities, and a new stature to the personality of the people. Maybe democracy is not the only form of government which can help to attain these ends, but most people in southern Africa believe that a democratic way of life is infinitely preferable to any authoritarian regime.[78]

However, whites in Rhodesia and South Africa had not embraced true democracy or majority rule, and the result was deadly for both countries:

> The spread of democracy in the past century has broken down the class system and the caste system. In southern Africa it could break down the race system and bring freedom to both oppressed and oppressor—for both are bound. But amongst our white people where could it get sufficient soil in which to grow? We have deceived ourselves into believing that we share already in a democracy. In fact there is nothing so grimly dead as a form which has lost its spirit. We do have democratic forms for whites. . . . This is not democracy and sometimes I despair of ever seeing it established amongst our peoples of the Republic and of Rhodesia. How can we make peaceful progress towards democracy when it is illegal to use the natural methods of getting there: free association, free discussion and the right to criticise? Democracy is not a perfection, it is marching forward together, a continuing fellowship allowing for differences of opinion, providing within itself the machinery for effecting peaceful change. Democracy is not only a system of government, it is a way of life. It has grown from the deep desire of men to develop to the limit of their ability.[79]

The speech was an amazing oration and it was unusual for South Africans to allow such a performance. Todd was not so lucky with his second Feetham speech in 1980.

Predictably, the reactionary Rhodesian government now in control did not want orations like the UN speech or Feetham lecture. Fearing a prophet, the Rhodesian governments often banned Todd's speeches or silenced him completely. Soon after the Feetham lecture

Ian Smith's government, the Rhodesian Front, banned one of Todd's speeches to be delivered at the Barbourfields stadium in Bulawayo under the Law and Order (Maintenance) Act.[80] Within a few days of this action, on August 26, 1964, the government declared a state of emergency, banned the leading paper for Africans, the *African Daily News*, and started detaining hundreds of African leaders in an effort to quell rising African nationalism.[81]

Todd's fears about a Unilateral Declaration of Independence (UDI) from Britain by Rhodesia were well-founded. The actions by the Rhodesian Front against Todd and the African nationalist movement in 1964 signaled Smith's actions for 1965. First, the fear of Todd's prophetic eloquence prompted Ian Smith and the white minority government to silence Todd. In 1965, two weeks before he planned to declare independence from Britain, Smith restricted Todd. On October 20, 1965, just minutes away from flying to England to deliver a speech at Edinburgh University, Todd was arrested and taken back to Hokonui ranch where he was restricted for the next year. This created a public relations nightmare for Smith, as it gave Todd worldwide celebrity.[82]

As soon as Todd was released from his detention he took up right where he left speaking out against Smith. For example, in 1967 at a protest meeting of property owners in Sinoia, Todd spoke out against a Smith government bill designed to prevent Indians and people of "mixed blood" from moving into white neighborhoods. Todd warned that Rhodesia's "doom would be sealed if it chose apartheid, a separation of races based on the South Africa pattern."[83]

Todd was arrested again on January 18, 1972. In 1971 Sir Alec Douglas Home, the British Foreign Secretary, negotiated an agreement with Ian Smith that Todd and most Africans considered a sellout to the racist whites. Britain sent Lord Pearce and the Pearce Commission to investigate the feelings of the Rhodesian people toward the proposed agreement. Todd and his daughter Judith spoke out in several public meetings against the agreement. After thirty-six days in prison, Todd was once again restricted to his ranch. No one was allowed to communicate with him from the outside or to directly quote him. Todd was barred from speaking or even writing letters. After four and a half years, Todd was finally released from detention on June 2, 1976.[84] At peril to his own life, Todd openly supported African rebels against Smith's government during his detention. Despite living in the midst of the heated battles of the civil war, Todd amazingly did not lose a single animal on his ranch during the fighting, and the Dadaya Mission remained open while many other missions were closed.

This detention also thrust Todd onto the world stage, making him more in demand as a speaker after he was released. Despite being sixty-nine years old, Todd once again began giving speeches to demand that full democracy be given to Zimbabwe. In January 1977 Jimmy Carter became the new president of the United States, so Todd began a lobbying effort for the African nationalists. He went on a tour of the United States in July 1977. During his travels he met with Andrew Young, the U.S. ambassador to the UN, Vice President Walter Mondale, Secretary of State Cyrus Vance, and on June 8 testified before the Subcommittee on Africa of the Committee on International Relations in the House of Representatives.[85] Todd talked to the UN Colonialism Committee on June 6, 1977.[86] Todd also spoke before numerous civic groups interested in African issues.[87] In these speeches Todd narrated the atrocities committed by Ian Smith against the African people to maintain white minority rule. For example, Todd told one group:

> Three or four of these guerrillas had held a meeting in this very remote place and 200 villagers women and children and men had come flocking in and they were singing and having talks and so on. The guerrillas were teaching them freedom songs and a stick of security forces I think 15 men came. They had been alerted because a couple of buses had been robbed in that area. So they had been sent down and they came up quietly through the bushes. Now they approached with their automatic rifles at the ready. So when a sentry fired a warning shot, they opened up with their automatic weapons and kept firing for seven minutes. When they moved into the village there were 35 dead, 31 seriously wounded. So our army does not mind killing 35 innocent villagers in order to kill one freedom fighter. Now that's only one instance of so many things that are happening because we have entered a time of complete ruthlessness. It is because of the tragic situation that I at the moment find myself in England and America.[88]

Darsey notes that prophetic self-evidence is radical because of "its engagement with society at its root."[89] He relates that Walter Bruggeman says the Hebrew prophet had to "move back into the deepest resources of his community and activate those very symbols that have always been the basis for contradicting the regnant conscientiousness."[90] Prophets threatened the very self-definition of a country by subverting how the government and the people understood themselves. Their self-definition was at odds with their very own ideals according to the prophet. As prophets judged moral wrongs in this way they usually alienated themselves from their audience. Todd not only was outspoken against white rule in his speeches in Britain, the United States, Australia, New Zealand, and the United Nations, but he also courageously did so in Zimbabwe.

All in all, in his prophetic *logos* Todd identified true democracy with the African nationalist cause. He challenged white Europeans to see that their form of democracy was not democracy at all but simply an authoritarian system perpetuating an authoritarian racism. He clarified the confused thinking of the whites, but like most elites they rejected the message and the messenger.

After Robert Mugabe's government came to power, Todd remained outspoken when freedom and civil rights were threatened. In 1980 Todd received his second invitation to deliver a Feetham lecture at the University of the Witwatersrand in Johannesburg, South Africa. When the South African government read the advance copy of the lecture, they refused to give him a visa. Unlike other times, the ban on Todd was circumvented. Students placed an empty chair on the stage at the university and had his speech published in the *Daily Rand Mail* on July 7, 1980. The speech became known by the title "The Speech that Says it All—in Silence."[91] From 1980 to 1985 Todd was a senator for Zimbabwe. As his differences with Mugabe grew, however, he soon resigned. In 1989, at age eighty-one, Todd spoke to a large group of Zimbabwean businessmen and leaders at the Hilton Hotel in Harare and warned that freedom could disappear even under black rule.[92] In his retirement Todd remained a critic of Mugabe's oppression of both black and white Zimbabweans.[93]

While Todd, unlike Christ, did not live in poverty, he did give away significant portions of his wealth. In 1988 he gave away three thousand acres of his ranch to create a farm cooperative for 50 civil war veterans and their families.[94] Later, in the 1990s, Todd sold his entire ranch and donated all the proceeds to create an educational scholarship for Zimbabwean students, the Garfield Todd Trust.

Even in the face of all these problems, Todd remained fundamentally optimistic as he protested against Mugabe, implicitly invoking a Moses persona (the people would achieve the promised land of a free Zimbabwe but he would not be there with them): "I would love to see a new constitution, for law and order to be restored and for the people to have enough food on their tables. Zimbabwe will get back on its feet, I am certain, but regret it won't be in my lifetime."[95]

For nearly seventy years Garfield Todd played an important role in Zimbabwean society. His Christian commitments and reasonable approach to religion and politics fashioned his hopes for African advancement in a multiracial society. He believed that Christianity would elevate the African to leadership on the world platform and educate whites out of their racial prejudice. While Todd was initially paternalistic toward Africans, his reasonableness eventually helped him to realize that all blacks had the right to the franchise and to self-determination—and that they should demand it. At peril to his own life and status, Todd took up a prophetic role to goad white leaders in Africa, Britain, and across the world to help Zimbabwe achieve its independence. At an age when most retire from public life, Todd, recognizing his status, continued his prophetic role when the Mugabe government began limiting the rights of all Zimbabweans. Clearly one of the most significant figures in twentieth-century Africa, Todd, through his life, rhetoric, and support for African rights, still speaks to the present as Zimbabwe and Africa face a daunting but important future on the world stage.

Todd's prophetic *logos*, *pathos*, and *ethos* nicely illustrates that a prophet is both an insider and outsider to his audience. He is alienated from them but at the same time compels them through shared premises. Todd's discourse was "both of the audience and extreme to the audience." Darsey's description of the prophet describes what Todd wanted to do through his prophetic discourse before various power elites:

> The prophet shares the ideals of his audience rather than the realities of its everyday life. He reminds the audience of that transcendent side of its culture that makes it larger than our individual wants and needs and aspirations and challenges us toward the achievement of that ideal. That effort requires exertion, sacrifice, and renunciation of indolence, and exercise of virtue. Prophetic discourse seeks to reshape, to re-create the audience in accordance with a strict set of ideals as commanded by God, revealed in natural law, and assented to in principle but unrealized by the audience.[96]

Whether that audience was Rhodesian whites, British politicians, South Africans, UN representatives, Americans, or later Robert Mugabe and the ZANU-PF government, Todd prodded all of them to give up individual or selfish aims and instead live up to their stated democratic ideals. Even in the face of repeated failure, Todd never deviated from this overall goal of remaking the audience by persuading them to live by their own best ideals.

Chapter 5

THE "HORRIBLE SPEECH":
TODD'S EFFORT TO END WHITE SUPREMACY

Todd arrived in New York City in March 1962 shortly before one of the most critical speeches of his career, given before a United Nations Committee. He immediately phoned his friend Hugh Foot, the British ambassador to the United Nations. Foot told Todd that Joshua Nkomo and Ndabiningi Sithole were meeting him that evening to talk about the 1961 Constitution for Southern Rhodesia. "I think it is a very good effort, don't you?" Foot asked. Todd replied that he believed the constitution a disaster. "Oh, my God!" Foot said, "Can I come around and see you?" Instead, Todd immediately went over to Foot's house where they talked and Todd convinced Foot to change his mind. Unaware of Todd's conversations, Nkomo and Sithole met with Foot. Nkomo later wrote, "Sir Hugh told me that he would soon have to resign in protest against the instructions he was receiving from London."[1] Within a few months Foot did resign from his position as UN ambassador from Britain. Such was Todd's power of persuasion.

On March 21 and 22, 1962, before a UN committee, Todd gave one of his best and most significant speeches. Todd's biographer calls Todd's speech "one of his finest hours."[2] Todd recalled that this speech "was probably the most important political speech of my career."[3] Yet during his speech Todd jarringly labeled it a "horrible speech." Why would he make such a seemingly incongruous statement? While most would use that label to judge his speaking effort as inferior, Todd was cleverly referring to the racist policies of Southern Rhodesia that he laid out in the speech. His opponents and their imperialist practices were "horrible," not his own rhetoric. Todd's speech of refutation used what Kenneth Burke called "perspective by incongruity" and was a masterful effort to refute racism in Africa.

By 1961 events continued to change rapidly in Africa. The British Empire was at its end. Britain was decolonizing and withdrawing from the continent. African nationalism continued to rise as more African nations broke free from European control. Liberals who wanted to gradually bring black Africans into British democracy and civilization were caught in the middle and becoming obsolete. White racists clung to the fiction that they could stave off African nationalism and maintain their lifestyles and political control. The Central African Federation was on its last legs as Zambia and Malawi emerged as independent nations. That left the troubling problem of Southern Rhodesia. Edgar Whitehead, who succeeded Todd as prime minister, introduced increasingly draconian and reactionary measures to maintain white control. The first instances of violent political protest and death in the colony since the early twentieth century occurred. Britain tried to create the fiction that Southern Rhodesia was a self-governing country with its 1923 Constitution granted by Britain. While the Rhodesian colonists enjoyed greater powers than most colonies, every major piece of legislation had to be cleared by the appropriate British secretaries in London before it could be considered by the Southern Rhodesian parliament. Britain maintained strong political control. Now however Britain wanted to withdraw from Southern Rhodesia as well as from other African colonies. In 1961 Britain began negotiations to create a new constitution for Southern Rhodesia. Despite involving Joshua Nkomo and other African leaders of the National Democratic Party (NDP), through British indifference and the cultural advantages that white colonists enjoyed, a constitution was proposed that ensured white supremacy for the foreseeable future.

Several things made the constitution objectionable. Two voting rolls were created: an "A" roll with high income, property holding, and educational levels, and a "B" roll with much lower income, property, and educational requirements. The "A" voters would elect fifty seats while the "B" voters would elect fifteen members to the legislature. Few Africans would qualify for the "A" roll, essentially maintaining white control of Rhodesian politics. Roy Welensky, the Federation prime minister, noted that the system was "intended to achieve two mutually irreconcilable objects: a rapid acceleration and a careful slowing down of the attainment of African majority rule."[4] Britain and the white colonists used the scheme to rhetorically posture to the outside world that they were committed to a gradual African franchise and that Africans would eventually obtain majority rule when they were ready to enter the modern world. To racist colonialists they argued that the new constitution perpetuated the current system and that white privilege would remain for a long time. This was a common rhetorical move creatively used in earlier days by Godfrey Huggins and Garfield Todd as enlightened paternalistic liberals. However, this well-worn tactic no longer worked in the new historical context; liberalism was dead as the Southern Rhodesians had to choose between belligerent racism and African nationalism. In addition in the new constitution, Britain gave up its right to approve or annul any legislation that it did not like (called reserve clauses), giving whites complete control and making them immune to British pressure to give Africans greater political rights and power.[5]

Nkomo and the NDP rejected the proposed constitution and urged Africans to oppose it. Garfield Todd joined Nkomo in opposition to the constitution.[6] With white voters and a few token enfranchised blacks the constitution was approved July 26, 1962, by a vote of 41,949 to 21,846, leaving 220,000 whites in control of 2,500,000 blacks.[7] In addition the Whitehead government outlawed the NDP, so Nkomo and his supporters reorganized as the Zimbabwe African Peoples Union (ZAPU). With their efforts thwarted, Nkomo and NDP turned to the United Nations for help.

The United Nations General Assembly passed a declaration on December 14, 1960, urging the implementation of independence for colonial peoples and countries. On November 27, 1961, the General Assembly established a seventeen-member (later expanded to twenty-four-member) Special Committee on Colonialism with a mandate to encourage the ending of European colonialism around the world.[8] Southern Rhodesia, over the objections of Britain, was the first place the Committee of 17 investigated.[9]

Recognizing Todd's stature and that he had essentially moved from liberalism to supporting African nationalism, Joshua Nkomo and other African leaders invited Todd to help them and apparently helped finance his trip to the United States.[10] The Committee of 17 and later the General Assembly overwhelmingly voted to urge Britain to suspend the new Constitution and extend to all the people of Southern Rhodesia full political rights.[11] The speech was delivered at the UN Headquarters in New York.

At first glance the speech is a brilliant refutation of the colonialist position on the new constitution. Nkomo recalled, "On this particular occasion his oratory was devastating. Facts against the 1961 Constitution flowed in fast sequence from his fingertips. . . . [H]e spoke like one possessed and he got a most thunderous ovation from all the delegates except of course that of Britain."[12] The speech certainly had excellent characteristics of a traditional refutation but more happened in this complex address. Todd spoke to the UN representatives, to Britain, and to white Rhodesians as an evangelist for democracy, asking them to reorient their understanding and to give the Africans their rightful place as the controllers of their own destiny. Burke notes that in secular and religious prophecy "it is held that certain important aspects of foretelling require a new orientation, a revised system of meanings, an altered conception as to how the world is put together. . . . [I]t is insisted that, if we change our ways of acting to bring them into accord with the new meanings (rejecting old means and selecting new means as a better solution for the problem as now rephrased), we shall bring ourselves and our group nearer to the good life."[13] While Britain and the Rhodesians had a commitment to democracy, their orientation, frame, or "piety" was radically different from Todd's. Burke says piety "is the sense of what properly goes with what."[14] For most whites, racial superiority, Christianity, civilization, and democracy went together and so blacks, the poor, the uneducated, and other "uncivilized" people were invisible or outside of democracy.

The paternalism of some and the racism of others made them reluctant to give up power. An imperialist fiction of democracy was in place as a "trained incapacity" to avoid seeing anything different.[15] For Whitehead, and for Sir Roy Welensky, the Central African Federation prime minister, the 1961 Constitution was a liberal and democratic document that would gradually bring all Africans into the political system. They were blind to the growing African nationalism and erroneously believed they could stave off radicals—white racists and African nationalists. Burke noted that a secular evangelist often has to be "impious" or shake up the old orientation by using "perspective by incongruity" or the "wrenching apart" of old language—"molecular combinations of adjective and noun, substantive and verb"—like a chemist who cracks up compounds when oil is refined.[16] For Burke the metaphors used by a speaker become the perspective by which he or she interpreted the world. By using creative metaphors or unusual perspectives, a rhetor tried to create incongruity in the audience's linguistic world to break through the trained incapacities and reorient listeners in new ways. In Todd's case he wanted the British and Southern Rhodesians to see the injustices of the whites' political practices and policies.

Several perspectives through metaphors emerged in the speech. First, Todd called the separate "A" and "B" voting rolls a "scheme," using Whitehead's own words and arguments against him. Whitehead argued before the Southern Rhodesian parliament that the "B" roll would allow whites to maintain control longer because eventually the votes of thousands of Africans would be severely devalued. It was, in Whitehead's own words, "a well thought out scheme." Chaim Perleman points out that an inadequate picture of the audience by a speaker "can have very unfortunate results." What is offered as support for a policy might incite opposition in an audience who would like to see a different policy. "Reasons for" now become "reasons against."[17] Todd jumped all over Whitehead's argument and word choice: "I think Africans would agree with the prime minister that it is a well thought out scheme, and they would recognize that the thinking was not theirs." Todd not only used Whitehead's argument against him but he also clearly reframed the constitution as a crafty, secretive scheme to disenfranchise blacks rather than Whitehead's idea that it was merely a plan to bring blacks gradually into democracy.

Further revealing the crafty and undemocratic side to the constitution, Todd incongruously called the Whitehead government's effort to persuade blacks to support it "devices." The government's persuasion was not democratic or free but devious, unjust, and possibly evil schemes meant to deceive blacks. He spelled out two specific practices for all to see. White employers were used to "assist" their black employees to register. Faced with this pressure, most complied. In British colonies, civil servants were not used in voter registration drives because of the potential conflict of interest. However, in violation of this the Rhodesian voter drive was declared to be "nonpolitical" so civil servants were used to obtain more black voters. Todd reemphasized that black registration meant that blacks accepted the constitution, accepted limited political power, and that whites should have greater power than blacks. Despite these "devices," black registration was "proved" in Todd's opinion "to be a failure." The blacks were able to see through the devious "devices" of the white government.

The new constitution also had a bill of rights, which the white government and Britain touted as evidence that the system was democratic. Todd shattered this perspective by calling it a "worthless substitute." He then again gave some powerful and compelling examples of laws passed by the Whitehead government that gave his metaphor fidelity and potency. Todd went through all twelve of the rights and refuted how they were allegedly democratic. For example, the first right said, "no person shall be deprived of his life save in the execution of a sentence of a court." Todd noted that in the past there was no reason to state this, because from 1896 to 1960 no life had been lost to racial conflict or police action. "But a new order has risen." Under Whitehead the police were more provocative. Thus at a meeting of five thousand in Salisbury, the police went directly in and arrested the speaker, prompting a riot in which one person was killed and many others wounded. The new rationale stated: "No person shall be regarded as having been deprived of his life in contravention of this section if, for example, it happens in order to effect a lawful arrest." This pattern repeated for most of the twelve rights. The supposed right was stated then followed by "but," "however," or "yet," making the constitution a worthless substitute for democracy. Todd's most elegant refutation was on the right to free speech. Since the government still decided what could be excluded for public safety and order, a person who might shout "'Up, up, up Nkomo!' and 'Down, down, down Whitehead!'" would have committed "a punishable offense." It truly was a "horrible" situation that called for a "horrible" speech.

Other metaphors were intertwined to make "worthless substitute" more compelling. Rhodes, Huggins, Todd, and other white liberals had long used the metaphor of partnership between black and white for their gradual and paternalistic policies. While it had a long history and was progressive in its time, it now was a dead metaphor or perspective for blacks and many whites. Todd provocatively called the "partnership" of the new constitution a "camouflage" for white supremacy, essentially deconstructing the old liberal strategy of trying to placate both black and white. In addition, further extending his impiety against white orthodoxy and offering a stunning reversal of white rhetoric, Todd said the voter registration was not "active citizenship" but a "political wrangle."

Rather than upholding democratic and human rights, the constitution meant whites trespassed and stole the rights of Africans. The constitution affirmed the right of free assembly, but the Law and Order Maintenance Act (1960) still allowed the police to stop anyone from speaking to an assembly or to enter a private house if three or more people were present and the police believed seditious or subversive statements were being made. African leaders were prohibited from attending or holding public meetings. Minimum sentences were automatically imposed thus removing the discretion of judges. The Federal chief justice resigned his position in protest, and Todd quoted his belief that the law "trespassed against almost every basic human right."

Todd did agree that one right was truly upheld in Southern Rhodesia: freedom of religion. However, the injustice of the law subverted even that freedom. Exhibiting Kenneth Burke's theory of impiety, Todd shockingly said, "the finest tenets of our faith are warped, twisted, suffocated by the unjust conditions which are maintained by the laws of the land." While protecting individual religious freedom "we fail to foster the life itself, the spiritual life of the nation." For white racists who wrapped their politics in the language of "Christian civilization" this was difficult to swallow.

Todd also used "perspective by incongruity" through carefully constructed sarcasm. Whitehead claimed that the new constitution made the Rhodesians masters of their own fate because Britain surrendered its power to control the country. However, Britain told the UN that it would continue to exert its power over Southern Rhodesia. Todd remarked: "The new Constitution must be a remarkable document if both of these things can flow from it truly, and it is certainly worthy of our attention." Todd gave it plenty of attention, as he skillfully picked it apart.

With these hard-hitting, impious, and incongruous perspectives—scheme, devices, trespassers, camouflage, worthless substitute, warped faith, and political wrangle—it would be easy to view the white Rhodesians as evil. Todd's role as the impious evangelist or truth-telling prophet would also lend itself to such a conclusion. Todd sensed this and near the end of his speech explicitly said that whites were not evil. Instead, they were merely corrupted by power. In the past he had thought that they were redeemable through appeals to reason. Now, however, he believed they needed guidance or even a nudge from another moral agent: Britain, even though she was part of the problem.

Todd believed that Britain was complicit in this effort to install white power. Britain participated in the nondemocratic "devices" of the colonial whites even when "all around were evidences of a deteriorating situation." Todd appealed to the British to become reengaged and work for a democratic solution: "The withdrawal of British influence from the affairs of Southern Rhodesia would be a tragic happening, for it would leave us to our own travail, to bloodshed, and to the eventual rout of the white people." Todd believed that only Britain could force white Rhodesians to make the necessary democratic changes. Britain was still redeemable and here he fell back to his reasonable approach; he thought his refutation could appeal to Britain's democratic instincts. Near the beginning of the speech he noted that he was using his New York platform "as a back door to London." He thought he could "prod" Britain into truly working for a democratic solution that would affirm equal rights for all.

Unsurprisingly, the reactions to Todd's speech broke down along racial and political lines. The United National Independence Party, which took the lead for Zambia's independence, praised Todd for having the "guts" to speak out against whites and added that he did a "first class job" with the speech.[18] Among whites, his appearance "caused a particular furor in settler circles."[19] Edgar Whitehead attacked Todd's speech as "a reckless attempt to worsen race relations" and labeled it filled with "irresponsibility."[20] Some MPs accused Todd of treason and sedition, and some whites wanted Todd deported.[21] This appearance, along with his 1964 speech before the UN colonialism committee, was one reason for Ian Smith to put Todd under house arrest just before Universal Declaration of Independence in 1965. Smith knew the power of Todd's eloquence; he realized that Todd, through his public speeches, could potentially stir Great Britain and even the United States to take direct military action against his rogue government.

Todd's rhetoric is filled with fearless and plain speech or *parrhesia* that according to West "unsettles, unnerves and unhouses people from their uncritical sleep walking."[22] Yet it is more than simply plain, unadorned speech; it is made more fearless and critical through what Plato condemned: rhetoric. Todd's speech was truly "horrible" as he broke apart the white and British fiction that Southern Rhodesia was moving toward democracy for all. With the impiety of an evangelist exposing a false orthodoxy and with the insight of a prophet, he accurately foretold: "I know that unless Her Majesty's government and the United Kingdom can now intervene, the prime minister must either be thrown out, as I was, or go on to the inevitable conclusion which will be one of riots, bloodshed and economic attrition."

The UN speech also is a perfect example of prophetic speech: "The especial aim of prophetic utterance," writes West, "is to shatter deliberative ignorance and willful blindness to the suffering of others and to expose the clever forms of evasion and escape we devise in order to hide and conceal injustice."[23] So here we find that Burke's impious evangelist using perspective by incongruity is also Darsey's and West's prophet spreading the democratic impulse through fighting against racism and oppression.

Chapter 6

TODD'S NARRATIVE RHETORIC: THE PREACHER OF DEMOCRATIC VIRTUES

> We recognize the worth of the individual and believe that God made all nations of one blood, of one common humanity, and that it behooves us all to walk humbly, remembering that the humble publican was acceptable to God whereas the proud Pharisee was rejected.
> — *Garfield Todd, 1960*

> I am horrified by the destruction of our economy, the starving of our people, the undermining of our Constitution, the torture and humiliation of our nation by ZANU (PF). Just as we stood with courage against the racism of the past, so today we must stand with courage against the terror of the present. — *Garfield Todd, 2002*

On February 13, 2003, a celebration of the life of the Todds took place at St. Martin-in-the-Fields in London. Reflecting their lives, the memorial service for the Todds was a truly democratic occasion. Oxford Professor and friend of the Todds, Terrance Ranger, reported: "The congregation was marvelously varied, ranging from Lord Carrington to the most recent Zimbabwean asylum seekers and including several former British High Commissioners to Zimbabwe, old friends and family of the Todds, and very many people with long-standing connections to Zimbabwe." Readers at the service ranged from former Dadaya students to the General Secretary to the Commonwealth. Ranger read messages from the queen, Tony Blair, David Steel, Jim Callaghan, and Garfield's old colleague, Hardwicke Holderness. Ranger recorded that "at the end of the service a great torch was lit and handed over to three young Zimbabweans who thus inherited the Todd tradition."[1]

Todd went where the truth as he saw it took him. Even in his final years Todd continued to evolve and build his legacy as a radical democrat and an exemplar of West's deep democratic tradition. Todd constructed a democratic tradition and legacy for all Zimbabweans, and a significant part of that tradition was his narrative rhetoric in the final stage of his life.

Todd's prophetic rhetoric underwent changes after Mugabe came to power although some of these changes were signaled toward the end of the Smith regime. Todd wanted Zimbabweans to remember the struggle against oppression and develop true democratic virtues. As Cornel West states, "Prophetic thought is preservative in that it tries to keep alive certain elements of a tradition bequeathed to us from the past and revolutionary in that it attempts to project a vision and inspire a praxis which fundamentally transforms the prevailing status quo in light of the best of the tradition and the flawed yet significant achievements of the present order."[2] Todd increasingly turned to narrative form to transform his audience of liberated Africans. He was an evangelist, prophet, and preacher for democracy, calling Mugabe and other African leaders back to their true heritage of full and deep democracy. Todd correctly feared that Africans would forget democratic legacies and opt instead for a postcolonial despotism modeled after the racist white colonial government rather than the true ideals of white and black democrats. Todd illustrated Richard Weaver's idea that language is sermonic. Todd wanted to keep Zimbabwe in the deep democratic tradition in the emerging postcolonial world, using narrative rhetoric to call them to remember the struggle against oppression as a guide to democratic virtues.

I will analyze five major speeches of Todd from 1979 to 1989 as the major expressions of his turn to preservative prophetic rhetoric. Delivered to diverse audiences all over the world, these speeches clearly delineate Todd's overarching ideal or metanarrative of democracy for Zimbabwe. In primarily epideictic speeches that were given at ceremonial occasions, Todd praised those supporting democratic virtues and blamed those who opposed those virtues. While Todd did not exactly follow Aristotle's prescriptions for epideictic rhetoric, he clearly spoke in the Aristotelian tradition of upholding the virtues that made for good moral character and sought to apply them to the larger community.[3] Otago University, where Todd took courses in education and English while studying at Glen Leith Theological College, granted him an honorary doctorate in 1979. Todd gave the commencement address on December 7, 1979, to four hundred graduates at a packed

Dunedin Town Hall. Otago University Professor R. G. Mulgan said in presenting Todd with the honorary degree, "New Zealanders may take pride that they have produced a statesman who has become an international champion of racial equality."[4] In 1980 Todd received his second invitation to deliver a Feetham lecture at the University of the Witwatersrand in Johannesburg, South Africa. When the South African government read the advance copy of the lecture, they refused to give him a visa. Unlike many other times, the ban on Todd was circumvented. The students placed an empty chair on the stage at the university, had someone read the speech, and published his text in the *Daily Rand Mail* of July 7, 1980. The speech became known by the title "The Speech that Says it All—in Silence."[5] The Tübingen Festival is an annual arts festival held in Tübingen, Germany, where lectures addressing key social, historical, and political concerns are given. The speech was delivered May 28, 1983.[6] In November 1988 Todd spoke for the final time to a World Convention of Churches of Christ in Auckland, New Zealand. Appropriately he spoke in his native country of New Zealand among the brothers and sisters of his religious heritage.[7] Finally, September 30, 1989, in Bulawayo, Zimbabwe, Todd delivered the keynote address at the dinner to celebrate Dr. Joshua Nkomo's seventy-second birthday and fortieth wedding anniversary.[8] While Todd used different stories and examples, they all point to the same conclusion. Because the speeches are international in scope, Todd saw Zimbabwe's metanarrative of democracy as relevant for the entire world. Implicit in his message was that Zimbabwe could be a shining example of democracy for Africa and the entire world. Todd the noble rhetorician, wanting to inculcate democratic virtues, was a preacher to the world directing "our passion toward noble ends."[9]

Narrative, as many have pointed out, is a staple of epideictic speeches, and Todd's speeches are no exception. As a preacher, Todd was very familiar with using examples to illustrate his sermons, following standard rhetorical advice for a rhetor trained in the usual enlightenment forms of rhetoric. Many of his earlier speeches, especially his sermons, had illustrations in them to enliven or throw light on his subject. The earliest sermon examined in this volume had many stories from his mission work to illustrate what the work was accomplishing. For example, to illustrate an African superstition about twin babies Todd told the following story:

"Come to my kraal, Missionary," pleaded a young man, "or otherwise they will kill one of my babies!" I went the 13 miles to Msipani and entered the hut in which the mother sat upon her mat on the floor with a little brown babe at her breast. With her were six or seven old women—the midwives—and one of them held the second little baby. "Take my wife and her two babies to the Mission," pleaded the young husband. "But they will surely not dare to kill the baby," I argued. "No, but only that first born boy will be properly fed and the second born baby, that one held by the grandmother, will soon die," he replied. "Take them today, please, for these old women will stay always with my wife, and I can do nothing." But the old women refused to let me take the mother and babies. I called in the head of the kraal and the old women then said that I should come back in eight days. Only after a great deal of difficulty was I at last able to take the mother and her twins safely with me to Dadaya Mission.[10]

Emory homiletics professor Tom Long points out that nineteenth- and twentieth-century preaching "rested upon a didactic, rationalistic, and conceptually oriented understanding of preaching" as a "means 'to bring light.'" When a preacher encountered an idea difficult to convey to an audience, illustrations were used to throw "some light on an otherwise shadowy subject." According to Long, sermons in the early twentieth century moved away from using persuasion to simply clarifying ideas.[11] Speaking practices never stand still. As Fred Craddock pointed out, "stories or anecdotes" in the sermons "do not illustrate the point, rather they *are* the point."[12] In late-twentieth-century political rhetoric there was a shift away from traditional enlightenment patterns to an electronic eloquence where narrative form dominates.[13] A similar transformation occurred in preaching with the rise of narrative preaching and post-liberal narrative theology.[14] Media theorists, McLuhan, Ong, Postman, and others have also traced much of the rise of postmodern electronic media culture.[15] Todd, while very conversant and interested in the development of electronic media, probably was not aware of the development of the influences of media on speaking beyond McLuhan.[16] Still, astute speakers make adjustments in their speaking, and Todd's later speeches clearly show a narrative cast more in tune with electronic eloquence.

Even in his narrative rhetoric, Todd was steeped in his Disciples democratic heritage. The Disciples tradition long has been interested in Christian unity, and Todd maintained that interest his entire life. In his 1955 speech at Rhodes University on the theme of Christian unity, Todd said: "I hold that the sin of division is in itself a most serious stumbling block to the carrying out of God's will upon earth."[17] In another speech on Christian unity, Todd said: "Where falsehood and pride entered, not only would the church be divided, but a chasm would be opened between the world and God."[18] In his banned Feetham lecture, after narrating the horrors and sufferings of the civil war—the destruction of schools, the closing of hospitals, "Operation Turkey," and the starving of the people—Todd told the story of Smith's repression and the victory of the nationalists. For Todd this story was significant: "From Rhodesia to Zimbabwe is not just a cold event in history, not just the mechanics of a guerrilla war but the emergence of a nation from racial darkness into the light of hope. Now we can dream again, we can laugh again, we can be happy together; we can sing, we can dance, we can clasp hands. We can fulfill the Christian ideal of being one in Christ."[19]

Todd saw the democratic virtues of unity (overcoming evil divisions and divisiveness) and peaceful reconciliation as a direct manifestation of the Disciples of Christ and Christian ideals of unity. The New Testament church ideal was a model for virtuous democratic society. While other democratic virtues cannot be so easily illustrated from his Disciples heritage, one should realize that Todd's Christian ideals served as the basis for his narrative democratic rhetoric. He saw no tension between his political and religious beliefs.

There were two intertwining stories that served as metanarratives for Todd's epideictic rhetoric: the history of Rhodesia turned Zimbabwe and Todd's own autobiography as a part of the country's history. Todd's own narrative was intertwined with Rhodesia's narrative and functions similarly for both the community and for citizens and leaders who want to live by democratic virtues. Todd believed that a life of service for racial reconciliation was worth living and right even when a person might not know exactly the right thing to do in a particular circumstance. The intertwining of Todd's own metanarrative with the metanarrative of Zimbabwe gave his rhetoric unusual evocativeness.

Campbell and Jamieson point to enactment as an important rhetorical form where "the speaker incarnates the argument, *is* the proof of what is said."[20] In Todd's narrative rhetoric, he became part of the proof for his argument as he incarnated the democratic virtues the story narrates. While he never directly stated "I have lived and believe in this story" everyone who heard Todd speak would instantly recognize that he embodied the narrated virtues. His incarnation and his actions in the drama gave Todd an even stronger *ethos* in these speeches. Once again he was the conscience of Zimbabwe, a preacher of democracy, one who lived by his story.

Todd started with the history of the colony of Rhodesia, which had been created by the defeat of the Matabele King Lobengula in 1893. For Todd this was the start of white oppression and the corresponding spirit of resistance by Africans. He cited the despairing message of the king: "Matabele! The white men will never cease following us while we have gold in our possession for gold is what the white men prize above all things. Collect now all my gold and carry it to the white men. Tell them they have beaten my regiments, killed my people, burnt my kraals, captured my cattle, and that I want peace." Todd then jumped to the 1930s, when life seemed to stand still for most Africans and only a handful of progressive parents wanted change. But he also pointed to the emergence of African nationalism through early leaders educated in the mission schools. The 1940s brought a revolution through World War II where Africans fought for a liberty which they did not have. With the influence of Christian education, Africans now especially demanded literacy for all their children.

In the 1950s a new African call came for a share in the political life of the colony. Joshua Nkomo and Ndabaningi Sithole became leaders in the nationalist movement. Moderate white leaders, including Todd, were rejected by the white colonialists. Todd incarnated his story in different ways as he retold important episodes of his life through the speeches. The civil war could have been prevented if his democratic ideals as prime minister had been followed. In the Tübingen speech he joked that the Germans "had the temerity, perhaps the foolhardiness to invite a 'failed politician' to speak on the subject of his failure, human and political relations in Southern Africa." The civil war, his ultimate failure, came because white Rhodesians rejected Todd's plan to share political power with Africans. Todd stated that his own white colleagues were shocked that he, as the prime minister, addressed a multiracial organization and suggested "that its aims should be the aims of the government."[21] In the Nkomo speech, Todd said he lost his leadership because whites thought he was a "security risk" for talking directly with Nkomo and the ANC.[22] Todd reported that leaders of emerging African countries were also distressed by his removal as prime minister. Kwane Nkrumah, the first prime minister of Ghana, the first African colony to achieve independence, said that Todd was "not able to do anything" to lay a foundation "for peaceful progress towards rule by the majority."[23] Todd, as prime minister, could not change the racism of Rhodesia, so Nkrumah asked "how can anyone seriously imagine" that Rhodesia's racism could "be changed by any group of [white] settlers?" Todd concluded, "Dr. Nkrumah was right: it had to take a civil war to drag Rhodesia to Zimbabwe."[24] In his World Convention speech Todd simply said that his "concern for African advancement, on which I believed white security was based, was neither accepted nor understood."[25] Todd presented an echo of his Christlike prophetic persona that first emerged when he was removed as prime minister: the belief that whites had rejected or crucified Todd for his progressive views on race.

The 1960s brought a period of selfishness by whites who refused to take a peaceful path by sharing political power or preparing Africans for true democracy. This continued with the repressive regime of Ian Smith. Black nationalist leaders and Todd were detained without trial; and on November 11, 1965, a Unilateral Declaration of Independence was proclaimed as Rhodesia broke free of Britain. The declaration was modeled after the American Declaration but as Todd put it, without its "soul": "Governments are instituted among Men, deriving their just powers from the consent of the governed!"[26] Under this rhetorical cover, a thousand-year rule of whites was launched.

The 1970s brought the failed Smith-Home agreement where Smith tried to trick Britain into accepting his control of Rhodesia, but the agreement was rejected by the Africans. A deadly eight-year civil war ensued with thousands killed and injured. Brutal tactics were used by both sides, but Todd and others supported the blacks because white racism, oppression, and unwillingness to give up power and establish a true democracy created the war.

Twice to international audiences Todd told the story of his suffering as a prisoner of conscience for his beliefs. In November 1971 Todd spoke at the University of Rhodesia (now the University of Zimbabwe) and "compared the decline in morality" of the Smith government "to the rise of Nazism." On January 18, 1972, Todd and his daughter Judith were arrested and thrown into prison. He was the only white in a prison full of Africans. On his first day a voice whispered to him "Are you alright, sir?" Later "a black hand rested on the ledge of the peephole and I placed my hand over it. I believe this is called solidarity!" However on the second day Todd heard a lot of cutting and hammering outside his cell and then found that a steel plate had been bolted over the peephole. Todd said, "I have always thought that the act of closing that tiny area of communication was symptomatic of our basic problem—a determination to prohibit understanding between black and white."[27] After five weeks of prison, Todd was put into detention: "Notices were placed warning people to keep out, a white policeman put on guard duty, and we were brought back home. No letters, no visitors, no telephoning, and a limit of 800 metres to our walking from the house!" Todd again reinforced his Christlike rejection or crucifixion by white Rhodesians through the suffering he experienced in prison and his detention.

The Lancaster House accords brought an end to the war. In 1980 the free nation of Zimbabwe was created and Robert Mugabe was freely elected as the prime minister. A pledge of reconciliation brought about a new day for Zimbabwe. While problems persist, Todd thought Zimbabwe could still learn from its history to be a shining example of democracy for Africa and the world. The narrative preserves the best of the story as a model for future praxis, but it also has negative examples of praxis to avoid. The story can be transformative of the status quo especially as Zimbabwe has not lived up to the ideals of the revolution. The Rhodesian narrative gives Zimbabwe a story to emulate and perhaps, someday, to live by.

Finally Todd, like Christ, was fully vindicated in the narrative. Both Zimbabwean independence and international recognition of his support for democracy against oppression were signs of this vindication. Despite doubts, Todd believed he was doing God's will in all his activities. Even though he made mistakes, he thought that if one lived by Christian virtues and practices, then even in the political realm one will usually and ultimately do the right thing or be a person of character. Like all prophets Todd remained optimistic about Zimbabwe, believing that he was "fortunate to be a citizen of Zimbabwe." In looking back over fifty years in Africa he told his German audience: "As a young man I saw visions and as an old man I can dream dreams. I am upheld in my hope for the future of my country for I know that there is a host of young women and young men in Zimbabwe today whose vision is of a country where liberty and peace walk hand in hand."[28] In his Nkomo speech the vindication was more oblique but it was clearly present. Todd recalled his first detention by Smith in 1965 because he "had actively associated" with members of Nkomo's group, ZAPU. Desmond Lardner-Burke, Smith's Minister of Law and Order, served the order based on "information which he was unable to divulge because of the confidential nature of its sources." Todd was angry "and thought he would ask the opinion of my lawyer—until I remembered that my lawyer was Desmond Lardner Burke." Todd then said, "But here I am, unrepentant, still associating with enemies of Rhodesia but who are now friends of Zimbabwe—people of Zimbabwe. I count myself fortunate to have lived to see the miracles that have happened in Zimbabwe."[29] In his New Zealand speech the theme vindication was his peroration. He won a papal medal while in his five-year detention. Mugabe brought a "policy of reconciliation" rather than a "Nuremberg trial" which resulted in healing rather than vengeance. Mugabe appointed him a senator saying, "It is time that people who denigrated you in the past, should now see you honored." He was awarded knighthood by Queen Elizabeth II. Todd admitted that throughout his prophetic period he was racked with doubt on whether he was doing God's will: "Could the horrors of civil war, of opposition to the government of the day, be justified?" He concluded: "Many questions are left unanswered, but in Zimbabwe today we live in an atmosphere of reconciliation and of hope. Grace and I emerge from our fifty-four years' service thanking God for His blessings and His mercy."[30]

Todd served as the trustworthy narrator for his own story since many in the audience knew the story, agreed with his version, and knew he incarnated the democratic virtues that he advocated. It made the rhetoric even more cogent and meaningful. He was advocating what rhetorical scholar Walter Fisher calls good reasons. Fisher offers that what makes a good reason or virtue valuable is that "it makes a pragmatic difference in one's life and in one's community."[31] Here Todd was addressing the difference these virtues made in his own life and implicitly the difference it made for all of Zimbabwe since he was a key actor in the story of Zimbabwe's liberation.

While many scholars have pointed out that speakers on the margins have effectively used enactment as a rhetorical strategy,[32] Todd represents a slightly different case. While he was out of power, he was not a completely marginalized person. He made the choice to become powerless by opposing the oppressive power structures of the day. Being a unique rhetor on the world stage, Todd did this in an unusual way: he challenged power by ultimately giving up power, a rhetoric act of *kenosis* or an emptying. Todd himself incarnated the democratic ideal that one should ultimately give up power rather than serve oneself; one should serve the common good and the country by helping others who replace you (or your administration). Africans and Zimbabweans had not learned how to practice this necessary aspect of democracy—a viable peaceful opposition and a willingness to give up power when the people wanted new leadership.

He also had the unusual opportunity of the prestige that came from being a former prime minister. Like former American presidents who carry the aura and prestige of the office with them for the rest of their lives, Todd was able to use his unusual power and status to oppose the very structure that he had upheld, a very rare occurrence in history. Again, he used his *ethos* in kenotic ways. For example, in his elegant ending to the Tübingen Festival speech, Todd said: "As for me, I would rather a thousand times be a Senator in a free Zimbabwe than be Prime Minister of the Self-governing Colony of Southern Rhodesia."[33]

Todd, while effectively using enactment, also pointed to other key actors in the story as exemplars of democratic virtue. Twice Todd narrated the story of a little-known National Hero of Zimbabwe, Masotsha Ndhlovu, who was buried at Heroes' Acre. In the Tübingen speech Todd called the story to mind to narrate the "spirit of resistance" and the "desire for liberty" that continued in Africans after the defeat of the Matabele King Lobengula. In the 1920s Ndhlovu was a leader of the African labor union, the Industrial and Commercial Union (ICU). He asked Charles Coughlan, the first prime minister of Southern Rhodesia, to allow Africans to use the sidewalks in the towns rather than having to walk on the streets. The government considered him "a dangerous revolutionary" and the Criminal Investigation Department surveiled Ndhlovu. Terry Ranger found extensive CID reports on Ndhlovu's activities and speeches. After a serious riot in Bulawayo the CID reported Ndhlovu addressing an African audience about the suffering: "If you had all been members of the ICU you would not have fought for you would have been brothers. The missionaries have come to tell us of the way to Heaven. The ICU tells us how to live on earth; and anyway, my brothers; we are living under the British flag and that stands for peace."[34] Todd continued and told of Ndhlovu's detention at Gonkudzingwa by Ian Smith. As a preacher in the Churches of Christ, Ndhlovu held meetings and the Dadaya Mission sent him money and clothing along with hymn books and Bibles. Ndhlovu came to Dadaya after his release to thank the mission. Todd continued, "The old man, with walking stick tapping, made his way down the aisle and entered the pulpit. As always his message was one of unity and peace. "There is plenty of room for everyone in our beautiful country," he said. Then as he was about to leave, he smiled broadly, showing two rows of very white teeth. "Anyway," he concluded, "I must thank the Government for they have made a young man of me. They have given me new teeth." Then Todd ended with the honoring of Ndhlovu with his state burial at Heroes' Acre. Todd was "surprised and delighted" at the funeral because Ndhlovu was "so quiet, so unassuming." Mugabe said at the funeral "his whole life was lived for unity and peace." Todd thought in honoring Ndhlovu "much honour also came to the Prime Minister and his Government."[35]

In the Nkomo speech the story was told in a slightly different way, but the past history of division between Nkomo and Mugabe loomed. Presumably most in the audience had known or knew Ndhlovu's political history, so Todd focused on details they probably did not know. His early history was condensed to the Coughlan story, and Todd stressed Ndhlovu's Church of Christ membership and the help Dadaya gave him while in Gonkudzingwa. He was "a frail old man," not simply an old man going to the platform. Todd summarized his point "that theirs was a wonderful and bountiful country with room for everyone" and then directly quoted Ndhlovu: "There should be no antagonism between black and white." Todd felt a "great debt of gratitude" to Mugabe for giving Ndhlovu the honor at Heroes' Acre. Todd stated: "Masotsha Ndhlovu was one of the earliest and most honorable of our fighters for peace and democracy. In his old age he could so easily have been overlooked. He owned nothing. He was modest. He fought injustice with a quiet resolution and a deep faith in God and in his fellow man."[36] Todd did not give an abstract explanation of the democratic virtues of peace and unity; the narrative of Masotsha Ndhlovu embodied them. In the Tübingen speech the virtues were advocated for the entire world. In the Nkomo speech these virtues were badly needed in Zimbabwe, and Ndhlovu provided them with an excellent Zimbabwean story to live by.

In the Nkomo speech, Joshua Nkomo, the honoree at the celebration, embodied democratic virtues. One of Todd's themes was that all had supported the liberation effort, but Nkomo and his wife had "especially suffered" through "pain, disappointments [and] long periods of separation from each other over far too many years." Todd also surprisingly stated, "Nkomo has had a greater influence on my life in Zimbabwe than any other man, which will surprise him as greatly as it no doubt surprises everyone else." In the rest of the speech Todd told of several key instances in their mutual history where their lives intertwined and where Nkomo played a key role in what happened to Todd. Todd recalled his prophetic call and the end of his political career in London in 1960. Nkomo read Todd's prepared statement for the British government and said, Todd revealed, "if I would add a recommendation that the United Kingdom should suspend the Constitution of Rhodesia and call a conference of representatives of the people, he would be glad to give his support in, of course, what would be my political suicide. Anyway I thought it was a good idea." Todd concluded, "that was the end of formal politics for me and I moved across to the informal sector with the Nkomos, the Msikas, the Dumbutshenas, etc."[37] Todd finished with an important final episode. In 1982 ZANU (Mugabe's party) and ZAPU (Nkomo's party) had a falling-out and the country nearly erupted into a civil war. Nkomo fled Zimbabwe in 1983. Finally in 1987 a unity agreement was signed between the two leaders, merging the parties and ending the threat of a civil war. Todd, now in retirement, accidentally suffered some severe burns requiring hospitalization and skin grafts.[38] Before the unity agreement was negotiated and signed Todd recalled:

> Another of my happy memories is of a recent experience. . . . Those marvelous nurses at Mater Dei Hospital had just levered me into a bath when a sister came rushing in to say, "The President and Dr. Nkomo have come to see Sir Garfield." I looked up and said, "There is just one chair. Get another and bring them in!" Well they got me out and into bed and in came my visitors. I was so glad to see the President but delighted that Mugabe and Nkomo had come together to see me, together again. Of course when they had departed the Matron came I think it was to thank me for my accident which had brought such important visitors to her hospital: a visit which had brought excitement and happiness to nurses and patients.[39]

Todd did not have to draw any conclusion or make any point, because the entire crowd knew what he meant; all could see the democratic virtues of peace, unity, and reconciliation that were apparent in the story. Again the narrative was a story with which all Zimbabweans could identify and also envision as a way to live their political lives.

Todd's enactment and the actions of Masotsha Ndhlovu and Joshua Nkomo were excellent examples of what Walter Fisher calls characterological coherence. Fisher says, "Whether a story is believable depends on the reliability of characters, both as narrators and as actors." Judgments about character, Fisher says, are "made by interpretations of the person's decisions and actions that reflect values." If a character's actions in a story are contradictory, change in sudden ways, or are seen as "strange," Fisher says, "the result is a questioning of character." Audiences want "characters who behave characteristically. Without this kind of predictability there is no trust, no community, no rational human order."[40]

This brings us to Robert Mugabe. While Mugabe does appear in Todd's narrative and, as we have seen, is pointed to at times as exhibiting democratic virtues early in his leadership, he never really is a central character. One reason is that Mugabe, after 1982, had been inconsistent in his actions. He tried to have Nkomo killed and Korean death squads were used to suppress ZAPU and Matabele opposition to the government. Todd eventually resigned as senator in 1985 and while there were numerous reasons that converged, a primary reason was his increased criticism of the government. By the 1989 Nkomo speech, Todd was a frequent critic of the repressive tactics by Mugabe. The democratic Mugabe became an oppressive ruler with a one-party state modeled after Ian Smith and colonial practice rather than democratic virtues. Todd continued his prophetic criticism of the lack of democratic virtues in the Mugabe government. In 1990 he told historian Graeme Mount that the business community in Zimbabwe regularly extended him invitations to speak. In May 1990 he had three speaking engagements and one scheduled for July. He said his message was "the idea of a one-party state is a disaster."[41] Mugabe's story simply lacked coherence when it came to democratic virtues. These inconsistencies also meant that Mugabe's life did not ring true to true democracy. In Fisher's terms it lacks narrative fidelity. One cannot believe Mugabe's rhetoric and life as a supporter of democracy.

Todd's life and the story of Zimbabwe is a narrative to live by for democratic citizens. For Todd the democratic virtues narrated in Zimbabwe's experience—especially peace, reconciliation, liberty, and unity—serve as warrants for future action. Rhetorical theorist Walter Fisher offers standards by which to evaluate Todd's narrative rhetoric. Borrowing from Gadamer, Habermas, and others, Fisher offers "good communication is good by virtue of its satisfying the requirements of narrative rationality, namely that it offers a reliable, trustworthy, and desirable guide to belief and action."[42] While many people do not share Todd's Christianity, persons committed to deep democracy would likely have few, if any, objections to Todd's democratic narrative as a guide for democratic action.[43] Fisher also holds that "all good stories function in two ways: to justify (or mystify) decisions or actions already made or performed and to determine future decisions or actions."[44] Todd's narrative rhetoric does both. He justified his own actions through his retelling of his story. His narrative and Zimbabwe's story for liberation can serve as a guide for future democracy.

While Fisher maneuvers all around the concept, he never explicitly develops the connection between memory (remembering) and narrative. As West reminds us, Todd as the preacher of democracy and as the prophet for Zimbabwe wanted to "keep alive certain elements of a tradition bequeathed" to Zimbabweans.[45] Previous theory about narrative rhetoric has little or nothing to say about the role of remembering. Narrative theologian George Stroop provides an important entry into the rhetorical dimension of memory in narrative:

> A community is a group of people who have come to share a common past, who understand particular events in the past to be of decisive importance for interpreting the present, who anticipate the future by means of a shared hope, and who express their identity by means of a common narrative. . . . What distinguishes a community from a crowd or a mob is a common memory which expressed itself in living traditions and institutions.[46]

Stroop points out that an "essential feature" of a community "is its shared memory and the common narrative by means of which it interprets the past."[47] In addition this memory and narrative becomes "an anticipation of the future."[48] The shared narrative of the community "is the glue that binds it members together." A true member of the community shares "in that community's narratives," recites "the same stories as the other members of the community," and allows "one's identity to be shaped by them." But memory is not simply an exercise of trying to reenact the past: "A person is a member of a community only when he or she re-members with the other members, only when the community's common narrative and the past it preserves are appropriated and extended into the future, both the future of the community and that of the individual."[49] Todd knew the importance of memory through remembering and interpreting the shared story in order to make the right decisions for the future. He chastised whites for not living up to their ideals of democracy in the British tradition. If they truly believed in democratic virtues they would practice them and give everyone the vote. In the same fashion Todd knew the danger for Africans was to forget the story of the struggle and its meaning for full democracy. For Zimbabweans to remain true to the ideals of liberation, they needed to remember the story and its democratic virtues. Todd's rhetoric served to function as one means for Zimbabwe to truly remember its democratic narrative. Todd was a constant presence and irritant through his speaking and simply through his existence for Zimbabweans to remember the virtues of democracy as a guide for the future.

All in all, Todd's narrative rhetoric exhibited what Aristotle and the Greeks called *phronesis* or practical wisdom: Todd sought good sense, good judgment, and practiced "equitable acts" with others.[50] Todd's narrative rhetoric, like his previous rhetoric, was reasonable for it met the criteria of narrative rationality Fisher set out: it made sense (coherent) and it rang true to human experience as it pointed to democratic virtues (fidelity). Fisher states about reasonableness: "These qualities, constituting narrative rationality, are particularly vital where equality of rights and freedom decide to exist as they do in any democratic, pluralistic setting. They are even more important in autocratic communities and societies, even though the nature and rules of 'coherence' and the limits of 'fidelity' are circumscribed."[51] For Todd, present-day Zimbabwe needs democratic virtues more than ever. For deep democracy to truly come, Zimbabwe and Africa need to heed the call of its preacher-prophet: to remember its story of liberation and go back to the road not taken. In so doing, they would not only be true to their real heritage, they also would once again bring honor to Garfield Todd and a host of prophets that span across time.

Conclusion

FIGHTING THE GOOD FIGHT

> Just keep throwing your bread upon the waters; if you're lucky; it will come back as ham sandwiches. — *Garfield Todd*

On February 13, 2003, a celebration of the life of the Todds took place at St. Martin-in-the-Fields in London. Oxford Professor and President of the Britain-Zimbabwe Society Terrance Ranger wrote:

> What none of us knew until afterwards was how appropriate it was that St Martin's was the venue. Michael Casey emailed Judy Todd and myself on February 27. He told us that Garfield Todd was named after U.S. President, James A. Garfield. When President Garfield was assassinated "Queen Victoria broke with the tradition of ringing the bells of St Martin's only at the death of a British monarch. She had the bells rung when Garfield died . . . the only time that St Martin's has broken with its tradition."[1]

The democratic tradition of the Churches of Christ lived on in Todd and his rhetoric. He realized the best of the democratic ideals of Alexander Campbell and James A. Garfield. His rhetoric and speeches are a legacy for the deep democratic tradition which will hopefully flower in Zimbabwe and Africa. He spoke truthfully, prophetically, and almost always remained optimistic in the face of daunting and discouraging circumstances. He incarnated deep democracy that ever opposed oppression and racism.

Todd's career also shows the importance of rhetoric. Todd stood in the civic tradition of Isocrates and Cicero as he put the public good above his own self-interests in his rhetorical leadership. I believe this is true even in his prophetic stage. Darsey correctly argued that prophetic rhetoric with its origins in the Hebrew prophets usually created conflict or an "uncivil" discourse because of its radical nature that challenged the ideas of society. He contrasts that with classical rhetoric that sought civility, compromise, and negotiation. He compellingly argued that democracy needs both traditions. Todd with his grounding in both the classical and the radical was able to creatively blend the two traditions. In a unique combination of circumstance, rhetorical adaptability, and staying true to his deep democratic beliefs, Todd accomplished this.

Todd was introduced to rhetoric through his religious training in the New Zealand Churches of Christ. The tradition was in transition from culture-rejecting sectarianism to a culture-affirming denominationalism. Todd picked up an implicit radicalism from the sectarian side and a more civil rhetoric from the denominational side. His formal training at the Churches of Christ theological college gave him exposure to mainstream Enlightenment rhetoric that stressed rationality, argument, and debate. He carried these democratic sensibilities to Africa and while Todd was paternalistic, unlike most whites he saw the advancement of Africans as something that was real and not symbolic. The full flowering of his efforts at education, the priesthood of all believers, and thinking for oneself was the development of African nationalist leaders who began to surpass Todd in pushing for African possibilities.

Todd then turned to become a mainstream politician in the Rhodesian parliament. Here he honed his considerable rhetorical abilities that he developed as an effective preacher. Todd quickly developed a reputation for eloquence even though he was a backbencher. His abilities led to his becoming the first missionary to become a head of state. Here he cultivated a rhetorical premiership paralleling the American rhetorical presidency and an eloquence paralleling American presidential rhetoric. These efforts were unprecedented in Rhodesian colonial history. Ultimately his rhetorical leadership failed with recalcitrant whites opposed to his racial policies; however, he developed considerable credibility around the world through his eloquence as he spoke in various venues as the Rhodesian prime minister. He continued this practice as the former prime minister in his prophetic stage.

When Todd found himself opposing an oppressive and racist society and after his modest gradualist approach was rejected by whites, he realized that the mainstream rhetorical approach of a head of state and a member of parliament did not work. He turned to prophetic rhetoric to bring true democracy to Zimbabwe. His removal by whites created his Christlike and Moses-like persona with Africans. Todd fully embraced this persona when the Africans called to him to be a prophet against the regnant racist white government. Prophetic speech was the only means to realize the civic ideals of classical rhetoric. Like any good rhetorician Todd responded to his audiences—black and white—but he did so as a prophet. Using his Christlike suffering persona, prophetic *pathos*, and *logos*, Todd demanded an immediate and full democracy for Zimbabwe. As we saw in his speech before the UN in 1962, he creatively combined traditional rhetorical approaches with perspective by incongruity to become the impious evangelist or prophet. He showed that the rhetoric of the whites was false and contradictory. Their call for a bill of rights was hollow as their own laws gutted any real effect these rights had. His "horrible" speech showed the horrible, unjust, and hypocritical actions of the white government to perpetuate oppression of Africans and entrenchment of white privilege in the name of democracy.

Todd's final stage as the narrative preacher for democracy illustrates another convergence between the prophetic and the classical. West correctly points out the preservative part of a prophet who calls a community to remember the best of a society's democratic ideals even if they are flawed. Fisher's narrative paradigm inspired by the Aristotelian rhetorical tradition of classical rhetoric illuminates how Todd created a *phronesis* for future Zimbabweans through his speeches that evoked the memory of the liberation. Todd wanted Africans to remember and thereby enact the ideals of their liberation. Todd also incarnated the very argument and story he narrated which once again gave him an extraordinary *ethos* with his audience. He wanted Zimbabwe to live by the same democratic story he incarnated.

Todd's example shows that the divide between the classical (Greek) and prophetic (Hebrew) traditions is not always stark. I suspect that even in the American scene prominent rhetors who stand in both traditions can be found. I also suspect that even some of the ones who move toward the prophetic pole still will use rhetoric from the classical tradition. Martin Luther King Jr. quickly comes to mind as a rhetor who at times could meld the best from both traditions.

West, in his important work on the deep democratic tradition, provided another key lens for understanding Todd's rhetoric. Todd stood in all three of West's democratic traditions: the Greek, the prophetic, and the tragicomic. Todd spoke fearlessly against the sophistry of the racist whites who pretended to be democratic. Todd decided to be a person of character and spoke out for justice and fairness for all Africans. Todd also spent much of his life developing a *paideia* through his educational efforts and speeches to create a critical citizenry that knew how to see through oppressive rhetoric. Todd did this even when it was unpopular to do so.

While West, at the beginning of his work, overlooks rhetoric in the Greek tradition, I hope that my efforts here will point to the critical role that rhetoric can play in developing deep democracy—a role that West acknowledges when he explores Emerson's rhetoric. While Todd and Emerson are worlds apart in many of their perspectives, Todd did share Emerson's Ciceronian concern to develop a rhetoric that keeps public officials centered on being ethical, honest, and focused on the common good. One cannot escape the central role that rhetoric must play in democracy. That legacy for deep democracy for better or worse goes back to the much maligned sophists who opposed Plato's aristocratic and totalitarian tendencies.

In all this talk of persona, impious evangelist, preacher of Christianity, and preacher of democracy, the final convergence between the classical and prophetic rhetorics in Todd's life is *ethos*. While certainly not identical, first Todd the "good man speaking well" and later the suffering servant of the Africans exhibited a sterling character worthy of the best that ascend to the pulpit each Sunday before a congregation. In all of his rhetoric his *ethos* was the key to his success or failure, depending on whom he was speaking to. Here Todd stood in the Isocratean tradition. Isocrates stated:

> The man who wished to persuade people will not be negligent as to the matter of character [*ethos*]; no, on the contrary, he will apply himself above all to establish a most honourable name among his fellow-citizens; for who does not know that words carry greater conviction when spoken by men of good repute than when spoken by men who live under a cloud, and that the argument which is made by a man's life is more weight than that which is furnished by words?[2]

Michael Hyde points out that "for Isocrates, *ethos* is both a legitimating source for and a praiseworthy effect of the ethical practice of the orator's art."[3] While at times Todd constructed his *ethos* through his discourse as Aristotle contends, most often Todd's *ethos* was brought with him into the rhetorical situations he encountered. Todd also embraced the prophetic persona to which the Africans called him. By the end of his career Todd was calling others to join him to live a democratic life and build a just and fully democratic society. His own *ethos* incarnated the very story that all Africans could live by in a fully democratic community.

Todd's rhetoric is important because it shows how religion can serve as a critical basis for political rhetoric. In Todd's case it is obvious because he was always the preacher for both Christianity and for democracy. To overlook the role of religion in Todd's life would be to fundamentally misunderstand him. His reasonable approach to issues and rhetoric, his love for liberty, democracy, education, reform, and human rights were inculcated in him from his New Zealand Churches of Christ heritage. He was a child of his religious heritage with all of its strengths and flaws. Even his prophetic rhetoric was an outgrowth of a rhetorical trajectory that originated with his Disciples' sensibilities: the right for a person to think for oneself and the priesthood of all believers. He saw what was true and defended it with all his might, even when he knew it could cost him his life.

Todd's rhetoric points to the need to explore the role of religion in the political rhetoric of other significant leaders, both in people who are religious and those who are not. This should be a fruitful line of inquiry to study anyone who was raised in a particular religious tradition. Many scholars know that large traditions or families of religious groups have similar outlooks on the world and introduce those worldviews through religious speech communities. Rhetoric scholars with knowledge of the symbolic webs and discourse of religious traditions and the individual religious groups within those traditions could conduct a rhetorical analysis of political discourse with those discursive patterns in mind. As noted earlier, the Disciples' tradition has spawned a large number of reformers and political leaders including three American presidents and one prime minister of Britain. More exploration of these leaders needs to be done. Most of the key reform movements in America and Great Britain have religious roots. Their full rhetorical meaning has not been adequately explored.

Todd embodied his democratic *ethos* to the very end. As a prophet he remained optimistic as he continued to battle Mugabe's oppression and reverse racism. Ironically, just days after he and his wife Grace were called white heroes of Zimbabwe and had three schools renamed after them, the Mugabe government, fearing Todd's symbolic power, stripped the ninety-three-year-old of his citizenship denying him the right to vote in the March 2002 election.[4] Instead of remaining silent Todd protested one last time against the growing chaos and evil present in his country: "I am horrified by the destruction of our economy, the starving of our people, the undermining of our Constitution, the torture and humiliation of our nation by ZANU (PF)." He added, "Just as we stood with courage against the racism of the past, so today, we must stand with courage against the terror of the present. Come what may I will, next March, be going to the polling station to claim my right as a very senior citizen to cast my ballot for good against evil."[5] This is consistent with Todd's earlier narrative rhetoric in the 1980s. In that rhetoric Todd reminded Mugabe of some of his democratic actions even as the prime minister began to oppress Zimbabweans for his own personal gain. Still Mugabe was an incidental character in Todd's telling of Zimbabwe's story because Mugabe's actions lacked narrative coherence and fidelity—his story was not truthful to Zimbabwe's democratic aspirations. Mugabe's final actions against Todd simply confirmed Todd's rhetoric in those final prophetic speeches.

Others caught Todd's vision of optimistic but tough-minded opposition to oppression. Lord Thomson of Monifieth (formerly George Thomson) told the British House of Lords: "We must not despair. I and other noble Lords, such as the noble Lord Hughes of Woodside, went to the extraordinary memorial service for Sir Garfield Todd in St-Martin-in-the-Fields. There was a huge congregation. That did something to lift up my heart and restore my faith in continuing to fight the good fight in terms of finding solutions for the Zimbabwean problem."[6] Todd would be pleased by such statements. His family and friends certainly hope that his legacy will live on in Zimbabweans who fight for the complete liberation of their country.

Todd certainly would have agreed that the conundrums of colonialism were and are difficult. In this postcolonial era too many have followed the legacy of white colonialism as they oppress both black and white for personal power and privilege. Todd's democratic rhetoric and the speeches he left behind can still serve as a possible basis for future democracy in Africa. They also can be a rich resource for democratic practice around the world. Todd championed the marginalized, and his Christian commitment was the foundation of his cause. Yet, Todd's vision was broad-minded and inclusive in the best of his ecumenical Christian tradition. He could work with all who were democratic: Christians of all stripes, secularists, people of all creeds and colors. That makes his rhetoric even more important in days of racial, ethnic, and religious division. His democratic story is worth pondering and further study.

"Rise Sir Garfield—'protect the poor and punish the wicked.'" These words, spoken at Todd's greatest honor, remind all of us that Todd's life and rhetoric calls democrats to be faithful in their service and practice of democratic virtues. As democrats struggle to uphold fairness and justice in society just maybe ham sandwiches will emerge from the democratic bread thrown on the waters.

Despite his outstanding ability and the numerous historically significant speeches that Sir Garfield delivered, he made no effort to systematically collect or preserve his speeches. This volume is designed to fill the void by bringing together, preserving, and making available some of the best speeches that Todd delivered across his long life.

The collection of speeches follows the three stages of Todd's rhetoric. The first six speeches are sermons he delivered in different venues around the world. Unfortunately, no extant sermon exists from his preaching in Zimbabwe. Even in recent years no one recorded an entire sermon. The next seven are from his parliamentary days. They are representative examples of his speaking style, as well as exemplars of important speeches that he delivered. Many excellent speeches, which can be found in the *Southern Rhodesian Legislative Debates* (1946–1958) popularly known as the *Southern Rhodesian Hansard* during his tenure as MP and prime minister, had to be left out of the volume. The next twelve speeches represent his prophetic stage and again were delivered in venues all over the world. Finally, another sermon closes the volume. This speech, showing that preaching is really at the base of all his rhetoric, appropriately overviews his entire career and states many of the themes that infused his whole life. Clearly one of the most significant figures of Africa in the twentieth century, Todd's life and speeches still speak to the present as Zimbabwe and Africa face a daunting but important future on the world stage.

SERMON TEXTS

Conference Sermon

This is the oldest extant sermon of Sir Garfield Todd. In 1950 Todd returned to New Zealand on a five-month furlough where he gave 116 speeches to an estimated twenty thousand people, delivered four live speeches on radio, and recorded five more.[1] During the Churches of Christ annual conference of April 6–10 in Invercargill, he delivered the conference sermon. Speaking on this occasion was a highly desired honor reserved for a prominent preacher in the New Zealand Churches of Christ. This speech illustrates the typical speech that he gave on the furlough and showcases his eloquence. The narratives of life in Africa are painted with striking, memorable, and vivid images. Grounded in his Christian worldview, the oneness Todd felt with the African people comes across. Listeners saw it as a "gripping address," and the entire conference "was greatly moved" by the sermon.[2] Near the sermon's end Todd quoted a justice of the high court in Southern Rhodesia who said, "in these days when we need a leader so desperately I have often wondered if our prophet might come from New Zealand?" Todd probably did not realize that eventually he would become that prophet. The text is reproduced from the May 1950 *New Zealand Christian*.

This evening drums are monotonously thudding in African villages and compounds while I who would be so much more at home within sound of them, stand here in Invercargill with the responsibility of addressing this great congregation.

Sixteen years ago I left the ministry of a church in Oamaru to go to Africa, and looking back, I know that although my ministry was a very happy one and the people were more than kind to their young and inexperienced pastor, I was glad to leave because I felt that I was not really needed in New Zealand. In Oamaru there were eleven ministers of the Protestant churches and the community appeared to be well served. My friends in the church were not in any particular need of my assistance and those not in the church were not much interested in what I had to say or was attempting to do.

Here was Africa calling, and to Africa we most willingly went. We went to join the throng of missionaries whose work it was to bring light where there was darkness, but our years in that great land were to bring light to our eyes, and an understanding of the needs of men—needs which in my own homeland of New Zealand I had been too inexperienced, too blind, too selfish to see. In New Zealand the casualness of my friends had quite deceived me—here were good homes, medical care for those in need, educational facilities, sport and wireless programmes, social security. The great majority of people apparently believed that the Kingdom of Heaven was being established in New Zealand by act of Parliament.

So with the feeling that everything had been accomplished in New Zealand we left for a land where almost nothing had been commenced, and for years our eyes saw only the differences—the difference in conditions, in the colour of the people and their customs.

Obviously things were different. Here were no fine homes but primitive hovels, vermin ridden. Here brown and black people squatted half-naked in the sun or crouched over little fires built in their huts—dark huts, windowless, like the minds of these primitive people. Here was no brightness of eye and intelligent speech, but dull, drinksodden folk living lives of deadening monotony—no education, no news from an outside world—just the magnifying of trifles with perhaps a quarrel or a fight to relieve the monotony.

Here the women were not well-dressed, educated, with rights and respect deserved and gladly given, but were poor creatures whose futures were decided by the older people of the kraal. Here were girls with no rights of their own, promised in marriage perhaps to polygamous husbands—promised while possibly still little children, taken to live with their husbands at twelve years of age. Here were women, old in appearance while still young in years, bearing their children while themselves still immature, walking their way dejectedly through a life of toil which brought them little reward.

The children in this new homeland of ours were not surrounded by intelligent love, with expert medical care and educational opportunity, but were lovable little brown babies—almost half of whom were doomed to die before they reached their first birthday. Figures cannot be exact, for there is no register of births even to this day in Southern Rhodesia. Here, instead of enlightened love, ruled deadly superstition—a power which would even condemn to death the second child of twins who might be born.

"Come to my kraal, Missionary," pleaded a young man, "or otherwise they will kill one of my babies!" I went the thirteen miles to Msipani and entered the hut in which the mother sat upon her mat on the floor with a little brown babe at her breast. With her were six or seven old women—the midwives—and one of them held the second little baby. "Take my wife and her two babies to the Mission," pleaded the young husband. "But they will surely not dare to kill the baby," I argued. "No, but only that first born boy will be properly fed and the second born baby, that one held by the grandmother, will soon die," he replied. "Take them today, please, for these old women will stay always with my wife, and I can do nothing." But the old women refused to let me take the mother and babies. I called in the head of the kraal and the old women then said that I should come back in eight days. Only after a great deal of difficulty was I at last able to take the mother and her twins safely with me to Dadaya Mission.

So we came to Africa and our hearts lifted as we looked out over the land and saw so much work that we could do, such deep need that we could meet. Wherever we looked we saw that need. The land was poorly cultivated, the houses badly built, there was so much sickness. Everywhere there was poverty, ignorance, superstition and evil.

Oh, where there is need the people welcome you. They welcome you even though you are not really skilled, even though you may make your instruments from fencing wire in an emergency. They thank you, and the look in their eyes smites you to your heart when you know your own inadequacy to deal effectively with a situation—when you know that the comfort of your presence is possibly the only effective service you can give.

And so we started our education through experience. I remember a certain moonlit night. The car bumped its way over terrible tracks, scraping its chassis over rocks which threatened to stop progress altogether. I was on my way to a village where a child was sick, but when I arrived there I found a beautiful little baby of perhaps fifteen months lying on a blanket. The babe had been its mother's delight—the hair was brushed, the body anointed with sweet oil, the only adornments a string of beads around the plump little body; and on her feet little white bootees. A most beautiful little babe, but dead. The hut was different from our homes, the surroundings different, but the grief— the heartwracking grief was the same as the grief of all mothers—Rachel weeping for her children and would not be comforted.

Sibanda is a Christian and his whole concern is for his family's welfare. It was a joy to see him marry and build himself a little cottage in burned brick with windows and a fireplace and chimney. It was something new in his part of the reserve, and many people watched him with interest. Sibanda works as a builder and makes £3 per week, which is a very large wage for an African. He was determined that his children should have every advantage, every opportunity that he had been denied as a child. His heart was very sad when his first born son was found to be suffering from so serious an eye defect that he would not be able to attend school. But this African man took the little boy to a specialist, waited in a hospital with him during the days following a serious operation, traveled in the weekends 120 miles by cycle to make sure that the little fellow was getting on all right and now has the joy of seeing him in school. Here is an African, coming from a primitive home himself, but by the grace of God finding within himself the determination, the unselfishness required to work and persevere in the interests of others.

But Sibanda has a brother—born of the same mother and the same father. This brother did not battle as did Sibanda to attend school, to make his decision to live a Christian life, but has taken the easy road. And what is that easy road? If you went to his village you would find the same primitive huts that his father had lived in before him, you would find dirty people, drunken people, children whose welfare excites little interest in their father. He is a selfish, superstitious, evil man, a man who lives to gratify his physical appetites and has neither ideals to encourage him or shame to spur him.

And then there was Ndlovu. Ndlovu many years ago decided to accept the Christian way and for some time he walked faithfully and he had his feet planted on the road that Sibanda has taken. But the right way, while being the most-satisfying way, the manly way, is by no means the easy and lazy way. Ndlovu grew careless. He left off attending services and began to look towards the old beer drinks and careless living. Before long he was not to be found in the Christian assemblies but at the beer drinks. His home was no longer a Christian home and his children did not go to school or to church. Soon there was no distinguishing mark between Ndlovu's village and any other heathen village, except that a man who has once professed his faith in Christ and made some attempt to follow Him never quite stills the voice of his conscience. Twenty years passed before Ndlovu stirred himself and realised what he had done—realised that having heard Christ's call, he had followed and then turned back. Ndlovu roused himself and came to the church, and expressed his regret. That was perhaps five years ago, and it was a sad sight to see this man coming to Dadaya with his determination to atone for his lapse. Ndlovu looked out of place amongst the other men, for you cannot live a careless, drunken, sinful life for twenty years without your face showing it very plainly for all the world to see.

Now Ndlovu's great determination was to have a Christian school established near his village. He worked and pled until this was done and Ngome school stands today, and to it go some of Ndlovu's grandchildren, but Ndlovu had come to his senses too late to save his own children. He had not accepted his responsibility at the right time, and his children were heathen. His son, a polygamist who has three wives, lives near his father's kraal, and the life of the son was so disgraceful that it began to prey upon the mind of the old man. In his son's heathendom he saw his own sin—the sin of taking life easily and refusing to set an example of right Christian living for his children to follow. There came such remorse that Ndlovu one day went away from his village and away from the tragedy of his son's kraal, and he was found hanging from a tree.

Mafala Matshazi was our local chief. Matshazi was a Mandebele—the Mandebele are an off-shoot of the Zulu people, and once they were warriors, but not today. They don't have to keep fighting-fit today, and if the crops are good they drink and quarrel. Matshazi had his good points and he was glad to have the mission near him. He even went as far as coming to an adult class once to learn to speak a little English. He made several attempts to send his children to school, if he didn't need them for herding cattle or cultivating in the lands, but there were many times when Matshazi was drinking while his children endeavoured to guide the oxen and the plough. Eventually the children got to about Standard 3, but when they were to come to the boarding school, Matshazi didn't quite get around to giving them their school-fees. It wasn't that he didn't want to help them—he wanted very much to get ahead himself, and to help his children too, but there were the beer-drinks and he didn't get time for other things. Then one day he fell ill and he called in his witch-doctors, but this time he realised that he was not going to recover. A message came for me to go to his kraal, but I was not available for some hours, and before I could go a message came to say that the chief was dead. I heard the rest of the story from one who was at the village when the chief died. Word had come back to Matshazi to say that I would not arrive for some hours and he evidently realised that I would not arrive in time, so he called his three little children to his hut and he said, "When I am dead you will dress yourselves nicely, and then you must go to Dadaya to the missionary and say to him that I have sent you, and that I am asking him to educate you." There are many people in Africa who don't quite get around to doing what they know they should.

And so we went on our way through the years in Africa, and as time slipped by, the strangeness of the land and its people became less and less noticeable to us, until the day came when we accepted colour and custom as being part of our daily life, until today when my children from Africa look at our European friends in New Zealand and search in their faces for resemblances to African friends. "Look at that man over there—isn't he just like Sibanda?" one will say.

With the passing of the strangeness there came a new awareness in our minds, and that was the fundamental oneness of the African savage with ourselves. I do not remember when I first began to realise this—I do not know if I was slower than most missionaries in recognising it, but I remember particularly one day when I had been called to a village where a young woman was in labour and the birth of the child had been seriously delayed. The home was an important one and the birth one of note. When I arrived about thirty or forty Africans were seated outside the hut looking serious and dejected. Inside the hut, lying in the semi-darkness, was the mother and with her several old women who were the midwives. I knelt on the ground at the side of the mother as hundreds of times I have done—but at one moment I remember raising my head and catching the eye of the old hag who in all her dirt of body was kneeling beside me to help also, and in her eyes I read the deep anxiety—anxiety for the young mother, and with it the readiness to help, and I thought to myself, "We are the same." In that hut differences of colour and culture and race no longer existed and we were one in sympathy with the mother—sharing her suffering as her babe was born. And I remember the old woman, as I held the babe in my hands, asking quietly if it were boy or girl; when I answered that it was a boy, she lifted up her voice so that through the inadequate walls of the hut the whole group might hear and called, "A son is born!" In the joy of that moment we all shared. In that instant I think I began to see more clearly and to recognise the common humanity of all men everywhere.

But in Africa the people were in desperate need while in New Zealand the people had little need of such as myself! In Africa I did not have to apologise for stepping in and helping to nurse sick people back to health. Wherever I went I was more than welcome—even on occasions when I went right into the huts of witch-doctors themselves to bring help to their wives or children. But then in New Zealand, if I had really been a doctor, I would also have been welcomed into the homes of the people, for my skill would have been sought and would have been appreciated. Then in this matter of health and of disease there was no doubt that the people were one—they were the same.

In Africa groups of people continually arrive at the mission pleading that we should come to their area and commence a school. In the papers today in New Zealand I note that from all over the country comes the demand for more and better schools and for more teachers. Then in this regard there is also a unity between the African in Southern Rhodesia and the European in New Zealand.

In Africa we teach better methods of agriculture, of the care of cattle, of the building of homes, but I am sure that all of these branches of life are also of great concern to my European friends in New Zealand. If I really were knowledgeable about such matters I believe I would be well received and what I had to say would be given attention. If people are starving, they will welcome the Red Cross workers and their trucks of grain—they will give them a royal welcome. If people are in sickness, their friends will wait at the front door to receive the doctor and welcome him into the home. Wherever there is a real need, a need which is fully appreciated, then the one who can meet that need can be sure of a hand stretched out in greeting.

But in Africa our work is neither altogether or even mainly concerned with medicine or agriculture or education in its narrower sense, or building or house-wifery or any other of the subjects we endeavour to teach; it is to bring to the people the Gospel of Jesus Christ. And with that message we go right in without any apology, for the need of it is as apparent as is the need of a diseased body for medical help.

When people accept Christ in Africa great changes come into their lives. No longer are they people without a purpose, no longer will they waste their time and their health in beer parties, no longer are they content to let their children remain uneducated, no longer will they pledge their daughters in marriage, no longer will they contract polygamous marriages with all the hatreds and jealousies which such marriages bring into a village. Women lift their heads, finding themselves people with honour and privileges. Oh, yes, Christ makes a world of difference in an African society, and no missionary has to feel embarrassed when stating His claims, when announcing to African people that bondage in Christ is perfect freedom.

Here, then, we place our finger upon the difference between the native of Africa and our people in this land—the African needs Christ, but the European does not! Is this really the case? Sixteen years ago, when I left New Zealand for Africa, turning my back on problems and difficulties which I did not know existed in the hearts of my own folk, I might have believed that the African needed Christ but the European did not; but my years in Africa have made me realise that in this respect more than in any other, the needs of African and European are the same.

In New Zealand the Christian religion has had a great influence; the coarser manifestations of heathendom have long since vanished from our land, and on the outside, anyway, most people look reasonably decent, reasonably honest. We have so complete a veneer of civilisation that we sometimes deceive even ourselves. Here is our great danger, as a people. New Zealand is today a wealthy country—a country of rich men. Almost everyone is rich today. My grandfather built a rough house and drew water from a well. My father borrowed his sister's shoes which were too small for him so that he might attend a social evening. When a sack of flour had kerosene spilled on it and was tainted with the odour, the family still had to persevere with tainted bread until the sack was finished.

Those days are past and I do not regret their passing, but is it necessary that the deep religious experience our fathers knew should pass with them? Must New Zealand be doomed to an era of civilised paganism? Will we have to learn by some yet unforseen tragedy that man cannot live by bread alone? Oh, the bitter need of this land, this wealthy, privileged land where so many beautiful homes are spiritually poverty stricken.

I hope that some of the things that I have said have been interesting, but I am not here to interest, or amuse, or entertain, but to endeavour to bring a message—an authentic message, gained from sixteen years of service amongst a primitive people, as the servant of a powerful Christ. But what is this message? Simply that the need of men, of all races and colours, is for hope, for ideals, for something worthwhile to accomplish and for the strength that is required to accomplish it. The answer to the needs of men is Jesus Christ—the risen Christ.

Let the Church recognise this—let it learn the truth again. And when I say the Church, I do not mean the Ministers or the priests but every Christian person. Let us recognise the need of the world! If we see a house on fire, we have no hesitation in calling for the brigade. If a child is lost we will arouse the countryside. When a man sees a real need he is provided with an incentive for action.

If our Christian people in New Zealand will recognise the need for Christ, how are they going to meet that need? It is not for me to lay before you a plan of attack on the forces of evil which are abroad today, but I do know some general principles. First, Christian people must recognise their own need, and make no plan without seeking the guidance of God, go no step without seeking His strength, and take no action except it be compelled by a love of their brother man.

The world needs a lead from somewhere today. The world needs Christian prophets today. I have a friend who is a Justice of the High Court in Southern Rhodesia and I lunched with him just before leaving home. He is a deeply spiritual man and he turned to me and said,

> In the 1914 war I had a good bit to do with your countrymen and I became a great admirer of them. None of us know, of course, but in these days when we need a leader so desperately I have often wondered if our prophet might come from New Zealand. It is a new land and the people are young and virile and they have done much in social leadership. Could they give us spiritual leadership?

I put it to you that if the Christian Churches really got going today, New Zealand might lead the world. If war comes you will send your finest men and women overseas and count the cost not too great. What is New Zealand prepared to do in the even greater difficulties that face us in the peace? To one who returns to this country after a long absence it appears that New Zealand has grown increasingly wealthy, increasingly self-satisfied, and that pleasure is her goal.

But I come from a land where 1 3/4 million people are living at a subsistence level and Southern Rhodesia is much more fortunate than other countries with vast populations. New Zealand is worried about her overseas balances, about her import controls, but few of the people seem to worry about the spread of Communism over the face of the earth. Spiritual leadership is called for—leadership in this land—leadership amongst the nations. But you always come back to the individual, and to the individual I address myself. I have learned in Africa that men need God, and I have learned that he who would attempt to meet that need must hold nothing back.

I feel that there is a danger of our churches thinking that they can legislate for a new order of progress, that better planning will bring them to their goal; but I would say that everything must be taken in its right order and that what the churches need is not legislation but consecration.

The world needs Christians. New Zealand needs Christians by the hundred thousand, men and women whose first interest is in the Kingdom of Heaven and whose income, family life, time are all made subservient to the Christ. What do you contribute in time to the cause of Christ? What do you contribute in money to the cause of Christ? Seek ye first the Kingdom of God and His righteousness, and all needed things shall be added unto you.

We know—of course we know. The trouble is that we appear not to believe the truth of what we know or we would put it into action. The cause of Christ awaits for men who know and who will act.

> We know the paths wherein our feet should tread,
> Across our hearts are written Thy decrees,
> But now, O Lord, be merciful to bless with more than these.
> Grant us the strength to fashion as we feel,
> Grant us the truth to labour as we know,
> Grant us the purpose, ribbed and edged with steel,
> To strike the blow.
> Knowledge we ask not, knowledge Thou hast lent;
> But, Lord, the will—there lies our bitter need.
> Grant us to build above the deep intent,
> The deed, the deed![3]

The Unfinished Task of Christian Missions in Southern Africa

The American Disciples of Christ, British Churches of Christ, and Associated Churches of Christ of New Zealand all had mission efforts in Africa dating back to the nineteenth century. British and New Zealand missionaries came to South Africa in 1896, Americans went to the Congo in 1897, Kiwis entered Zimbabwe in 1898, and British missionaries first came to Malawi in 1909.[4] Despite very little contact and coordination, Basil Holt, an American Disciple based in Johannesburg, realized that these Southern African mission efforts had ninety thousand members in their churches. Holt proposed that these mission efforts form a convention "for mutual understanding and some coordination of their work" that would meet every four years.[5] Garfield Todd was inducted as the first president of the All Southern Africa Convention of the Disciples of Christ. He delivered this presidential address at the convention opening at the Linden Christian Church, Johannesburg, on September 20, 1954.[6]

Todd defended Christian missions for the good that they brought to Southern Africa, especially the influence of civilization and morals—a common topic for Todd in his political speeches. In segregated South Africa Todd pled for the church's leadership in race relations which was clearly the meaning of the speech and its title: "The Unfinished Task of Christian Missions in Southern Africa." Todd believed that Christianity and spiritual values, not the secular enlightenment, would be the basis for solving the problems of society. The sermon also stressed a theme that Todd's daughter Judith said exemplified Todd's Christian political philosophy: "Love thy neighbor as thyself and if you do that then you have no worries political or otherwise."[7] The text of the sermon is reproduced from the *Southern African Sentinel*, November 1954.

The symbol of the Christian Church is a cross. From Calvary onwards, it has been associated with suffering, but the crucifixion was followed by a triumphant resurrection, and through nineteen centuries of history, the Church has had her victories. The world took little note of the birth of Jesus at Bethlehem. The young boy with the inquiring mind who set questions to the Doctors of Law at the Temple at Jerusalem grew to full manhood, trained as a carpenter, and at thirty years of age set out upon the work which it had been ordained he should do.

His friends were conscious of his goodness. Andrew brought his brother Peter to see Him. James and John were ready to leave Zebedee, their father, to follow the young prophet. Matthew left the Custom House. Thomas was ready to follow also—his doubts were to come later. Judas Iscariot thought it worth while to join the band. Here was a little group—a mere handful of men to start a world crusade. The work of the Church began in Jerusalem and, over the years, flourishing under persecution, extended to the farthest corners of the world.

The philosophies of man are constantly changing. Policies and politics of the state are never long stable, but the Church is the guardian of eternal truths, and to be worthy of its name, it must be true to God. The Church and its message cannot be moulded and restricted by the thoughts and desires of men, whether they be individuals or whether they be governments. The Church works amongst men, but its commission, its authority, and its power come from God Himself, and the truths that it preaches are enshrined in the Scriptures.

The missionary zeal of the early Church soon took the message of Christ throughout the known world. Its influence was felt in northern Africa in the very early days of Christian history, but many centuries were to pass before the Christian message was preached in Southern Africa, and, north of the Limpopo, we have this year celebrated with deep thankfulness the one hundredth anniversary of the coming of Christian missionaries to Southern Rhodesia.

It is not my concern today to trace the history of the work of the Church and its Missions, nor shall I attempt to evaluate the work that has been accomplished over the years. This present age has its very serious problems and the hearts of men are inclined to fail them, but the Christian message in the twentieth century is more than ever a Gospel of confidence, of hope, and of good will. Africa's debt to Christian missions is great, as a study of even its byproducts—the Christian mission hospital, Christian schools—will show.

There are those who believe that the African would have been better off if Christian missions had not come to this continent, but such an opinion can be held only by two types of people. The one group are those who have had no knowledge of what life is really like in a primitive African village. The tourist who makes his way to a remote and picturesque village up on the hillside, with its little brown huts and perhaps its fat babies playing in the sun, might be forgiven if he thinks that there dwells innocence and happiness. Those who know the people know of the sickness and of the disease, know of the babies born so soon to die, know of unhappiness, the frightful ignorance, the killing boredom of life in a native village. They know of the frightening power of witchcraft and the terror which it can bring to the heart and the frightful deeds which from time to time it inspires. They know of spiritual darkness in the souls of the people and of their need, their great need, physically, mentally and above all, spiritually.

The other group who hold that missions should not have come to Africa are those who would deny the African the full stature of Christian manhood and womanhood; who would, for their own selfish ends, have preferred to have kept the African where he was before Christianity came to the continent—and that was at a level little higher than the animals. For all that has been accomplished by the Christian Church in South Africa we are deeply grateful, but our great concern is for what remains to be done, for the task of Christian missions is a task unfinished. On the one hand, there is still much of the primitive in Africa today. Anyone who wishes to serve his country must be prepared with open eyes to face the facts, and our police records show that a belief in evil—that a fear of the supernatural is still a very potent force in African life.

Only a few months ago in my own country, the papers had a story which featured an old African man hiding behind the path which led up from the lands to the village. Coming along the path was a little boy of two years of age. With old age, we associate kindliness and a love of children, but this man took the little child and sold him for £10 to another who wished to kill the babe, which he did and used parts of his body for making medicine which, supposedly, would guarantee the success of a business venture in which he was interested.

All too often terrible deeds similar to this occur. What is almost more distressing in my mind is the fact that there is no wave of indignation amongst the people regarding such a thing. Of course, all Christians, whether they be brown or white, condemn such crimes, but there are still many amongst the African people whose condemnation and indignation are overlaid to some extent by almost an understanding of, if not a sympathy with, the reason for such a crime.

Christianity is, however, concerned not only with the villages and with the primitive people who may live in them, but also with those who live in towns, for the needs of the people in Johannesburg, for example, are just as great as the needs of the people in primitive villages. Christianity is deeply concerned, not only with the African people, but with the whole community in Southern Africa, and, although the work of the Church may for greater effectiveness be divided up into work amongst children, work amongst the youth, work amongst Africans, work amongst Europeans, it is not really a work that divides, but a work that unites.

There are many aspects of the Christian message. The first one is that concerning a man's relationship with his Maker. The message of personal salvation is of the utmost importance to every man, woman, child, and here missions are on non-controversial ground. When men recognise their need of God and seek salvation, no one will criticise missions in their work of guiding a man so that his need may be met. As long as men are born, the Church has its work to do—whether that work be done through the special agency of missions or in other ways. But when a man becomes a Christian, his life is changed and his attitudes are changed. There is no such thing as a common Christian, for when a man becomes a Christian he enters a new relationship with God. He also enters a new relationship with himself and his neighbours.

The Christian message has a good deal to say regarding a man and his neighbour. We remember that when Christ was questioned regarding the greatest commandment, his reply was that a man should love his God with all his heart, his mind, and his soul, and his neighbour as himself; and when he was asked to define "neighbour," he told the story of the man who went down from Jericho to Jerusalem and fell amongst thieves. Then came a picture of those who passed, the priest and the Levite, good men of high repute, but who were not prepared to go out of their way to give assistance. Then came the one whom Jesus held to be "neighbour," a Samaritan, a man thought to be very lowly by those who listened to Jesus, for they were orthodox Jews.

The Samaritan, however, was prepared to go out of his way to help someone whom he did not know, but whose need attracted him.

It is very possible that if Jesus were with us today, in Southern Africa, he would have used a different parable to denote a "neighbour." He would very probably have said that a man walked through the suburbs of Johannesburg and was set upon by thugs, was stripped of his belongings and left unconscious. He might then have pictured a European passing in a car and not stopping to render assistance, and followed by an African who was prepared to give of what he had, who was prepared to meet the need of the unfortunate victim.

We have made distinctions between the Church and missions. We too often think of the Church as being the European Church and missions being that particular agency of the Church which serves the African or other coloured community. That distinction is not a real one and it is not held firmly by the Church, but it is often popularly so held. Some times the distinction in the minds of men between the Church and the mission is, on the one hand, of a body of people at rest, and on the other, of a special group of Church members who have an evangelistic fervour. I hold that the Church, to be a Church in reality, must be a body of people militant in their endeavour to extend the borders of Christ's Kingdom and to build up the faith of those who profess to be His followers. I believe that, as the years pass, there will have to be greater unity between the Church and missions, and that what we call the indigenous church will have to be truly indigenous in that there will be a very much greater unity between African and European within it.

At the present time, the whole world is concerned with problems concerning neighbours. This is by no means a new problem, but in earlier years, a strip of salt water between two countries tended to simplify the position. Whether this holds good today is a matter of much doubt, but certainly in Southern Africa there are no natural boundaries to simplify problems between us, and there are those who hold that the Church is inclined to make the difficulties even greater. From a certain angle this is no doubt true, but on the long-term view, I believe the Church holds the solution to our problems, and I know of no solution other than that which Christian teaching can bring.

Admittedly, in this process of change which goes on inexorably, the Church and the State are inclined on occasions to tread on one another's toes; and yet there need be no antagonism between the two if each keeps to its own sphere. The Christian Church is concerned with matters of high principle. The teaching of Christ can show a man how he should regulate his conduct on the one hand with God, and on the other with his neighbour. The ideal which is set before us is a very high one, namely that we should love

God with our whole being. A person who even endeavours to carry out such a precept is obviously a very special kind of person. The second part of the commandment is that this man who has achieved so high an ideal for himself should be prepared to love his neighbour as himself. Love, in my estimation, is no sentimental, weak passion, but denotes strength and respect, as well as affection. Sometimes there are those who criticise governments and their legislation and their general conduct and feel that a government should be so guided by the highest Christian principles that it should be much further ahead in these things than the community at large. But in our human conditions and environment, a government cannot do better than express the ideals and aspirations of people as a whole, and where a government is criticised in any particular way regarding its lack of ideals, the Church might examine itself more fully to see whether perhaps its work is not being done as well as it should. There is no doubt regarding the responsibility which lies at the door of the Christian Church. It is a very heavy responsibility, and one which it cannot shirk.

Governments are concerned with carrying out the will of the people. Admittedly, today almost all governments take a very much more intimate interest in the affairs of the population than used to be the case. Many governments today are concerned with the provision of medical facilities for the population; with providing education for all the people; with providing even housing and transport. It is because governments have taken over a practical interest in many of these things which affect us in our day to day lives that we are more than ever critical of their work. Governments have to lay down laws, governments have to use coercion to see that law and order is maintained.

Governments have always had power over the body, but the Church has always maintained that a much more important power is that which is exercised over the soul, over the spirit of man. How much power is the Church exercising today in the life of the community? It is true that too often there is a form of godliness, but that the power of God is denied; and I do not think that as a whole, the European population of Southern Africa does give the worthy example which might be expected of it, taking into account the years of Christian civilisation which we have enjoyed. It is true that times without number, we whose skins are white demand special privileges, a special place in the community, because we say we are the civilised section of the community. It is a very human failing to demand rights, but to be chary of accepting responsibilities. I believe that the European population in Southern Africa has very special responsibilities and that a great deal of our trouble today is that we are not accepting the responsibilities, but at the same time, demand our rights. I believe that if we were prepared more fully to accept our responsibilities, many of our problems would automatically be solved.

It is true that the problems which the Church faces are by no means confined to the continent of Africa, for perhaps the greatest problem before the Church today is the materialistic age in which we live. It is not a new phase in the lives of men that people are tempted to place their trust in goods rather than in values. Christ had much to say on this point nineteen hundred years ago and said of one who had amassed great riches, "Thou fool, this night thy soul shall be required of thee."

The European section of the Church in Southern Africa has to face the problems of a materialistic age, but it has also to face the racial problems peculiar to Southern Africa, and this is perhaps asking almost more than man can face up to. But we have no choice in this matter. The challenge is before us and the Church alone can face it.

Our responsibility as Christian people is to do our part in making the Church a vital living force within the community. Where the Church is strong and worthy, its influence will be felt very definitely by all the people who live in our society; and as long as men live, the task of the Church, whether of that as a Church or as missions, is unfinished.

Now in my talk this evening, what new thing can I speak of? We all have a thirst for news, and what news can there be in this address? I have stated the need. I have spoken of the need of a man for his God. I have spoken of the need to work out a formula for good neighbourliness between the races. But in what way can this be done? I am afraid I have nothing new to say. In each country, the Church can find ways of making its influence felt. The Christian missions in many parts of Africa have had special privileges, and too often those privileges have not been taken advantage of. There have been churches in the home countries who have decried the opportunities which their missionaries have received of working in schools and colleges. They have said that their work was not concerned with education but with the saving of souls. As if it is possible to divide up a man's intellect and his spirit and his social relations as you can his stomach from his heart!

There are still in most countries in Africa opportunities for the Church and its missions to work in schools, to work through hospitals, and, of course, through the churches and their ordinary agencies. Some of these opportunities are determined by set policy, but in all British countries anyway, opportunity is given for the church, and I believe adequate opportunity to exert its influence much more fully than it is today.

In New Zealand, which was my home country, it was true that for many years and certainly all the years I was at school, by law, the schools were secular, free, and compulsory. While it was legal to teach philosophies within school, it was not legal to name the name of God nor to teach the Christian religion. I believe the reason for that was that in the earliest years, there was so much denominational rivalry, that it was felt that the children could well depend upon the Church and the home to provide adequate religious training. In recent years, it has been found that the churches and the homes have not been giving the spiritual training necessary to work a democracy, let alone to save the souls of the people, and the schools have been opened to some extent Christian teaching. I have no doubt that whatever attitude a government may take to its African schools particularly, that opportunity will continue to be given for the teaching of Christianity and its spiritual values.

In Southern Rhodesia, the missionaries still conduct most of the African education which the children enjoy, and Southern Rhodesia, like most other parts of Africa, lies under a great debt to Christian missions. It may be that for many years our work will continue under the control of missions, but already in the towns the state is taking an increasingly greater part in the provision of education for African children, and many big schools are now completely controlled by the government. However, in these schools, Christian teaching is given for half an hour a day.

I could not over-emphasize the responsibility which rests upon the Church. The state has certain powers, but those powers are of necessity limited although they may seem great and widespread; for they concern the material things more than the spiritual, and I believe that the answer to our greatest problems is not material but spiritual. To whom, then, can we go for the solution of our problem if the Church has lost its power? If the salt has lost its savour?

The opportunities for the Church today are in many ways greater than ever, but it does not use the opportunities which lie to its hand. The churches use different methods, and recently we have seen in the Billy Graham mission in London a very full use made of propaganda, of loudspeakers and many modern methods of spreading the truth. These methods are used greatly by forces with whose views we do not agree—for example, the force of Communism. And why are we so backward as a Church in using modern methods? Another thing which should strengthen us in these days is the fact that the enormous distances which used to exist physically between other churches in the mother countries and their missions in Africa have been annihilated. It is so easy for representatives to move around the world. It is so easy to take news backwards and forwards quickly. It is so easy to use films and other modern ways, giving a much more adequate knowledge of the need of the people of Africa to the people in our home churches.

I know that there is sometimes a certain reticence on the part of governments to allow people of other countries who come as missionaries to have free access to our lands, but I do not think that very much hindrance is usually put in the way of people from the Churches overseas. The Church itself knows no national boundaries, but on occasions natural boundaries do form a certain hindrance to its work.

I speak tonight in a church which has been fostered by the Disciples of Christ of America, a body of people more than two million strong who have played and play today a very worthy part in the life of the Church and the nation in the United States. I believe that the National Council of Churches in America can be of great help to us all, and I for one welcome growing interest which is being shown by Americans of all the Christian Churches in the States. I believe that the bonds between us as nations are very important ones in this troubled time, but that the bonds between the Churches are of even greater significance and can inspire a sense of brotherhood between us which can have far-reaching effects in the lives of our nations.

Circumstances change and the world that is evolving is very different from what it was even fifty years ago. Change is always frightening, but Christian people should be confident. We should remember that while atomic power and speeding transport are very new to us, they are not new to God, who created all things. The Creator who packed this universe with power so many aeons ago is not surprised when at this time he has permitted men for the first time to tap these incredible resources. Sometimes I think Christian people believe that God Himself is frightened by change and that the things that happen today are a surprise to Him. Our attitude should be completely different. We should realise that God, whom we endeavour to serve, is in these days allowing man to take into his hands power which has always been available to him but of which he had not until recently even dreamt. We should realise also that the spiritual forces which alone can make use of the power which we are tapping must come from the One who created all power, both physical and spiritual.

Does the Church today give to the world the impression that it is the body on earth of the Son of God Himself? For that is what it purports to be. Does it give the world the impression that the power of God is manifest within it? I believe that the Church and its missions face a task of enormous magnitude and that the world wants today to see if we can bring the power we claim to have to solve the very real problems which lie before us.

We should not be faint-hearted. We should not wish that our task were other than this, for we have been promised that no challenge will be given us through God's grace which we cannot answer, which we cannot meet. But let us remember it is "not by might, nor by power, but by my spirit," said the Lord.

Christian Unity, Christ's Prayer

Starting in 1949, the Peter Ainslie Memorial Lecture, delivered annually at one of the English-medium South African universities, existed to promote Christian unity. The American Disciples of Christ, through an administrative council, the Council on Christian Unity, sponsored the lectures to commemorate Dr. Peter Ainslie, a distinguished ecumenist (1867–1934) and minister of a leading congregation at Baltimore, Maryland. Todd was the first Disciple to deliver one of the lectures. Other Ainslie lecturers included the luminaries Alan Paton, author of the anti-apartheid novel *Cry the Beloved Country*, and Dr. George MacLeod, founder of the Iona Community, Scotland. This sermon, the seventh Peter Ainslie Memorial lecture, was delivered at the University of Natal, Pietermaritzburg, on June 1, 1955.[8]

The audience was mostly faculty and students with several local clergy and their spouses. Basil Holt reported that the "lecture received a good press" and the city's leading newspaper editorialized on June 2: "If Mr. Garfield Todd's words will have enabled the words 'Christian Unity' to be firmly planted in the minds of church leaders of all denominations, his visit to Natal and last night's lecture will have been well worth while."[9]

This is an important sermon. First, Todd articulates two classic themes in the history of his tradition: Christian unity and Christian primitivism. His positive Christian and ecumenical spirit shines in combination with his plea for grounding Christian practice in the biblical witness in a classic restorationist manner. In addition to arguing that "Christianity is an objective belief based on definite facts" which "are binding upon all Christians," he pleaded for the use of reason and the examination of issues through "the light of New Testament scriptures" and for listening "to the judgment of the sanctified scholarship of the Church universal." Todd explained, "God has given us reason and, in matters which are controversial, we can make an appeal to the scholarship of spiritual leaders of the Church in all ages and throughout all its communion." This ecumenical attitude is rooted in his primitivism: "I believe . . . that while we must treasure everything which we believe to be part of the true lineament of the body of Christ, we must also be ready to cast aside anything which is out of harmony with what we might term 'original Christianity.'"

Finally, Todd grounded his ecumenical primitivism in ethics. He turned to baptism and the Lord's Supper noting their prominence in Churches of Christ stating, ". . . they considered them, not in relation to metaphysics and mysticism, but in relation to action and ethics." He explained, "In the sacraments the real action of God became sealed in our response and in this way the believer himself, ethically responding, became partaker of the divine action. . . . To the personal action of God, we must make a personal reply." And so Todd the Christian responded to the moral question of racism both in his life and later in his prophetic speeches. The following text is reproduced from the pamphlet, R. S. Garfield Todd, *Christian Unity, Christ's Prayer* (Grahamstown, S.A.: Rhodes University, 1955).

As a very young man, less than two years after leaving theological college, I came to Rhodesia with my wife and little daughter to work amongst African people in a Native Reserve. There was so much to be done, seven days a week, in building, in farming, in medical work, in teaching and preaching and pastoral care, and my wife and I were for more than 13 years the only European workers in the Lundi Reserve.

My College Principal had warned me that, as a missionary, the jobs of each day and the isolation in which I would work would sever my link with theological thought, and it is true that the writings and thoughts of the great theologians of the Church, over the last 20 years, have largely passed me by. Most regretfully I must admit that I can make no pretence to great scholarship or deep learning.

You may ask then, why I have the temerity to give this address, and I answer: because I have belonged all my life to a Church which has concerned itself deeply with the need for unity; because I have seen the transforming power of the Gospel of Jesus Christ and I know that it cannot be fully effective in a divided Church; because, having been called to lead a government, I believe implicitly that "except the Lord build the house, they labour in vain that build it; except the Lord keep the city, the watchman waketh but in vain."

If this is the basis of our belief as Christian people, then how important to society, to the world, is the Church, and how deeply concerned we must be for its welfare—this holy and catholic Church.

There are those who believe that denominational differences are good, and speak of healthy competition. There are those who think it a good thing to have different kinds of churches to suit different types of people, but who confuse a desired unity with an unnecessary and in fact undesirable uniformity in worship.

When our Lord came to this earth to reveal to men the perfect love of God and to set up His Church, He had no delusions about the worth or the dependability of mankind; in fact His love was high-lighted against the background of the unworthiness of men. The unity of the inner circle of His twelve disciples was broken by the betrayer, Judas Iscariot; but it was also threatened time and again by such weaknesses as the ambition of James and John, the denial of the apostle Peter, and the doubts of Thomas.

The resurrection and the fellowship which the little band of disciples enjoyed with the risen Son of God brought them such courage and determination that their loyalty to their Lord did not again come into question but, even in those days so near to Christ Himself, error began to creep into the Church. The apostle Paul wrote to the church at Rome and said, "Now I beseech you brethren, mark them that cause divisions and offences contrary to the doctrine which ye have learned; and avoid them. For they that are such serve not our Lord Jesus Christ, but their own belly; and by good words and fair speeches deceive the hearts of the simple." These words of Paul strike all the more effectively because of the fact that they follow chapters in which Paul exhorted the brethren in Rome to be kindly one to another, to live peaceably with all men, to recognize the greater unity even amongst the differences between them, to refrain from judging one another. However, when it came to those who would cause divisions in the Church of Christ, in the body of Christ, his warnings were clear. In Paul's first letter to the church at Corinth, immediately following the salutation and his giving of thanks for everything that was good in the church at Corinth, he came straight to the point regarding their divisions, "For it hath been declared unto me of you, my brethren, by them which are of the house of Chloe, that there are contentions among you. Now this I say, that everyone of you saith, I am of Paul; and I of Apollos; and I of Cephas; and I of Christ. Is Christ divided, was Paul crucified for you, or were ye baptized in the name of Paul?"

As we read these words, we recollect with sadness the time when Jesus prayed for the unity of His Church. Christ was approaching the culmination of His work, with the shadow of the cross already reaching out toward Him, when He lifted up His eyes to heaven and said, "Father, the hour is come; glorify thy Son that thy Son also may glorify Thee." And then came the prayer for His beloved disciples; for the world at large; for those who would yet believe on His Name, "Neither pray I for these alone, but for them also which shall believe on me through their word; that they all may be one in us; that the world may believe that thou has sent me."

In the light of Christ's prayers, there is no room within His Church for the divisions which mark its beauty and holiness. And yet they are there and have been for nearly 2,000 years. The fact that they have been in existence for so many years should not, however, blind our eyes to their sinfulness. We believe that Christ is the hope of the world. We know that He works through His Church and we must recognize the great responsibility which rests upon that Church and upon every Christian person today. We cannot speak of a healthy competition between denominations when Christ himself prayed that, through the establishment of unity within His Church, men might be led to believe in His divinity and in the authority of His work and of His Life. I hold that the sin of division is in itself a most serious stumbling block to the carrying out of God's will upon earth.

In this interesting world in which we live, there is such diversity; diversity of forms, of species, of colours, of sounds, and each has its own attraction. The peoples of the earth too, differ in colour, in traditions, in outlook. But in God's eyes the people of the world fall into two clearly marked groups. The only division which is of real significance is not the division between Greek and barbarian, between bondman and freeman, between male or female, but the division between those who seek God and His righteousness and, on the other side, those who refuse to ally themselves with God and the good. What makes this difficult for us all is the fact that the line of demarcation is not as clear as it should be. Within our own ranks, and unfortunately within the life of each one of us, evil creeps in. Our standards are not high enough. We may refrain from doing evil and glory in our triumph over small temptations but, at the same time, the measure of our love is not great enough and we fail miserably in our positive work for Christ and His Church. These are the faults which Christ so clearly foresaw, and these are the faults which have brought disunity into His work. The desire for unity however has never been absent from the Church at any point of its history and great efforts and sometimes very wrong ones have been made to achieve it. The Church of Rome, particularly, has worked in every possible way to achieve a unity of the Church within its own fold. Through the centuries, the Roman Catholic Church has laid down one policy, demanded allegiance to one creed and brought into being an amazing physical unity and organization which has spread across the world. But this sort of rigid unity and uniformity led to a very wide and deep cleavage between those who were prepared to accept the will of God as interpreted for them by men, and those who sought for themselves to determine the will of God as revealed in the Scriptures: The authority and organization of the great Roman Catholic Church today is not acceptable to hundreds of millions of other Christian peoples. But desire for union has not been limited to those within the Roman Catholic Church. The Peter Ainslie Lecture which I have the honour to deliver this year, is in itself, an expression of the desire for union on the part of a body of Christians known as the "Disciples of Christ," a body of Christians who claim as their reason for existence a great passion for the unity of Christ's Church. Their history goes back over more than 150 years to a time when the American nation was very young. I wish to speak of this movement for it is my mother church, the church into which I was born, and I believe it has made a worthwhile contribution to the cause of unity.

The beginnings of the movement lay with two Presbyterian ministers, Thomas and Alexander Campbell, both scholarly and devout men who had come from Great Britain to America to shepherd the members of the Antiburgher branch of the Presbyterian Church. At that time the Presbyterian Church in Great Britain was split into a number of sections. There were, for example, the Old Lights and the New Lights, the Burghers and the Antiburghers. The tragedy was that Presbyterians going overseas from Britain took with them all the divisions of their church, just as we so unfortunately have brought all the divisions of our own churches to Africa.

When Thomas Campbell arrived in America, his son, Alexander, was still at university in Glasgow. Amongst the new settlers, Thomas Campbell found some of his own branch of the Presbyterian Church, but also Presbyterians of other sections and the foolishness and sinfulness of the divisions and barriers between the various branches of his church so distressed him that eventually he decided to invite all Presbyterians, no matter what their particular branch, to come to his service. That might have been tolerated, but he also invited them to partake of the Lord's Supper and this invitation to the Holy Communion was more than the authorities of the Antiburgher Church would tolerate. Eventually Thomas Campbell found it impossible to continue his work and so withdrew from the Presbytery. However, although the Synod was against this very humble essay into church union, the Christian congregation had a very different attitude to it and, in 1809, the people to whom he had been ministering set up the "Christian Association of Washington," whose object was to restore to the Church of God her original purity and unity.

From this small beginning there developed a movement towards union which spread very rapidly at that time throughout the United States of America. It was deeply disappointing but hardly avoidable that this group, which aimed at unity, should become another denomination with its own accepted teachings, even though they were not put into creedal form. Unfortunately, also there were from time to time very serious divisions and quarrels, by no means all of them being on major matters of doctrine.

Nevertheless, amidst the bitterness and sectarian strife of the day, the Disciples of Christ or "Churches of Christ" made considerable progress and, in America alone, there are now almost two million members. In other countries also, churches were established and the "Restoration Movement" as it was called made known its plea that, to obtain the unity which was not only so desirable but which was commanded by our Lord, we should return to scriptural ways.

Away to the south in New Zealand, over a 100 years ago, the Restoration Movement became known and churches were established. My grandparents, who had been members of the Cameronian branch of the Presbyterian Church and who had settled in the south of New Zealand eventually joined the Restoration Movement after much deep thought and prayer. They did not change their allegiance lightly, but the call to work for unity fired their imagination and they left the Cameronians and for the rest of their lives gave their full support to the congregations known simply as Churches of Christ.

Eventually I was born into the movement and did not join the church because of a particular desire to further the cause of union but because I wished to be a follower of Christ—just as other young people in their own churches make their decisions and take their place. Eventually I came to believe not only in Christ and His atoning work, but also in the special plea of our churches for unity. I also must confess, that in my youth, I considered that my own church held the key to the problem and that all truth was with it.

I was rudely jolted out of my self-satisfaction when I came to Africa. I well remember a service shortly after I arrived in the Lundi Reserve. An African evangelist, a fine old man, gave an address, not on the power of the risen Christ to save the souls of men, but on the superiority of our particular church over the churches round about. "Not," he exhorted, "the Methodist Church, not the Roman Catholic Church, not the Dutch Reformed Church, no, but the Church of Christ." How right he would have been if he had been speaking of the catholic Church of Christ. How wrong when he was referring to our own work, our own churches in the Lundi Reserve. Never had the warning of Paul struck home to me before as it did that day. "Now this I say, that everyone of you saith, I am of Paul; and I of Apollos; and I of Cephas; and I of Christ."

I was appalled, as all those who work in Africa must be appalled, with the desperate need of the people. On every side there was poverty and filth, disease and drunkenness and, worse than these physical things, was the witchcraft, the fear and the degradation of the souls of men. Yet we, with so many others, were walking into the villages and offering these people not the simple Gospel message, but the Gospel as we saw it from our denominational standpoints and, whatever may have been our motives, our high intentions, none of us was entirely free of these faults.

As the months passed, I was most happy to find that the greatness of the need of the African people did have its effect upon the various missionary societies working in Southern Rhodesia. I found that we got together much more readily and easily than did our respective churches in the homeland. I found that many of my brethren in other churches, whatever their authorities may have held, recognized that the need of the people must be met, not necessarily by setting up more churches of their particular denominations, but in endeavouring to find pastoral care for Christians who might be transferred from one mission area to the area of another church. I found that this urge to care for the souls of men was great enough to make men rise above their denominational walls and make overtures to other churches to ensure care for their members who were being transferred to another district. And so my own course gradually was made plain to me. We endeavoured, through churches and schools, to open the Scriptures to enquiring minds and to lead as faithfully as we might, learning ourselves as we went on our way through the years. We endeavoured, not only to build up faithful groups of followers of Christ, but also to get them to recognize their common brotherhood with all those who accept Christ as Saviour and who endeavour to do God's will.

There are two things which should compel us along this road towards union. The one is the great need of mankind and the other the greatness of the love of God. If my house were burning down, I would not be greatly concerned whether it were a Roman Catholic or a Presbyterian who directed the fire hose on it. What I would want is enough water on the blaze and, if mens' souls are in jeopardy, the important thing is that they should be saved. We are told that there is "none other name under heaven given among men, whereby we must be saved" except the name of Jesus Christ of Nazareth. Let us thank God that, down through the centuries, despite the quarrelling of men, their smallness and unworthiness, despite the conflicts within the Church, the grace of God has always been bountifully available to all who have called upon His name. Our sin is that, because of our divisions, the Church has been unable to give that united witness which would have made this world a very different place from what it is today. Before Jesus ascended into heaven, realizing better than anyone else how great and how desperate was the need of men, He gave instructions to His disciples. His instructions were simple and He did not appear to foresee the need of interminable conferences, the analysing of differences, the careful phrasing of creeds. His words were, "Go ye therefore, and teach all nations, baptizing them in the name of the Father and of the Son and of the Holy Ghost, teaching them to observe all things whatsoever I have commanded you and lo, I am with you alway, even unto the end of the world."

This is the second consideration, "and lo, I am with you alway, even unto the end of the world." As Paul put it, "Who shall separate us from the love of Christ? Shall tribulation or distress or persecution or famine or nakedness or peril or sword? Nay, in all these things we are more than conquerors through Him that loved us. For I am persuaded that neither death, nor life, nor angels nor principalities nor powers, nor things present nor things to come, nor height nor depth, nor any other creature shall be able to separate us from the love of God which is in Christ Jesus our Lord." That is the love which binds us to Christ and which should bind us to one another. I am afraid that the obstacles which have been erected between us, as Christian brethren, are obstacles which also come between us and Christ Himself. How carefully and wonderfully balanced is the Christian life. We may not pray for the unconditional forgiveness of our sins—we shall be forgiven as we are prepared to forgive. We wish to have full union with our Saviour but we may not achieve this without accepting the same degree of union with our brethren in Christ.

It is urgent and most important that we should turn our eyes from the things that divide us to the things which unite us and how many and how wonderful are the treasures we share in common. We look back over the years of Christian history and give thanks for the many outstanding men and women who have lived for Christ and sometimes died for Christ. They may have belonged to some particular denomination, some particular branch of Christ's Church but, in their greatness, their denominational ties are forgotten and they are shared by the Church universal.

We give thanks for the memory of Gregory the Great because he was the instrument chosen to bring Christianity to Great Britain. The fact that Saint

Francis of Assisi was not a Methodist does not spoil his memory, nor do we think the less of Livingstone because he was a Presbyterian.

Our hearts were stirred within us when we heard during the days of the Nazi persecutions of faithful Christian witnesses, and our pride in them was not conditioned by whether they belonged to the Lutheran Church or the Roman Catholic Church, or some other section of God's people.

We rejoice in the work that Billy Graham is accomplishing and we give thanks for every man and woman, every boy and girl, who has found a new allegiance to Christ through his work. The fact that Graham is an American and a minister of the Southern Baptist Church of the United States, does not lessen our appreciation of his work.

I say that even as Christ is too great to be claimed by some denomination, so every outstanding Christian is too great and too valuable to be hedged in by denominational walls. His work, his life, belong to the whole Church of Christ.

Last year I spent a couple of weeks in Nairobi and, while I was there, I was told by the Director of Prisons that in the Nairobi jail there were 150 men waiting to be executed. I was told by the Director and also by others that a Roman Catholic priest was giving his whole time to the care of these condemned men. I did not have the honour of meeting that man, for I would not have asked him to give me of his precious time when he had so much to do, but I was told of how he would sit there on the prison floor, hour after hour, surrounded by the next group of men who were to mount the gallows—murderers and men who consorted with murderers. Representing the church was a Roman Catholic priest who had taken upon his shoulders the responsibility of bringing to men who were rightly the outcasts of society, and yet still the children of God, their last chance of accepting a salvation which can be extended even to murderers. When I heard of this man, I felt very humble, for I doubt if I would have the courage to face such work but I also was grateful that there were men within the Church, faithful and ready to meet any service.

By this time you may be saying that I appear to be a man without convictions for, if I am so ready to accept the work of people of all churches, I probably also argue that all are right and that it really doesn't matter at all to which church a man belongs. I must make my position clear. The movement to which I have belonged all my life, while it has always been prepared to accept as Christian brethren all those who acknowledge Jesus Christ as Saviour and sincerely attempt to carry out God's will, at the same time, has always placed great emphasis upon sound doctrine.

In my views on these matters I am particularly indebted to certain outstanding scholars of my own church and especially Dr. William Robinson,[10] who have worked for unity on the foundations laid by the Apostles.

In seeking union, I believe we must start by recognizing each other's churchmanship, whatever may be the matters that divide us. We can surely accept the sincerity of other Christian people, even though we may not agree with all that they hold. Christianity is an objective belief based on definite facts. It is not a flimsy theology which can be shaped or twisted to suit any man's ideas. I believe that most people have a deep love for their mother church and it is right that we should hold precious everything that is good and true in the teachings which we receive. I believe, however, that while we must treasure everything which we believe to be part of the true lineament of the body of Christ, we must also be ready to cast aside anything which is out of harmony with what we might term "original Christianity." This has been the attitude of my own people down through the years and it is possibly achieving fulfillment today in the work of the Faith and Order Movement of the World Council of Churches.

We may sum up by saying that we should get together on those things which are universally accepted as being of Christ and, at the same time, be ready to give up, or at least not make a test of fellowship, those things which have been added by men. I do not mean that everything in the New Testament which is concerned with the early Church should be accepted and used by us today, for some things, such as the washing of feet, were matters very local both as to place and time. We must recognize, however, that the Church is part of the Gospel of Jesus Christ and that it was given to us by God, not something which has come to us from the imagination of men.

Christianity does not exist without the Church. The Church is Christ's body upon earth—a visible society of people—and if we wish to join that body we must comply with the conditions which have been laid down by God himself. The Church as God planned it and as Christ prayed that it should be, is one and undivided. It is indivisible in the mind of God; it should not raise partitions between nations or races, or classes. The divisions which exist within the Church are to our shame.

To what authority must we turn in our desire to find a way towards union? There is only one standard of authority and that is in the New Testament scriptures, for here we have the record of the birth and growth of the Church. I do not mean that there should have been no development of thought since the days of the Apostles. Again I do not hold that everything concerned with our church life has necessarily been laid down in the New Testament, but what I do hold is that all theology, that all the thinking of men down through the last twenty centuries. should be continually checked against the standard revealed in the New Testament.

The interpretation of the Scriptures has always been a difficult matter and private interpretation has led many into serious error. On the other hand, most of us, as Christian people, are not prepared to accept an ecclesiastical hand-out. Fortunately, there is another method available to us. God has given us reason and, in matters which are controversial, we can make an appeal to the scholarship of spiritual leaders of the Church in all ages and throughout all its communions. My own fathers in the faith were always ready to examine matters in the light of the New Testament scriptures and listen to the judgment of the sanctified scholarship of the Church universal.

In Christianity we don't have a set of abstract truths, or arguable philosophy. What we do have is a set of historical facts, a record of happenings which can be examined and checked, which must be accepted or rejected. A person lived and that person was Jesus Christ. He lived a life, a record of which we have. He died and was raised from the dead. This is something very different from speculative theologies which are the explanations of these facts in the thought forms of a particular age. Here we have a body of facts which are of major importance and which are binding upon all Christians. The scattered forces of the Christian Church cannot be brought together on theologies, but we endeavour sometimes to do this. Theologies wax old, they become out-of-date and the forms which seemed alive in the generation of their day, have no attraction for succeeding generations. I would not in any way despise theology, but I do say it should be given its correct place in relation to the historical facts.

Our acceptance of Christ is not based on a knowledge of the inner mysteries of the Trinity, or of the incarnation, but on a personal acknowledgement of Jesus as Lord and Christ, as Redeemer and Saviour of men. The most primitive baptismal creeds are simply, "I believe that Jesus is Lord," or "I believe that Jesus is the Christ, the Son of the Living God." Paul pointed out that, having accepted Christ, his followers must grow in knowledge and grace that they must be fed on the milk of the Word and graduate from their position of babes in Christ to that of men, but the foundation of their faith would not change—it was still the acceptance of a personal saviour. Our own churches have always given great prominence to the sacraments, but they considered them, not in relation to metaphysics and mysticism, but in relation to action and ethics. "A positive institution" was for them something done in the realm of reality—it demanded personal action. In the sacraments the real action of God became sealed in our response and in this way the believer himself, ethically responding, became partaker of the divine action.

This approach prevented the sacraments from being confused with magic and, at the same time, they were given a position of particular significance within the Christian Church. To the personal action of God, we must make a personal reply.

The challenge to definite belief and personal action brought conversion back from the shadows of experimental religion and set it again in the realm of reality. When Peter was asked on the day of Pentecost what men should do to be saved, he gave a definite answer.

In our attitude to the sacraments especially we should be guided by the New Testament example. In our attempt to do this very thing, our churches have for example always made the Lord's Supper the central act of worship each Sunday morning, as it was for more than 400 years after the crucifixion. It was a corporate act of worship by the whole church. At the Lord's table the Church, remembering the sacrifice of Christ, receives new strength. The sacraments both of baptism and the Lord's Supper must be given the rightful place for which they were divinely designed.

And so I would turn from this incursion into the history of the Disciples of Christ, to reaffirm two fundamental beliefs. The first that we, in our desire for union, should recognize our brethren in Christ in all love and humility and the second, that we should recognize that the Church is of God's designing and therefore it behooves us to measure our ideas about it and our plans for it alongside His standards as set forth for our guidance in the New Testament.

Those who love Christ must love His Church. Those who would serve Him must actively, prayerfully and intelligently strive to restore the Church to its Apostolic simplicity and beauty—that the world may believe.

Our Timeless Missionary Mandate

The World Convention of Churches of Christ, a meeting of all groups around the world historically associated with the entire Disciples movement, is currently held every four years. Garfield Todd had a long and historic association with the World Convention. Todd spoke at the fifth convention held in Toronto, Canada, in 1955, the first of four conventions that Todd addressed over the course of his career. An American Disciples publication called him "one of the most notable delegates" and "one of the most outstanding figures" of the Toronto convention. This journal said, "Starting from a Christian point of view, the one-time missionary has led in working out a new political, social and economic program whereby it is hoped that the natives and the country's 165,000 whites can live together in harmonious relations."[11]

The sermon articulated important aspects of Todd's Christian vision. The emphasis was on evangelism and how the gospel can transform people and society. Todd mostly narrated stories of his own mission experiences but the focus was on how Christianity can change all aspects of life. For Todd medical, educational, and spiritual needs of people were intertwined. When people are brought to Christ, the quality of their lives is improved as all their needs—physical and spiritual—are met. He said, "We had lived amongst a responsible people and our crowning joy was to see thousands of men and women added to the Church of Jesus Christ." True to the Churches of Christ emphasis on instruction and knowledge, Todd concretely pointed to the development of the school at Dadaya and the development of Christian African leaders in all types of vocations.

This sermon was delivered at the World Convention of Churches of Christ, in Toronto, Canada, on Wednesday, August 17, 1955, in the evening session, at Mapleleaf Gardens. The text is reproduced from a manuscript from the Garfield Todd papers, Disciples of Christ Historical Society, Nashville, Tennessee.

Not so long ago in the history of our race, the world seemed secure. In those days, people did not rush like frenzied ants around the world, nor did anyone feel an urge to stake a claim to lands on the moon. I wouldn't suggest that those were good old days; the time when most people were still firmly attached to the land and when industry, new-born, appeared a most unpleasant infant. The human race has since been jolted out of its security by world-shattering changes. Gone is the assurance of a leisured way but, let us be honest, there are few here who would be prepared to go back to the old order and such an admission means that, although science has admittedly given us a number of new problems that we don't like, it has nevertheless presented us with gifts which we prize.

In the ever-changing scene around us, one symbol of warning, of encouragement, and of hope, stands immovable. Almost two thousand years ago it was placed there by wicked men and stood as a symbol of their sinfulness and shame. On it was crucified the Son of God but from it, for almost twenty centuries, has flowed the abounding love of God.

In the changing and imperfect world around us, we labour that we may make progress for ourselves and for our children. Towering above our labours, our weakness and our sin, stands this symbol of God's love. If we raise our eyes to it, our whole life is put into true perspective for, in the cross of Christ we have perfection; we see the love of God for men proved triumphant and eternal.

In the light of the fact that we have changed the face of the earth, that we have raised living standards, that we are making our world bring forth abundantly for the needs of men, do you not find it amazing that the cross of Jesus Christ should be so topical, so attuned to our modern need? Like every age that has preceded us since the dawn of Christianity, we find that the cross of Jesus Christ is especially topical, especially challenging to our own age. "What will it profit a man," said Jesus, "if he gain the whole world and lose his own soul?"

We have netted the seas, we have scaled the highest mountain, we have conquered the air, we have dug up the treasures of the earth and we have fashioned from God's material gifts useful and beautiful things for the delight of ourselves and our children. Have we not come very near to gaining the whole world and, as a race of men, do we not stand in danger of losing our own souls?

This is the real war—the only significant battle—and waged throughout all generations since the fall of man. This is the reason behind the churches of Christendom. This is the reason for our gathering at Toronto. This is the background to our prayer, our watchfulness, our Christian striving. Great and powerful forces battle for the souls of men and so very many millions of God's children are content to fashion with their hands gods of their own from the material blessings which were given by the Almighty God to be of service to his children, not to be worshipped by them.

We have not met here thoughtlessly to condemn other people, for we do not have to look beyond our own hearts to see the wrongfulness of men. We know that we must go outside ourselves to find the comfort that our souls require. We condemn the children of Israel, but we have some understanding of their action, when so soon after their miraculous delivery from the hands of the Egyptians, they gave in to the temptations to fashion from their golden ornaments a God that they could see for themselves, a God who was under their own control, who would have the qualities they wished to ascribe to him.

That is the kind of God that we are tempted to wish for also, a God who will be under our own control, who will be fashioned according to our own wishes. We would like to replace the Almighty, who is a disturbing God, a challenging God, with one whose demands are not so far-reaching, whose standards are not so high, whose service is not so demanding. Here, I believe, is the crux of the matter. I do not fear the materialists. I do not fear the Communists so much as I fear the materialism which has crept into the Christian Church, which infiltrates into our own lives.

Twenty centuries ago, one man, the Son of God, was not afraid to face the materialism and corruption, of the whole world. Today, it is estimated that approximately 700 million people are Christians. In other words that almost one third of the whole population of the world is nominally Christian. One person out of every three. Those are the figures. If they were really facts we wouldn't have to fear the future. Can you imagine what it would be like if we really had 700 million people seeking first the Kingdom of God and His righteousness, 700 million people whose desire it was to do the holy will of God? In actual fact we know we don't have one person who is wholly consecrated to the service of Christ, who walks without error in the footsteps of his Master.

However, thank God, we do have millions of men and women, boys and girls who are consciously endeavouring to live the Christian life, who are manfully striving under God's guidance to serve Christ faithfully. Amongst this throng of God's elect stand proudly so many of our own Church members. We who are gathered here in Toronto tonight stand in the ranks of that army and it is particularly to you and to the members of our Churches throughout the world that I speak.

What is the challenge that faces our Churches? I believe it can be stated in two quotations from Christ himself. The first is a portion of Christ's prayer as given in the 17th Chapter of St. John's Gospel, "that they all may be one, as Thou, Father art in me and I in Thee, that they also may be one in us: that the world may believe that Thou has sent me." Here we have stated the necessity for unity between God and ourselves and also the same need for unity between Christian and brother Christian. Such unity is required as a basis for our Christian life, for our very existence.

The second part of the challenge is given in the last Chapter of Matthew when Jesus said, "Go ye, therefore, and teach all nations, baptising them in the name of the Father and of the Son and of the Holy Ghost; teaching them to observe all things whatsoever I have commanded you, and lo, I am with you alway, even unto the end of the world." There we have the challenge. On one side the need for that strength which comes from unity with God and unity with one another and, on the other, our duty to the outside world—our programme of action. This is the purpose of our being, this is our timeless heritage.

I am not concerned in my address this evening with the unity and strength of the Church in the homeland, except to say that the success of its mission to the world outside depends entirely upon the spiritual condition of the Church itself. In this address I will not concern myself with what might be called home evangelism or home missions, but I will limit the remainder of my address to what I might term the responsibility of the Church in privileged lands to the under-privileged peoples of the world: in other words, to what we term "mission" work or "foreign mission" work.

Tonight we have the great privilege of meeting with members of Churches from many countries and a place of honour in this service is given to missionaries who are at present home on the American continent. It has been the great privilege of my wife and myself, as representatives of the Churches of Christ of New Zealand, to work in Africa for 20 years.

For the first 13 years of that time, we were, with our small daughters, the only Europeans in a large area in which more than 20,000 African people lived. Those were very precious and very happy years, during which we made the intimate acquaintance of the people amongst whom we lived and worked. During the whole 20 years of our service in the Lundi Reserve, we never doubted the worth of each day's service for the need of the people, spiritually, physically, intellectually, socially, was so great that we could never fully meet it. I can speak intimately only of the work in a small district in the centre of southern Africa but, if it were possible tonight for my missionary friends also to stand and give their stories, we would be giving widely diverging pictures of life in so many lands, of customs, of problems, of victories and of defeats, of sorrows and of great joys. In the varying tapestries which might be woven before your eyes, there would however always run a common thread, the need and sinfulness of man—the eternal, forgiving love of God.

More than 21 years ago, my wife and small daughter and I landed from New Zealand at Durban in the Union of South Africa and made our way north by train for 1200 miles until we crossed the Limpopo river and entered Southern Rhodesia. Southern Rhodesia is a self-governing Colony, not quite big enough or important enough to be a dominion but no longer under Colonial Office direction. Twenty-one years ago it was a country of 1 1/2 million Africans and about 50,000 Europeans. It depended for its existence at that time largely upon the production of gold. The government was by no means rich and the African people were primitive in the extreme. Any education that was given was carried out by the Missions with a minimum of help from the government itself. In fact the total government spending on African education was $200,000 only.

We made our new home in the Lundi Native Reserve at a small mission station named Dadaya which had been founded quite a number of years before. There we found a few buildings and 20 African boys who were in a little boarding school. One boy had reached the sixth year in school, which we call Standard IV and the others were all in lower classes. My wife was the first trained educationist to come to that part of the country and she made the school her special charge. Throughout the Reserve were another 12 little schools and our total staff numbered 15 Africans. The income which supported the schools and teachers and ourselves amounted to less than $5,000 that first year.

Forty miles to the north-east there was a fine Mission belonging to the Church of Sweden where a doctor was stationed but the roads between us were little more than tracks. 14 miles to the east there was an asbestos mine with one doctor also, but both of these men had more work at hand than they could do. In our area, for the 20,000 Africans there was no doctor at all, so that anything that was given along the line of ordinary medical help had to be given by ourselves.

The little schools throughout the Reserve went only as far as Standard I, the third year of school life. Churches had been established throughout our area, but it was so very difficult to build up the spiritual life and knowledge of a Christian congregation when the pastors themselves found it very difficult because of their lack of education even to spell out most haltingly the words of the New Testament.

But we were young—just in our early twenties—and it was all fascinating. There was a wet season which lasted four or five months of the year and in which anything up to 20 or 30 inches of rain might fall. The rest of the year was dry and, although we were in the tropics, the altitude of the country is such that nights are cool, even though the days may be fairly warm. We were welcomed by the people, by the local Chiefs and Headmen and we felt ourselves to be among friends from the very beginning, a feeling which deepened as the years passed so quickly by.

The people amongst whom we lived were Matabele who are an off-shoot of the warlike Zulu people from the Union of South Africa. Until 65 years ago, these people used to raid the much more peaceful Mashona peoples of Rhodesia and steal from them women and cattle and grain. The Matabele were always warlike and were great hunters but were not as far advanced on the ladder of civilisation as the Mashona people who knew how to smelt iron and make their own primitive tools. Dadaya Mission was built in the heart of a Matabele encampment but a few miles further out the Mashona people lived and most of the churches and schools were established in their country.

So it fell to our privileged lot to work amongst these tribes. In the schools and churches we taught and preached and endeavoured to guide a slowly awakening people. In the villages we bound up wounds, delivered babies, ministered to the sick. While I could tell you personal stories of being treed by a lion, of leopards in the kitchen, of the ravages in our small family of malaria, bilharzia and typhoid, of anxious days and weeks, I thank God that I have no stories to tell of up-risings or of massacres in our land for it is almost 60 years now since the last person lost his life in a racial riot of disturbance.

We are very proud indeed of the good relations which have existed between the races for so many years in Southern Rhodesia and we are most anxious that our record will be maintained unblemished. But, while I am glad that I have no stories of that kind to tell, there were many other terrible happenings. There were the regular accident cases—children caught in burning huts, babies burned by boiling water or hot porridge; encounters with wild animals or snakes or crocodiles; but, while these things happened and the giving of help was part of the duties of a missionary, the more terrible things were those which happened because God was not in the villages.

The drums would beat, the people would assemble from far and wide for great beer drinks. There was a lack of understanding, a lack of thought and of love. I am not saying that mother-love was extinct for that was not so and mothers, according to their limited knowledge, gave loving care to their babies and their children. Sometimes one even saw evidence of father-love, but marring it all was the influence on primitive peoples of the power of the notorious witch-doctors and the general fear of evil spirits.

Some of the beliefs were amusing and not harmful. I remember one day, when a number of the old and supposedly wise men of a tribe came to me to ask my intervention with a certain European who had apparently killed a crocodile and left the carcass unburied. A drought raged and the old men came to me to ask if I would persuade this European to allow them to go and bury the crocodile because, they said, it was quite obvious that there could be no rain while the crocodile lay unburied.

That was naive, but not naive was a happening on the following year when again there was a drought. The elders of a tribe in the nearby Belingwe hills demanded of a man that he should tell them where he had hidden the tail of a jackal that he was supposed to have killed. Until the tail of the jackal had been buried there could be no rain, said the old men. The accused probably had never killed a jackal, but, anyway, he could not produce the jackal's tail and, in anger and frustration, the men picked up stones and stoned him to death. The tragedy was deepened because they believed in what they had done. They believed that unless the gods were propitiated, their wives and families could well starve and, in self-defence, they rose up against the man whom they believed was holding back the life-giving rain.

In the villages, the lives and personalities of children were not sacred. Despite British law, in some places the custom of pledging little girls to old men still was maintained and girls as young as 8 or 10 were sometimes sent to take their place, against their wish, in the home of the man who had purchased them.

Into this life of ignorance and evil came the dynamic power of the Gospel of Jesus Christ and let me say with all sincerity that, when Christ walks into a village in Africa, when he takes his place in the heart of any one person in a village, changes follow. The mission, with its missionaries, its African teachers and preachers became the hands and feet of Our Lord and, in the degree to which these servants were faithful, so came blessings to the people; so came light into darkness.

The hardest thing to bear was our inability to meet the widespread needs of the people. Our budget in those first years, as I have said, was only a few thousand dollars a year and, with this, churches and schools had to be run, wages had to be paid, medicines had to be purchased, food had to be provided.

We had come from New Zealand, a land which has in its short history always been famous for its enlightened social legislation. Every child in New Zealand is educated, every sick person is ministered to, every old person receives care. With a background such as that it was so difficult for us to accept the fact that we had to choose in giving help; that we had to make up our minds which was the more deserving case. We were young and the responsibilities were great. It seemed so unfair and so heart-rending that we could not give to all as they needed. There was an element of bitterness in that and I think it first struck home when, sometime after we arrived, I held in my hands a newly-born baby which would not breathe. It was just a little after 4 o'clock in the morning and I took it into the warmth of our kitchen and gave artificial respiration. Such a tiny little brown body and it would not breathe. I breathed into its mouth and lungs and felt the little heart pick up and the beat become normal. I kept it up for a little while and then stopped; still no breathing and the heart-beat began to slow. I breathed again and again until the morning came; but every time I stopped for a few moments the heart would slow. 7 o'clock brought with it all the varied duties of a mission station, all the claims that were made upon one's time. I was not a trained medical man and I had done what I could. I had to say in my heart to the little one, "I have given you a chance; you have not been able to take it." In distress I laid it aside. Not to be able to meet the need is the bitterest part of any missionary's life.

Our mission became a place of refuge. A place to which girls who were given in marriage against their will ran for freedom, a place to which boys and girls, often without money, came to receive education and work in school holidays to repay something of the service that the mission gave wherever it was possible to give.

A few months ago I saw in the *Christian Science Monitor* the picture of an African named Ndabaningi Sithole who had just arrived at a theological college in the United States to study for a B.D. degree. In the story it told of how, many years ago, he came without money to Dadaya Mission and how we allowed him to help in the dispensary and so to earn enough to keep him at school. Sithole has his Bachelor's degree and many years of service behind him now and today he has the privilege of being a student at an American college, fitting himself for mere adequate service amongst his people. So many boys and girls came to Dadaya Mission soon we had 150, then 300, then 600. So many accepted Christ as their Saviour. Such changes came to their lives and in due course Christian homes were set up and our hearts were filled with a great thankfulness, for the Christian religion really works in the lives of those who accept Christ. We all know that from our experience in the homeland, but the transforming effect of the coming of Christ is seen even more forcibly in a primitive heathen village. There everything seems to change.

Thirteen years flew quickly by and we were joined by a second couple from New Zealand and, in the next 7 years, 10 more helpers came. Our African staff, on whom the work so greatly rests, grew from 15 to more than 150, many of them well qualified and particularly fine people. More than 4,000 children attended our 33 schools, with almost 600 in residence at Dadaya Boarding School. A secondary department and a teacher training department were added in due course.

We saw children grow up and take their place as Christian leaders. Young men returned to us after having taken a degree at university. Young women qualified as nurses. The income grew from $5,000 in 1934 to $130,000 in 1953. We had enjoyed 20 happy years when I was called to leave the mission work and take the position of prime minister of Rhodesia.

We had lived amongst a responsive people and our crowning joy was to see thousands of men and women baptised and added to the Church of Jesus Christ. How I wish it were possible for me to paint a more adequate picture of the wider mission field. The colours would not always be bright throughout the world but let me underline one phase of all mission work everywhere; that is the great need, the impossibility of fully meeting the opportunities which confront the workers.

I speak tonight to members of churches in privileged lands and I plead for an awakening concern for our brethren overseas—for the less privileged peoples of the world. In the love of God all men stand equal. However, there is not equality of opportunity and to whom much is given, from him much is expected—that means much from you and much from me.

In the vision which confronts the Christian Church, there can be no racial differences, no national boundaries for the love of God is as wide as his creation and includes all his children.

The challenge to the Church is the age old one to disciple the nations. "And I, if I be lifted up will draw all men unto me," said Jesus. We have, in our timeless heritage, beauty and love and power—a compelling message—the only answer to the problems of our age. We have a command which we cannot escape: "Go ye into all the world and preach the Gospel, and lo, I am with you always."

The Church Knows No Boundaries

During the 1955 World Convention of Churches of Christ, Todd was elected a first vice president for the sixth convention, which was held in Edinburgh, Scotland, in 1960. "The Church Knows No Boundaries" is his vice presidential address at that convention. Major changes had taken place in Todd's career since the Toronto convention. In 1955 he was prime minister of Southern Rhodesia but in 1958 he had been sacked and Todd had also lost his seat in parliament. The speech takes place a little over one month after his call by the African people to be a prophet for the nationalist cause—the call he accepted with his letter to Lord Home that was jointly signed by Joshua Nkomo on July 26, 1960. That letter ended his political career.

While many of the same themes endure in this sermon, one can detect a harder prophetic edge to Todd's thoughts but an edge still infused with high idealism, as the sermon title indicates. Todd wanted Christians to think of "the church as Christ wills her to be," not of the church defined by our human limitations of service. Todd acknowledged the difficulties: "The Christian must love with an intensity which does not flinch even at a cross, though the cross for him may be just hard and discouraging work." Showing his shift to a prophet, Todd rejected a purely political means in service, saying, "We do not place our hope in human systems." And later he was uncertain about the economic challenges, because "we cannot see how the material problems [of Africa] can be solved." However, he was optimistic about improvement in human relationships: "but a far greater challenge rises before us in the realm of human relations, success in this field depends first upon our relationship to God. If that is right then we can turn with confidence to our fellows." The speech text is from the *Christian Standard* of September 10, 1960, 579–80.

Jesus, who knew no bonds and recognized no boundaries, called His church into being and gave His disciples the task of teaching and baptising the nations. Upon that task He set His seal and said: "All power is given unto me in heaven and on earth—therefore go ye."

From the days of Peter and Paul the gospel has been preached to Jew and Gentile, to the slave and his master. We give God thanks that the church—despite the weakness which results from its sins of division—has been able to bring the challenge of Christian discipleship to every nation.

The message has often suffered because it has been handled by men and there have been deep disagreements between Christians concerning the doctrines themselves. While such error has tarnished the message itself, nevertheless the power of God has been able to work through it and the love of God has brought hundreds of millions of people into the church.

While the gospel has been preached in every country, it has not been applied in every situation; while the church has not recognized geographical limits, it has all too often set boundaries upon its sphere of influence. In the early centuries of the church the call to keep oneself unspotted from the world brought monasteries into being. Men endeavored to attain higher standards of Christian virtue by withdrawing themselves from the world and its temptations and giving themselves to the adoration of God.

The number of Christian people who would have opportunity, even if they so desired, to be members of such orders is very small indeed; but the number of men and women, within the church who show something of the seclusive spirit is large. Through all the ages we have been prone to make divisions within our lives in such a way as to allow God one part but to refuse to recognize His lordship over every situation.

We say that the church knows no boundaries; but when we make such a statement we are thinking of the church as Christ wills her to be, not of the church made up of ourselves and our brothers. Our congregations are no nearer perfection than are the people who comprise them. Christians are forever setting limits upon their service, and the thought of entering fully into the life of the world around is as unpleasant to many as the sight of Jesus consorting with publicans and sinners was to the Pharisees. When I speak of the church breaking boundaries and concerning herself with the affairs of the world, I am not visualizing the church as a great machine, organized on an authoritarian basis, wielding power upon earth through force and intrigue. I have in my mind an ideal church, congregations of humble men and women, deeply concerned for their fellows and ready at any cost to themselves to serve effectively so that the leaven of the love of God may permeate every situation.

Our history has shown that all too often the involvement of the church with the world has changed the church more than the world. Most of the social sins from which men have suffered have been blessed by the church in some form and in some era. The church has associated herself with wicked rulers and with the worst abuses of capitalism. Too often her sins have included a refusal to define the wrong in definite and recognizable terms, and a failure to right it.

Thus Christian people have been tempted to call upon men to love one another as if, some simple way without striving, without suffering without spending of effort and blood could easily be put right. We ascend the mountain of worldly privilege and self satisfaction and, looking out over the troubles of our fellow men, we thank God for our own good fortune, our own superior wisdom, our own Christian graces, and then we meet together with other fortunate people like ourselves and pass resolutions, neglecting to implement them. Today I plead with myself and with my brethren in Christ for our fuller participation in the cares and problems of the world. I plead that we do away with all boundaries and enter the life of the community and the world to battle in the name of our Savior. Our Master was so greatly concerned that God's will should prevail that He steadfastly set His face towards Jerusalem even though he knew that the road He would take would lead not only into the city but through the city and out onto the hill of Calvary.

The road we should take leads out into the world—into a maximum participation in the affairs of the community and of the nation—a wise participation, guided by clear ideals and high principles and based upon a full dedication of our efforts.

With all the power in the world at our service, men today have never been so weak, so powerless to ensure their own safety. With an unprecedented power over natural phenomena in our hands, we have never in history been so afraid of what that control may mean to us. We have never been less confident in God or more afraid of our fellowmen. Said the dean of Yale College:

> We must acknowledge that the loss of faith in our world, our destiny, our religion, is the cloudy and dark climate which most America finds itself living in today. The individual may do what he likes to further his own gain. The man of wealth owns a whole district, of slum dwellings, and feels no pangs of conscience for the hunger, squalor, and disease he encourages. The aggressive salesman makes outrageous claims for the product he wishes to sell. The novelist writes a scrofulous book in hope of being on the best seller list, and television corrupts the public taste.

The need for a sense of direction, for a new statement of faith, was stated recently by the president of Harvard University:

> To many, not just the colleges but the whole Western world, has for sometime seemed a drift with little sense of purposeful direction, lacking deeply held conviction, wandering along with no more stirring thought in the minds of most men than desire, personal comfort, and safety.

This is today's challenge to the Christian faith and we must not be dismayed by the fact that men have turned from God to science as if materialism could be the answer to man's need. We recognize the wonders which are being revealed, but these revelations of order and of power should bring us to a new reverence for the Creator who placed them there, who established their order. Increased knowledge has not of itself brought men satisfaction. Power, as an answer to our need, has now revealed its own absurdity and its own impotence. We need a message for this age when armaments have failed us. And that message must come from the one who said, "Not by my might nor by power, but by my spirit."

Christians start with an advantage when they take their part in the world around them, for we know the nature of men. We are kept fully aware of the weakness and sin in the world, for we are always conscious of ourselves. We do not place our hope in human systems. We know that pride is the greatest sin and that power is something so to be feared that it should be placed only in the hands of the humble, of men who recognize that they are stewards answerable to God. We recognize the worth of the individual and believe that God made all nations of one blood, of one common humanity, and that it behooves us all to walk humbly, remembering that the humble publican was acceptable to God, whereas, the proud Pharisee was rejected.

And so we turn to our own countries, and our own circumstances, in a world where distances are shrinking every day and where the far countries of yesterday have become our near neighbors of today. I turn to my adopted country of Africa, the birthplace of my children, and our home. At this hour, no country's need is greater than Africa's. In terms of today's political philosophies this is the one great uncommitted continent. Will she join the "free nations," or will she seek her future in a materialistic communism?

When my wife and I went to Africa more than twenty-six years ago we believed ourselves to be especially fortunate, and so we were. To us had come the opportunity to serve among twenty thousand African people whose need was great. We had come in the name of Christ, supported by our brethren of the churches of New Zealand and sure of the work that we were called upon to do. Churches and schools had to be built; medical help was required. The work was hard and the days were long, but our life was filled with happiness and deep satisfaction, and as the years passed we saw the fruits of our labors. To the great continent had come missionaries like ourselves from many countries and churches, and although we did not fully realize what was happening, we had brought a message which not only saved souls but also brought a new dignity and a thousand new questions.

The seeds of Christian civilization were being sown and even a little truth inspired thoughts of freedom. But what is freedom? In 1957 I walked though the streets of Accra, the capital of Ghana, and saw the happy throngs of people on Independence Day; saluting each other with raised hand and call of "Freedom." But a survey of what people thought freedom meant showed that their concept ranged from a hope for dissolution of the police force and a sharing of all available public funds, to a belief that it all would be just a lot more hard work.

Twenty years ago life was simple in Africa. Colonialism was strong, and despite inherent weaknesses and much faulty thinking, it continued to bring assistance and training to a people who were soon to rise up and proclaim their own manhood. But circumstances were beginning to change, and the powers being developed in individuals at mission schools and churches were ready to make themselves felt in the outside world. Where my way had been clear in the earlier years I now felt an urge to follow through and take the next step to move out with the people as they entered upon another era where they found themselves with new urges, new capabilities, yet living in circumstances in which those in power refused to take more than limited notice of the changes which should be made, or give opportunities for development which the people called for.

If there is one sphere of human endeavor from which many Christians would isolate themselves, it is politics. When, after much thought and prayer, my wife and I decided that I should stand for election to government, we met opposition from some members of our New Zealand churches. Happily a majority agreed with us and, while continuing wherever possible with the work of the mission, I gave my time to public life in central Africa.

I hope that my work has had some success. I am well aware that it has often failed, but I take some encouragement from the degree of opposition which is shown me from people who hold that "the church" should not interfere in politics—meaning that Christians should pray but not act, worship but not serve.

The Christian, with all his imperfections, is Christ's representative on earth. His duty is to see with the eyes of Christ. He must understand with the comprehension of the one who called first for allegiance to God followed by a responsibility to our neighbors. The Christian must love with an intensity which does not flinch even at a cross, though the cross for him may be just hard and discouraging work. We have promised not only to adore the good but to do it.

The Christian gospel is a disturbing force in Africa, and Christians are challenged to make it a conquering force. In the great continent of Africa, south of the Sahara, live 60,000,000 brown and black people who have, during their history, been despised and rejected by their fellows. In our generation they are destined to rise to nationhood and to share world leadership.

Very wonderful things are happening in Africa, along with frightening and evil things also. People who have seemed to sleep for centuries have awakened, and men and women are struggling to fulfill their destiny. When that struggle is expressed in Christian terms it is a wonderful thing to see, and it has been our good fortune to watch many of these battles waged successfully. The leaven works in the life of a people—sometimes imperceptibly, sometimes spectacularly. In Dube's village a mother made her decision to follow Christ and that set many things in train. The children attended school, where they learned not only the basic subjects of literacy but also the Word of God. Old customs were supplanted by new, and even customs of eating and drinking were modified. Instead of the men and boys being served first and then the women and girls eating later in another hut, the family ate their food together. Instead of people sitting on stones around a central place they sat on chairs around a table and individual plates were provided. Spoons took the place of fingers, and while many of the changes did not stem necessarily from the fact that Christ had come to dwell in that kraal, the grace which was said before meals acknowledged His lordship over it.

From that village have come fine young people, and one is now assistant editor of an important newspaper. From worse circumstances came the head of a secondary school; from a completely primitive family has come a Christian minister of great influence. Hundreds of other young men and women have come from our churches and schools and have moved out into the world of men to bring something of our Christian heritage to changing Africa.

In our continent we are faced with enormous difficulties—with the problems of government in circumstances of poverty, of primitive social services, of inadequate development capital. We cannot see how the material problems will be solved; but a far greater challenge rises before us in the realm of human relations, and success in this field depends first upon our relationship to God. If that is right then, we can turn with confidence to our fellows. There is no place in the world of men where relationships between people are not the greatest challenge of the day. There must therefore be no boundaries to the work and influence of Christian people, for we are God's servants committed to work for the day when His will shall be done on earth as it is done in heaven.

My World and its Need

Todd was invited to address the World Convention for a third time in 1970 at Adelaide, Australia. The Australian Churches of Christ have had a long admiration for and interest in Todd's mission work and political activities. The speech was delivered October 23, 1970, at Apollo Stadium. The editor of the *Christian Standard*, an American publication of the independent Christian Churches, E. V. Hayden, summed up this sermon as "an informed and informative presentation of the theme he has sounded ten years earlier in Edinburgh, Scotland. . . . It was the theme of his own life and ministry, that Christians must be involved in the affairs of life and state, to the ameiloration of men's manifold ills." He added, "Friends from many nations felt the stimulating warmth and generosity of conversation with this tall Rhodesian in Adelaide. He seemed eagerly grateful for each friendly contact and shook hands warmly at parting."[12] James J. Christiansen from the Lindenwood Christian Church in Memphis, Tennessee, thought that Todd's speech "fittingly concluded Friday night's session of the convention." He believed that Todd's "statesmanship manner which . . . characterized his Christian witness . . . frequently pricked the conscience" through his questions "what does the church have to offer?" "What hope can Christian Church give the world today?" "What is the programme of your church?" The speech serves well as a philosophical and theological stage for his political speeches that follow. The text is from Sir Garfield Todd's personal collection and was provided by Todd.

So God created man in his own image: in the image of God he created him; male and female he created them. God blessed them and said to them, "Be fruitful and increase, fill the earth and subdue it, rule, over the fish in the sea, the birds of heaven and every living thing that moves upon the earth. . . . So it was; and God saw all that he had made, and it was very good."

God's command "Be fruitful and increase, fill the earth and subdue it," is the one divine commandment that man has accepted and obeyed with enthusiasm. When we speak of "My world and its need" we today contemplate 3000 millions of people but as we cannot visualise one million, we are 3000 times less able to bring into focus the total of our brothers and sisters for whom we are commanded to be concerned.

We attempt to simplify the concept by speaking of "developed" countries and "developing" countries. By "developing" countries we mean areas which are poverty-stricken in comparison with the West. In such countries 1000 million children, one third of the world's population, live in sad circumstances. Of each 100 children, 20 will die in the first year. Of the 80 who survive, 60 will have no access to medical care as we know it. They will be undernourished and may suffer irreversible mental and physical damage. Just over half of those who live to be seven years of age will enter a school; and of those who do, fewer than 4 out of ten will complete the elementary grades. Neither God nor anyone else could look out on the family of men today and say that it is very good.

But it is not only in developing countries that there are problems, that there is injustice, that God's handiwork is being spoiled. Do you know the "Song of the three children" from the Apocrypha? It is a song of nature, of an undefiled earth. Here are a few lines from it:

> O ye sun and moon, bless ye the Lord:
> Praise and exalt him above all for ever.
> O ye fountains, bless ye the Lord.
> Praise and exalt him above all for ever.
> O ye seas and rivers, bless ye the Lord.
> O ye whales and all that move in the waters, bless ye the Lord.
> O all ye beasts and cattle, bless ye the Lord.
> O ye children of men, bless ye the Lord:
> Praise and exalt him for ever.

It is a far cry from the crystal fountains and sparkling rivers of that hymn of praise to the reports of the pollution of air and rivers and of the sea itself, with which we are becoming all too familiar. From north and south, east and west come reports of man's need, of injustice, brutality and greed—and from our Lord comes the command to love God and our neighbour as ourselves: our neighbour from Asia, from Africa, from the Americas, from Europe.

The world and its people, the world and its needs, have changed little in essence from that time when, because of sin, the Lord God drove man out of the garden of Eden to till the ground from which he had been taken. Admittedly there are more people, there is booming industrialisation, there are fantastic changes in communications—and also much truth in Reinhold Neibuhr's declaration that "history is the record of an ever-increasing cosmos creating ever-increasing possibilities of chaos." Neither history nor the New Testament is a record of human progress: neither portrays evil as being steadily overcome by good.

This is the world of need which confronts the unbeliever, the world which was thought by 19th Century liberals to be steadily improving so that one day a generation of the blessed, having climbed on the shoulders of so many former generations of dedicated workers, would emerge into a heaven upon earth. Two world wars have killed that easy liberalism.

This is the world that confronts the Communists. They believe that man has at his disposal all the knowledge required, all the power needed to subdue the earth. The Communists believe that the real problems of men are production, distribution, communications and the provision of all services necessary for the welfare of the world-community. They hold that these are matters which can be placed on a drawing board and solved by scientific knowledge, checked by computers. Obviously, with the knowledge and power already at the disposal of men, it is possible in theory to solve problems of production. It is possible to distribute goods throughout the world. Almost any project, from cleansing the air and rivers of pollution to educating and caring for the needs of mankind, is within our powers to accomplish.

This is the world of need which confronts the Christian Church today. We have our place within that wide brotherhood: what is our reaction to the needs of men? Two generations ago many good churchmen looked out upon the world with hope, held that enlightened political policies would establish the Kingdom of God in their generation; called with the Prophet Jeremiah for social change; "Mend your ways and your doings, deal fairly with one another, do not oppress the alien, the orphan, the widow, shed no innocent blood in this place . . . then will I let you live . . . " then God's will shall be done on earth. The Prophets, despite their grim warnings, were essentially optimists. They were hopeful because they believed in the rightness and beauty of God's purposes: they believed that his will would eventually be done.

Christians are exhorted by Christ himself to pray "Thy Kingdom come, Thy will be done, on earth as it is in Heaven." Our Lord's final words of comfort to his disciples were, "And be assured, I am with you always, to the end of time." What does it all add up to? Where does the Church stand today, what is its message, what its hope? What do we think is meant when we read Paul's assurance to the Church at Philippi "My God shall supply all your wants out of the magnificence of his riches in Christ Jesus." What were the needs of the Christians at Philippi . . . what the extent of Christ's riches?

Some of us have lived many years in the faith of Christ. Would we care to draw up a balance sheet setting forth the data of our Christian life—the assets and liabilities—the receipts and payments? How wide has been our enterprise, how enthusiastic our endeavour, what hopes have been fulfilled? Fifty years ago I responded to what was termed the simple Gospel message. "Believe, repent and be baptised." I know that that was not the full content, for Paul, writing to the Romans, stressed that we should rise from that baptism to walk in newness of life. In practical terms what did that mean 50 years ago? What does it mean to the new Christian today?

In the past fifty years we have suffered the hell of a world war; we have all been contaminated by an attempt to wipe out the people who brought us the Bible and with whom our Lord was numbered. What hope can the Christian Church give the world today? I fear that many people, especially young people, have little respect for the church as they see it . . . as they see us. Too often our record has been uninspiring. If we have been the leaven of change then something has gone wrong for, after 2000 years, too little of the lump has been affected.

"Lift up your eyes," you may say, "lift up your eyes to that other country, so beautiful that Paul found no words to describe it: that land where God's will is done now in full justice and love." With all my heart I thank God for the promise of life after death, for the other world which will be our home; but we must remember that Jesus Christ came to this earth to atone for the sins of men. In the fullness of time God became flesh and, as man, dwelt amongst men. He began a ministry which his disciples continue upon this earth. From the cross on Calvary Christ called all men to a new relationship with God and with one another—then—at that moment: now—at this moment. Then came the resurrection of our Lord and indeed all things had become new. Weak and sinful men became powerful ambassadors of God, fearless in service, loyal to death. The Kingdom of God had been established.

Let us face the truth. The crucifixion of Christ is the measure of the power of evil and it is that same evil which confronts us in the world today: man's flight from God, man's inhumanity to man, e.g. label a man a Communist and he is no longer man, no longer our neighbour. The resurrection of Christ brought from the apparent disaster of the crucifixion a new era of possibilities, both for man's relationship to God and his relationship to his brother. So was established the Kingdom of God in which our Lord is reconciling the world unto himself.

We, as Christians, hail Christ as the Lord of history, clothed with power and authority. Here, in the fullness of time, came God's answer to the sin which had separated men from himself: which had spoiled that good creation. God is the God of history. Jesus Christ lived under Pontius Pilate and died outside Jerusalem. He promises us heaven but calls us to serve him upon earth. "Go forth therefore and make all nations my disciples; baptise men everywhere in the name of the Father and the Son and the Holy Spirit, and teach them to observe all things that I have commanded you." That's it! you say, "Let us stick to the Gospel!" I agree, but we must all agree that the Gospel has no limits to its interests, to its concerns, to its love.

The writer to the Hebrews exhorts us to "stop discussing the rudiments of Christianity. We ought not to be laying over again the foundations of faith in God and of repentance from the deadness of our former ways . . . . Let us advance towards maturity; and so we shall, if God permits." What is the program of your church? Is it to keep itself alive . . . or is it to leaven the community in which you live and to make your nation a Christian force ready to contribute to the worldwide brotherhood of men for whom Christ died?

Our times are significant for God; what is equally important is that we who are Christians should be significant in our time. Of course the Kingdom of God is eternally in heaven and all creation awaits the ultimate culmination. However, until that day comes, our responsibility is upon us and it is clear. We are to participate in the continuing incarnation of Christ, of his incarnation in men, in the social order of our day. Men must be forgiven, the whole creation redeemed.

I ask again, what is the program of your church? Does the Gospel as you preach it reach out in loving concern to the under-privileged, to drug users, to those in jail as well as those in hospital, to the aged and the unwanted, to the homes of those robbed by car accidents of fathers, mothers, children? You are saved by faith . . . but my brothers, says James, what use is it for a man to say he has faith when he does nothing to show it? Can that faith save him? Suppose a brother or a sister is in rags with not enough food for the day, and one of you says, "Good luck to you, keep yourselves warm, and have plenty to eat, but does nothing to supply their bodily needs, what is the good of that? So with faith, if it does not lead to action, it is in itself a lifeless thing."

I would fail in this address if I left the impression that we, the Church, are to meet the world's need by ministering from the inside to those outside. Our task is to extend the borders of the Kingdom, to bring men to accept Christ and to share full citizenship within the Kingdom: full brotherhood within the family. I would be unrealistic if I were to suggest that if our love is deep enough, our concern intense enough, we will persuade all men to accept Christ. We remember that Jesus himself said to his followers, "And yet there are some of you who have no faith." We are told that "from that time on many of his disciples withdrew and no longer went about with him."

We can feed men and clothe them, we can share in their struggle for political freedom but we cannot save them from death. Death is certain. Philip of Macedon had a slave whom he had instructed to come every morning, no matter what the day or the King's business, and to shout in his presence, "Philip, remember that you must die." We work, we plan, we hope, but the future is unpredictable: nothing is sure except that, sooner or later, we die. This knowledge is ours and it is a perception that we do not share with animals and plants, which also die. We know that we will die but we rebel against it: we believe that we were not made to die. Death is not a natural and acceptable fact in the experience of man who is not simply a natural being but is a creature made in the image of God. Death offers us a choice: faith or despair. This is the pivot of my world's greatest need. To this point come all men, of all races, of all countries. Only Christ can meet this need. Only Christ has a message which makes sense of our battles, our hopes, our despairs.

The Bible shows history coming to an end, not in blind and senseless chaos but in God's ultimate victory. History is fulfilled in the divine purpose of creation. The Gospel of our Lord which we are commissioned to preach to all nations, that Gospel alone, can meet the needs of my world. The Gospel is the message of God's creation, of man's sin, of God's salvation. It is the gospel of Abraham's faith, of Peter's denial, of the Good Samaritan, of the fatherhood of God and the brotherhood of men. As history is lost in the new heaven and the new earth the promise will be fulfilled that "at last God has made his dwelling-place with men! He will dwell among them and they shall be his people. He will wipe away every tear from their eyes; there shall be an end to death and to mourning and crying and pain; for the old order has passed away," and the ultimate need of my world will have been met by God the Father out of the magnificence of his riches in Christ Jesus.

POLITICAL SPEECHES

First Campaign Speech

While the exact date of Todd's speech cannot be determined, this text represents his stump speech given when he campaigned for his seat in parliament. The text is taken from two sources: "U.P. Candidate on Native Affairs," *Rhodesia Herald*, March 21, 1946, 7, and "Native Standard Should Rise," *Bantu Mirror*, March 20, 1946, 1. The *Rhodesia Herald* serves as the base text because the entire speech is reported either by direct quote or a close paraphrase and summary of some parts of the speech. The *Bantu Mirror* provides some excerpts which fortunately cover some of the paraphrased or summarized sections of the *Bantu Mirror*. Footnotes will indicate which parts are taken from each source.

There were fully 200 people present at the Hotel Nilton, Shabani, last week when Mr. Garfield Todd the United Party Candidate for Insiza District gave an address on Native Affairs.

At the close of the meeting Mr. L. N. Papenfus, an 1890 Pioneer congratulated the speaker on the soundness of his policy. Mr. V. E. Slater was in the chair. In the course of his address Mr. Garfield Todd said that it was unavoidable that when a large illiterate and very backward race lived in close proximity to a small civilized white community there would be many difficulties to overcome. The difficulties had become more pronounced as the years had passed, mainly for two reasons. The first was that the white population was now a settled community and the new generation of Rhodesians wished to be quite sure of their stake in the country of their birth. The second reason was that although the native population as a whole was still very backward, there were plenty of signs that they were capable of much advancement as they came into closer contact with western civilisation.

Economic and Political Aspects

"This is the background to our first problem, which is the fear that a rising primitive race may swamp us economically," said the speaker. "The fear is not so much that the black man may rise but that in the process of his doing so he will undermine all the economic standards of the white man.

The second problem is just as serious. It is the fear that the native may soon exercise a growing political power and that eventually that power will be greater than our own."[13]

"Intelligent, thinking Africans do not wish to see the European standard of living lowered. Their wish is to see the African standard raised, and anyone who argues that one must come down before the other can rise is stating that the wealth of this world is limited. If it is, then even a free and equal distribution of all the wealth in this country between black and white would give none of us as much as £20 per head p.a. It is in the interests of the country that the native standard should rise."[14] The European standard, however, was guaranteed by the law of the land through the Industrial Conciliation Act.

The second fear was that the law of the land might soon come into the hands of a people quite immature politically. As the franchise now stood any person who owned property valued at £150, or who had income, salary, food allowances, etc., which came to the value of £100 per annum and who was also able to fill out the form of application unaided might vote.

Unsatisfactory Law

"I believe that the law as it stands is quite unsatisfactory from the viewpoint of the European, but I believe that it is even more unsatisfactory from the point of view of the African," said Mr. Garfield Todd.

"The European fears the chaos which would result from the exercising of thousands of votes cast by natives just sufficiently educated to fill in a form and who are without any reasonable political experience.

The native, who is much more concerned with making a living than in gaining a vote, sees in the minimum amount required to qualify more than his maximum income ceiling. Except to the very few politically-minded Africans, the vote has an over-rated value, and it is fairly obvious that most employers would not be willing to give the African a wage which would automatically make him eligible for a place on the voters' roll.

The United Party recognises that the time has come to make changes in the electoral law. It believes and I believe with it that such changes must be made for the good of all sections of the people. The policy of the party is that legislation will immediately be introduced to stop further Africans being placed on the electoral rolls of the country. At the same time, Europeans—it is suggested two in number—will be elected to represent native interests in the House. The system of Native Councils, which has already been started, will be extended throughout the country, with the aim of teaching the African people the democratic way of life.

I would, therefore, point out that if this is done the European section of the country will be able to put its fears behind it and face with full honesty, and without prejudice, the question of bringing full development to this country. I believe that the African situation has much to do with any possible development, and it is only when satisfactory standards of living and of the maintenance of democratic government are assured that the European community will be ready to face the problems in a way which will benefit all the peoples of this land."

Land and Living

"Now, with our fears forgotten, let us first consider the Land Apportionment Act. The main purpose of this Act is to divide the country into two zones, one for Europeans and one for natives. As a general plan, it has much to be said in its favour. We must recognize the fact, however, that we Europeans are determined that the African people shall not live apart from ourselves. In theory we may say that we would like to live our lives apart from the primitive people of this country but that theory does not satisfy the practical considerations of life in Southern Rhodesia."[15]

"In the year 1943 we find that a total of 6536 Europeans were engaged in farming and mining operations in this country. What was their attitude toward the complete segregation of Natives? The answer is those 6500 Europeans called almost 200,000 Natives into the European areas to work for them. In this country there are about 28,000 Europeans doing one job or another. Those 28,000 wage-earners employed more than 25,000 Native domestic servants. This does not sound like segregation to me."[16]

The full picture showed that 28,000 European wage-earners required at present more than 303,000 native assistants of one kind or another to carry out the work of home, farm, mine and industry, equal to one-quarter of the total African population. Efficiency and health of native labour was essential, so that on the very lowest considerations, upon the most selfish motives, they must raise the African standard of living. Any man who felt that by a policy of keep the native down he would keep his own standard up, was betraying the future welfare of the country.

The Frankel Report had stated: "We are convinced that the main causes of the relatively low efficiency of native labour throughout the Colony are malnutrition and disease." Any government, then, must set about with increasing vigour to raise the health standards of the native people.

The Liberal Party candidate recently stated that the health of the native people was deplorably low and he stated that, should the Liberal Party be returned, it would subsidise the food of the African people.

"I believe," said Mr. Garfield Todd "that that is no way to approach the problem, nor do I think that our present European population could bear the burden of such an undertaking, even if it were willing to do so. The African people, I believe, can do much for themselves. In Rhodesia we have land enough and to spare. What is required from us is help and guidance. Already some measures are being taken. Reserves are being planned better; agricultural demonstrators are at work; water conservation is being carried out. But all real improvements in the food position, in the state of health of the people, come down to a basis of education, of the enlightenment of the people.

When the mass of the people of this country are educated, then measures taken to improve agriculture, to raise dietetic standards, to make hygienic methods of life part of the ordinary life of the people, will soon be successful. There is no other real way to set about these vital problems."

Cost of Education

The Labour Party had stated that should it be returned, the State would take over native education. "That is quite all right with me," said the speaker. "It is also quite all right with many other missionaries, although there are some who would not wish it. There is however, the question of cost. At present it costs the State only £180,000 per annum to finance the whole educational project including its own schools. I estimate that if the missions [were] handed over to properly-paid government officials, the cost would immediately rise to £1½ million. Many of the missionaries, including myself, do not get one penny grant of any kind towards salary. Not that we do without wages, but Churches in America, England, Sweden, New Zealand, etc. pay our full wages.

I believe the day will come, and I want it to come, when the government will be able to take over the full system, but by that time the native people themselves should be able to pay the bill involved, or at least to pay a larger proportion of it than they could at the moment.

The Liberal Party candidate said recently that if the Liberal Party were returned to power they would 'control' all native schools. When pressed for an explanation he had nothing more to offer. To say that the government would 'control' schools is a delightfully vague statement. If it is meant that the government would be responsible for the syllabus of instruction in schools and would see that any particular syllabus was adhered to, then I beg to point out that the United Party has already made sure of this. The present government tells the missions what they are to teach, pays them on results of that teaching, and can close them down at any time if there is reason to believe that the schools concerned are not being run on what the government considers to be sound lines. "If the candidate meant that, the government would take over the whole system and run it with Civil Servants, then my only criticism is that I do not think the Liberal Party has counted the cost."

Kind of Education

"What is the content of this education? There are the three R's, the vernacular of the child and the English language. There are religious education, practical hygiene, training in good manners and discipline and subjects on the practical aide. All of these things are good and form the basis of progress. The education of the native is of great importance to the European, for it is to our advantage when we deal with Africans, they should be clean, respectful, intelligent and as capable as possible.

It has been suggested that all mission-trained natives are—to put it bluntly obnoxious in the extreme. I do not agree. Not that I would suggest that there are no very unpleasant types in existence, but if a little learning is so dangerous a thing, then the remedy is to do the job better.

An educated person, whatever is his color, is of more use to a country than an uneducated person. I know that the schools in the locations of the big cities, I know that the school in the compound in Shabani, are all having a big influence upon the children—an influence for good. I know also that our own school cannot begin to cope with the demand for trained girls and boys. A product that is so greatly in demand cannot be so bad."

Native Contribution

The cost of the present system of education was £180,000 per annum, so that the cost to the government was—as far as schools in that area were concerned—about £1 per pupil per year. The cost to the government of European education was approximately £30 per head and, if further concessions which the United Party have guaranteed to country people are given, it was going to be more than that. On this basis, then, native education was carried out very cheaply. The native helped to pay for all that he got. One tax the native paid was poll-tax. This amounted to £450,000 per annum.

"Let us take this one sum. Let us add to it the cost of maintaining Native Department. We get a grand total of £411,000. In other words we still have £36,000 in hand. There is much more that is carried out by the government for the development of the African people, but I would point out also that there are many other ways in which the native contributes revenue. The native, at the present time, pays for a big proportion of what he receives."

The Good of All

"On the question of native affairs, there will always be great differences of opinion. Almost everyone here has a feeling that he or she has some fairly sound ideas on what should be done. Let us respect each other's opinions on how things should be done, but let us be as united as possible in our determination to face the situation honestly, to be just in our judgments, to seek the true welfare of this land in which we are finding life very pleasant, and putting aside any master-race theories, for the abolition of which so many people of ours have died; let us strive for the good of all."

Maiden Speech
June 3 and 4, 1946

This speech is covered and analyzed in chapter 3, "Moving Toward Democracy." The entire text is given because a maiden speech is usually very important in the British and Commonwealth political tradition. The speech is important for Todd, as I argued earlier. The text represents an accurate transcription of the proceedings (including reactions from Parliament members), unlike the American *Congressional Record*. The speech is reproduced from the *Southern Rhodesia Debates of the Legislative Assembly*, vol. 26, part 1, pp. 140–54.

Mr. Todd: Mr. Speaker, the Budget statement given by the Hon. The Minister of Finance was awaited with great interest and high expectation by the people of this country, and I am sure they have not been disappointed. The proposals the hon. the Minister has made will set this country further on the path of progress, which it is already treading. The Budget serves to remind us that a chapter of this country's life is closing, the chapter during which this country was exploited for private individuals, and it is encouraging to see large sums set aside for the development of our natural resources, for the raising of the water table of the country, for the development of the roads, of the telegraphic system, of the electric power system. I am sure that the large grants which are being given towards the agricultural and mining industries, together with the much happier state of taxation, will be of very great benefit to them and to the country at large.

A notable feature of this Budget is the sum which is set aside for advances to private people that they may develop their own factories, their own mines and their own farms. The decision of the State to set aside such large sums for the development of private enterprise must meet with a large degree of unanimity throughout the country. But there is, of course, one thing which this House must watch, and that is that when the State sets out to give such help to private enterprise this House will see that the money which it provides will definitely be used for the benefit of the whole country and not just for the enriching of certain individuals. (Hear, hear.)

I am afraid that I for one must disagree with the hon. Minister in his decision to withdraw £1,000,000 of the £3,000,000 which had been set aside as a reconstruction fund and in the meantime as an interest free loan to Britain. It seems to me at the present time, when so much money is available and when rates are not high, that it would have been a very good thing to have left the £3,000,000 untouched. I think there are a number of people who would like to see that £3,000,000 as an interest free loan left as a gesture. But it is not only a matter of sentiment. I feel to some extent the policy of the government, as stated, is not being fully carried out. The £3,000,000 was definitely set aside, and I think it was the intention of many of us that it should not have been touched during this year. We have felt that it was a good thing to put aside a certain amount of money. We feel that to put aside even the whole surplus of this last year as well would have been a very good thing. The country could easily have afforded to get the money which is required in loan funds at the present time. We do not know what the future holds. It may be that in a year or two's time there may be more difficult conditions than there are at present. When these times come, and even now, when we do not know if these times will come or not, the country would feel much more secure if it had extra assets at its back, and I do not think the hon. The Minister has given adequate reasons for touching the million pounds at this particular time. (Hear, hear.)

The criticisms that I have of the Budget are not so much concerned with what is listed, but with what is not included in it. I would not forget, and would not like the House to forget, the very large sums which the government has provided for social services at the present time. For such things as education and public health the total is very large indeed, but nevertheless I would have been grateful to have seen the hon. the Minister make a courageous gesture to the people in the matter of social services, and I think that that gesture could have been made under the vote to hospitals. The House will realise that at the present time the government pays 78% of the total cost of running the hospitals of this country, and the total amount now paid by patients in fees is only a matter of, about £105,000.

Now, it seems to me that if we can afford to pay 78% of the total cost of hospitals, we could very easily afford now to provide free hospitalisation for all people of this country. (Hear, hear.) If that is the case, then I think if the hon. the Minister cannot now give an assurance that we will have free hospitals in this country, at least he might give an assurance on the lines that no family will be charged more than a maximum of say £10 or £15 hospital fees in any 12 months. That would be a help to the people. I do not think that a 10% reduction in hospital fees is sufficient evidence for this government of its avowed policy of providing full social security for this country, as the country can afford to pay for it. Now, Sir, as the hour is passing I would like to move the adjournment of this debate before I proceed to the main part of my address.

[House adjourned at 11 minutes before 6 o'clock p.m. June 3. Debate resumed at 2:15 p.m. June 4, 1946]

Mr. Todd: The atmosphere of the House seems to be conducive to changes of heart. As I may not have many opportunities of congratulating the hon. members of the Opposition I would not like to let the opportunity pass of congratulating the hon. the Leader of the Opposition on his change of heart in relation to social security. I remember some time ago when I happened to cross swords with him at a public meeting he was very definitely against social security, and I happened to be on the side of social security. It is heartening to see that so many people are now becoming of the opinion that social security has a great deal to do with the future of this land.

With regard to the three million loan to Great Britain, the hon. the Leader of the Opposition suggested that this amount should be given as a straight-out gift from this country, and on the face of it that appears to be a very generous gesture, but the government has to accept responsibility for the development of the country, and even if it is promised the support of the Opposition in doing something which is irresponsible, that is not sufficient reason for us to do it. The people of Great Britain are interested in Southern Rhodesia. They know how much development has to be done; they know the very large proportion of our population which is needing a great deal of assistance; they know of the extensive areas which are not developed, and I do not think the people of Great Britain would appreciate a gift of three millions, when so much development work remains to be done in the country. As an interest free loan, the gesture is appreciated, and I am sure the gift would not be. It appears from the estimates that more than £500,000 is to be spent during the current financial year on subsidies of one sort or another. Later in the session we will, no doubt, be told more about these subsidies. I expect quite a lot of them have to do with the food of the country, and it is in connection with food that I would now like to speak.

I notice, for example, that we are going to spend £100,000 on subsidies for maize. We know that the maize situation is not as sound as it should be. We have heard of the increase in price guaranteed to farmers for the production of maize next season. I am sure the hon. the Minister will not be deluded nor will the public be deluded into believing that even an increase in subsidy will necessarily guarantee the supplies of maize required for the life of this country. We have seen in past days that subsidies have been given and at the present time the natives are eating very musty meal from the Argentine, and we have been unfortunately put in the position of having to spend a quarter of a million by giving it to a country with which we would rather not trade to such extent at the present time.

The hon. Minister of Agriculture is new to his job and I know he will have the good wishes of all sections of the House as he goes forward to endeavour to assure to this country the food supplies it needs. I am hoping that he will make immediately a very broad survey of the whole food potentialities of the country. I would suggest that maize is the basic food of the native and not of the European. The native himself might be encouraged to grow much more of the food which he eats than he is doing at present. We are guaranteeing large subsidies for the production of maize on the one hand and on the other hand the natives, e.g., in the Bikita area, have just had their price for maize raised from 6s. 6d. to 7s. 6d. a bag. That is no encouragement whatever to grow maize, and I am sure that this policy has already been shown not to be in the interests of the country. While we pay 6s. 6d. or 7s. 6d. a bag to the native farmer, we provide a quarter of a million to import maize from the Argentine.

Restrictive legislation in connection with maize may have been all right in years of surplus, but legislation which is designed to deal with a surplus is certainly not the type of legislation required to deal with famine conditions. Throughout the whole of the country restrictive legislation has actually made the food position worse. In the Belingwe, Filabusi and Shabani areas the mines used to provide a good market for locally grown maize and many thousands of bags were traded, but since restrictive legislation has been brought in the sale of maize has practically ceased in those areas.

In Filabusi one case was brought to my notice where last year a native had 200 bags of maize for sale which a large mine nearby would have been glad to buy, but it was not permitted to do so, and that maize had to be transported a large distance to Balla Balla, for the market. Actually months passed and later on the Native Commissioner of the area made enquiries regarding that particular maize and he was told by the native concerned that the costs of transport were so great that the whole 200 bags had been turned into beer. I admit that that sounds like a Dr. Olive Robertson story,[17] but I have had it authenticated by the Native Commissioner of the district concerned. Not only has restrictive legislation stopped the production of maize or deterred it, but at a time like this when transport is at such a premium we find that the big mines in the area I represent have to bring in their maize and meal in trucks which could well be spared for other purposes. Now, Sir, in connection with food, I would warn the House that the present policy of the Native Department concerned with the native and his land is not in the country's interest.

We know, of course, that in past years the native lands, native reserves, have been suffering greatly from erosion, from all sorts of malpractices in agriculture, and we are all convinced that such things have to be stopped and the land gradually built up once again. We know that the Natural Resources Board has brought great pressure to bear on the Native Department—if the Native Department required that pressure—to have things remedied. Now I believe that the Native Department has in the past, tried to get more land for native occupation, and that the ex-Minister of Lands has not been willing to provide sufficient land for the purposes required. I would suggest to the House that this denial of sufficient land to the native is going to have a very adverse effect upon this country. It is already having a serious effect, but if we carry out the policy, even before it is completely carried out we will find ourselves in a very grave situation. For the denial of the land and the restricting of a native family to five or six acres of arable land; not necessarily good land, will mean that soon the natives will be able to produce only enough for their subsistence. In other words, they will have very little over to sell, and the growing population of urban natives which could well eat the surplus which the rural natives can produce will have to be fed by highly subsidised European production, and if there are famines and droughts, as do occasionally come to this country, we will find that the native on his restricted area of land will also have to be fed from heavily subsidised sources or else again we will import maize at high cost from other countries.

I know, too, that in past days there has been a great outcry against the native being permitted to have large herds of cattle. If some had had their way, many years ago native herds would have been greatly reduced, and in the time of need which this country has been experiencing in these last few years, we would have been unable to call upon the great reserves of native owned cattle which have been at our disposal. The number of native cattle which has been brought forward to help this country in its time of need and to assist us in our war effort has numbered hundreds of thousands. Now our policy at the present time is to restrict the native herds, to bring each native family down to 6, 8 or 9 cattle per family.

I feel that to the interests of Southern Rhodesia we should be producing as many cattle as the country can run without detriment to the land, and if there are going to be wide areas of the land which are not going to be grazed, I would suggest that these areas should be opened up to those who can graze cattle on them. It does not matter really for the true welfare of this country whether these cattle are owned by white or black. The main thing is to have the maximum production of cattle.

Speaking of cattle I would like to turn for a few moments to the report of the Cold Storage Commission. There are many good features in the report, and I presume that sitting on this side of the House I should look for all the good points, but I am inclined also to look for some of the bad points. When we consider the effect which Public Utility concerns have on the country, it is right that we should seek out and find any ways in which the situation might be improved.

There is one point in connection with the Cold Storage Report which I feel is a very serious one. It relates to the wastage of cattle in condition and by death. Now the House knows that there is an agreement between the Cold Storage Commission and the Native Department by which the Cold Storage Commission has guaranteed to the Native Department that it will take all the native cattle that are offered to it. A blank and unlimited agreement like that is not good business. It has been proved not to be good business last year when it led to the death of very many cattle. If we say native cattle, some may say it is a pity, but after all, the native does not really matter quite so much; but I would point out that when we speak of native cattle in connection with the Cold Storage Commission we have to remember that these cattle were cattle purchased by the Cold Storage, and when they wasted and died, they were no longer native cattle but cattle belonging to the country in the name of the Cold Storage Commission.

This agreement works in this way. We know that as we come towards mid-year and cattle come into better condition, sales are held throughout the native reserves, and it may be that as many as a hundred thousand head of cattle begin to make their way towards the Cold Storage Commission's works. Now, unfortunately, under the Land Apportionment Act no provision was made by which we could change the seasons as between natives and Europeans, and so in the European areas at the same time great numbers of cattle also come into full condition, and Europeans also have large numbers to sell to the Cold Storage Works. The Cold Storage Commission is then on the horns of a dilemma. It has bought possibly one hundred thousand head of native stock and at the same time it can hardly refuse to deal with the European stock which is offering, so what does it do? Last year it accepted European stock and allowed the native stock, which was Cold Storage Commission stock, to be put out to grazing. The grazing was not adequate, and when the rush was passed, it brought in the native stock to its slaughter yards. By that time the cattle had lost condition very seriously, and also there were large losses through death. Now, Sir, that is bad business at any time, but when famine stalks the world it is inexcusable unless it is absolutely unavoidable. And I do not think it is unavoidable.

Also, there is another side to this matter. The Cold Storage Commission has had a very good year despite the fact that it has had these losses, and despite the fact that the cattle bought in the native reserves had lost very seriously in condition before it could bring many of them to the slaughter pens. Who was it that guaranteed the losses which were not experienced by the Cold Storage Commission? Obviously in the prices which were allowed to the native expectation of loss was allowed for, and so the native actually made good the loss through the death and the falling off in condition of the fifty thousand native cattle slaughtered last year.

Now I would suggest that it is in the interests of the country that the highest direct prices be paid to the native producer. It has been said that he cannot take part because of technical difficulties in the bonus system which helps the European farmer. As we find that a great number of native stock did not get into the slaughter pens until they were on their last legs, it is obvious that the bonus system cannot be applied to native stock, but I would suggest that if through wise guidance our great native resources are developed, the future of the secondary industries of this country may well exceed our highest expectations. We have got to give the native the highest possible return for what he can produce if we are going to get the greatest amount of money from him to help in the development of our secondary industries. Therefore this matter is not an academic one, but one that is concerned with the real development and welfare of this land. I suggest that these matters have a great deal to do not only with the present food situation, but with the laying of sound foundations for the future. If the hon. the Minister of Agriculture can, by wise guidance, make sure that all the resources of this country are fully utilised, then we will have a firm foundation on which to base our dreams of developing Rhodesia so that she may go forward and take a worthy position in our Commonwealth.

But, Sir, the food situation is not the only problem which confronts us at the present time. We all appreciate that if this country is going to be developed, if we are going to attain satisfactory health standards for the whole community, if we are going to bring about an adequate measure of immigration, then it is necessary that we should provide adequate housing of the right type and at the right price. On the estimates we find that there is a sum of £126,000 set aside as a government housing project. As a gesture, this is greatly appreciated, but I hope that the government intends to tackle this matter in a very much more courageous and determined manner than a vote of £126,000 would indicate. I feel—I may be wrong—that the government is chary of tackling this very big problem, and yet I feel that only the government can do it. Not that I think that the housing of this country should be nationalised. I do not think that. But if we leave it completely to private enterprise without the guidance and assistance of the government, we will never get out of the wood. Perhaps hon. members do not realise just what a great part the government already plays in building and construction work in this country. The sum of £126,000 by no means tells the whole story. If you look at the estimates you will find that the government during this financial year intends to spend more than half a million pounds on building and construction work of one kind or another, including many houses for its civil servants.

The two problems that face us are these, that we must provide enough houses of the right type, and they must be provided at a price which is reasonable. I feel that a government that is already spending half a million pounds per annum on building might be able to help very materially in the provision of the necessary materials for house construction at a price which is not too heavily loaded by the various middlemen in the industry. It appears to me that an organisation that is spending half a million pounds has ways and means of making sure that materials can by provided without too heavy a profit. I know that is not the only difficulty. I know that the building trade itself is so hopelessly behind in its structural mechanics that it will take some time to catch up. I am not suggesting that we begin to experiment with these things in Southern Rhodesia but I do suggest that we should keep in close contact with other countries, profit by their experience, and make use of new materials as they become available. Even at the present time there is a great deal we can do.

I feel, for example, that the government can standardise quite a number of plans for houses. Now this is not acceptable I know to a number of people who immediately visualise whole rows of houses with two windows and a door, but that is not my thought when I say that the government should standardise houses. This is an emergency, and the emergency will last as long as we are short of housing facilities. When we manage to catch up the time of emergency will pass and people, if they wish, will be able to build £5,000 or £10,000 mansions.

Take for example motor cars. We do not each want to construct one of our own particular model and design, provided we can have a choice of 40 or 50 standard models, most of us can find something which is satisfactory to us. The assembly line puts a good car within our means. They would not be within our means if we endeavoured to build cars to suit our own particular tastes. In the case of building similar things could be done. By standardisation and in procuring fittings in bulk and simplifying construction, we would expedite the building of houses. When you are working to a simplified plan you know approximately how many man-hours can be expected in the building, but if everybody tries to build his own particular mansion there is little gained and it takes longer to build.

There is a third matter in the building of houses which I think demands our attention, and that is in connection with restrictive legislation. No one is more determined than I to make sure that European standards of living are maintained and raised, but I do not see the justice for denying to members of the community the joy of living in houses just because of the fact that by law we are unable to make use of the potential skill of the greater part of our population. On the estimates it will be noted there are votes for the building of native hospitals, native schools and native houses. The need is very great. Are we going to see these built with European labour while Europeans are waiting for homes to live in? It seems to me that restrictive legislation is striking at the welfare of the community. It is time that we awakened to the fact that the maximum skill and service of every member of the community is required if we are going to ensure the maximum development of the country.

New Zealand has been quoted as being an example of a country where houses of the right kind are built in the right way. I agree. When I was in New Zealand in 1942 I looked over some of the housing schemes and was very much attracted by the thousands of new houses erected. In that country there is cheap capital—often most erroneously held to be the one and only reason for cheap homes—there, is standardised building to a wide variety of plans, and of a splendid type. Hon. members of the Labour Parties will be delighted to hear that these homes are built by private enterprise, under contract to the government. (Laughter.) I would urge the government to plan, to purchase standardised materials in bulk and erect, by contract, if possible, sufficient homes of the right type for the people of the country.

In addition to food and housing, there is a third major matter on which I would like to comment and that concerns the African people in their relation to the welfare of the land. From the estimates we see that three-quarters of a million goes to the Native Department and the Native Education Department and if you look at the loan votes, you will find a total of £315,000 goes to the Native Department. Those are large sums of money. The House has certainly more than an academic interest in the native people. It is only quite recently that we have awakened to the fact that the native areas affect us. If we had been wise and had wakened to the dangers of the deterioration which was going on in the native areas some years ago, we would have saved ourselves millions of pounds which it is now going to cost us to reclaim wide areas of land which have been allowed to fall into ruin. At this time when our resources are taxed to their utmost, we would also have had the help of better production from native areas which would have been in better condition than they are. I would urge the House that as we have neglected the native areas for so long to our own hurt we do not make the mistake any longer of neglecting the native people themselves.

The native people through their labour are essential to us for the development of agriculture, for the development of industry, and for the development of mining. I know that growing attention is being given to the distribution of native labour. While it is right to pay attention to the distribution of native labour, I feel that the House must go right back and show a more intense interest in the native people themselves in their conditions, in their opportunities or lack of opportunities for developing, in the potentials which exist in the native population for the development, of this land. We might expect a population of one and a quarter million to produce a very great total of wealth during any one particular year, but when we look at the wealth they produce, we find that the total is miserably small. I regret to say that until now we have been inclined to consider the native people from a very selfish angle, from the point of view of labour for our own particular industry and not from the broader point of view of the full welfare of the land.

I would ask that we consider more and more the native people from the angle of their value to the whole country. I would suggest that we start by removing from our minds the picture which so many have of one and a quarter million peasants, each one scratching his own piece of land with a hoe. There is no hope for the future in a picture such as that. I would ask that we put in its place a picture of a progressive people, native farmers, who are able not only to produce enough for their own subsistence but enough to help with the feeding of the large native population which will come to the urban areas to take their place in our secondary industries. I would like you also to realise that if such progressive farming is introduced into the reserves, it will require all sorts of safeguards, and it will require also a great deal of encouragement which is not now forthcoming, but we will then have a picture of the native farmers in this country having enough to buy something of what is produced by our own secondary industries. These things interlock. The interest of all the people of this country interlock. Unless there is cooperation, the country cannot reach its zenith of development.

I would think it is necessary for us now, and I am sure most of us realise this, to get a new respect of labour and to eliminate the great wastage of labour which goes on through the country. There is nothing so noticeable in this country as the wastage of native labour and I would suggest that if we took the matter seriously within the next five years we could train 20,000 female domestic servants and release from our homes 20,000 male natives whom we have no right to have here during this time when labour is so much needed for the development of the land. It is time that we considered very seriously the sources of supply of our native labour. Distribution is only the last step. Distribution is a kind of rationing by which we make the best use of restricted supplies. It is good up to a point, but it does not solve the problem. We must get back to the very fountains of the supply of our labour. I know that the question is a very complex one and it has to do with such things as nutrition, health standards, education, the opening up of the minds of the people and instilling into them a sense of responsibility, giving to them a greater desire to progress and make them worth the wages we ought to pay.

I would suggest that the whole question of the development of natives and the native labour of this country comes right back to something which most people do not recognise, right down to a basis of native education. Unless you open the minds of the people and make it possible for them to receive the tuition which they will need as they take their place in industry and in the mines and in the many avenues which will be opened to the native people, they will not be able to satisfy their employers.

I would suggest that all these things have a basis in education. For example, we know we have to raise the health standards of the native, but yet how can we get down to the health measures unless people can understand. It is all very well to teach a native how to use a thermometer, to place it in disinfectant, but if he wipes it on his trousers before he inserts it into the patient's mouth, who is to blame? We cannot instill progress until we give the whole native race a basis of education. If we realised the importance of it, we would stop playing with it as we are now doing.

We realise the importance of European education. I think that the Budget tells many stories to those who have eyes to see, European education, now costs us more than £600,000 and, provided the money is being well spent, we not only do not grudge it but we would gladly provide more if and when necessary. It costs us about £10 per head of the European population for the education of our European children.

The Budget tells just as enlightening a story in connection with native education. We see in that respect not £10 but less than 4s. per head per annum being spent on native education. I am not suggesting that it would take £10 per head for the native population in order to give the native the education required to enable him to take his right place in the development of the country, but I am sure the House recognises that you cannot educate the native race on less than 4s. per head per annum. I am not now dealing with the question of principle, but I would plead that the whole development of this country is intimately and inescapably bound up with the development of the native people and that the development of the native people is based on education. If that is so, I would suggest that it is time we got on with the job.

I have complimented the hon. the Minister on his Budget, I have made one or two suggestions, and I have possibly made a few more criticisms than might be expected, or even welcomed, from an hon. Member on this side of the House, but it is because I believe that the hope of this country is placed in the government of the day that I am determined to say anything that I think should be said for its welfare. (Applause.) I am sure that the people have the greatest confidence in the hon. the Prime Minister and in his government, but their hope will only be sustained so long as the government steadfastly follows its policy and does not deviate either to the right or to the left, only so long as the government keeps its actions in harmony with the broad outlook of the hon. the Prime Minister himself; for it is in that principle of humanitarianism that the people of the country have placed their confidence and their hope. I am quite convinced that if this House is willing to see that all the potentialities of the country are used to the full, then the future of Rhodesia is assured. (Applause.)

Speech on Federation
June 23, 1952

In the early 1950s federation—the uniting of three British colonies of Northern Rhodesia, Southern Rhodesia, and Nyasaland—was seriously promoted. African nationalists opposed federation because they correctly believed that it was one more mechanism for whites to prolong colonial power and white control. White right-wing extremists who were later to become the leaders of the breakaway independent white Rhodesia also opposed federation, believing it would slow down Southern Rhodesia's ability to become an independent dominion.

Southern Rhodesian Prime Minister Godfrey Huggins and the United Party promoted federation primarily on economic grounds, believing that federation would spur economic development and growth for Central Africa. Huggins believed that a gradual emancipation would take place for Africans through a partnership between the races. Todd, a United Party member working within the political system, endorsed the partnership metaphor. However, Todd interpreted it as allowing all blacks who were educated and "civilized" to be placed on an equal footing as whites. He also believed that Africans were more rapidly achieving civilized standards than Huggins and the rest of the United Party. It was a paternalistic approach but more progressive than Huggins's vision.

Todd stated in this speech in support of federation: "It has been suggested that the Home Government wishes to use Southern Rhodesia as a brake on the development of strong African nationalism. I do not believe that that is the motive for the proposed federation. . . . We are committing it to a policy of racial cooperation." Todd, as will be seen in a later speech, admitted that he was wrong about racial cooperation. Federation came into being in 1953 and Huggins vacated the Southern Rhodesian premiership to become the new federation prime minister. Todd ascended from the back bench to replace Huggins as prime minister of Southern Rhodesia. This speech is an excellent example of Todd's loyalty to Huggins and the United Party that resulted in his surprising choice as Huggins's replacement. The speech text is from *Southern Rhodesia Debates of the Legislative Assembly*, vol. 33, pp. 2668–78.

Mr. Todd: Mr. Speaker, when I first came to this country, I came to serve one section of the population alone; that was the African section; but as the years pass we all come to love the country for its own sake. We come to realise that the interests of all the people in the country are essentially one, and that anyone who serves the interests of one section well, serves the whole. I have felt in recent years—as the Colony has been developing, gaining strength and taking a more important place in our Commonwealth, the very great privilege of being a member of this particular country at this particular time.

In considering an important subject such as the one which is before us, I feel that we have got to use our very best intelligence and goodwill so that eventually we may come to the right decision. We are fortunate (I feel myself fortunate) this afternoon to have heard the three hon. members who have spoken, because they are hon. members who attended in person the Conference in London, who know all the things that were said and discussed, and all those little points which are not included in the official reports. I have been helped by what I have heard, and I have had certain matters made clearer to me.

We realise, even from the first three speeches which we have heard this afternoon, that there are definitely two sides to this proposal, and the job of the electors of this country is to make up their minds as to which is the better choice and to vote accordingly. I hope that the hon. the Leader of the Opposition, when he spoke of the referendum as being the result of a motion brought before this House by the Opposition, did not really imply that without that motion there would not have been a referendum, because I am quite certain that every voter—every person who is interested in the matter—would have demanded that a question of this kind be settled in no other way.

We know that there are two sides to this question. On the one side are those who are sure in their minds or are growing in certainty, that this proposal is desirable and which, although it may be beset with difficulties, is not beyond our capabilities. On the other side are those who, from one motive or another, believe that Federation is not in the best interests of some section—one section or another—of the population, and in this particular group I believe we find very varying ideas; it is rather amazing to see the extremes in ideas to which the various people within this group subscribe. Some are completely against federation, because they believe that it would not be in the best interest of the African population. Some of those, particularly Europeans, are our friends in Britain who have been quite vocal. Then there are others amongst us who believe that in the interests of the European we should not have a Federation of States in Central Africa.

Amongst this group, who oppose federation, are many Africans not only in the North but also in Southern Rhodesia, and I would think that most of them are concerned really with an African nationalism and that they are attempting to play on the fear of their people. I remember very well 13 years ago when Lord Bledisloe and his friends were in this country considering amalgamation, that the Africans who spoke at that time concerning the question were—most of them—against amalgamation—for the reason that they believed that if we had amalgamation with the North then the very great progress which was being made amongst the native peoples of this country would have to be shared with the African people to the North and that their numbers were so great that the money available would not go round, with the result that, with an amalgamation they believed that African progress in Southern Rhodesia would be slowed up.

Today, there are many educated Africans (or quite a number anyway; most of those who talk on this matter) who are against federation, but it is very difficult to find from them what are their exact reasons. I think the Rt. hon. the Prime Minister has stated the position rightly when he says that they feel this is a time for bargaining, and while they are not really against federation they would like to bargain and "give" us federation, as I heard one group say, on certain terms. This group is not very large and there is a very much larger group of educated Africans who are concerned, rightly, not so much with federation or Dominion Status or any other form of government, but with the definite advancement of their own people. If they are convinced that that can be speeded up by a form of association of countries in Central Africa, they will be completely in favour of it. Then there is the great mass of the people who do not know anything about it but who, because of their very low status in civilisation, can be fairly easily influenced by those who care to work upon their fear.

There is a belief in Britain amongst certain people that there was in the old days an idyllic state for the African people that the coming of the Europeans has destroyed that state and the African people are much the worse for it, and that federation would be a still further worsening of their position. I will say more about that later.

Then I believe there is a group of people who would be quite prepared to federate if they believed that it could be done satisfactorily: if they believed that the outcome would be the advancement of Southern Rhodesia as well as the other countries concerned. I heard one eminent member of the legal profession refer to the White Paper as rather a "creaking structure," and I am sure that it can be described by that term because, after all, federal government is quite a new thing. It is a modern form of government, less than 200 years old, and in all federations there have been difficulties to overcome; there have been considerable quarrels at times between the states and the federal government itself, and at some periods I am sure there were people who thought that perhaps it would have been better if they had not federated. When, however, we see the result of the outstanding example of federation, such as the United States of America and the Commonwealth of Australia, we realise that despite the difficulties the results have been very good indeed.

The hon. the Leader of the Opposition speaks of this White Paper being open to improvement and I hope it is. I am sure, anyway, that as the years pass we will find just what has been found in other Federal States that we have to make alterations from time to time as circumstances change. Right from the beginning there are certain things in the White Paper which make us, perhaps, a little apprehensive, and one is the African Affairs Board which might perhaps be better called the "Human Rights Board." Then it might not be concerned only with African Affairs as its name implies. I believe it is unnecessary and that it could cause a great deal of trouble and difficulty, and could do, perhaps, more harm than good, but if we look for all the difficulties which may arise in any system of federal government, then I know we may be disheartened, but so would anybody else who had ever thought of federating other countries. Others have persevered and succeeded, and we have before us a challenge to attempt, to persevere and to succeed.

Also there is the matter of racial representation in the Federal House. I, for one, am not at all happy about that; not that I am against having members of the African population, if they are worthy of their place, in the Federal House, but I think we, in Southern Rhodesia, are doing very much better by having a common roll and giving the opportunity for those who have the qualifications, who have the ability, to eventually make their way and take their place in the seats of Government.

Well, Mr. Speaker, I realise that any proposal for federal government in Central Africa which would suit Great Britain and suit everybody here would be an ideal beyond our accomplishment. Therefore, any system which is suggested will not find complete favour in the eyes of any one of us but, having read the White Paper, having this afternoon heard the speeches of the three hon. members who have spoken, I am convinced that this is a fair attempt to set up a system of federal government and one which has a substantial hope of success.

Now, I am concerned not only with economic values (although I realise their importance) but I am concerned with human values, and I believe that in Central Africa we could build a great nation, not of white people only but of all the people who are lawfully in these countries. I like the statement in the White Paper that the people who are lawfully here are truly the inhabitants of these countries and have a right to be here. When the Rt. hon. the Prime Minister spoke of federation as being a means to the abolition of the fear of want and also other fear, I wholeheartedly agree with him.

When we turn to the federations of the Commonwealth of Australia and the United States of America, and even Canada, we find from history that originally the strongest motive for federation was common defence. They felt that for reasons of defence the people of those countries, people scattered over big areas, should form a united front against any possible common foe. I do not think we can say that that motive moves us, but I think we might say that we should get together for a united assault on all the things in Central Africa which ought to be improved, those things which are bad and ought to be done away with, and that if we join forces and find a system of government that is satisfactory we will be able to do a great deal for all the people of Central Africa and set up a state which will be worthy of its place in the world.

Years ago British people were very proud of themselves, not in a boastful way, but they believed that they had a real and worthy contribution to make, and when those people came to Africa, for example, they came not only to gain but also to give. I believe that they were right in their belief. I believe that Cecil Rhodes was not governed only with an idea of amassing wealth and power, but that he believed that British rule was something which was a boon and which, being introduced into countries where the people were primitive, would bring to them great blessing.

It rather seems that there is a feeling in the British Commonwealth of Nations that our exploits of past days ought to be apologised for and that really we have not anything to give that primitive peoples have not got already in their civilisation, or in their way of life if it is not a way of life which we would term civilised. But when we turn even to the history of this young country of Southern Rhodesia and see what Europeans have already brought to this country, we can believe in all fairness that the coming of the European, while being in some ways a mixed blessing, was of tremendous advantage to the people of this country.

There are difficulties today which have to be faced, some of which have grown out of the fact that British people came here 50 years ago. One of those is the fact that the African population has grown so much. It would not have grown so quickly if there had not been a civilising force and law and order established here. In the early days, and not so many years ago either, more than half of all African children died in the first year of their life, but as medical services have been built up the people have multiplied at an almost alarming rate. The holdings of cattle when the Europeans came here were pitifully small, but over the years, as veterinary knowledge has been shared with the people and services provided, cattle have also multiplied at a very great rate, and today there is a very different position in Southern Rhodesia, one which is very much happier than many African people realise.

Some of these Africans, who are very vociferous in their condemnation of the Europeans and of the treatment they get at the hands of the Europeans in this country; are perhaps not old enough, or their memories are perhaps not good enough, to remember just what conditions were like only a comparatively few years ago in this country. But when one speaks to older men, people whom we know well and can call our friends, who remember what conditions were like 30, 40, and 50 years ago we find that they are very thankful indeed that British justice has come to this country. Even today, when chiefs' courts are getting more power, there are many Africans indeed who realise that there is no justice yet to compare with British justice and that when they go to a magistrate's court their chances of getting fair treatment are very much better indeed than they are when they go to the chief's courts. I believe that we have given the Africans a great deal and, as the hon. the Leader of the Opposition has said, there is very much that Southern Rhodesia can give to Central Africa.

But where I disagree with the hon. the Leader of the Opposition is this: He says that, while we have the ability and the power as a State under our present government to exert a great influence in Central Africa, we are about to lose that power. Another statement which he made was that he has not a great deal of respect for the ability of the Colonial Office, and I would think that those statements, taken together, mean simply this: Southern Rhodesia is apparently giving up certain powers to a federal government. Those powers which it gives to the federal government are fully surrendered to the federal government by the Colonial Office. On the one side, the hon. the Leader of the Opposition deprecates the fact that we are surrendering certain powers to the federal government, but, on the other hand, I am sure he must rejoice at the fact that the federal government will be taking from the Colonial Office a variety of powers in Central Africa which it enjoys at the present moment. We therefore free a large part of Central Africa from certain Colonial Office powers which the federal government will take over, and in the federal government we, as people with much experience have considerable influence. In other words, we are giving up certain powers, but we are not giving them up entirely. We are surrendering them as a State and taking part in them in a federation. By giving up a little, I think we are sharing more largely in the whole of Central Africa. That, of course, is a matter of opinion, but I believe that is the position.

Now, Mr. Speaker, I want to see the influence of civilisation made more manifest and more widespread throughout Central Africa, and I believe that can be done much more rapidly and efficiently by a federal government than it can be done by the governments of the three states as they are at present. After all, while we may rather decry economic gain, while some may say we are really selling our birthright for a mess of pottage, we have to realise that a great deal of the benefit that can be conferred upon ourselves and upon the African people of the three territories, can only be conferred if we can find the money necessary to set up the services we want. Social advancement is not something separate from economic advancement and I do not think there is any need to state that again because every one of us in this Chamber wishes to give the Africans extended social services. We want also to extend the social services to our European population, but whenever we speak of this the hon. the Minister of Finance is quick to show that the biggest obstacle in the way is that very mundane thing, money. We have not enough of it. We realise that not only do we need funds from taxation to run our social services, but that, if we are ever to extend our social services fully, we have to develop the country.

And so we come to another form of money, not the ordinary revenue of the country, but the capital resources, not of this country, but such capital resources anywhere as we can tap for the development of this country. It is obvious that those who wish to see a great social advance in Central Africa realise that we have to find very large capital sums. I do not think there is any doubt that the three States taken together are a better investment, a better surety for the investment of capital, than taking any one of them singly. Not only that, but I believe—and I think the Rt. hon. the Prime Minister mentioned—that the proposed federation is something which is in line with the vision of Cecil Rhodes. I believe there are many people who have money, as Cecil Rhodes had money, who are prepared to be spurred by a vision similar to his in these mundane times.

I believe one can work up a great deal more enthusiasm for a Central African Federation with all the possibility of building a great and wealthy nation which can give its very great donation in material things—as well as, I hope, some day in intellectual and spiritual things—to the world, than in trying to work up the same enthusiasm about three small states. I believe, Mr. Speaker, that if there are—and apparently there are—very substantial economic advantages to be gained by a proposed federation, that there we have the basis for the development of social services for the people of this country—education and health and so on. But we must face many problems, and one of the most serious problems is simply this: Have we in ourselves what it takes to make this federation a success? The hon. the Leader of the Opposition ran through a list of countries, not British ones, where federation had not been successful.

Mr. Stockil: Mr. Speaker, on a point of order, I did not refer to federation in connection with those countries. It was a question of British control and influence.

Mr. Todd: I withdraw that statement. I misunderstood the hon. the Leader of the Opposition.

Well, Mr. Speaker, I shall, myself, give an instance where federation has not been a success. Let us take the continent of America. We have spoken about the United States of America, and I think most of us realise that they would never have attained their present wealth and power if they had not been able to come together and demonstrate the old adage that unity is strength. But there are many people in many small states in South America, and while they make their contribution to the world, when we think of wealth and power and world leadership it is not the states of South America that spring quickly to our minds. It is the United States of America. While I am sure there are other differences between the North American States and the South American States than just their difference in unity, I believe that the fact that States of South America have not been able to federate or unite is one of the chief reasons for the fact that they do not lead in the world today.

But why have they not been able to unite? Instead of building up a federation of states there, we actually have instances where unity has been obtained for a certain time and has disintegrated again because the people did not have what it takes to remain united. They did not have the ability to overcome their difficulties and so they split off once again and became smaller states.

But what is our ability? What is the measure of our ability? The measure of our ability will be seen if we decide to federate in what kind of a job we make of the proposed Federation. It may be that we have not got the ability. I can hardly believe that. I believe that, as the States of Australia have been able to federate, so we, too, should be able to make a united nation. But I realise that our difficulties are very different in kind from some of the difficulties which were before the States of the Commonwealth of Australia when they came together. Our difficulties are very different from those of the United States, although in some ways there is a similarity. We have particular problems to face because of the fact that we, as Europeans who hold in our hands the gift of civilisation, are so small a minority.

But difficulties surely need not dissuade us. When Lord Bledisloe was here 13 years ago, one of the reasons why he and his commission did not recommend amalgamation of Southern Rhodesia, Northern Rhodesia and Nyasaland at that time was because the small European population of Southern Rhodesia was inexperienced. But there have been many changes since that time. We have lived through a great war and we have seen this country develop and our system of self-government has proved itself sound. We have proved that we are able to run our own affairs satisfactorily so that, when the committee met in London to draw up the report which we received a year ago it was felt that the situation had completely changed as far as the experience of the European population of Central Africa was concerned, and I believe it has. We have shown in our short history of self-government that we are able to take a reasonably balanced outlook. We have had no Native Affairs Committee to check on the Bills that have come before this House, but we have seen a complete change made in the life of the African people in a very short space of time. There is very much to be done still and although in some ways one might say we have only begun upon the great problem of civilising the indigenous population, still I say great strides have been made in the last few years. I believe that what we have done should not only assure our friends in Great Britain, whose great responsibility towards the African people is very real and very great, but it should also give us confidence that we can take our leading part as senior partner in a proposed new federation. Thirteen years ago, Lord Bledisloe and his friends were not at all sure about our native policy. They put it kindly but they said that the Colonial Office native policy and our own were different and it was too soon yet to say which would be to the best advantage of the African people. But when the Committee sat last year they said that the apparent difference had more or less resolved itself. They said the aim of both policies was the improvement and the advancement of the African people and in many ways Southern Rhodesia had advanced further by its policy than had the Northern Territories.

In one way they said we were behind, and that was that the political development of the natives in the North had been faster than the political development of our own Africans. I believe that is a misstatement. I believe it is a wrong idea. I cannot subscribe to a racial type of government and while, at the present moment, one has maybe to accept certain racial representatives in a Federal House, I hope that the day will come before long when that position is changed and there will not be the need for racial representatives. I believe that Southern Rhodesia, in its reaffirmation of the Common Roll on a basis of satisfactory qualifications has the right policy. I believe that Africans qualifying on that basis to share in our political life are further advanced and on a much sounder basis than on that of universal franchise which could and would lead, I believe, to universal chaos.

Now, the hon. the Leader of the Opposition speaks of the fact that under our own Constitution we have reserved legislation when the legislation is differential, but now there is a new term and that is "disadvantageous." Well, as far as I am concerned—and I think there are many people, and I trust the majority in this country who feel as I do—if legislation is definitely disadvantageous to a section of the people, then ultimately it is disadvantageous to the whole country, and while we may face all sorts of difficulties under a ruling such as that, we have to resolve those difficulties because eventually we must see that the things that are done under the Federation are done for the good of all.

We have entered a critical period. It has been suggested that the Home Government wishes to use Southern Rhodesia as a brake on the development of strong African nationalism. I do not believe that that is the motive for the proposed Federation. I believe that the motive is obvious, that federation brings a new strength, better opportunities and advantages, that it is the right and sensible thing to do and that the time has come to act. Of course, it is an important decision to make. If we federate these three countries, we are committing Central Africa to a liberal policy. We are committing it to a policy of racial cooperation, which I believe we are not so fully committed to under our present State Government. I believe that it would be easier to swing back from such a policy at the present moment than it would be when we are on a Federal basis. If this is a disadvantage of federation, then people must consider it and vote accordingly because I believe that, if we create a federation, we shall commit Central Africa and ourselves and our children to a policy of full cooperation with the African people, as they rise to a civilised state.

Now, Mr. Speaker, I know that propositions such as this are fraught with danger. There is going to be some uncertainty, but surely we have within us the vision and the courage that will be necessary, and the ability also, to make the propositions which are set before us in this White Paper a reality which will bring benefit to all the people of Central Africa. Let us set about establishing a great Central African State which will benefit our British Commonwealth of Nations and contribute to the good and to the peace of the world. (Applause.)

1956 Congress Address by the Prime Minister

This was one of Todd's most controversial speeches during his tenure as prime minister. The disparate views of partnership were emerging between the Federation, led by Huggins, and Southern Rhodesia, led by Todd.

The speech was delivered June 22, 1956, at the United Rhodesia Party Annual Congress. Todd decided to use the party congress meeting as the occasion "to bring into the open in a forceful speech the problems of relations with the federal government which, it appeared had been exasperating him and his Ministers for some time."[18] The federal government limited immigration and opposed raising outside capital funds for economic development. Todd believed that increased immigration and capital funds were cornerstones for the economic development needed to spur African advancement. Todd also criticized Huggins for cutting back on funds for European education while Todd was funneling more money into African education. Todd rightly feared that whites would not accept the perception that their needs were being shorted in favor of the Africans. Todd was also upset that indigenous African aspirations based on racial considerations were not being deterred in the Federation—essentially an abandonment of Huggins's traditional multiracial policies. The African National Congress and other groups wanted immediate and universal control for blacks whether blacks were educated or not. Todd believed this undermined Southern Rhodesia's plan to gradually bring all civilized people together regardless of their race. The speech created division within Todd's party with those who supported Huggins becoming upset with Todd. Roy Welensky, Huggins's deputy prime minister, who was to succeed Huggins as federal prime minister in a few months, made a sharp and antagonistic reply to Todd. The speech illustrated some of the difficult and treacherous political currents that Todd had to navigate while prime minister. The text can be found in the Roy Welensky Papers, Box 516, folder 4, fols. 11–18, Rhodes House, Oxford University, Oxford, England.

The publication of our Mid-term Report makes it unnecessary for me to look back over the work of the year and review it, as I would normally do. I am, therefore, going to take the opportunity to look forward and consider our position as a party in relationship to the present political scene.

Two and a half years ago we considered ourselves almost a part of the Federal Party. Our general policies were similar, our supporters were largely common to both parties, but we were concerned with Territorial matters while the Federal Party concerned itself with the Federal aspect of each territories life and policy.

The decision, in Southern Rhodesia, to keep the two Parties separate—one for Federal functions of Government and the other for Territorial functions, was a deliberate one. Eventually in Northern Rhodesia a different course was taken and the Territorial side of politics is the concern of a territorial division of the Federal Party.

During the two and a half years of our existence we have cooperated in every way possible with the federal government. We have endeavoured to meet them and in actual fact we have pled for fuller cooperation and consultation between our two governments. Our conscience is quite clear as far as this aspect is concerned. On the other hand differences in outlook have become increasingly apparent along certain lines. On the policy of partnership between the races we have been in agreement with the Federal Party and our attitude in this regard has been maintained. We agree with the federal government in its decisions regarding Kariba and we believe that the project will prove of inestimable value to Northern Rhodesia, to ourselves, and to the Federation as a whole. A main disagreement with the federal government stems, never-the-less, from Kariba itself, and is concerned with the effects of the scheme on present development. The federal government holds that

Kariba is so big that it must dominate the entire economic scene until power is flowing from it. The Southern Rhodesia Government believes that the decision to build Kariba has as its corollary the necessity to press forward widespread development, with such immigration as is required to make possible this development, and with the provision of all the services that are required to absorb a rapidly growing population.

The United Rhodesia Party Government is deeply concerned with the progress of this country and of the Federation. We are working for the development of all, with special emphasis on the African people but we recognise that the quicker we get a million immigrants—not to take jobs but to make jobs—the better for the future of us all. We hold that it is not in the best interests of the Federation to limit immigration to an arbitrary figure of 20,000 people a year. Our government considers that we should welcome whatever number of immigrants are required to make possible maximum development both in primary and secondary industries, and that services should be planned on an adequate scale to receive these people.

The United Rhodesia Party Government in pleading for maximum development, differs from the Federal Party Government in its attitude to loan funds. The federal government states that loan funds are so difficult to obtain that it is not possible to raise the money necessary to give us a completely adequate transport system and also provide the roads, schools, hospitals, etc. which would be needed by a fast growing population. We hold that there has been lack of planning, that no adequate programme has been formulated and that the outlook of the federal government on this matter precludes any hope of obtaining the necessary funds. We feel that if the vision were there and the planning done, then the funds could be found. We believe that our capital requirements, in relation to world capital, are so small that they could be found if the will were there. I have said before that our needs are such that I firmly believe that we are wrong to limit our overseas borrowing to the United Kingdom. I know that we are also receiving funds from organisations, such as the International Bank, but I believe other sources, including non-government organisations in the United States and Canada, could be tapped.

I believe that the Southern Rhodesia Government was completely right in organising an industrial drive as and when it did in the United Kingdom. We want to get industries on the drawing boards now so that when power from Kariba is available, industries will be preparing, or even ready, to use that power. It must surely be recognised that there is a time-lag of up to three years between the first decision and the commencement of production.

We want to plan the agricultural future of the country so that the needs of a growing population can be met from the potentials of our own land. We welcome, wholeheartedly, e.g. the efforts of the Rhodesian Selection Trust to prove the Kafue Flats and will be greatly encouraged if it is shown that this great area of irrigable land could provide wheat and rice and other crops for our people.

But all of this projected development requires funds. Local authorities must plan to take their full share of the responsibility of such development and their need for loan money should be met. This is a matter, it can be held, for the Territorial governments, but the economic outlook is conditioned by the federal government, and if new sources for loan funds are to be tapped, the federal government must do it. On these matters there is a difference of outlook between the federal government and the United Rhodesia Party Government. This is so fundamental that we could not join their camp unless the attitude of the federal government were to change radically. On the other hand we believe that there are very many people in all territories who are supporters of the Federal Party and who feel as we do that Kariba should not impede progress but should stimulate it—not from 1960 onwards, but from today.

We have grown away from the Federal Party Government and this is an embarrassment. While we have cooperated with the federal government wherever possible, we have had little contact at the planning stage. I do not hold that Territorial governments should necessarily take their cue from the federal government, but its influence in economic matters especially is great and frequent consultations between all governments should be held. For example, we have been greatly embarrassed as a government because of the fact that, when we launched a progressive plan for Native Education it appeared concurrently with statements from the federal government that the Treasury could not make money available for the provision of necessary school facilities for European children. A further example of this apparent conflict lies in announcements, on the one hand, from our government of sound plans for improvement of African farming, and on the other hand from the federal government that European immigration must be limited, to 20,000 a year, thus implying curtailment of European progress.

I am sure that the governments in Northern Rhodesia and Nyasaland also suffer embarrassments of this kind. They can only be overcome by the general development of the whole Federation, planned and implemented by a much closer cooperation between the four governments.

Our worries as a party, however, are not confined to the economic sphere. We are the present government of a people who pledged themselves in 1953, in a great act of faith, to become partners in a Federation with Northern

Rhodesia and Nyasaland. In that act of faith we handed over important powers to a government jointly responsible to three territories. We understood that we were to work for the abolition of racialism. We believed that there was to be partnership between the races. Long ago we freely decided in Southern Rhodesia to leave colour out of politics and to push forward with sound policies for all the people, both European and African in education, health, housing, and general social services, in agriculture, in industry. We face, because of our decision, enormous problems, but these are mostly on the side of finance, on the general production of wealth, not because of any opposition from the majority of our people.

Under our Federal Constitution we have certain members of Parliament elected or nominated as racial representatives to the Federal Assembly but it has been generally accepted that, as more Africans advance and are able to take their full part in the political life of the Federation the present special representation of one race will fall away.

We believe we had the right to expect that the political pattern agreed upon between the partners in Federation would have been the pattern for all political development within the territory. I do not know if it is possible to disassociate the local Colonial Office representatives from the policy of the Colonial Office itself, but I would like to do this for I do not complain of the calibre of local officials or of their service, which I am sure is devoted. What I do object to is the political pattern in Northern Rhodesia and in Nyasaland—the jockeying for seats in the Legislative Assemblies on the basis of race, the continued and increasing underlining of colour; all of which augurs badly for the future of a multi-racial land. The background of Colonial Office experience makes it an unsuitable guide for our people in the north in the development of their political life within this Federation. The division resulting from two governments being under the Commonwealth Relations Office and the other two under the Colonial Office is not only an unhappy one, but is fraught with some danger. I have had no experience of the Colonial Office other than what I have seen of its policies over the past two and a half years in our Federation, but from that experience I am led to wonder if it has accepted Federation, and certainly if it has accepted the political pattern of working for the elimination of colour in politics.

We are not prepared to run Southern Rhodesia on the basis of a struggle between different races. On the contrary we are committed to government by civilised people of all colours working together in full cooperation to ensure the development of the country along with the maintenance of sound standards. At the same time it is our policy to give every opportunity and encouragement over the years ahead to bring every citizen up to a decent and civilised standard of living and conduct with full participation in the political life of the country.

As a government we have demonstrated beyond doubt that we are wholeheartedly in support of such a policy. Our housing projects, our Native agricultural policy and our five-year plan for education set the seal on our honesty of purpose. Our Commission of enquiry into conditions for the franchise is the outcome of our desire to place the government of the country safely and for all time in the hands of responsible and able citizens.

The fact that the Federation has different policies for different areas is a serious weakness and is of the greatest concern to us all. Any policy of racialism in any one of their territories of our Federation is a threat to every section, and African racialism is no more acceptable than European racialism.

There are organisations within our Federation today which are abusing the constitution and working for its destruction. There are political bosses who labour to bring the masses of uncivilised people into a disciplined subjection to their orders. All of this is a negation of democracy, a threat to our political institutions, and may I say, to the personal safety of our citizens.

For example, why should law-abiding Africans in the North not be permitted to buy from Indian or European shops, or from any shop that they choose? If the people whose rights are being interfered with were Europeans, we would certainly be stirred to greater action. If any European leader endeavoured to exert such dictatorial influence over a section of our people as the Congress leaders today are building up, there would be deep concern not only in this country but throughout the Commonwealth. The whole issue of colour and race is confusing our thinking, and I believe it is high time that it was cleared. Is it not time that we laid down our standards very definitely and also honestly and generously abided by them? Or are we going to continue to think in terms of black and white?

I believe that the wish of the majority of reasonable people of all races in the Federation is to think in terms of a united people, but for some time we all recognise that there will be one section, a comparatively small section, made up of both black and white who will have to carry a particularly heavy responsibility both in the fields of government and of taxation. If we think along these lines we will be concerned to see that the people who are just awakening from barbarism are led, not into paths of insurrection and lawlessness, but towards the balanced development of their talents and eventually to their full participation in government and in bearing their load of taxation.

We, the people of the Federation, require self-government at the earliest opportunity, but until we can have self-government we should see that our policies are aligned as closely as possible, and that the relationships between us are strengthened.

When I speak of self-government what do I mean? There is no political party in the Federation today, unless perhaps the Confederate Party, if it is still alive, which holds that government should be by Europeans only. It is an accepted fact that the electorate holds that government should be in the hands of civilised people of whatever colour they may be. The electorate does not hold that government should be in the hands of one race but the African National Congress does believe that. It works for a racial government and that aim is directly in conflict with the Federal Constitution and with democratic thought throughout the free world. We all want self-government but it must be true self-government.

It may be asked on what authority I speak of Congress activities. It may be held that I am interfering in the affairs of Northern Rhodesia and Nyasaland, but I would remind those who would criticise in this way that the Nyasaland Congress in particular is active throughout Southern Rhodesia. From time to time meetings are held in various places in Southern Rhodesia. At these meetings anti-Federation songs are sung and people are harangued by leaders who are not concerned with the truth, but are concerned with swaying an uncivilised people by every device they can muster. Those audiences are regularly told, for example, that Nyasaland is not a part of the Federation, that the degree of Federation which we have is only on trial and that the African people in Nyasaland can secede from the Federation at will. At these meetings money is collected to further the work of this seditious organisation. We have waited in vain for the Colonial Office authorities to take action against Congress.

We are a territorial Government—linked in a Federation with partners whose destinies are too greatly influenced by politics in the United Kingdom. As a Government we recognise the dangers which beset our people and our political ideals and we must take every possible action to combat these dangers but this will mean a definite change in our position as a party. As we stand today the United Rhodesia Party Government is so exclusively a territorial organisation that we are unable to assist our friends in the north, both European and African who wish to be free of Colonial Office inaptitude and espouse bolder policies.

The whole question of constitutional development is one near our hearts. We see change and development taking place in various parts of the Commonwealth and recognise that but for our multi-racial pattern, we would be far nearer Dominion status than we are today. As a Federation we are economically sound: we have the necessary leadership amongst us and the economic opportunities available will in themselves attract the capital we require for the development of our land. But one of the most important things that must be maintained is stable government. We have no jealousy of the present Federal Party Government—we have no jealousy of their present or future leadership. What we require is a more dynamic policy, a wider vision, a greater determination to press forward with maximum development, accepting the implications that this brings. If such a policy were in evidence, there would be overwhelming support for the Federal Party and it could look forward to governing this Federation for many years to come.

Our Federal constitution has made of us one people living in one country which is decentralised into three states. In the future, I realise that it must continue to be decentralised in one form or another. More important, however, than the type of decentralisation which must exist are the common purposes which should be ours, the common aims, the increasing degree of cooperation which should be in evidence as we press forward to raise living standards and provide opportunities for progress for all the people of our great Federation.

I recognise that there may be widespread criticism of my speech. It may be said, for example, that constitutional issues are already being considered and carried through by the federal government. I do not know if this is so; but we welcome the statement by Sir Roy Welensky that Dominion status is near. I do not know what plans the federal government have for further constitutional changes, but I do believe that in a democracy the people should have a wider say in these matters and that it should not just be reported to them at some time in the future that all is well between the federal government and the United Kingdom Government and that agreement has been reached on certain principles.

I believe that these vital matters should be discussed in Congresses such as these. We do not live in a country where the future is sure and sound, but one in which almost anything can happen. The circumstances call for the greatest of vigilance and for an overriding unity of purpose amongst the electorate.

We see a pattern evolving before us in which it is quite clear that unless action is taken we are going to be subjected in the years ahead to a constant threat by political bosses who could use a disciplined mass of people as a threat against established law and order. There will be no future for this country unless the laws are respected and obeyed. Alongside of sound laws and just administration must go an increasing degree of civility and consideration of one person for another regardless of colour. On the other hand civility and consideration on the part of one person for another will never be brought about by mass threats, either economic or otherwise.

And where, you may ask, does the United Rhodesia Party figure in all this? My answer is that if we do not figure in it—in wider economic planning, in constitutional changes—then we are heading for extinction for there is no future for a political party which concerns itself in isolation with territorial matters only—no matter how diligently it may endeavour to carry out its tasks.

What then must we do? There are two possible alternatives. We could put this speech forward as an invitation to the Federal Party to consider our views and perhaps at their Congress in September to give a reply. At that Congress, no doubt, they will be considering their own future policy, for policies of Governments are rightly made and altered in Congress. If in Congress the Federal Party feels that there is merit in what we say and if it is ready to improve its own policy and make it acceptable to a greater proportion of the people of the Electorate in Nyasaland, Northern Rhodesia and Southern Rhodesia, then we should link up with them for the benefit of the Federation, and in Southern Rhodesia as in Northern Rhodesia our Territorial affairs would be the concern of the Federal Party.

Here let me state unequivocally that should the Federal Party gain and accept our support, I would in every way possible give my personal backing to Sir Roy Welensky when he takes over the leadership of the Federation. But if new policies regarding immigration, general economic planning, and constitutional development are not advanced by the Federal Party—policies which are acceptable to ourselves and to the great number of people in the three territories who are critical of the present government, what does the United Rhodesia Party do?

I believe that we must have a part in these wider issues. If this view is accepted by Congress and if the Federal Party does not make it possible for us to join them, then we must seek a liaison with people of like mind to ourselves in Northern Rhodesia and Nyasaland, and together with them, challenge the Federal government all along the line.

This I would bitterly regret but our whole future is at stake—the success of the Federation—our high hopes for the development of a progressive and happy society—all of these things depend upon courage, upon vision, upon action—now!

Franchise Speech

The franchise was one of the issues that eventually led to Todd's demise as prime minister. In March 1957 a commission led by Sir Robert Tredgold, the chief justice of the Federation, made several recommendations to enlarge the number of African voters. One proposal was to retain a common roll favored by Todd and a rejection of a dual racial roll favored by Welensky and the Federal Party.[19] While the Tredgold Commission's proposals were hardly radical and did not threaten white rule—the number of eligible Africans for franchise were severely limited by educational and financial requirements—the white right-wing reacted in anger.

Todd wanted a modest six thousand educated Africans added to the voting roll. On June 15, 1957, Todd made a speech at Salisbury before a liberal group of whites and Africans called the Interracial Association of Southern Rhodesia at their annual meeting. Todd threatened to resign unless these Africans were given the right to vote. Todd's opponents in his own party were incensed by this demand.[20] However, a compromise emerged and after an exhausting campaign where Todd spoke to large and small groups all over the country, a franchise bill was passed by parliament on August 21, 1957.[21] Unfortunately no text is extant for Todd's speech before the Interracial Association. This speech was the first one Todd delivered before parliament on April 30, 1957, and contains his main arguments in favor of wider franchise for educated Africans. Todd's conservatism and opposition to universal franchise is clear in the speech. African nationalist groups criticized the conservatism of Todd's policy but many still appreciated his efforts that were liberal for its day.[22] They knew that Todd, despite his paternalism had their best interests in mind, something they knew was not true for other white politicians. This text is from the *Southern Rhodesian Legislative Debates*, vol. 39, pp. 1241–51.

The Prime Minister: Mr. Speaker, I think it is very useful that we have an opportunity today for a preliminary canter without legislation before us and with no vote at the end of our deliberations. I am sure that, as has already become evident, opportunity will not only be taken to discuss the Tredgold report, but also to bring forward any particular theories which we may hold ourselves. I have been delighted to hear the hon. the acting Leader of the Opposition say that we should keep this above party politics and I completely agree with him. But as a government we do also represent a party and it is our responsibility at a later date to bring legislation before this House. I would therefore like to remind this House that as a party we did promise the electors to take whatever steps we could to preserve racial harmony, to avoid the undesirable principle of separate representation on racial lines, to build up security and confidence within the Colony and without the Colony and to set up a commission or select committee to give people an opportunity of putting forward their views and generally also to assist us in preparing such legislation as would ensure that the government of the territory remains for all times in the hands of civilized and responsible men. We declared 1956 a franchise year. Unfortunately, we were not able to complete the work of the Commission during that year, for reasons which everybody knows, but during 1956 a great number of people and organisations gave much thought to this particular problem and last year we fulfilled our promise to the electorate by setting up a commission which was to consider and report on a system for the just representation of the people of the Colony in its Legislative Assembly under which government is placed, and remains, in the hands of civilized and responsible persons.

The next step following this debate will be the formulation of legislation to bring into being such system as this House will eventually agree upon to realize our ideal. Now, we are indebted to the Commission. Much has been said on this already, so I will only say we are indebted to the Commission particularly in the first place, for its recommendations, which I may say immediately are not binding upon us, and can well be ignored if we can bring before this House better recommendations. We are indebted to the Commission also for its statement of the case for the just representation of the people, for its careful research and for argument so compelling that we dare not ignore it. The Commission has stated emphatically that the just representation of the people is of fundamental, of overriding importance. Let us honestly recognise that this concerns particularly the African section of our population.

I would like to back up the observation which the Commissioners have made with one which was made just the other day. I think it was made in the Union of South Africa Parliament, but anyway it was made by Mr. Harry Oppenheimer, M.P., who said: "It is obvious that if there are no recognized and legitimate channels through which the natives can make their power felt, they will make it felt through undesirable or illegal channels."

Now, let us consider what is this just representation. First of all, we might turn to one other matter and that is I think you can say that in general people who approach these problems approach them from two different angles. In other words, there are two different groups of people as far as their ideas are concerned. There are the theorists who will have nothing less than universal adult franchise. These are the people who believe that in the very granting of democratic institutions one generates political maturity and ensures democracy. Now, the hon. the acting Leader of the Opposition has spoken about this from the point of view of Athens and has read something that the last Prime Minister of Southern Rhodesia quoted in this House, but I do not know that it is true to say that the Athenians fell because they tried to be too democratic for linked up with their democracy was also the owning of slaves. Their conditions were very different from ours. In fact, it is very difficult to compare the two and they were certainly not so democratic for right up to the end they did keep their slaves.

Then there are the practical people, I hope no less idealistic, who while accepting the sovereignty of the people at the same time regard the system of elections as an instrument of government which must be used by capable people but not necessarily even by all the adult people and that it must be used further for the good of all the people. Now, it is true that we do not have representatives of the first group in this House. We are all representatives of the second group, and although we may have differences of opinion we are all pragmatic in our approach to this subject. We are fortunate in that the Commissioners were also of the same group and were also practical in their approach to the problem, so much so that they have been criticized on that point. I saw in one Communist newspaper which came across my desk—I am not its advertising agent, so I will not give the name of the paper—the following: "The Commission claims to have produced a scheme which provides a common roll for Europeans and Africans which rejects resolutely any form of racial representation," and then comes the comment of the paper: "Nothing could be a greater misuse of the English language."

It goes on:

> The Commission is quite brazen in giving its reasons for these regulations. The European section of the electorate would feel itself adequately protected against the possibility that it might be politically overwhelmed by backward and illiterate sections of an African population susceptible to unreasoning appeals to African nationalism.

Of course, what the paper did not take into consideration was this; that it was not the race of the people that one had to be protected from, but one requires protection from the backward and illiterate sections of any population which might be susceptible to unreasoning appeals of any kind.

We are fortunate that we have had a Commission which was so practical and sensible in its approach. We are not only concerned with the theory of the problem; we are concerned with how these things will work out. We have, for example, the pressures that are brought to bear at election time. We must take into consideration the state of the people—their education, their background, their experience or lack of experience of political systems, their susceptibility to persuasion, and in this country their persuasion through witchcraft and sorcery.

As I say, we are not theorists, ready to accept the universal adult franchise because that may be the ultimate aim in democracy. On the other hand, I am sure we would not wish to swing to government by an oligarchy.

Some have said that by providing for "special qualification" voters, the Commission is making provision for those who are less than responsible, and I heard one of our members ask the other day "How many irresponsible people does it take to make one responsible person, or how many special voters are equal to one ordinary voter?"

If we consider a community such as Canada, Australia or New Zealand, we can say there are several groups of people: There is the (A) group who through their profession, or work, or industry, or service to the country, are people whose names have become household words throughout the country, and whose public services are widely appreciated. Then you can say there is another group, the (B) group, whose services within a city or district are well known, who are very responsible, give much of their time to the public interest and who, although perhaps not as well known throughout the country, are certainly first class leaders within their own areas, and I do not think any of us would ask: "How many of the (B) group does it take to equal one of the (A) group?"

Then there is the much wider group which we may call the (C) group, a much greater group of responsible people in professions and businesses, housewives, people of education and of sound economic position; then there is another group which we might call the (D) group, the group of labourers and people who may not be so stable or so responsible; but to whom no one in their own country would think of denying the vote. Then, Sir, we come to another group the (E) group, which we do not find in Canada, Australia or New Zealand, or if we do find some of them, they are so few that no one notices them, but which in this country is the major group. Those are the people who have not emerged yet from the dominance of the witchdoctor, who are illiterate and who do not understand party government or democratic principles.

I believe that those first three groups—A, B and C—are those whom we could say our European people in general fall under plus a fairly small number of Africans at the present time. I think there is no doubt that all of those people are well worthy of the vote, and there would be no argument as to whether they should get the vote. These are the people whom our Commission has defined under ordinary qualifications, and these three groups would make the top group.

Then there is the (E) group, the great illiterate group in Southern Rhodesia which we do not find in the United Kingdom or New Zealand or Canada, but I do not think there is any argument in this House about the fact that they are not ready for the vote. They should not be enfranchised. Admittedly, though this is not the day for discussion of this subject, aids should be available to help those who are determined to leave this bottom group and enter the middle group, and perhaps in time join the top group.

I would like to focus the attention of the House for a few minutes on the middle group—in Southern Rhodesia the emergent group—the group which lies between those who without doubt are worthy of the vote, and the great group who without doubt are not ready for the vote. This middle group of emergent people are not irresponsible. One cannot say they are irresponsible. It may be they are less responsible than the top group for there are as many grades of responsibility as there are people, but they are certainly less advanced and certainly less capable than the top group. In Canada or Australia or the United Kingdom, our middle group—this emergent group—is their lowest group, and so their situation is very different from ours. In a modern, progressive country, I believe that the top group represented by our ordinary qualification group make up such a large proportion of the country that the people here who are our middle group—that would be the bottom group in Canada or Australia—can be accepted as voters with equanimity and as there is no grade which is equated in those countries with our bottom grade, civilization, security and general progress, based as they are on the top—I think it is true they are based on the top group—will not be threatened, but unfortunately the top group in Southern Rhodesia is not the biggest group. The largest is the bottom group. Even the middle and top groups together are not as large as the bottom group, so I agree with the hon. member for Hatfield (Mr. Aitken-Cade) if he is thinking along these lines—which he is not—that it is fair enough that the minority of the country should rule at the present time, but the minority which I mean is the top group, combined with this emergent group, with the safeguards laid down by the Commission.

There is one thing that this House must make sure of, and that is in fixing qualifications for the franchise we must be sure we do not allow the power inadvertently to fall into the hands of the people who comprise the bottom group of this country, for if we did we would prejudice the future of the whole community.—[HON. MEMBERS: Hear, hear.]

Now, Sir, that is not our only danger. If this emergent, middle group which is by no means a majority in Canada or Australia or New Zealand, should over the years become the dominant group in Southern Rhodesia, it could be that our future would be prejudiced. If we define our middle group and set financial and other qualifications as its boundaries, it would be incumbent upon us also to make sure that those boundaries are not broken down eventually by the lowest group. We will have to take that carefully into consideration; but where I disagree with the hon. member for Hatfield (Mr. Aitken-Cade) is in his argument that really the election of government should be left in the hands of the top grade only, those of ordinary qualifications, and I gather from what he says that he would not leave the qualifications as they are today but that he would advance them. However, he has not gone into detail on that.

It is not enough in a democracy to have power in the hands of those best qualified. It is dangerous to be governed by an oligarchy, even if it is an aristocracy, even in a homogeneous community, but I believe it is even more dangerous where the top group to whom you are going to give the franchise, to whom you are suggesting the franchise is to be restricted, is mostly from the race which is a minority, and in this country, a small minority. But anyway, Sir, in Southern Rhodesia all through our history we have eschewed racialism in politics and we have also laid a claim to democracy.

I hold that our dangers are two-fold; first, that we must see that we keep the government in the hands of responsible people. "We are entirely satisfied," say the Commission, "that a country is amply justified in making an endeavour to confirm the franchise to those of its inhabitants who are capable of exercising it with reason, judgment and public spirit. It is in this sense that we have interpreted 'civilized and responsible persons,' as used in our Commission."

But in our efforts to do that we may fall into a second danger, and that is that we may be tempted to keep the qualifications so high that we are no longer a democracy and our political edifice, being so narrowly founded within our people, will be pushed over by those very people who should be an integral part of its strength. I hold that that second danger is just as great as the first and that no security can be achieved unless the franchise is given to the greatest number possible, and I think I have already clearly shown what I mean by the word "possible."

The Commission particularly underlines that second danger, that of basing the electorate on too narrow a foundation within our people. I am quite sure there are no hon. members who will cavil at the ordinary qualifications as suggested by the Commission. They are high, and surely there is no doubt that those who can attain to them are worthy of the vote.

Our problem today therefore is the problem of our middle group, the emergent people. How will those people be represented? How will they have its say? We have been tenacious in holding on to the common roll in Southern Rhodesia. There have been times in our history when parties have guaranteed to an electorate that if they were returned they would take the Africans off the common roll and give them special representation, but those threats or promises were never realized and I believe that today feeling is stronger than ever throughout the country and we are determined to hold on to the common roll principle so that any one of any race who holds the necessary qualifications can be enrolled; in other words, while one can use the word "common" in a number of ways, we think of it particularly as being common to the races and also in Southern Rhodesia that the candidates are common to all the electors.

Now, Sir, the qualifications for the roll must on the one hand ensure democratic representation and on the other hand they must do that without imperiling those same democratic principles and organizations, and we are asked: "Is £15 and literacy a fair test?" It does not sound very much. £15! Wherever you go throughout the Commonwealth today you might say: "What sort of a person is only getting £15 a month?" but that is not a fair question in Southern Rhodesia—at least, perhaps it is a fair question in Southern Rhodesia.

What would not be fair would be to make up one's mind that anyone in Southern Rhodesia only getting £15 a month obviously could not be worthy of the vote. Is it fair to say: "What sort of people in Southern Rhodesia get only £15 a month?"—[MR. KELLER: You must be thinking of the old age pensioner.]—The old age pensioner is fully catered for in this report if the hon. member will support it, as no doubt he will, being an honest, sincere and intelligent gentleman.

In Southern Rhodesia we find, according to the report of the Commission, that the number of people who get only £15 a month include people who hold quite responsible posts in the life of the community. We may say to ourselves: "Why is it that this peculiar situation is found in Southern Rhodesia when it is not found in Canada or Australia," and the answer is that we have a national income which is relatively low, and unless we take this fact into consideration our judgment can well be prejudiced.

If in Canada we asked if trained teachers, transport drivers, experienced policemen, should be given the vote, no one would doubt that they should be given the vote; but it is true, as is pointed out by this Commission, that there will be young trained teachers who will not get £15 a month. There will be policemen of some years experience who will not get as high as £15 a month, there will be transport drivers, who, in their earlier years of service, will not get £15 a month.

The economic set-up here is changing rapidly I know, and we are fortunate in that, but our economic set-up means that people who in other countries are considered because of the work they do and the responsible part that they play in industry and in the life of the community, capable of having the vote, in Southern Rhodesia they might not get a vote, simply because our national income, is as yet very low. If our national income were higher, if it were possible for the government to bring in the taxation which is required to pay its servants both black and white, the rates they would get in any ordinary country, then teachers would not be being paid £10 or £12 a month, but the lowest of them would be getting £30 and more a month. But we cannot do this. It is not that we would not like to do these things. We are faced with economic problems which, although we are endeavouring to overcome them, and are overcoming them, cannot be overcome in one year or perhaps fully even in ten. But because we are not on the one hand able to overcome these problems at present, is that really just cause for withholding the vote from people who on their other qualifications, should get it. Surely not.

I know it is very difficult to determine what sort of tests one should apply. We know how difficult it is, and how especially difficult it is to determine character. How are we to judge it? We can only judge it by secondary manifestations and some of those are difficult to bring under examination. The man who has a steady job, who year by year is working well, who is getting his increments, and who is partially educated, and can express himself in English, perhaps we could say that on the average his character and judgment are probably reasonable. He may have some failings in his character. He may have moral failings, but in general he is a responsible, steady-working citizen.

Now, the Commission also suggests that the income qualification should be on the basis of at least two years' standing, and that is another check and a useful one. The Commission asked the Department of Labour to make a survey to find out what kind of people were getting £15 a month today in Southern Rhodesia. The survey showed that in general an African drawing £15 a month has passed well beyond unskilled labour and may be regarded as a reasonably responsible person.

There are those hon. members who may say "Why the hurry? Why not let things slide? We have got on all right for 60 years. Why all this fuss?" Well, there are a number of reasons for this fuss. Times have changed. The African people themselves have changed. They are not the primitive people whom we met here in 1890, and their change has made them demand changes of us also. As the Commission points out, this is not just a constitutional issue, it is the first and basic step in the settlement of the whole future of race relationship in the Colony. If you admit that statement from the Commission, there is no need to go further in pointing out what an important matter this is. However, if we do need anything else, I would remind you of another matter. I would remind you of the Communist threat to Africa, and it is a real threat. There is no doubt whatsoever about that. To the south of us, the Union of South Africa is most sensitive about it. Americans who have been through this continent lately have also, on their observation, pointed out that there is a real Communist threat. Richard Nixon put it in its full magnitude the other day in these words: "Africa is a major target of Communist infiltration and intrigues, and if the Communists were to succeed in controlling it, they could control the world."

That gives some idea of our part. It may be a small part, but it is a most important part as far as our responsibility is concerned.—[MR. KELLER: He wants America to control it.]—Well, if it comes to the point of America controlling the world, or Russia controlling the world, should I agree with the hon. member or disagree with him. I would prefer to see America controlling the world.

Sir, our relationship also to the federal government is of importance. There has been some comment lately to the effect that we are perhaps not playing our full part in making the Federation a success, and there have been some who have rather pictured us as letting the side down. I would refute any such suggestion. We have been concerned over the years with a non-racial approach to the franchise in Southern Rhodesia, and it is up to us to endeavour to have that non-racial approach not only enshrined in our own legislation and regulations, but if possible also in the Federal regulations.

I recognize that the federal government has been forced to accept the racial approach—I know that it is on a temporary basis—by the United Kingdom Government; and I know that because of the racial representation within the Federal Parliament, they have problems to face which we do not have in our own House.

Before the recent conference in Great Britain, we had assured the Federal Prime Minister not only of our acceptance of his plans to enlarge the Federal House and make certain other changes which would require constitutional amendments, but we had told him of our enthusiasm for his plans, and that we would support such constitutional changes as would be required to bring them into effect. Where we did disagree was on the question of Federal franchise in so far as it affects our country of Southern Rhodesia, because we do not want to accept any system which has a racial basis. However, we do recognize how important it is, if it is humanly possible, to get agreement on these matters and regarding this particular matter I would point out that the federal government does not depend upon our permission to legislate, as it does depend upon our permission when constitutional issues are before it.

Sir, we all want to see the machinery of Government for the Federation strengthened and we will cooperate in every possible way. Within Southern Rhodesia, agreement between the federal government and ourselves on qualifications for the franchise would mean one set of electoral rolls, which is, if not the only consideration, a very important matter in our electoral system. I believe it is possible for us to come to agreement on this matter, so that the one set of rolls would do for both Federal elections and for our own, although the delimitation of constituencies would of course be different.

This is a very urgent and practical issue that we are facing and must face, not only in this House, but also in cooperation and consultation with the federal government, because I believe that both governments will require to bring forward legislation in their Budget sessions this year.

Besides this immediate issue there are wider issues which also confront us, and these are none the less urgent. Because of the fear of being too early with progressive measures, some would condemn us to waiting until we are too late; to wait until that moment when, because we have lacked imagination and courage to grasp our present problems, we find ourselves overwhelmed by a tide of black nationalism or world Communism.

I believe, Sir, that that is not putting the matter too highly. The problem is great. I have faith that if the government puts forward sound, liberal legislation before this House, the electorate will back it, and I hope that the members of this House will have confidence not only in the electorate but in themselves and will put on the statute books of this country the kind of legislation which will promote sound racial relations and lead to a period of peace and prosperity.

Immorality Debate Speech

In April 1957 two members of Todd's party moved to amend the Immorality Act that forbade sexual relations between black males and white females outside of marriage proposing: "That the Immorality and Indecency Suppression Act be amended to prohibit illegal sexual intercourse between a European male and an African female." Todd and other liberals in the Rhodesia United Party wanted to abolish the act, believing that the law was anachronistic, unenforceable, and simply racially motivated. Ian Hancock argued that Todd's opposition to the Immorality motion marks Todd's transition to a true liberal that set him on a collision course with his cabinet and party.[23] Hardwicke Holderness explained that whatever were Todd's "reasons and however well expressed," his opposition counted "as an indelible black mark against him as a politician looking for white votes and as a Prime Minister depended upon by his colleagues to command them."[24] Holderness correctly noted, "Garfield's speech was well-researched and as conciliatory as possible but uncompromising."[25] Todd presented carefully crafted arguments refuting the protection the law supposedly brought to women, exposing its racial nature, and showing it was unenforceable. He also thoroughly researched all the previous legislative debates from Rhodesian history. It shows Todd's reasoning and argumentative abilities at his best. Despite Todd's efforts the vote was 15 in favor of the motion, including all four of Todd's cabinet ministers and 9 against, including Todd.[26] The speech text is from the *Southern Rhodesian Legislative Debates*, vol. 39, pp. 1327–39. The speech was delivered May 1, 1957.

The Prime Minister: Mr. Speaker, I do not think any of us, whether we are for the motion or against the motion, are particularly happy this afternoon in this debate; but I know the hon. member who brought the motion forward did so with the very best of intentions, and I am sure whether we are for or against it we are all sincere in our intentions.

At first glance, the motion which is before us seems perfectly clear. It is concerned *prima facie*, anyway, with morality. It sets a high standard and it treats European men and African women in the same way as the law of 1903 treats European women and African men, and on the face of it that would seem to be fair play. I would like to be on the side of morality and fair play.

But, Mr. Speaker, this is frankly a racial measure and not a measure which is concerned with morality.

The hon. member for Eastern (Dr. Alexander) came nearer the point. I do not know whether he said he would support a Bill, but he almost went as far as to say that there should be a Bill to make all sexual relations outside of marriage illegal. That, at least, is being honest and going the whole way.

I believe that the Act of 1903 has nothing whatever to do with the present situation, has nothing whatever to do with the protection of the women today. I would be the last person to suggest that we do away with any law which is really there to protect the women and girls of either the European race or the African race and if we do not have enough legal sanctions to protect the women of both races, then I would certainly agree to sponsor such legislation in this House. But let us consider the legislation which we have already on our statute books and also, of course, to the provision under common law for some of the protection that is provided. Indeed, a great deal of it comes under the common law. As far as assault of any kind, whether ordinary assault or rape or attempted rape are concerned there are no statutes, but these matters are covered by the common law and covered fully. Then, in regard to indecent assault of any kind we have the Criminal Law Amendment Act of 1953 and against other assaults of different kinds, immorality and so on, we have the Immorality and Indecency Suppression Act, Section 4. I hold that we have adequate laws to protect the women and girls of all races in this Colony.

Then you may ask why was the law of 1903 put on the Statute Book—there was a very special reason. Other hon. members have taken the trouble to read up the debates, and I also have spent a great deal of time on these early debates and I think in putting forward what I have to say I am putting forward the truth as it stood then. In 1901 the brothels in this country were closed under an Immorality Suppression Act and in 1903 it was pointed out that there were a number of European women in Southern Rhodesia who were of such a low type that they were consorting freely with native males. There were very few European women in Southern Rhodesia in 1903 and they put forward their view that the actions of these unfortunate people, all of whom were known to the police, were placing them in a very serious and unfortunate position in relation to African men as such. They held that the actions of these dissolute European women could lead Africans to believe that all European women were of this type and for that very particular reason the law of 1903 was put on the Statute Book and it was possible to carry out the provisions of that law because every one of the dissolute women were known to the police. There were not many of them.

In 1916 the law came up for revision and apparently in the 1903 law you could not convict unless you could prove that these particular European women had consorted with Africans for gain and so in 1916 the phrase "for gain" was taken out of the law and the Attorney-General stated in May, 1916, in the second reading of the Southern Rhodesia Immorality and Indecency Suppression Ordinance: "It was special legislation to meet actual needs and was not based on moral considerations. It was a law to preserve the prestige of the white race and to prevent anything which might endanger the honour of white women." I am going to make it specific, as I said it was specific in 1903. "There were still," he said, "a few degenerate women against whom complaints had been made." That was the reason for the passing of that law in 1903. The reason was still there in 1916 and because of that special reason that law was amended and today we are being asked to be just and to apply the same provisions on the other side when the circumstances have passed long ago.

By 1921 apparently things were changing and Sir Charles Coghlan, the first prime minister, said: "Let them take away in this country the law against the special danger to which it was found women were exposed in 1903." It had been moved that in the cause of justice the law should apply also to European men and African women and Sir Charles Coghlan said that the way to meet this matter and to give real justice was to take away what was no longer necessary, that special law which was passed to meet a special danger in 1903.

Now, the hon. member for Eastern (Dr. Alexander) has stated that in the years of his experience as a doctor he has only had three or four cases where he has attended European women who were pregnant by a native male and that in each case the women were of a low mentality and also the circumstances under which they had lived had cut them off from ordinary social contacts, and yet we find in this supposedly civilized country that those people were put in gaol.

I have discussed this matter with two learned judges, both of whom have had experience in other countries and both of whom have had experience in this country and both of them told of the unfortunate things which had happened and which do happen today under the provisions of this Act. One of these learned judges said to me:

> I have never in my judicial life had a case of this type before me where I wanted to use the law that is provided. All the cases that I have had

during my experience have been the most pitiful and heart-rending cases and I have been obliged to declare these people criminals on top of the tragedy which they already faced.

All the same, I can hardly believe that this is the right time to dispense with this law, for we should first give it such careful consideration as would assure the European women and others in this country that they do not depend for their protection upon its clauses. But if the House wishes, the government would be prepared to give further consideration to the matter and then after full consideration would give the House the opportunity to repeal this statute.

Over the years this matter has come up from time to time and maybe it is to be wondered, if the case were as clear-cut as the hon. mover has endeavoured to point out, that legislators down through 54 years have turned down the suggested amendment on each occasion. It has come up every five to ten years in one guise or another, a question or motion or in some other form, yet on every occasion it has been turned down.

I was interested to see that in the Hansard debate, I think of 1921, Mrs. Tawse Jollie stood against those who were prepared to make the Act applicable to European men and native women. She spoke at some length on it. I cannot go into all the things she said, but she eventually stated that there should be further investigations, and she regretted she could not support the motion.

Mr. Speaker, when Mr. McChlery, who has been mentioned today, moved the adjournment of the debate in 1921 he said that it was the legislation that they had in the country that had occasioned that demand on the part of the women of the country. He would like to see it repealed, but the women did not want it repealed. Perhaps if he had put to the women that their safety did not in any way depend upon it, they might have had a different idea. That is why I suggest that the House would probably be unwise to accept the amendment which has been moved by the hon. member for Bulawayo East (Mr. Abrahamson) this afternoon because I know they probably believe that their safety depends upon it.

Now, the Union of South Africa Government has introduced a number of Immorality Acts. They introduced another two or three weeks ago. In 1927 they passed the straight one between white people and black people. Since then they have taken further steps, in this evolution on a racial basis. Where we are prepared, apparently, to allow coloureds, Indians and so on to consort with either Europeans or with Africans, because it is not suggested we should have legislation covering these relationships, they have decided that the white race will be restricted and protected by law in every particular. As the hon.

member for Bulawayo East (Mr. Abrahamson) has pointed out, and I think absolutely rightly, this would only be the beginning of a long series of Acts in this country also. When you start legislating for moral matters and particularly for racial matters, I am sure you just have to keep on legislating. You will be forever finding holes in the legislation you have and you are committed for all time to patching up the legislation. Anyway, in 1927 the Union of South Africa prohibited illicit carnal intercourse between European men and native women. There are very great difficulties if you introduce such an Act. It is very difficult for the police to get convictions. What the accused would have to do would be to prove that there was some colour either in the one person or the other. If he could prove that or even if he could throw enough doubt on the racial side, then it would not be possible to get a conviction.

In 1929 in this country there was a petition from the coloured community and the officer commanding the Criminal Investigation Department then said: "I submit that any such action, and moral influence deprecating miscegenation will combat this evil more successfully than any legislation, the general enforcement of which would, in my opinion, be impossible and not intended now, and still less in the future, with appreciable result."

1930 came and Mr. Huggins then moved in this House: "That the government take into consideration the advisability of introducing legislation on the lines of the Union of South Africa Act No. 5 of 1927." Mr. Huggins during his address pointed out that he had not thought up this bright idea for himself. He had been asked by the Premier to introduce the motion because, it had been brought forward to the Premier by a women's organization. Mr. Huggins, during the course of the debate, did not show a great deal of enthusiasm for the measure. As the hon. member for Gatooma (Mr. Buchan) mentioned, in conclusion, Mr. Huggins spoke of the bad press that Rhodesians had got in London recently on the matter of liquor and then he said: "If there is no real necessity for this suggested legislation it would be as well if no Bill were introduced on the subject because otherwise we shall have the London press pointing out that we are not only drunkards but beasts."

In 1930 there was another demand on the part of an organization and the police again made this comment:

> In my opinion preventive legislation is not required and, even if it were adopted, would—as in the Union of South Africa—be practically unenforceable in view of the difficulties of detection, especially in the case of voluntary intercourse; moreover, I am entirely in accord with the opinion expressed by the hon. the Premier that the necessity for this drastic legislation is past.

But in 1931 the Government did at least have a shot at preparing a Bill in case it were needed and there is on record the typescript of what purports to be a Bill to prohibit cohabitation between European males and African females which was to have had the title "Immorality Act, 1931," although as far as we can find it was never read in this House. The Bill provided the punishment of offenders with a fine of £200—which would be worth about £600 now I suppose—and imprisonment for three years which is still worth three years, it has not been devalued—or both, as well as deportation.

But interestingly enough, not all women's organizations were in favour of this type of legislation and may I say that not all European women today are in favour of it. I have no societies backing me in my address this afternoon but there are a number of European women of intelligence and repute who are in agreement with what I am saying today; in 1931 the Matabeleland Women's Institute sent forward this resolution:

> That this Federation, having regard to the upholding of race purity and the unhappy lot of the innocent offspring, condemns the offence of miscegenation in any form, but it deplores extremely the idea that legislation should be introduced for the punishment of the offender, as it considers that such punishment would only tend to lower his or her standard of life, and that the question of legislation should be considered very carefully in relation to the offspring of such unions and their relations to the poorer Europeans.

Another three years passed and in 1934 there came a motion before the Reform Party Congress in September 1934. It was resolved at the instance of its Women's Branch, to recommend legislation to combat miscegenation, but at that time the hon. the Prime Minister, Mr. Huggins, expressed himself averse to any legislation likely to make criminals, and felt that the matter was best dealt with by public opinion.

Then there was a long silence. From 1934, for 17 years I can find no trace of anyone bringing this matter up, but in 1951 Mr. Eastwood in this House asked the hon. the Minister of Justice and Internal Affairs whether he would introduce legislation in regard to miscegenation to enact the same penalties for European males and Native females as now apply to European females and Native males. The hon. the Minister in his reply suggested that Mr. Eastwood should raise the matter as a motion in the House so that it could be debated, and nothing further was heard of the matter.

Now, Sir, much has been said about the offspring of Europeans and Africans, and it is true that many of them are being brought up in surroundings which do us no credit and do the country no credit, but if there is any suggestion that these people are a lower breed or less capable, then I would refute that completely.—[AN HON: MEMBER: Hear, hear.]

It is suggested that we do not know of Euro-African shorthand-typists but that is only because we have had a secondary school for these people for only about four or five years. There has been a great lack of willingness by Europeans to accept the responsibility which should have been accepted long ago with regard to these Coloured children.—[AN HON. MEMBER: Hear, hear.]—Not only that, but certain statements made this afternoon are, I think, an insult to the Coloured people in general. There are a great many other Coloured people who from legitimate marriages have produced children, one I know myself has nine children, who have helped to swell the total over the years from 1,000 to 8,000. I, myself, have many friends among the Coloured community who are worthy people. Amongst them are fully trained mechanics, teachers, drivers, nurses and people in positions of responsibility, and holding some place in the community of Southern Rhodesia. (Applause.)—[AN HON. MEMBER: In spite of their drawbacks?]—It was said that when these people grow up they reproduce people of their own kind. What can be taken from a statement like that? We can only gather that people of their own kind are not worthy. We, in this country, are all against miscegenation. Under the circumstances which exist in Southern Africa, it is very unwise, to say the least of it, but I am quite amazed at the action of the churches. I also, would like to be on the side of the churches, but I wonder if the hon. member has put before the churches what is involved. This is not a moral question; it is a racial question. I cannot understand the churches—and so many of them—giving their backing as so many of them have apparently given their backing to a motion which is just as racial as anything in the Union of South Africa, except that on the face of it admittedly it gives justice. I have said that *prima facie* it seemed a just measure, but it is a racial and not a moral measure.

As far as the Africans are concerned, it has been suggested in recent comment and also this afternoon that the African people were feeling so angry about the fact that European men were consorting with African women—and a number of them do—that it had led to murders. That has not been proved, but I think we can say without any fear of contradiction that the number of African people who would be prepared to back any such assault of that kind is small indeed.

I think it is unfortunate that the work of some maniacs has been interpreted to mean that the African community at large will go to such lengths to stop immoral relations between European men and African women. I do not believe it and, Sir, all the evidence goes to the contrary.

It is true that in the reserves there have been a number of African girls who have brought forth Coloured children and I, going through the reserves and knowing the people as I believe I do, have seen many instances of this but I have not found any violent reaction. In fact, I would like to pay a very warm tribute to the African people for their kindness and readiness to have in their villages the offspring of these illegitimate unions. Over the years they have looked after these children and there is much to be said in appreciation of the action they have taken. Not only that, Sir, but in general I believe the Africans have shown that while they do not like miscegenation, they have not reacted so violently that they would go to the lengths of assault and murder.

I have spoken about this matter to Africans including a number of leading Africans in this country. So far I have not met one of them who demanded that we pass the amendment under discussion this afternoon, but they want the law that is on the Statute Book repealed, and I think there are many reasons why it should be repealed. The first reason is that it is an insult to the European women of this country today.—[HON. MEMBERS: Hear, hear.)—(Applause.)—The second reason is that on the face of it, it is a completely racial law and is not just.

Last month a very similar motion to this was brought before the Northern Rhodesia House. Mr. Gaunt, on the 27th March, moved: "That this Council is of the opinion that miscegenation should be made a criminal offence when it takes place between non-Africans and Africans as defined in the Interpretation Ordinance, Chapter 1." I am not going into the debate. It was not a tremendously long debate, but an African spoke and his speech so impressed me that I want to mention it. I have not taken it all. Some of his English was a little difficult to follow. I am reading it in his words. Mr. Chileshe said:

> The House is being asked to make miscegenation a criminal offence. I think that this motion can be very well intentioned. From many aspects of life, we know that this type of association is not a desirable one. Those of us who through contact have seen the results of that type of association, particularly as the hon. member for the Midlands Electoral Area has explained, with regard to their offspring. Some people in the African community think the offspring are really much better off. They are better regarded and they are better cared for than their African counterparts. I think it is a matter of raising the moral standards of the people. It is a

matter of getting the people to know that the colour of a person or whatever it may be does not matter. What matters mostly is the personality that is within him and, secondly, that if he is going to continue to exhibit the purity of his kind it is really his duty to see that he did only those things which would help to preserve the identity, the qualities and those characteristics which are particular to that species to which he belongs. That is really the fundamental law which would abolish all of this, and if people had this understanding in them, even if they associated, it would be mere association, like any other person would associate with another person, for mere exchange of information, but it would be a sad thing if by a motion like this, if when a person of the European race, for instance, might be seen moving about with my daughter and just chatting, people say: "This is one of the undesirable ones. He is in the company of that black girl. What do you think?" Similarly, if an African man is found in the same way in association and people begin to talk, that is where it is most undesirable that a thing like this motion should come before this House, because it begins to suggest in the minds of some that there can be no other association, which I deplore, because some of us have got to enjoy the conversation and talk about what we have and nothing more. I will not support a motion of this kind because it is exhibiting things really that are unnecessary and which I understand that the best of our men and women on both sides would not want to indulge in.

I think that is a remarkable speech and one which would do credit to anybody.

Now, Sir, coming to the year 1957, in Southern Rhodesia, the police advise us that if such legislation is enacted it would be easy to enforce against the comparatively small number of European males—I think about 70 are known—who co-habit more or less openly with African females, but it would be more difficult to detect the more numerous clandestine associations which take place between European males and African prostitutes in the larger urban centres. Legislation might deter many potential offenders as well as remove the grounds for complaint against discriminatory laws, but the difficulties of detection and the opportunities for blackmailing activities by prostitutes and their protectors should not be overlooked.

Sir, there is a great deal of truth in that and any one of you who knows the African people and who knows the outside districts will know that there are some surprising names among the Coloured children and I am certainly not convinced that all of those names are rightly given to those Coloured children. After all, if you have to find a European name for your child, why not give him the best you can find or at least one of the good ones, and I am not convinced that a number of the names really belong to the children who bear them. If they do, there are a number of . . . We will not say any more.

If we are going to pass a law like this, if we are a government worthy of our name we will do our best to enforce it, for it is most distressing and frustrating to have laws that are not enforceable.

I have been particularly concerned with the liquor laws and what has particularly disturbed me is the fact that we are not successful in enforcing some of them. One of the most difficult ones has been the law concerning the selling of liquor to Africans. It is broken continually, and it just makes a farce of the law if you are not getting the cooperation of the people or if there are other practical difficulties which make it impossible to have it properly upheld.

Sir, I hope that all the laws we will pass in this House will be practical laws that we will really have a hope of enforcing. The motives behind the motion today are good ones; I do not doubt that in the slightest, but I think that in the first place the position was not fully known, and in the second place it is impractical to say the least, to bring forward a motion of this kind. I said, Sir, that it would be difficult to get convictions. I have a letter here. I will not say who it is from but it is from someone who has known for some years past, conditions in the Union of South Africa. I would like to read a paragraph. Let us see if you would like to see this sort of thing happen in our country:

> I may also state that it frequently happens in practice that the Native female involved makes a confession or intimates that she will plead guilty to the charge. Her case is then tried first, and after conviction, she is used as a witness for the Crown against the European male. Too often the Crown relies upon her evidence to secure a conviction of the male accused, and fails because corroboration of her evidence is required. The result is that the less guilty party is punished, and the other escapes, and the Native regards this as a racial injustice. To obviate this, prosecutors now charge the two accused jointly in cases of this nature, and as the Court must consider the evidence against each accused separately, even in a joint trial, prosecutors now see that they are furnished with proof of the crime in defence of the plea, or confession of one of the accused before they institute proceedings.

That gives us some idea of the difficulties that are being experienced in the Union of South Africa. Sir, I do not believe that anybody in this House—in fact hon. members have indicated that—wants to go the way the Union of South Africa has gone. The reason for the motion today was to do justice, to treat things fairly and to endeavour to stop a practice which we do not like; but of course the practice which we should really condemn is immorality in general, and nobody has gone as far as saying that we should legislate against that. We also reject miscegenation, but remember that miscegenation is the mixing of species, and that miscegenation is not in itself an illicit thing. We are prepared to carry on and legalize miscegenation in marriage but it is outside of marriage that we wish to make it illegal. If we are going to allow people of mixed race to marry, we are not being as honest as the people in the Union of South Africa, and I would not like to see us go as far as they do. There they say:

> You shall not marry. If you go out of the country and marry and come back again, your marriage is annulled. If you are married and one of you is coloured and the other is white, and you believe that you are both white, and after a few years it is found that one of you is not fully white, then your marriage must be annulled, but the children that have been born in the meantime will be counted legitimate.

Those are the extremes to which this sort of legislation, unless we are most careful, could bring us. It is a long time since we have passed a completely racial law in this House, and I hope that we will not decide to pass one now.

Sir, I believe that as far as this motion is concerned, it does almost reach back into the past to hit our Coloured population. A number of these people are married and the children are legitimate; others have not been so fortunate, but there is nobody in this House in their attitude to illegitimate children, who is going to make it more difficult than is possible for them. I believe that is so I hold that the passing of a law of this kind is certainly not going to make things easier for the Coloured people of this country.

Now, Sir, I would like to give you the latest comment that we have had from the police on the legislation which is suggested today. This is the last paragraph of the report which has been given to us. "From the police point of view it must be said that any such legislation, although it might serve as a nominal deterrent, could only be enforced by a continued clandestine observation and intrusion of a type that would probably not be tolerated by our people."

There are many points of view, but I do think it would be unwise to instruct the government to bring in the legislation that has been suggested. I think it would be unwise to accept the amendment which is before the House. I have the greatest sympathy with those who have brought this motion before the House today. I hope that they will realize that while I have fought perhaps vehemently, I have fought because I believe it would be very much in the worst interests of this country to contemplate such legislation; not only because of the effect overseas—and it would do us enormous damage overseas, it would be high-lighted throughout the free world—but because of the damage it would do us here and we cannot have the young men of our police force used as vice squads, or at least I do not think we can.

The belief that public opinion is not a strong factor is, I believe, wrong. I believe that the churches, that public opinion in general, that all good people both on the African side and on the European side, will recognize that it is inadvisable, to put it at its lowest, and most unfortunate for white and black that there should be miscegenation—either the illicit miscegenation which is being deplored today—or even marriage—in this country at the present time anyway and also as far as we can see into the future. I hope that hon. Members may support an amendment which I feel I must move and that is, Mr. Speaker, that we omit all the words after "That" and substitute "miscegenation be deplored."

Reply to the Toast "Southern Rhodesia" by the Prime Minister of Southern Rhodesia at the St. Andrew's Night Banquet at Bulawayo Saturday, November 30, 1957

Tradition held that the prime minister would give an important speech at the Caledonian Society's celebration of St. Andrew's Night on November 30 because so many white Rhodesians were of Scottish descent. The African National Congress, organized under the leadership of Joshua Nkomo and George Nyandoro, was the main organization pushing African nationalism. As the ANC became increasingly militant, Todd was caught in the growing tensions between white extremism and African nationalism. Unlike later prime ministers, Todd knew the African leaders and was a personal friend of Nkomo, so Todd would meet and talk with them. Whites and some of Todd's cabinet were alarmed over this personal contact, the new franchise laws, and other perceived pro-African actions on Todd's part. Africans sensing Todd's pro-African stance pressed for more and faster liberalization or a real partnership. Todd recalled, "I felt that I must put a brake on the nationalist demands so as to give the white electorate some assurance that the Government was in control of the situation."[27] The speech contains attacks on African nationalist agendas that can be found in his earlier speeches as prime minister, included in this volume. However, Todd was in transition, on the verge of his ouster as prime minister. Todd states, "At the time, and increasingly since, I was unhappy and eventually ashamed of that speech, especially the tone of it."[28] Todd was increasingly uncomfortable and soon to be too impatient as the politician working within the system trying to balance the impulses of contradictory constituencies. Soon he was to be a prophet calling for African democratic rights and challenging the system to correct injustices. The text is reproduced from the press release of the speech text and can be found in the Todd papers in possession of Susan Paul.

We all know that if a freedom-loving people wish to keep their liberty they must be eternally vigilant. One of the most difficult tasks of government is to balance responsibility on the one hand with the desire to make further concessions towards the growing liberty of the individual citizen, particularly the African. The Southern Rhodesia Government has pursued a vigorous programme designed to extend the influence of private enterprise, and to provide an increasing degree of liberty for the individual. Liberty is not just freedom to do anything one wants but opportunity to fulfil one's finest potentials and it can be regarded both from the individual's standpoint and, taking a wider view, from the angle of the country itself.

In the wider view, the denationalising of the steel industry, the sale of the State sugar enterprise, have brought new freedom, fresh opportunity, and a great deal of new capital flowing in to the country. The setting up of various courts and boards, for example in Town Planning, has taken power from officialdom and placed it increasingly in the hands of local residents. The introduction of the Land Husbandry Scheme promises to three hundred thousand African peasant farmers a greater degree of freedom than had ever before been contemplated. The immediate results of giving ownership and dignity are seen in a doubling, and even a trebling, of production per acre. Another example of the policy is the granting to Africans of a ninety-nine year leasehold of land near industry and the provision of such assistance as had already made it possible for thousands of Africans over the past eighteen months to acquire their own homes in town.

It is quite obviously in the best interests of Rhodesia that our population should be strengthened as individuals and that increasing freedom should be granted where it can be demonstrated that such concessions will be accepted responsibly and not debauched into licence.

In line with such a policy has been the introduction of legislation to ease the Pass laws and allow greater freedom of personal movement. In four years of work our Southern Rhodesia Government, with a marked unity of purpose, has worked to a programme providing the type of climate in which private enterprise can flourish, and has taken the strongest action in extending the privileges of property ownership.

A far-sighted plan for the extension of a sound and practical educational programme was introduced two years ago and the African people as a whole responded splendidly to the challenge that they should contribute an extra half million pounds a year to make the scheme financially possible.

A select Committee of Parliament has for the past two years worked unremittingly on the principles and details of a new Industrial Conciliation Bill designed to maintain European standards of attainment in skills and wages and at the same time to make possible increased African participation in the industry of the country. Also envisaged is a gradual extension of democratic bargaining in the fixing of agreed wages and conditions of service.

Through all our planning has been the determination to maintain our standards, but our policy has never been in conflict with that deep purpose of liberality which has always been the mark of the Rhodesian. It was in the best interests of the country that while this liberal spirit continues to be demonstrated in the maintenance of colour-free electoral laws, the qualification for the vote should have been raised to a standard which ensures the future political stability of the country.

And now I announce that we have been, for the past three months, concerning ourselves with the preparation of further security legislation which is of course of a restrictive nature; legislation which could be used to restrict the freedom of both individuals and organisations.

What follows is said in the hope that public opinion, both European and African, will be so roused in the support of freedom for the individual and the maintenance of good relationships between the races and between the forces of law and order and the people themselves, that we may yet be able to refrain from bringing our new security measure before Parliament in February next.

In Southern Rhodesia there is no cause for alarm, and in general the relationships between our peoples are good. However, the farmer who takes no action when he sees the beginnings of erosion, when it is at that point easily controlled, has only himself to blame if, after a few years of neglect, he faces a situation which can only be set right at great cost and enormous effort. Our feelings are just as deeply affected when we see in Southern Rhodesia signs of erosion amongst the people. My government has at no point in its four years of service shirked taking a firm line when that was considered necessary, and our present actions are based on the belief that prevention is better than cure.

Some months ago, when the African National Congress was formed, I was asked for my views on its significance and for the reactions of the government. I said that we would wait and take careful note of what happened. At that time there were one or two matters which concerned us, but Mr. Nkomo, to whom had been given the leadership of Congress, was known to be not only well-educated and capable, but a responsible person. The choice of the name "Congress" was not reassuring for its popular appeal was likely to be on the lines of the northern Congresses whose influence in Southern Rhodesia has grown. The Constitution which was accepted was a reasonably responsible document but we did not know whether Mr. Guy Clutton-Brock and the others who helped frame it meant it to be a rule of conduct for Congress members in Southern Rhodesia, or propaganda to place in the hands of the Africa Bureau and other friends overseas. We did not know what influence Mr. Clutton-Brock would be able to exert, or how responsible other leaders, official and unofficial, would be.

The best thing to do was to wait and see the kind of fruit the tree would bear and here are some of those fruits. It may be that Congress will feel that my criticisms are not just, and it is my endeavour to disclaim responsibility. We have seen in Northern Rhodesia, where Congress has been allowed to pursue its unfortunate way, that when a major crime is committed which is a natural outcome of a campaign against constituted authority, that both Congress and the individual who wrecked the train hasten to proclaim that it was not the act of Congress. It could well be that it was not the direct responsibility of Congress, but can Congress really side step the guilt when its actions and statements build up an atmosphere of boycott, strike and violence in a country?

In Southern Rhodesia Mr. George Nyandoro has in effect supplanted Mr. Nkomo in effective leadership and, with other Congress members, campaigns against those Africans who wish to take their place amongst the civilised and responsible community which governs Southern Rhodesia. Africans who join the present political parties are termed "sellouts," "Judas Iscariots," "foolish people" and they are warned that they will be dealt with in due course. A leading member of the African Congress inferred in Salisbury last week that the Congress would determine what is in the African interests, and "that those who pursued courses which were detrimental to the African interest should be dealt with accordingly."

At a recent meeting in a Native Reserve another leading Congress member instructed that European store-keepers in the Reserves should be approached for financial support and that if they refused they should be reported to Congress. "I will know what to do with them," said the speaker.

At recent Congress meetings held in reserves near Salisbury the chiefs have been flouted and members of the police force humiliated. There are no laws governing such matters and there should be no need for them. African people have very strong traditions of courtesy, but what shocks them today in the undignified and irresponsible conduct of some Congress leaders, could well attract them tomorrow.

In a totalitarian country resistance and violence may be the only means which are available to the people, but in Southern Rhodesia there are democratic ways of approach to authority. In Southern Rhodesia pressure on Government can be exerted by the vote, and the franchise law has no racial restrictions.

The ways of democracy are slower, more normal in their growth and sound, and the European people of this country have shown themselves liberal in their outlook and ready to accept into the voting and governing circle all citizens without regard to race, who show goodwill and who meet the requirements laid down in law.

Congress, on the other hand, does not concern itself with voters, but is endeavouring, by its actions, and in conflict with its constitution, to discipline a mass-machine whose powers would not be exerted through the vote, but through some type of mass action. As part of this plan it must find ways of prohibiting Africans from taking part in the democratic life of the country and this it is doing by threats and by endeavours to humiliate.

If the Federation is to fulfil its great promise and become a worthy democratic nation we need to bring into our political parties now all courageous, capable Africans who are ready to cooperate and I would compliment Mr. Winston Field on the many meetings he has recently held with Africans. What lies before us—cooperation or unrelenting racialism? It is the first duty of the government to provide protection for all our people, and this we will continue to do, even if it means introducing further legal restrictions. If, on the other hand, leaders in Congress and particularly Mr. Clutton-Brock and Mr. Nyandoro would throw in their weight with the forces of law and order, if they would give their support to the cause of racial harmony, we could in the next three months halt the erosion which has started and make further restrictions unnecessary.

Times of change, of development and of adjustment are always fraught with danger, and in such times powerful emotions can easily be stirred. May I give the solemn undertaking that the government recognises these things and that we can be depended upon to keep firm control and not delay decisions when the security of the country may depend upon our action.

PROPHETIC SPEECHES

Statement against the "Colour Bar"
March 10, 1959

On March 16, 1959, Todd made four successive extemporaneous presentations opposing the continued efforts of white Rhodesian society to segregate the races and maintain white privilege. The audience at the speeches represented at the time the largest gathering to ever hear a public speech in Southern Rhodesian history. Unfortunately no extant recording exists for any of the four presentations. However, a copy of Todd's statement given a week earlier that eventually prompted the speeches is reproduced below. The statement contains the ideas and arguments that Todd presented in the March 16 speeches. When compared with what liberal whites were saying in the United States in 1959, Todd's proposals were extraordinary. No one was making comparable arguments in such a public venue, nor was anyone with Todd's stature as a former head of state saying anything comparable. The statement is reproduced from the *Rhodesia Herald* of March 10, 1959, 1, 3.

The whole future of the Federation is being threatened and we are indebted to governments, to our police and our troops as they work to restore order.

Under the circumstances which obtain when military and police action is taken on a wide scale innocent people suffer as well as the guilty and every citizen should give full support to the government so that the emergency can be brought to an end at the earliest moment.

All that we have worked for over the years is in jeopardy and time has run out. Party politics and individual political ambitions pale into insignificance as we face our problems and our future will depend upon whether there are enough Europeans and enough Africans of any party who are today ready to implement the policies of partnership which we have talked about, for the past five years.

The Federal Prime Minister has said: "But when the price is paid and, I trust, the lesson learned, all races will have reason to be most hopeful for the future of this country." The Prime Minister is not explicit regarding what are the lessons, or who is to learn them, but I suggest that there are many lessons to be learned and that the greatest responsibility for the future lies with the present almost entirely European electorate, for with them alone lies the power to make the necessary changes.

There is only one policy which can guarantee the safety of all our citizens and that is the policy of partnership, but that policy cannot flourish in a country where there is a rigid colour bar. These two concepts are irreconcilable.

Under our present circumstances the colour bar is the responsibility of Europeans not Africans. However, unless it is broken massively and immediately, it will not pass from this land and within five years it will be used by Africans against Europeans and partnership will become an impossible ideal. The great majority of our white people are of British extraction and they should be able to break down a barrier which is foreign to the best in our tradition.

The Rhodesias and the Union of South Africa are the last countries of importance where a man is judged by the colour of his skin, when actions and personal relationships are so greatly influenced by race. After five years of so-called partnership in Rhodesia, an African citizen, educated, clean, well dressed and ambitious for the progress of his family and his country remains a second-class citizen in his own land; unable to enter, for example, cinemas, and unable even to become a fireman on the government-owned railways.

The serious mistakes which the federal government has made threaten the whole Federal structure. The federal government should not have limited the main electoral roll through high qualifications, to an almost entirely European electorate, and then under such circumstances to have announced that it would seek dominion status in 1960, for this is a policy designed to place the entire control of the Federation in the hands of an almost exclusively European electorate—the very antithesis of partnership.

While this situation remains we are without hope, and an immediate statement should be made by the United Kingdom and federal governments to the effect that dominion status will neither be sought nor granted until a satisfactory degree of confidence has been achieved between Africans and Europeans and the Electoral Act has been so changed as to allow responsible Africans, even if their present economic status is low, to have a vote of equal value in the government of the Federation.

Instead of a meeting of governments in 1960 to consider dominion status we need immediately meetings of governments to consider such matters as:—

- The economic advancement of all sections of the community on terms of complete equality of opportunity;

- The political development of the Federation with planning to achieve full powers for all governments within the Federation at the earliest date consonant with the growing ability of the people of each State to govern themselves and to share in the government of the Federation;

- A survey of the whole field of human relations, with consideration of such measures as may build up a respect between the races and lead to a complete destruction of the colour bar as such.

We have made too many mistakes and the latest one is the determination to keep Africans and Europeans apart in post offices. The new proposals have made thoughtful Africans angry instead of grateful for this is a perpetuation of the colour bar by the federal government itself. If an African can sell stamps and give change, why should he not sell stamps to Europeans as well as Africans?

Let us recognise that these so-called pinpricks are wounds which will not heal until the irritations are stopped, and let us also realise that a great deal of what has to be done lies with ourselves in our daily contacts, with shop assistants, with employers and with men and women of different races as they work together.

This is our country—and the quicker we are freed from the embarrassments of our relationships with warring political parties in the United Kingdom the better for our national health, our progress and our very safety. However, we must recognise that "our" stands for seven million Africans, Asians and Eurafricans and 300,000 Europeans. Leading Africans must also be convinced that such freedom is in their best interests and this will not happen until such Africans share with us in government and in all the benefits of the development which is coming to the Federation.

Our Federation must become, without any further delay, a country where race or colour do not matter, and where the only criteria asked for are decency in living, consideration of the needs of others, a readiness to work hard and a determination on the part of all to uphold the law for the safety of our land.

After Independence, What? Political Imperatives

From his days as prime minister and for the rest of his career, Sir Garfield traveled extensively in the United States and Britain. His speaking ability, high credibility, and extensive knowledge of the African continent as Africa was emerging from colonialism made him a popular figure at colleges in the 1960s. Wellesley College, in Wellesley, Massachusetts, an outlying city of Boston near Harvard University, is a leading American liberal arts college for women. As a part of its intellectual life and interest in current political affairs, Wellesley sponsored a symposium on Africa and invited Todd to speak along with Julius Nyerere, who was touring the United States before he became president of Tanganyika (Tanzania).[29]

Even though it was less than two years since Todd was removed as prime minister, a dramatic shift had occurred in his political stance. Freed of the constraints of the office of prime minister and no longer a Southern Rhodesian MP, Todd now firmly advocated positions that only the African National Congress had articulated in the 1950s. Todd now fully realized that for real democracy to emerge in Rhodesia, the majority of black Africans would have to rule. He also knew that it was inevitable that Africans and not Europeans would run all the African nations. His paternalism was fading away. He was optimistic that Africans had the ability, if given the proper training and opportunity, to embrace what he called the "sweet reasonableness of democracy"—an idea undoubtedly reflecting his Churches of Christ background. Todd still placed great emphasis on the need for education, a consistent theme from his earliest political days, however the focus now was on developing a true democratic system for Africans where minority rights would be protected and war prevented. The speech indicts colonialism and eerily spells out the problems of postcolonialism if Africans were not properly helped. Todd pled for America and the West to work with Africa to develop African democracies. Like a true prophet his warning still has currency: "The free peoples of the world must work to ensure that freedom, liberty and opportunity be made the heritage of all men. We, who believe in democracy, cannot evade our responsibility, for liberty is threatened in America when it is denied in Africa; peace is in jeopardy when the minds of men are at war." The speech was delivered on Wednesday, February 17, 1960. The text is reproduced from a manuscript found in the Dr. Emory Ross papers, Disciples of Christ Historical Society, Nashville, Tennessee.

An American citizen introduced us to Africa when we first arrived in Bulawayo from New Zealand. "Don't make the mistake of thinking that the people here can't reach any standards you can set," he advised. "Give them of your best and believe in them. They won't let you down."

For more than 25 years, my wife and I have endeavoured to follow that advice and we have found it dependable. For those who do not know Africa, may I repeat it in other words. There are differences of colour and appearance, differences of custom, but if we wish to generalise, we will make fewer mistakes if we say that there are no differences at all between us—whether we are white Americans or brown Americans, whether we are white Frenchmen or black or brown or white Africans. We are all members of the great family of men, of one blood, and within us we have that divine spark that lights the hearts of all men.

It was no more remarkable for Jefferson to say that men had the right to "life, liberty and the pursuit of happiness" than it is for men in Africa to band themselves together to express this compelling belief in demands and actions. That is just what has happened, and to such effect that greater constitutional changes are in progress in these months than have been seen before in Africa in fifty years. 1960 will see two-thirds of all our people independent, 150 million citizens in seventeen free countries. Here are our new companions in the fellowship of Nations. They have arrived so suddenly and so unexpectedly that they have caught us unprepared. What welcome will they receive? How significant is this appearance? What are the great political imperatives that will carry Africans upon their way?

Africa, south of the great desert, appeared to sleep in the sun through the centuries, her people showing little desire to share in the struggle towards knowledge and more complex living. Twenty years ago, in Rhodesia, we were giving presents to children to entice them to school, and while boys would come, few girls were permitted to do so. Parents recognised that education has a powerful influence upon children and that girls who had been to school developed very definite views about whom they would marry. This was a discovery made by our own people many generations ago! But these attitudes have passed and throughout all Africa education is worked for, sacrificed for, lived for.

Today there is no going back to simple and primitive tribal ways. Independence cannot be used to turn a people back again to a type of life which, after all, can be lived only in seclusion and where there is almost unlimited land. The pressure on the land itself has increased so greatly in the past fifty years: probably the population has trebled in that time. Communications have destroyed privacy and Africa today is open to all the pressures and influences of the outside world.

Probably these very pressures brought three different colonial policies—so different in their outlook and methods—to bear the one fruit of independence, and at the one time. The British governed by indirect rule through the traditional authorities, the Chiefs. The whole system was controlled by one man, the Governor, who was answerable to Her Majesty's Secretary of State for the Colonies in London. In general, the system was a liberal one, designed to transfer power eventually to new African nations. It is said that in 1947 the Colonial Office prepared a splendid thirty-year plan to bring Ghana to independence. That story may be untrue but it highlights Britain's problem of recent years. She says thirty years to independence, the people say fifteen, and eventually it is ten.

The French were fortunate people. They had the finest citizenship, the widest liberalism, the freest freedom in the world and they were enchanted to extend these gifts to the farthest corner of overseas France. Government was from Paris, but to Paris came representatives from the Cameroons, from the Ivory Coast, from Chad and every overseas province. But with all the official desire and effort for liberty, equality and fraternity, economic standards of white Frenchmen were incomparably higher than those of Africans, and even on the political side, the vote of a Frenchman in France might well be worth the votes of a dozen French Africans.

The Belgians were a hard-headed practical people. Not for them these liberal and idealistic notions of sharing political power. Economic opportunity was something that Africans would understand. All you had to do was to control the press, forbid independent trade unions, isolate the people from outside influences, but give them a practical education. What the Belgians had to learn was that it is not possible to develop one side of a man's intellect and yet keep men from concerning themselves with freedom.

All these roads, heading, it seemed, in different directions, have led to freedom and self-government. Only the Portuguese know the dark road which does not appear to lead into the sunlight of freedom; but I believe that their road will prove to be just a few years longer. So the people come to govern themselves. Great political imperatives thrust the people to freedom and the same strengths must now carry them forward; but the leaders face changed conditions. It is relatively easy to lead an awakening people against an antagonist who can be seen—who stands out clearly white against a background of colonialism. But when that battle has been concluded, must there be another enemy—must it be the Chiefs, or the Opposition, or a neighbouring state; or will the new leaders be able then to turn to the great challenge of meeting the needs of their people? Will they be able to turn from fiery speeches to hard work, to careful planning, to wise statesmanship? The need of every African community is so vast that it could provide a challenge to unite the people, a task to test the strength of the finest leaders.

There are few parts of Africa today where every man could work on his own plot of land and produce from it all he needs. Anyway, that standard of existence is no longer acceptable and there are enough progressives in every community to leaven the whole. There can be no retreat to the simple life. One hundred years ago 80% of the people of America lived on the land; today, fewer than 20% produce the food for the whole community, and frightening surpluses besides! Every community throughout the world wants to walk this prosperous road, and Africa has joined the march.

The people of Africa are impelled to advance though few of them, as yet, could express their feelings in words such as these—words whose influence upon mankind cannot be measured:

> We hold these truths to be self-evident, that all men are created equal, that they are endowed by their Creator with certain unalienable Rights, that amongst these are life, liberty and the pursuit of happiness. That to secure these rights, Governments are instituted among Men, deriving their just powers from the consent of the governed.

Whether we watch from New York or London, we should recognise that these new nations can be understood—that their people have our weaknesses, our strengths and similar ambitions. In Africa there is greed but there is also unselfishness, there is hate and there is love—but in Africa, too, bad is bad and good is good—and whatever may be the barriers of speech, there are no barriers to the language of the heart.

The people of Africa have demanded that their leaders bring them to freedom and those leaders have responded; but this is just the entrance to a new age. There are people who do not know what freedom looks like—what it feels like. In Ghana, in 1957, a newspaper made a survey of what the people thought freedom would mean. One man said it would mean that they could now divide up the Cocoa Stabilisation Fund and everyone would receive ten pounds. A woman said it would mean the disbanding of the police: "The white man brought them. We don't want them," she said. An African farmer told me that he expected freedom would mean just a lot more hard work; but however limited may be the understanding, the people expect their leaders to meet their great and growing needs.

But the future of the new nations may well be determined by the welcome we give them, by the assistance that is made available to them. The world has changed since almost two hundred years ago when you stood upon the threshold of nationhood. You may go back two hundred years in your own history and read of the planning, of the resolves, of the Constitution-making, of deep differences of opinion, of long and learned argument; from all of which grew the American outlook and way of life—a nation was born.

But your nation grew and developed in comparative isolation and the tempo of your progress was relatively slow. Your lands were spacious and no industrial revolution had yet introduced a world of machines and made possible a high standard of living.

But the new nations of today will not be satisfied with slow development. Admittedly they have arrived late but they feel that this just means that they have lost so much already that nothing must now stand in their way.

America had to pull herself up by her own shoelaces. It was a long and hard struggle. There were no international funds available for construction and development and some of today's great industrial empires were started in a shed, with a few hundred dollars and a determination to find a way. No doubt much of your strength grew from this struggle but it is too slow for today, and anyway there are two competitors in the field to win the allegiance of new peoples—the free nations and the communists.

Three great forces are brought to bear upon the development of new nations in Africa—the continuing drive from the people themselves, the influence of the Western group and the influence of the Russian bloc.

The drive from within the nation is complex. The Colonial powers have endeavoured to transplant their own political institutions in the new territories, and the foundation in most new States is a universal franchise. It would give us all great comfort and confidence if we had reason to believe that a universal franchise guaranteed a democratic order. What it does do is to make sure that the majority group takes over the government of the country, and while that is one side of democracy, it is the other side which gives democracy its strength and makes it the finest known system of government. The other side is the security of the minority; the right of these people to state their views, to exert their influence, and to work openly and freely to take over the government at a later date, by changing the opinions of the people and gaining a majority of votes.

The only argument that can justly be used against the universal adult franchise is that people who vote should know what they are doing. It appears desirable therefore that educational facilities for all should go with a universal franchise, and preferably precede it.

The people of Ghana or Nyasaland know that America and Britain, Australia and Canada are great democracies and that these countries have a universal franchise. What they are not so clear about is the fact that either by tradition, or by the provisions of a Constitution, minorities in these countries have rights, and that it is the proudly accepted trust of the majority to limit their own power so that the rights of the minority are not prejudiced. In general it can be said that security, liberty and opportunity are based upon the rights of each individual.

This, I believe, is the most difficult concept to get across to the people of the new nations. The upholding of such rights requires real stature and maturity within a community. Not only that, but whatever may have been the theories behind Colonial rule, in fact, the Governors and District Commissioners leaned towards autocracy and the experience of the peoples whom they governed was not always one which taught them the sweet reasonableness of democracy in action. When governments of the people are established, they recognise that they take the place of the Colonial Government and are, I am afraid, all too prone to believe that they will also have to be very firm, because they too will work for the good of all and therefore any opposition is an unwarranted hindrance to the sound development of this country, and should not be tolerated.

Dr. Nkrumah put it to me recently in rather a different way. He said that until Independence the people had been united in their determination to obtain the freedom of their country. Now that goal had been reached, a great bond had disappeared and it would take some time for the form of government and opposition to evolve. He said that it was not easy for the opposition to clarify its differences with government, for not sufficient time had elapsed for alternative policies to be framed, and that the one compelling thought which overshadows all other opposition policies, was a militant determination to get the government out and get themselves in.

I am not making a judgement on the fairness or otherwise of this statement, but it does high-light the need to substitute new bonds and to find new and satisfying goals once independence has been gained. It also underlines the problems which face a people when the colonial authority transfers power under a system that requires for its satisfactory working that the monolithic unity of the people give way to two or more parties.

This is a problem which is not easy to solve because government, supported by an adequate majority, can carry on quite efficiently under a so-called democratic system which actually produces authoritarian rule.

In America you have your Constitution and your Bill of Rights: you provide access to the Courts for those who hold that their rights have been denied to them. While you would not hold that this has actually accomplished all that was intended of it, there is no doubt that it had the greatest significance. It is to be hoped that Nigeria, which will have a comparable provision in its Constitution, will similarly benefit. If it is shown that Constitutional safeguards can be made to work in Africa by a Court which is not corruptible, there will be more reason than exists at present to believe that Africa can become the home of truly democratic states. The influence of a democratic nation of 34 million people in West Africa could be a compelling example to neighbouring states.

But the political direction of the new nations of Africa will be profoundly influenced by nations outside of Africa. The African nations will not stand on their own for many years to come, and in this modern world, no nation, even the greatest, is unaffected by others. Today, countries at extreme distance from us are yet our near neighbours. The nations of Africa are especially open to influence, for there is so very much that they need, and which they must obtain from the developed countries. We have seen Russia's great eagerness to penetrate into the countries of Africa. We know something of the painstaking preparations which are being made in Russia to prepare envoys to win the confidence of the various peoples of Africa. I am sure that the interested European countries and America also will not underestimate the importance of the challenge which confronts them. The influence of America in Africa could mean much for freedom and democracy as well as for economic development. But in the realm of political forces, what is America's policy towards new African nations; towards those that are nearing self-government and towards those in which freedom is being limited?

That America, the Commonwealth, and other free countries, should have clearly-stated and helpful policies is greatly to be desired; but it is also desirable that these policies be directed to the development of states in which liberty and opportunity are the rights of every individual. Only to the extent that governmental policies in Africa are in harmony with these concepts, should support be afforded by the free nations. I believe that this attitude should be made clear and that all actions should be unequivocal.

But in the picture that I have given, I visualise such countries as Guinea, Ghana, Nigeria, the Cameroons, Tanganyika and the nations of the French community. Not all the countries of Africa fit into the picture I have painted. Conditions in the Belgian Congo are so confused that it is difficult to speak with knowledge about it. Here is a great country of thirteen million people who have received no training at all in the responsibilities and administration of government, and yet stand on the verge of self-government. If nations, which have been led deliberately to self-government and whose people have been made familiar with democratic institutions, face almost insuperable difficulties in establishing sound regimes, what will be the future of a country which has known only completely authoritarian rule? The compelling imperative was to break away from Colonial control, and a violent and irresistable force has been released. It has burst the dam and threatens to spread out and devastate the country. This cannot be allowed to happen but it is not yet clear what may be done to assist.

The key to any measures which may be suggested must be "assistance" to a new nation. It is unlikely that the Belgian Government can do much more and it would probably be unwise for any single nation to try to take the place of the Belgians, so it may be necessary for the United Nations Organisation to offer help. Perhaps I am being pessimistic about the Congo, but it has great significance for my part of Africa, and within its own borders the good government and progress of thirteen million people are at stake.

While the course of the new African nations will be difficult, their problems are simple in comparison with those of the so-called multi-racial countries: Kenya, Central Africa and the Union of South Africa.

The Union of South Africa has been an independent country within the Commonwealth since 1910. The political imperatives which brought that country to independence came from the white people, the Afrikaaners and the English. It is not possible here to go into the deep troubles which precipitated the Anglo-Boer war at the turn of the century, nor the reconciliation which it was hoped would lead to a full merging of the two white races into one people.

Fifty years ago when the South Africa Bill was debated in the Parliament of Great Britain, Mr. Asquith referred to the Constitution as a "magnificent monument of freedom and conciliation." No note was taken of the fact that only Europeans had attended the Convention and that no non-Europeans had been consulted about the Constitution. In the Cape Province there was a non-racial franchise and some Africans were qualified to vote in elections, but it did not disturb politicians or the general public, either in Britain or in South Africa, that the new Constitution specifically denied to all non-Europeans the right of membership, either in the Assembly or in the Senate.

This is jubilee year for the Union of South Africa; it will be a jubilee for whites only, but not even for all the whites. It is a year of mourning for people of other races for the nationalist Government has taken away what meagre representation they had in the management of the country's affairs. The doctrine of separateness has been pushed to its limits and whites are separated from people of mixed race and both are separated from the Bantu. What are the political imperatives which have motivated people in the Union of South

Africa since Independence? Antagonisms, and policies of racial supremacy, feelings of deep hurt and hatreds.

The great majority of the white people believe in separation. The Afrikaaner people hold that they are a special nation called into being by God. They are a nation of the Bible; but greatly influenced by Old Testament doctrines. The fact that at this late stage in history their nation has been formed, is held to have a special, a divine significance. Following upon this, it is argued that God must have had a special purpose in His work, and that it is the duty of the Afrikaaner nation to fulfil that purpose. To do this, however, the people must keep the race pure—and so the argument proceeds. Once you have accepted the fundamental premises, the argument advances with some logic, and branches out into the responsibility of whites for blacks, and the need to ensure that equal, though separate, ways of development are provided. Today the talk is of the establishment of black states called Bantustans. Here will be concentrated millions of African people who will discuss together the injustices which they suffer; here their numbers will continue to grow and with each menacing year the threat to white domination will increase. There is no future for democracy under such conditions, there is no knowing what the future will bring, nor how long superior force can withhold from eight million people the free pursuit of life, liberty and happiness.

But here are powerful political imperatives within a free state; great forces in dangerous conflict. But the Union of South Africa is not self-sufficient and the free nations must have a policy towards her also. The denial of liberty by whites to blacks in South Africa is in essence no different from the denial of liberty to a minority in one of the new nations. The South African example is nevertheless particularly hated within Africa itself for feeling is heightened by the racial aspect of the government's policy. The essence of our concern is to bring our maximum influence to bear upon efforts to ensure the liberty of all men.

In the past, America has had close relations with the great European powers and has run the risk of being associated with them, and with criticism of them, in the African mind. Now France may be about to clear herself of further criticism and suspicion, Belgium will be out of the picture and Britain will continue for some time to occupy a position of some embarrassment. America's duty seems quite clear: it is to support and assist democratic causes in every possible way, whether through direct action or remote contact by way of international organisations. It also requires that she refrains from supporting governments whose policies, as they affect the lives of their people, are out of harmony with those accepted in America today.

Africa is a very large continent and no one person can know intimately its peoples and its problems. I have spoken about the new states, about the Colonial Powers, about those nations which advance towards self-government, about the Union of South Africa. I may appear to have spoken with great confidence but there is so very much that I do not know. I suggest that, if you are really interested, you should seek your knowledge both widely, to keep the general picture in view, and intimately, to get to know some country and its people.

I have tried, through study and travel across the continent, to get some grasp of the general situation; but I have also had the great privilege of living in Rhodesia for twenty-six years—just exactly half my life; but the best half so far.

Without going further, even to consider the political imperatives behind the pan-African movements, I wish to take you to that part of Africa which I call home, to the country in which my children were born, and of which we are citizens—Rhodesia. The Rhodesias, north and south, together with Nyasaland, were joined in a Federation in 1953, and I regret many of the events which, over the past two years, have made us head-line news.

Nyasaland is a small and beautiful country in the North-East, lying alongside a lake as big as a sea. She has the largest population of the three states—three million people, almost all Bantu for there are only seven thousand whites and perhaps ten thousand Asians and people of mixed race in that country. There are differences of opinion regarding the potential wealth of the country. Tea is grown, there are possibilities for irrigation on quite a large scale, and there may be workable deposits of bauxite and other minerals. No one really knows, but what has been obvious for many years is the poverty of the people. More than a hundred thousand of Nyasaland's young men are always away from home working either in the Union of South Africa or in the Rhodesias. Nyasaland is governed by a Governor who is responsible to the Secretary of State for the Colonies in London, and by a Legislative Council which is controlled by the Governor although it has elected representatives of the people as members. A number of the functions of government in Central Africa, such as external affairs, communications, trade and industry, are controlled by the federal government in Salisbury.

Northern Rhodesia is the biggest of the three States and by its production of copper and cobalt provides more than two-thirds of the value of the exports of the whole Federation. Northern Rhodesia is a Protectorate like Nyasaland and her government is similar, except that greater control is vested in the local government and less in London. In Northern Rhodesia there are two and a quarter million Africans, about seventy thousand Europeans, and perhaps ten thousand of other races.

Southern Rhodesia has about two and a quarter million Africans, fifteen thousand Asians and people of mixed race and two hundred thousand Europeans. In 1923 self government, with certain restrictions, was granted, and since then the country has had its own parliament of elected members.

The Union of South Africa lies to the south of the Limpopo River and Southern Rhodesia lies to the north. One-third of her white population comes from the Union and the influence of South Africa is very strongly felt in our country and, to a lesser extent, throughout the Federation.

The Federation of Rhodesia and Nyasaland was established with the agreement of the Government of Great Britain, the Governments of Northern Rhodesia and Nyasaland, which are still appendages of Her Majesty's Government, and the Government of Southern Rhodesia. The electorate of Southern Rhodesia, in a referendum, decided by two votes to one to enter the Federation. The Constitution stated that this union would ensure that the eight million people of Rhodesia and Nyasaland would be governed in such a manner as "would conduce to their security, welfare and advancement." Our experience over the six years of Federation has shown that the Constitution was not as wisely framed as our circumstances required.

But just as important as exercising exquisite care in the framing of a Constitution is the need to have it accepted by the people whose lives it is to affect. It was not enough to postulate that the Constitution was a good instrument and that it would eventually bring the country to full membership of the Commonwealth. It was fundamental that its terms should apply to all our people and that the benefits it promised should be enjoyed by all, without distinction of race or colour.

In 1953, those in authority believed that the African people in general were not sufficiently advanced to be able to understand what Federation meant or what great benefits it would bring. If those responsible believed that it was right or at least practicable, to impose the Federal system without its immediate acceptance by a majority of the people, then they should have recognised that the only way to make it succeed was to make its advantages manifest to a majority of the people without delay, and also to ensure that those benefits were experienced in the actual day to day life of the people.

Six years of Federation have brought considerable economic development, particularly in the Rhodesias, but while such advancement is of great importance, it is limited to a small section of the wide field of "life, liberty and the pursuit of happiness." Only when economic progress is accompanied by the extension of liberty, by the growth of security, and by the strengthening of bonds of partnership and cooperation, can it fairly be held that the Constitution is fulfilling its purpose.

Some plead that more time must be allowed before judgements are made. Many people hold that an expanding economy will itself meet the needs of our people: bread, not votes, can save the Federation.

If the consent of the people is not won, then it can only be a matter of time before authority comes into disrepute and the further maintenance of law and order will degenerate wholly into a police and military exercise.

The vital test of the good faith of the European is his readiness or otherwise to remove colour from politics. The Constitution provided that qualifications for the Federal franchise should be decided by the First Federal Parliament, in which the majority of Members was European. Here was the acid test of partnership, here was opportunity to show good faith by extending the franchise as widely as possible within the limits of literacy and responsibility. If this had been done, the whole course of Federation would have been changed. In 1957, however, parliament flouted the danger of denying political rights to Africans, and while making a pretence of non-racialism, it used the device of the artificial economic colour-bar to maintain a political colour-bar. Only a few hundreds of Africans were able to vote alongside the 80,000 white electors at the following election. The Electoral Act of 1957 is the greatest single blow to a possible unity and it is designed to hold almost all power in European hands for the foreseeable future.

Our Federation was based, not upon a community of men, free, equal and independent; but was placed in the hands of 80,000 white electors, the majority of whom would, at the most, admit that Africans in general might sometime in the distant future become capable and responsible fellow-citizens. In these circumstances government can hardly escape appearing to be completely arbitrary in the eyes of the majority of the people. In our Federation men of only the one race have consented together, and this is our great weakness.

A serious omission from our Constitution is a Bill of Rights. Some of the most important aspects of human relations cannot be determined by law but it is essential that a standard be set, and that every individual be guaranteed liberty, security and opportunity to the extent that the law can provide. So much of our present distress and uncertainty stems from fear, and if people could be shown that their fears were unfounded we would banish most misunderstanding.

The free peoples of the world must work to ensure that freedom, liberty and opportunity be made the heritage of all men. We, who believe in democracy, cannot evade our responsibility, for liberty is threatened in America when it is denied in Africa; peace is in jeopardy when the minds of men are at war.

We hold these truths to be self-evident, that all men are created equal, that they are endowed by their Creator with certain unalienable rights, that among these are life, liberty and the pursuit of happiness. That to secure these rights governments are instituted among men, deriving their just powers from the consent of the governed; that whenever any form of government becomes destructive of these ends, it is the right of the people to alter or to abolish it, and to institute new government, laying its foundation on such principles and organising its powers in such form, as to them shall seem most likely to effect their safety and happiness.

Letter Delivered to Secretary of State for Commonwealth Relations
July 26, 1960

This is a full text of the controversial letter delivered to Lord Home and then released to the press where Todd called for a suspension of the Southern Rhodesia Colonial Constitution to help move the colony to independence under African majority rule. Joshua Nkomo and other nationalist leaders signed the letter which called for the intervention of British troops if needed to guarantee that the white government would step down. Todd realized the letter meant the end of his political career. This letter marks his call to a prophetic ethos by the nationalist movement. The text is located in the Welensky Papers, Box 676, Folder 4, fol. 54, Rhodes House, Bodleian Library, Oxford University.

The Secretary of State for Commonwealth Relations: My Lord,

For some years we have pleaded with our governments to extend the franchise so that we might enjoy political stability in Central Africa. The United Federal Party governments, however, have chosen to play politics with the even more reactionary Dominion Party and have paid scant attention to the voice of eight millions of voteless people. When protests have been made our governments have used the pretext of maintaining law and order to stamp out criticism and dissent, and have not hesitated even to use their military might to do this. Government policies are now maintained by force of arms and are directly responsible for the present unrest.

Ranged against the great mass of our people are 200,000 whites with police, an army and an airforce: four percent of our population, in the name of civilisation, have ranged themselves against the great body of people of our country, refusing liberty, denying justice and flouting the lessons of history.

It is imperative that Her Majesty's Government accept the responsibility for taking immediate action to establish a new and democratic regime in Central Africa. At present Britain is supporting an undemocratic and unjust form of government which, if left to itself, must soon disintegrate, causing widespread suffering to all sections of our people.

If Britain finds herself unwilling to intervene decisively in this situation within her colonial sphere, a situation in which 80,000 voters are permitted to govern 8,000,000 by military might, then Her Majesty's Government must state this clearly and now. Those people who are now protesting against their governments in Central Africa will then know that they must depend upon their own strength to gain liberty. We recognise that eventually this would lead to intervention by the United Nations Organisation but that there would be much regrettable and unnecessary suffering before this happened.

We pray that Her Majesty's Government, justly proud of having, in recent years brought some five hundred million people to freedom, will not flinch from the task of upsetting the present regime and of guiding and assisting the establishment of democratic rule by the people of our land.

Because of our deep concern to see harmony between the races and justice and opportunity for all citizens, we ask

1. That an immediate statement be made to the effect that Her Majesty's Government will intervene in the affairs of Central Africa to establish democratic governments so that the will of the people is implemented.

2. That the Constitution of Southern Rhodesia be set aside and a democratic order substituted for it.

3. That Her Majesty's Government come to immediate agreement with the federal government that no troops from the Union of South Africa will be called upon, or permitted to intervene in Central Africa. If South African troops were to be used in Central Africa, it is doubtful if there would be a healing of wounds in the next twenty years.

4. That, following an immediate statement of intent to set aside the Constitution of Southern Rhodesia, adequate armed forces should be made available from the United Kingdom to ensure that changes in government are made peacefully. It must be recognised that

should British troops be sent to Southern Rhodesia to support the present Government against the people of the country, the prestige of Her Majesty's Government would be so damaged that it would be extremely difficult for Britain to assist in any later attempts to establish a democratic regime.

5. That all necessary measures be taken to bring each of the territories to self-government within the next five years and that elections at the point of self-government should be based upon a universal adult franchise.

6. That immediate moves should be made to transfer powers from the federal government to the States. Concurrently with these changes the three territories should be given equal control over what remains of the Federal machine, which should then become the servant of the territories and no longer their master.

London, July 26, 1960.
Enoch Dumbutshena, Paul Mushonga, Joshua Nkomo, Garfield Todd.

United Nations Speech 1962

Todd viewed this as one of his most important speeches in his career. The speech is extensively explored in chapter 5, "The 'Horrible Speech': Todd's Effort to End White Supremacy." The speech was delivered at the UN Headquarters, New York, on Wednesday, March 21, 1962, at 11:30 a.m. and on Thursday, March 22, 1962 at 10:00 a.m. The text is from the United Nations General Assembly, *Special Committee on the Situation with Regard to the Implementation of the Declaration on the Granting of Independence to Colonial Countries and Peoples Verbatim Record of the Sixteenth Meeting*, A/AC.109/PV.17, and United Nations General Assembly, *Special Committee on the Situation with Regard to the Implementation of the Declaration on the Granting of Independence to Colonial Countries and Peoples Verbatim Record Of The Sixteenth Meeting*, A/AC.109/PV.18.

Mr. Todd: May I first express my appreciation to the Committee for its readiness to give me a hearing this morning. I regret that I have not been able to obtain the complete records of what has happened in this Committee regarding Southern Rhodesia, but I have the report of the proceedings of Friday, 16 March 1962, and have particularly taken note of the statement of the representative of the United States of America.

Now, if my understanding of the situation was as expressed by the representative of the United States, I might say that I would not be here before the Committee this morning. I think that there must be something wrong somewhere, that some of the evidence on which he has founded his statements must be different from that on which my understanding of the situation is based.

I hope I am fair in saying that I gather from the statement made by the representative of the United States that the general reaction in a normal situation would be to ask the administering power to relinquish its limited authority, but that in the peculiar situation in Southern Rhodesia it is a fact that several delegations had asked Great Britain to retain her powers. It appears to me that the statement further says that under the circumstances, as they are understood, a number of delegations would agree that the United Kingdom should not at this time grant Southern Rhodesia independence; and further, that the United Kingdom should not wash its hands of its responsibilities in relation to Southern Rhodesia.

From the statement, it would appear to be agreed that the United Kingdom had some continuing responsibility to encourage and to help the people of Southern Rhodesia to move towards a form of government that would give each element of the population an equitable share of opportunity and responsibility. It appears that there might be differences of opinion amongst the delegations regarding the degree of that responsibility, but that there is a unanimity that there would be no denial that it existed.

The representative of the United States went on to say that, judging from the statements made by the United Kingdom representative, the present situation in Southern Rhodesia allows for peaceful change, and further, that progress is being made towards the objective of greater African participation in government. I was interested to learn also from this statement that when the United Kingdom representative had described the new Constitution

> ... as a step in the direction of such African participation he referred to it as only a beginning, and he quoted with evident approval from a statement of Sir Edgar Whitehead to the effect that the new constitution is bound to lead in time to African majority, and that that is something for Europeans to welcome. (A/AC.109/PV.15, pages 4–5)

The representative of the United States continued:

We are convinced that all concerned would agree that efforts should be made to work out agreed solutions that will permit all the people of Southern Rhodesia to achieve without violence a free and prosperous future. Such solutions should be based on the freely expressed will and desire of the people and should lead to harmonious inter-racial relationships that will permit all elements to play a full part in the political, social and economic life of the country. (Ibid., page 5)

Further, he felt sure that all members considered that

... every effort must be made so that change in this territory will be brought about through orderly, constructive, peaceful processes, and not through violence. In this way, a firm foundation may be laid for a society based on equal rights and prosperity for all. (Ibid., page 6)

The representative of the United States felt that the United Kingdom ". . . will play a very substantial role in the process of moving towards the achievement of these objectives in Southern Rhodesia" (Ibid., page 6), and that the Committee should endeavour to keep the United Kingdom to its task.

Now, I agree with the general sentiments so expressed. But I would go further; I would point out that if the facts with reference to the United Kingdom were as stated, if the will to assist were undoubtedly there, then I would not be here. Frankly, I am using New York as a back-door to London; I am here to endeavour to prod Great Britain into taking the very attitude which the representative of the United States says is its attitude, into accepting the responsibilities which the representative of the United States says are acknowledged to be its responsibilities, and into using the powers which the United Kingdom representative apparently admits Great Britain still retains.

Before I begin my own evidence, I must admit that I am to some extent a prejudiced witness. I came to Southern Rhodesia in 1934 as a missionary from New Zealand. In 1946 I went into the House of Representatives, the legislative assembly in Southern Rhodesia. In 1953 I became Prime Minister of Southern Rhodesia on the basis of agreement with federation, with which I completely agreed.

In 1957 I found myself in considerable trouble with my own party, although I had a great majority in the House. To a large extent, the trouble arose from a determination to raise the wages of the African people and to extend the franchise to the African people. Today's Prime Minister of Southern Rhodesia, in a message of farewell but perhaps not of good wishes to me, pointed out that with a huge majority in the House I had not done as much as he has to improve the lot of the Africans. And there is much in what he says. But I do know that the little that I endeavoured to do in those years at least cost me my political head.

But I must admit that I have particular interests and am, to some extent therefore, a prejudiced witness. And I will point out that Mr. Nkomo and I shed light on this subject from rather different angles. Mr. Nkomo's feelings are deeper than mine. He has had the problem of finding an education under very difficult and adverse circumstances; he has had to suffer from the colour bar when he went to get a job, to get a position in industry; he has been pushed around by the police; his party has been banned. He is, in a way, bruised and battered and frustrated, and he is particularly concerned for his people and his children.

If in Southern Rhodesia circumstances had affected me so harshly, I think I might well be incoherent. It amazes me how Africans can be as pleasant and as balanced as they are. I cannot say that I have suffered at all because of conditions in Southern Rhodesia, as Mr. Nkomo has suffered. But I am here today because I believe that my country of Southern Rhodesia is in grave danger, and because I am concerned that Great Britain shall play her part in the future of our land. My petition to the United Nations this day is to endeavour to achieve this, and no doubt I differ to some extent with Mr. Nkomo in my approach.

I had intended to go into some detail regarding the situation in reference to self-government in Southern Rhodesia, but from what I have heard this morning, I gather that it is quite unnecessary for me to do this. Apparently, it is generally agreed that while Southern Rhodesia has a large measure of self-government, it does not enjoy complete self-government. I will, therefore, just sketch one or two things roughly in my evidence.

In 1923, Southern Rhodesia was given self-government, put under the Dominions Office and taken out of the Colonial Office. When the Conference of Prime Ministers was instituted, the Prime Minister of Southern Rhodesia went there by special invitation only and, I think, to a large extent, the particular position given to Southern Rhodesia and the special honour given by the other members of the Commonwealth was based upon the personality of a great man, Lord Malvern. For his times, he had great insight and was a just man. While there are many criticisms that might be made of him, in his time he was a very forward looking statesman.

The 1923 Constitution limited the powers of the Southern Rhodesia legislature considerably. Various matters concerning land, discrimination between the races, and so on, had to be held over for the pleasure of Her Majesty. There has been a great deal of misunderstanding regarding this, particularly amongst the electorate in Southern Rhodesia, for many of my European friends believe that the British Government never interfered at all in our legislating.

Lord Malvern himself sometimes rather proudly said that the United Kingdom Government had never vetoed one law that Parliament had passed. But he was not always frank regarding what happened behind the scenes; for behind the scenes there was certain legislation which had to be cleared before we could bring it into Parliament. I, after all, was Prime Minister for four and a half years, and am well aware of the fact that any legislation which could be reserved for Her Majesty's pleasure had to be discussed in detail with the representatives of the appropriate Secretary of State, and that until the legislation was cleared, we would not bring it first to our caucus and later to the House.

I believe that in July 1960 certain matters came to a head. At that time I had talks with the Secretary of State for Commonwealth Relations, Lord Home and because of the riots during that month and the bloodshed and deaths in Southern Rhodesia, had pleaded for the setting aside of the Southern Rhodesia Constitution. Lord Home assured me that it was not possible, under the powers which the United Kingdom Government retained, for them to bring pressure to bear on Southern Rhodesia to have a conference similar to those held for Northern Rhodesia, Nyasaland, and other colonial territories.

Mr. Nkomo and I at that time wrote a letter to Lord Home, pleading for the setting aside of the Constitution of Southern Rhodesia. We pointed out that the sort of constitution that Southern Rhodesia ought to have would be one which would be unwelcome to the European population although eventually in their best interests, and that because there might be trouble, it would be necessary to have security forces available in Central Africa.

We suggested that, in consultation with the federal government, the British Government should send the Security Forces necessary from the United Kingdom. In our parliament in central Africa, unfortunately, it was suggested that we had asked for an armed invasion of Southern Rhodesia, and no one at that time had the fairness to read the letter we had written to Lord Home, even in the face of calls that I be impeached for treason, or threats that I be hung upside down from a lamp post. This was a sad and unworthy chapter in the history of our parliament.

However, by what methods, means or influences we do not know in actual fact, a constitutional conference for Southern Rhodesia was called, with the

Prime Minister of the United Kingdom in the Chair, and from that Conference has come a new Constitution. This is the Constitution which apparently, the United Kingdom representative assures you, will lead to an African majority, something for the Europeans to welcome.

However, when the Conference was called, as Mr. Nkomo has told you, no doubt, the Prime Minister had no intention whatsoever of inviting delegates from the African Nationalist Movement to be present at the Conference. In fact, at the last moment, as the Prime Minister was about to board the plane and when Mr. Nkomo had said that he would go to London anyway, without invitation, the Prime Minister was asked what the position would be if Mr. Nkomo turned up at the Conference door. The answer was that it would be a matter for the British police.

Now there are differences of opinion, quite obviously, between the views of Mr. Nkomo and Sir Edgar Whitehead as to what actually happened and what the results of the Conference were on the constitutional position; but I believe that certain things are quite clear. In the first place, the main reason for calling the constitutional conference, as far as the Government of Southern Rhodesia was concerned, was to get rid of the United Kingdom influence in Southern Rhodesia. It is also clear that the National Democratic Party, which was headed at that time by Mr. Nkomo, wanted a universal franchise. It was also clear that the outcome of the Conference on the political side was to give 220,000 white people fifty seats in the House, and two and a half million African people fifteen seats in the House. It is also clear that this division is based on two rolls, and that at best, it could be only an interim measure.

Now how much of this the National Democratic Party accepted is for them to say. But it is quite obvious that they did cooperate to a large extent and I, for one, would honour them for their cooperation; but if they did accept in any way the findings of the Conference, they soon had no hope whatsoever of putting them across to their own followers.

Before anyone had time to say anything, the Prime Minister of Southern Rhodesia stated that this was not an interim measure, but a final measure, the phrase used being "for all time." A second thing was that the Prime Minister of the Federation sent his congratulations, saying that it was a better arrangement than he could have expected.

It seems to be without doubt that Southern Rhodesia achieved a great victory over the United Kingdom in this matter, for all the legislation that used to be reserved for Her Majesty's pleasure is now in the hands of an almost entirely white electorate.

I must point out that while the Prime Minister did say—to use a quotation supplied by the representative of the United States of America—"the new Constitution was bound to lead in time to an African majority," he did not say in what length of time. And I would point out that the Federal Prime Minister not so long ago stated that it would take about 200 years for Africans to be equated with whites, but even he would be ready to admit that it was bound in time to happen.

However, in Africa, and in our part of Africa also, there is not that sort of time available for either the Federal Prime Minister nor for the Prime Minister of Southern Rhodesia, nor for the Constitution of Southern Rhodesia. The representative of the United States was unable to quote another Minister of the Cabinet in Southern Rhodesia, who explained the matter to the European electorate. He said that if and when Africans would get similar educational facilities to whites, they would certainly challenge the rule of Europeans, and would eventually take the place of the majority. But he assured them that there was nothing to fear, for at the present time we spend £4 million on 550,000 African children, and that to give them the same facilities as we give our European children would cost us not £4 million but £50 million. It was quite obvious that in the foreseeable future this could not happen. It is true that today we spend something over £100 per head on European children for their education, and something over £8 per head on the education of African children. But I would point out that the Minister was wrong in his comparisons, for it is not true to say that the one system, although it is so much cheaper, is only one-twelfth as efficient as the other. And I, who have had a great deal to do with African education, am quite sure that, although there are not the facilities and buildings and other expensive equipment and processes, nevertheless the junior education given to African children is fairly good. However, I cite this simply to bring before this Committee an attitude of mind which is an important attitude of mind.

We must recognize that it is difficult to consider Southern Rhodesia in isolation from a very complicated federal system, which, of course, in its turn, is not self-governing. And there I might pause just for a moment to point out that I am sure there is no doubt about the position of Nyasaland and the fact that it is not self-governing. There is also no doubt about the position of Northern Rhodesia, and there should be no doubt at all about the status of the Federation itself within the federal sphere. For, in 1958, the Federal Prime Minister stated that he would get dominion status—in other words, full self-government—for the Federation in 1960. And I believe he might well have done that but for Dr. Banda. I doubt whether the United Kingdom Government would have stood in his way.

However, in 1958, African nationalists in Nyasaland told me that they had lost confidence in the Government of the United Kingdom and that, because of this, they would fend for themselves and that there would be violence. As they said, this is the only thing which the United Kingdom Government eventually understands. They took this action in January and February of 1959.

Mr. Nkomo told you, I understand, about the proclamation of an emergency in Southern Rhodesia at that time, not because there was an emergency in Southern Rhodesia but because it gave us the control there so that we could safely send reinforcements, security forces, to Nyasaland. Anyway, the upset in Nyasaland clearly killed the thought of dominion status for the Federation in 1960. There then came a lesser call from the Federal Prime Minister for independence for the Federation in its own sphere of Government for 1961. This, he said, could not be delayed beyond 1961. But, of course, it has been delayed beyond 1961. And now it appears that not only may there be no dominion status, or no full independence for the Federation within its own sphere of government, but it may be that Britain will have to dismember the Federation. After all, the United Kingdom Government created it, and it may have to destroy it, for we in Central Africa—fortunately for ourselves—do not control our own destinies as far as the Federation is concerned.

Before that excursion into federal matters, I was saying that it is difficult to consider Southern Rhodesia in isolation from the Federal situation. But that is really, of course, what we are attempting to do. At present, we in Southern Rhodesia are still governed by the 1923 Constitution as amended. However, we are now entering the era of the new Constitution, which will be fully effective legally on the so-called appointed day—the day that the present parliament is dissolved.

Now, what of this new Constitution? Apparently, Britain says it is designed to maintain its own position of influence and power in Southern Rhodesia. Perhaps Britain does not say that; I am not sure. But I am sure that it does not maintain that influence and power. Southern Rhodesia politicians say that it is designed to give us—"us" being the white people—control of the affairs of Central Africa, control of our own affairs, included in which is the destiny of 2.5 million African people.

May I suggest that, apart from the virtues of the document itself and its weaknesses, there is one vital ingredient—the one upon which its success depends—which is entirely missing. It is that the Constitution is not acceptable to the people. If there was anything that the Monckton Commission of 1960 said, it was that no Constitution could succeed unless it was acceptable to a majority of the people, no matter how wonderfully phrased or clearly thought out were the terms of that Constitution. It is customary amongst our white people to say that Africans really do not understand politics—and a great many of them, of course, do not understand the party system, because a great many of them are uneducated and are unable to read of course. But all of them do concern themselves with, and are deeply affected by, the situation regarding schooling, the situation regarding the land, the number of cattle that they may own, the opportunities which exist for their children. And it appears to me that these matters are, after all, the blood and bones of politics.

The great problem of our country is the division which exists between 220,000 whites and 2,500,000 blacks. And this was recognized particularly by the Monckton Commission, which said that racial bigotry in Southern Rhodesia might well wreck the Federation. "It follows," said the Monckton Commission, "that no form of association is likely to succeed unless Southern Rhodesia is willing to make drastic changes in its racial policies." And, of course, on the wider issues, the Monckton Commission said: "No new arrangement can succeed unless it obtains the support of African opinion."

When Britain and Sir Edgar Whitehead contrived this new Constitution, they contrived a really remarkable document, which apparently allows Sir Edgar Whitehead to say in Southern Rhodesia that we are self-governing, that Britain has surrendered its power to intervene in Southern Rhodesia, that we are masters of our own fate—and yet allows the representative of the United Kingdom in the United Nations to state that all is well and that Britain will continue to maintain its interests and its power to influence Southern Rhodesia. Or does he say that? Again, I am not sure. But at least the representative of the United States feels that he can say: "The United Kingdom did not appear to be even considering the possibility of washing its hands of Southern Rhodesia." The new Constitution must be a remarkable document if both of these things can flow from it truly, and it is certainly worthy of our attention. This Constitution permits—in fact, requires—a two-roll system of registration for elections. Until now, we have had one common roll in Southern Rhodesia. It has had high qualifications, designed, in the words of the present Federal Minister of Law, speaking in the Southern Rhodesia Parliament in a moment of truth, to keep Africans off the roll. However, those Africans who did get on the roll enjoyed full rights.

But now we are to have two rolls, an A roll with high qualifications electing 50 members to the House, and a B roll with lower qualifications electing

15 members to the House, and these two sets will have interplay to the maximum extent of 25 per cent—the B voters on the A candidates, the A voters on the B candidates. This is, supposedly, the African break-through into politics in Southern Rhodesia.

The Prime Minister said of the Electoral Act in which these changes are made under the new Constitution: "The passage of this bill is an essential step on the route to our independence." In the same debate the Prime Minister said that, after a study of all the different categories of workers and their financial conditions, he was prepared to defend his statement that between 50,000 and 60,000 Africans would be eligible for the B roll, and that this was a reasonable and conservative figure. He said also that these voters would have full influence at the present time on A candidates—in other words, that their votes would not be devalued because they were few in number—but that this would change with the years, and, to quote again from the Prime Minister's statement, "There will no doubt come a day when there will be hundreds of thousands of B voters, and then devaluation will be severe. This is a well thought out scheme." That is the Prime Minister's statement, not mine, but I think Africans would agree with the Prime Minister that it is a well thought out scheme, and they would recognize that the thinking was not theirs.

This is the type of electoral law—though, I believe, a much fairer one—that the federal government passed in 1957. In 1957 the federal government, brought in a two roll policy, and at that time I pleaded with Lord Home, the Secretary of State for Commonwealth Relations, that the British Government should exercise its powers and not permit the passing of this unfair electoral law. However, the British Government believed that this was a reasonable forward step, and it approved the law although it had power, if it had wished, to set it aside. In 1960, only three years later, the Monckton Commission, on which served a number of people from the Federation of Rhodesia and Nyasaland, said of this electoral law that its passing in 1957 was a death blow to the last hope that a success might be made of the Federation. It is such a pity that we do not appear to learn.

It was thought when that federal law was passed that at least 50,000 Africans would enroll on the B roll and go to the polls, so that, although they would have very limited powers, we would have the partnership of seeing 50,000 or 60,000 whites and 50,000 or 60,000 blacks going down the roads together and entering the polling booths together. But instead of 50,000 doing this, only around 800 of the Africans—I have not the exact figure, but it was under 1,000—actually enrolled and went to the polls. What was the explanation? It was said that the Africans were not interested. The truth was they were so greatly interested—so interested and so understanding—that they were not prepared to register as second class citizens in the land of their birth.

But there came a more enlightened franchise policy—for which we thank the United Kingdom Government in Nyasaland. It appears to me that the United Kingdom Government is able to act very morally and very objectively as long as there are not too many white people concerned in the country under examination. In Nyasaland there were only 9,000 white people and nearly 3 million Africans, so that when the franchise law was introduced there recently, although it had an A and a B roll, and although the A roll had high qualifications and the B roll had low qualifications, the A roll was responsible only for electing eight representatives to the House whereas the B roll elected twenty representatives to the House, and the Africans immediately recognized the power that there was in such a roll.

In just over one month 114,000 Africans registered on the rolls in Nyasaland, and yet in Nyasaland the Africans have not had as great an advantage in educational facilities as have the African people of Southern Rhodesia. And they were prepared to cooperate, although they were not even given the universal franchise that they wanted, because they recognized that here was really a substantial step forward towards self-government by the majority of the people.

Now in Southern Rhodesia the first thing that had to be done under the new Constitution was to get the Electoral Act working. The Prime Minister believed—and I am sure he did believe—that he could succeed in doing this. He was allowed a choice of the time under the constitution. He could make the time for registration, as little as two months, or as long as six months, and he chose the longest period available, six months. And yet in Nyasaland, where the new electoral law was welcomed by the African people, in one month 114,000 people registered.

The Prime Minister made a tour of Southern Rhodesia to sell the new Constitution to the African people. For various reasons he did not inform the press where he would be holding meetings, and the press had the greatest difficulty in following him at all. He did not allow the people to come in great numbers because he was afraid that the reception would not be good, so that in most meetings the people came by invitation. The Prime Minister had police protection, and yet he failed in his attempt to sell the Constitution, for I doubt—and again I have not the exact figures, but I think my figures are very conservative—if anything like 3,000 new African voters have registered in the first two months of the six-month period, and this includes approximately 500 chiefs and headmen who were registered because of their office. And yet, to get the figure which the Prime Minister says he must have, or ought to have, a figure of around 50,000 Africans participating in the elections in October, he would have to get 8,000 Africans registering every month for the six-month period.

It is clear that the African people are not ready to accept the fifteen seats given to them under the new Constitution. Nor are they ready to be enrolled as second class citizens. The Electoral Act under the new Constitution simply does not permit an adequate representation of the people, and because it does not permit an adequate representation it has failed to win from the people—despite the use of very doubtful devices—the representation which it does allow.

Speaking of devices used to persuade the people to register on the B roll, I shall mention only two. There have been appeals made to employers to assist in getting their employees to register. Now it is very difficult for an employee, faced by an employer, not to register when he is asked to do so. In our countries civil servants are not used in drives to get people to register, but the drive for voters was declared to be non-political, and therefore civil servants could be and were used in the drive.

If there was a common roll then a drive to get people to register would really be just a matter of active citizenship, but in the situation arising out of our new Constitution we have actually not a non-political situation but the most highly charged political wrangle of the day. The United Federal party used every device to get Africans on to a B roll, where their very registration implies (1) that they accept the new Constitution, (2) that they are prepared to accept limited political power on a racial basis and (3) that they agree that white people on the A roll—for there are very few Africans on the A roll—should be given greater power than they have. Anyway, the methods of gaining African participation under the present Constitution have already been proved in my estimation to be a failure.

Under this new set of circumstances, quite unforeseen I believe by the United Kingdom, will Britain now intervene and together with the Southern Rhodesia Government and representatives of the people—for the Government, I regret to say, does not represent the mass of the people—devise a new electoral measure? Or must Britain at this point admit that it has given up most of its power in Rhodesia under the new Constitution, and that it has done this and taken this action at the most critical time in our history?

I would quote from a White Paper published by Her Majesty's Government, Command Paper 1399, where it says bluntly:

In 1959 the Southern Rhodesia Government proposed to the United Kingdom Government that the Constitution of Southern Rhodesia should be revised with a view to transferring to Southern Rhodesia the exercise of the powers vested in the United Kingdom Government.

Further, the proposed new Constitution, which is based on the conclusions of the Conference, will reproduce many of the provisions of the existing Constitution. It will eliminate all of the reserve powers at present vested in the Government of the United Kingdom, save for certain matters set out in paragraph 50, and it will confer upon Southern Rhodesia wide powers for the amendment of her own Constitution. It will also contain a number of important additional features, such as a Declaration of Rights and the creation of a Constitutional Council designed to give confidence to all the people of Southern Rhodesia that their legitimate interests will be safeguarded.

Mr. Chairman, if you would wish to adjourn the Committee, from my point of view I have finished the quotation and it would be a suitable time.
[Speech resumed 22 March, 1962, 10:00 a.m.]

Mr. Garfield Todd: When the Committee adjourned yesterday, I had just completed reading certain extracts from Command Paper No. 1399, published by Her Majesty's Stationery Office, which stated that reserve powers held by Her Majesty's Government were being handed over to the Government of Southern Rhodesia. So, in the case of the protection that the United Kingdom might provide, the people of Southern Rhodesia are given a Declaration of Rights and a Constitutional Council, these designed, it is said, to give confidence to all the people of Southern Rhodesia that their legitimate interests will be safeguarded.

Why then are the people not confident? Why is Mr. Nkomo at the United Nations? Is he just being unreasonable? Are his fears groundless? Is he mistaken about the suffering that he is enduring? When Great Britain participated in the framing of this Constitution, in the provision of the Declaration of Rights and the Constitutional Council, did she really believe that these devices would achieve their purpose, when all around were evidences of a rapidly deteriorating situation, in which it was obvious that whites and blacks were drawing apart?

Did Great Britain, as she withdrew from her responsibilities in Southern Rhodesian really believe that she could expect a racial minority, hard pressed by 90 per cent of the population, to make a Declaration of Rights effective when, to maintain its position, that minority was being forced, even as the Declaration of Rights was being framed, to introduce further restrictive measures?

One commentator has said that the words of a Declaration of Rights would be quite ineffective, unless the passion for liberty and justice flamed in the hearts of the people. There is truth in that statement, but a carefully devised bill of rights which faced the realities of the situation, and which was justifiable, could be of great assistance.

However, I find it difficult to believe that any Declaration of Rights is worth the paper it is written on when it is being given to a people as a substitute for the vote. I hold that this Declaration is a substitute for the vote, and on that consideration alone, it is quite useless and therefore is not acceptable to the African people, who compose 92 per cent of our population.

This Declaration of Rights does not have the power to free any of the men whose movements are still restricted; nor does it give one iota of protection against the repressive laws which, in the past three years, have been added to our statute books, namely, the Unlawful Organizations Act, the Vagrancy Act, the Preventive Detention Act, and the Law and Order Maintenance Act. The Declaration of Rights has been used to justify the decision of the United Kingdom to hand over powers which she might have used to protect the African people of our country, to hand over those powers to an almost exclusively white electorate.

The withdrawal of British influence from the affairs of Southern Rhodesia would be a tragic happening, for it will leave us to our own travail, to bloodshed, and to the eventual rout of the white people. Now this is a very serious statement for me to make and a most unhappy one, but I believe that an examination of the provisions of the Declaration of Rights will bear out what I have said. Such an examination will show that we have been given a worthless substitute for British protection.

Do not forget that present legislation in Southern Rhodesia is not disturbed by the Declaration of Rights. The provisions of chapter 6 of the new Constitution of Southern Rhodesia are designed to afford protection for the following rights and freedoms. Every individual has the right, whatever his race or colour, to: (a) life, liberty, security of the person, the enjoyment of property and the protection of the law; (b) freedom of conscience, of expression, and of assembly and association; and (c) respect for his family and private life.

The first right says that no person shall be deprived of his life intentionally save in execution of sentence of a court. Until recently there was really no need even to state this; everyone would have accepted it because it was the order of the day. It was our proud boast that no life had been lost in any racial conflict, in any police action, from 1896 to 1960. But a new order has arisen and its effects are excused by the following saying; "However, no person shall be regarded as having been deprived of his life in contravention or this section if, for example, it happens in order to effect a lawful arrest." Recently there was a meeting of about 5,000 people in an African area of Salisbury. The police took exception to the statements of a speaker, and instead of waiting until a propitious time to make an arrest—the police in our country used to be discreet—they went straight in and arrested the speaker on the platform. This action provoked remonstrance and the throwing of bottles. Riot-guns were immediately fired on the crowd and there were wounds and one death. On 14 September 1961, the officer commanding the Salisbury Urban Riot Party stated in court that he had instructions to arrest intimidators and stone-throwers by shooting if necessary.

The second right says that no person shall be deprived of his personal liberty save as may be authorized by law. But as Mr. Nkomo has pointed out, the government has taken to itself powers to detain people without public trial, though it does bring accused people before a private tribunal. I appeared personally before such a tribunal on one occasion and I found it very distressing, and also very difficult to believe that I was in a British country. The accused men were kept in the yard outside the court. They did not hear my evidence nor did they have opportunity to question me. From 1959 to this date some of these men have still not regained their right of free movement. Mr. Nkomo is in New York today probably because the Government of Southern Rhodesia has served papers upon him, and upon thirty-eight of his friends including a professor of history at the University of Rhodesia and Nyasaland, forbidding them to attend any political meeting for a period of ninety days.

Further, under this second right, in section 5, it is said that any person who is unlawfully arrested or detained by another person shall be entitled to compensation. Yet when British ministers collaborated in drawing up such a right, did they not recognize how incongruous it would appear to the African people, who would compare it, for example, with section 11 of the Unlawful Organization Act, which is not affected by the new bill of Rights and which says:

> In relation to any act or anything whatsoever done under the provisions of the Unlawful Organizations Act, no action, indictment or other legal proceeding whatsoever shall be brought in any court of law against the Government or its servants.

So when, not so long ago, a man was arrested and detained for some weeks because of a mistake in the name, he had no power to claim compensation.

The third right says that no person shall be held in slavery or servitude, or required to perform forced labour. However, there is a phrase which says that for the purpose of this section, the expression "forced labour" does not include any labour which forms part of normal communal or other civic obligations. I myself would not have much protest to make, but I do know that many African people, in the light of their past personal experiences, would not regard this provision as an adequate protection against what they have considered to be unacceptable demands for labour in native reserves.

The fourth right states that no person shall be subjected to torture or to inhuman or degrading punishment or other treatment. However, against this, Africans arrested in the sweep of 1959 tell of security forces unceremoniously pushing their way into the homes of the people in the middle of the night, and of the fact that men were taken to police stations while still inadequately clothed. I myself took grave exception to a recent action by the Prime Minister, who sent troops into country districts to surround certain villages and to frighten the people while revenue men collected overdue taxes. My telegram of remonstrance had no effect, but I am convinced that from every angle this was the most expensive tax we whites have ever collected.

The fifth right concerns protection from the deprivation of property. But this right has been written in the face of section 7 of the Unlawful Organizations Act—section 7, which allows any police officer, without warrant, to enter any building where he has reason to believe that even documents of an unlawful organization may be found, and cause to be seized all property which he may have reasonable cause to believe to belong to such organizations.

Mr. Nkomo has no doubt told you of what happened when the National Democratic Party was banned. The government seized their office equipment, confiscated their motor-cars and set back the African nationalist organization by many months. This is a very serious matter, for if the new Constitution had been acceptable to African nationalists, the action of the government would have made their task of organizing for an election extremely difficult. When the terms of the Constitution were announced, the Prime Minister stated that his party would get not only a majority or the "A" seats, but a majority of the "B" seats, the African seats, as well; for, as he said, perhaps rather picturesquely, he would "knock the living daylights out of Joshua Nkomo." This objective has been pursued by (1) banning the nationalist organization; (2) seizing their transport and equipment; (3) not allowing any political meetings to be held anywhere for a period of two months after the referendum; (4)

forbidding all political meetings in African reserves; and (5) prohibiting forty of the outstanding African leaders from attending any political meetings anywhere for ninety days. Mr. Nkomo is still restricted by that ban.

The sixth right says that no person shall be subjected to search of his person or to entry into, or to search of, his dwelling-house. Africans simply could not visualize such a change of attitude on the part of the authorities. Our daily papers have carried several news items during this very month telling of widespread early-morning sweeps and searches with the arrest of many scores of people—and I have already mentioned section 7 of the Unlawful Organizations Act which says that any member of the police may, without warrant, enter any house or building in which "he has reason to believe," etc.

The seventh right is concerned with provisions to secure the protection of the law. Section 2 (a) says that every person who is charged with a criminal offence shall be presumed to be innocent until he has been proved guilty. To demonstrate how distant this is from today's reality, I will just quote section 9 of the Unlawful Organizations Act, under the heading so appropriately termed "Presumptions" in which is set out a list of offences of which the accused, until the contrary is proved, shall be considered guilty.

The eighth right is concerned with the protection of freedom of thought and of religion. I believe that this is the situation today, in general terms. Anyone can be a Catholic or a Hindu, an Anglican or a Muslim, an Atheist or a Pentecostalist without fear. What concerns me, under the heading of religion, is the fact that the finest tenets of our faith are warped, twisted, suffocated by the unjust conditions which are maintained by the laws of the land. We are ready to protect the right to spiritual and intellectual freedom, but we fail to foster the life itself, the spiritual life of the nation.

I hold that neither the British Government nor the Government of Southern Rhodesia showed real concern for the realities of the situation when they compiled our new constitution. Now, I hope I am not being too unfair, but how different was the attitude of Her Majesty's Government when the matter was important, when it had to do with finance. In this matter, there is no use for vague terms such as "Her Majesty's pleasure." Now we use the term "Her Majesty's Government" in the United Kingdom.

The British Government, which vacillates and procrastinates over a constitution for Northern Rhodesia, shows no sign of indecision in section 32 of the new constitution which says that any law which has been assented to by the Governor and which appears to Her Majesty's Government in the United Kingdom to alter, to the injury of stockholders, any undertakings given at the time of issue of Southern Rhodesian Government stock may be disallowed by Her Majesty's Government; further, that if it is disallowed, the Governor of Southern Rhodesia shall publish the fact in the Gazette. Again, any such law shall immediately, upon publication in the Gazette, be as if it had not been made. I am not really disagreeing with the terms of section 32, but I do stress that the life of the people, their rights, their opportunities, should weigh, at least as heavily with Her Majesty's Government in the United Kingdom, as do the interests of the stockholders.

The ninth right deals with the protection of freedom of expression; but the government retains the right to decide what is in the interests of defence, public safety, public order, public morality and public health. So today a man who shouts "Up, up, up Nkomo!" and "Down, down, down Whitehead!" commits a punishable offence.

We have even lost our sense of humour: Some of our police reserves have blue uniforms; so have our girl guides, our girl scouts. Some months ago, an African was fined £20 for calling a police reservist a girl guide; and when a second case came before the magistrate, a fine of £25 was levied—two months' pay for an African—as we could not permit people to make fun of our police.

The tenth right says that no person shall be hindered in his freedom of assembly and of association. In 1960, we passed a Law and Order Maintenance Act, the terms of which were so objectionable that, although it was state legislation, the Federal Chief Justice resigned his high position in protest against its adoption. The Federal Chief Justice, Sir Robert Tredgold, stated that, in his opinion, this legislation trespassed against almost every basic human right. The provisions of this act are so wide that a police officer may, at a gathering of persons, forbid any person from addressing such gathering; may enter and remain on any premises, but not including a private house, at which three or more persons are gathered, if he has reasonable grounds for believing that a breach of the peace is likely to occur or that a seditious or subversive statement is likely to be made. Under this act, for certain offences, the discretion of magistrates and judges is set aside and minimum sentences are prescribed by the act itself. This act controls processions, public gatherings and meetings, takes the right to prohibit individuals from attending public meetings, as is the case with Mr. Nkomo and others today, and forbids the holding of meetings in open public places, streets and squares.

The eleventh right says that no written laws shall contain any discriminatory provisions. I recognize the legal implications of that, but I wish to point out, that, under the terms of the same constitution, it is permissible to divide the citizens of the country into three groups: (1) citizens with an "A" vote who are given supreme political control, and who happen, almost exclusively, to be white; (2) citizens with a "B" vote who are given the shadow, but not much substance, of political participation; and (3) citizens who are denied a vote of any kind. Such a situation, under the law, prejudices the judgement of a citizen who is offered the comfort of the 11th right.

The twelfth and final right is that there shall be protection against discriminatory action, but whatever may happen in the framing of the laws from now on, the African people are still discriminated against, in comparison with Europeans, by a lack of schooling facilities, by a lack of hospital facilities, by a lack of technical training, and, pre-eminently, by being denied freely elected political institutions.

However, not only have we a Declaration of Rights: but we have a Constitutional Council, also provided to give confidence to all the people. The main functions of the Constitutional Council, we are told, are to advise the Legislative Assembly as to whether its bills are in conformity with the Declaration of Rights. This is, no doubt, commendable, as far as it goes, but it has no impact upon the present situation; it provides no relief from present laws.

The structure of the Council is complex; the qualifications for membership in it are high; it is an intricate and, no doubt, beautiful machine, the pride of some constitutional lawyers, and designed for a good purpose. But it has no fire in its belly. In this situation of rapid deterioration, a condition emphasized unmistakably by the deterioration of our laws, by the rapid growth of our military and police strength, in this situation, Great Britain is handing over her reserve powers.

In the face of all that the Monckton Commission has said about gaining the consent of the people for a new constitution, Britain is party at this moment to imposing a new constitution upon an angry and unhappy majority. Contrary to the definite advice of the Monckton Commission, Britain supports a two-roll electoral system which provides for an almost exclusively white A roll, with supreme political powers while offering the African people a B roll with limited political power. This is designed as a political remedy in a country where today eight per cent of the population holds 95% of the votes.

This has been a horrible speech: a most distressing speech from my own point of view. For I understand the problems of the Prime Minister of Southern Rhodesia. Who should understand them better? I know that every law he is bringing to his aid, every extra policeman, every restrictive regulation, every tear grenade, every riot gun is needed. And there will be no end to that need if he must pursue his present policy of political supremacy for whites, even though it is camouflaged as partnership. I also know that unless Her Majesty's

Government and the United Kingdom can now intervene, the Prime Minister must either be thrown out, as I was, or go on to the inevitable conclusion which will be one of riots, bloodshed and economic attrition.

The Prime Minister—and honour to him—has already risked his position by his readiness to break down the colour bar, but he will not give the African people the one thing that they will not be denied—the vote. He has done much in the four years of his office, much that is repressive and regrettable, but also much for which I might have spent more time commending him. But the Prime Minister has failed to get the African people to accept a new constitution and he is failing to persuade 60,000 Africans to enroll on the lower B roll.

Does this situation then not demand some action of the United Kingdom? If the constitution had been willingly accepted, if it had been shown to be a sound and dependable vehicle to convey the African people upon their forward political way, that would have been an entirely different situation. In such circumstances I would not have been present today at the United Nations. Surely the terms for the getting of the new constitution to Southern Rhodesia included the ready acceptance of it by a majority of the people of Southern Rhodesia.

What, then, must be done since the people will not accept it? Surely Britain must find a constitution which will be acceptable to the people. Is it not quite obvious that only the United Kingdom can assist the white electorate in making the changes necessary, even to save themselves? The white people of Central Africa are not evil people. They should not be termed typical Europeans but should be understood as typical human beings. In earlier years, we found ourselves in very pleasant circumstances where privilege came to us easily; now, in changed times, we are confronted by an awakening: people who outnumber us by twelve to one. We find ourselves unable to make adjustments in our thinking quickly enough. We hold supreme political power. We can justify our every action in law. Being human, we will not, of our own, indeed we cannot, divest ourselves easily of our privilege.

I am pleading for my country; for white people, as well as black people. The Europeans have made, and could continue to make, a magnificent contribution to the development of Central Africa. All of this, however, will be lost unless great changes are made now. We, the white people, have been made judges in our own cause, and no man is good enough for that. I believe that if the United Kingdom does not act today—and I plead with them to act—then the United Nations will have to act tomorrow.

Can Christianity Survive in Africa?

Todd considered this speech one of his "better efforts"[30] and it clearly is one of his best. The speech laid out a Christian view of political action for social change on a national level. Todd saw African nationalism as a child of Christian missions. White missionaries brought the wider world to Africans but as long as whites remained paternalistic they mostly engendered frustration. The churches had a duty to consistently apply the Christian message of social justice and support the African cause. There are many excellent thoughts in this speech but two are vintage Todd; for instance, "The Church must never evade her responsibility to choose the right, to protest not only against the violence but also against the use of repressive laws backed by force." And, "The nationalist cause is not in itself anti-Christian; in fact in so far as it presses for freedom of the individual, for social justice for all, without distinction of race, its principles are Christian." The overall mission for the Church in political action in Africa was "to achieve an atonement between black and white." The speech was broadcast from the Federal Broadcasting Corporation, January 2, 1963. The text was provided by Sir Garfield Todd.

Africans have burned down Churches in Angola, they have expelled a Bishop from Ghana, they have wrecked missions and shamefully treated missionaries in the Congo. I have been asked whether, after consideration of such terrible happenings, it should be concluded that African nationalism and Christianity are incompatible? or simply, do I believe that Christianity will survive in Africa?

The question itself came as a real jolt because the possibility of Christianity failing had never entered my mind so I have had to do some new thinking. What about African nationalism—what do we mean by it—and also what do we mean by Christianity?

Some people endeavour, for the convenience of their own arguments, to equate African nationalism with Communism. We know that Communist thought is atheistic, and so it is argued that African nationalism is also a godless movement.

But while African nationalism is a comparatively new phenomenon, nationalism is not. We should have learned our lessons from Irish nationalism, Indian nationalism, Cypriot nationalism—American nationalism. Looking back over many, or few, years on the great forces that one by one have wrested power from Britain to establish governments of the people in Eire, in

India, in Cyprus, in what has grown to be the great United States of America, we surely are not naive enough to hold that these forces were wholly evil. Admittedly, they were all accompanied by the suffering of many innocent people, and every nationalist movement has been accompanied by excesses and often by atrocities. Each, in turn, was bitterly condemned and resisted by a large section of the English people. Yet, only a hundred years ago, the people of England themselves came very close to tragedy when their own privileged classes bitterly opposed the extension of the franchise. However, at the last moment, those with legal power showed their good sense in withdrawing their resistance to the passing of the Reform Bills. The nationalist struggle is new in Africa but it is not new in world experience. The circumstances in each African country differ but the struggle is essentially the same, an uprising of the people in a demand for their full share in government, which means government by the majority; one of the requirements of democracy.

But why burn the churches, why destroy the schools, why harm the white missionaries? Some of the reasons may be neither complex nor significant. In the first place not only churches are being destroyed, but also dip tanks, contour ridges, railway lines, homes, motor cars, the lives of men and women. Many of these happenings have no deep significance in terms of the nationalist struggle. It cannot be suggested that because schools are burned down, African nationalists hate education. The first thing that each new nationalist government does is to send young men and women for training overseas, and the portfolio which is given the most generous treatment is that of education. Nigeria has five thousand students in Western universities. Nyasaland works to establish her own university. The methods used by some African nationalists to express their opposition are on a level no higher than that of the man who kicks his car when it won't go. I am sure that many schools and churches in Southern Rhodesia have been burned simply because they make torches of protest, easy to fire and perhaps safe from observation.

But there could be deeper psychological reasons for attacks upon churches and missions. The Christian gospel is concerned with men as individuals. To each man the Christian missionary brings a message of freedom; freedom from sin, freedom from ignorance, freedom from despair. In the name of Christ, the missionary brings medical healing, new methods of agriculture, new learning, besides the message of salvation. In our country one section of the Christian Church went out into the reserves, and awakened the people, telling them that all things were possible for them. Another section of the Church became almost part of the establishment, erected beautiful buildings and catered, if not in theory, certainly in practice, for the European privileged class. It is a contradiction in terms that Christian Churches, in which all men are equal before God, should be racially divided but this unfortunately happened.

From the mission schools have come an ever growing number of young men and women, some with poor qualifications, some with fine qualifications, but all finding that they had missed the most important qualification of all—a white skin. In the past, black people in Southern Rhodesia have been paid according to their standard of living, and standards of living were based upon race.

The missionaries gave opportunity to learn but had no power to condition the circumstances which their pupils would meet when they moved out into the wide world—missionaries in colonial countries were actually educating their students for frustration. Education for frustration: could anything be more dangerous?

What is the effect upon a man who is educated by the church when he finds that white Christians assume attitudes of superiority and align themselves with a minority government of their own race? Perhaps it would not be surprising if church and mission targets were sometimes deliberately chosen for attack.

But even if missions, and missionaries, have been singled out in this way, the attacks cannot be proved to have been leveled against the Christian religion itself. It is both the weakness and the strength of Christianity that it depends so heavily upon men, while at the same time being entirely of God: His gift to men, His free salvation for men. We who are Christians never do justice to our religion, never carry out its precepts as we should, lack the burning zeal for the welfare of our fellow men which should be the hall-mark of our faith.

The Christian religion will not fail in Africa for while it has been brought by white men, and may have suffered in transit, it is of God and it is good. If it is suggested that Africans as a people are rejecting the good because some Africans commit crimes against their neighbours, the same argument could be advanced against every people of every nation—and in our own time, especially against the German people.

But while I believe that the religion that defied the power of the Roman Emperors, the religion whose very fount was a crucifixion, whose growth has been nourished by martyrs down to our own day, will not fail in its worldwide purpose, I do recognise that the Christian church, as we know it in the work and worship of its local congregations, may be seriously affected by the evil, bitterness or catastrophe of a particular age. Today, from many areas it is reported that church attendances are falling. At the same time racial bitterness increases and crimes are committed against life and property. The nationalist cause in our land is accused of using violent means to gain its ends and is exhorted by the government to turn to constitutional methods. The reply is that it has not been the policy of the nationalist party to plan violence: but that when people experience great frustration it is natural for some to turn to violence; especially when there seems to be no open road to negotiation.

But the Christian church can have nothing to do with violence; Christians are exhorted to be ready to suffer; even to sacrifice life for friends; but we are explicitly forbidden to suffer as murderers or thieves in any cause. If success for a cause depends upon violence then the Church cannot support it—which means, not that Bishops or priests are forbidden to participate, but that it is not a cause with which any Christians should be associated.

But is the nationalist cause necessarily an unholy one? Is it fair to judge the cause itself by the violent excesses of some of its supporters? May it not be that violence stems, not from an evil cause, but because the Church is allowing a just cause to go by default? Or if the nationalist cause is not entirely just, or worthy of the support of Christian men and women, perhaps the Church is failing in other ways. Even where people are critical of nationalist claims, the Church has a duty to do—not necessarily to support wholeheartedly either one side or the other, but to do her work of conciliation. All men, privileged or underprivileged, brown or white, are the concern of the Church and the objects of Christ's love. It is an evil thing when anger is aroused, when men consider themselves to be unjustly treated or discriminated against. If such things are true the Church cannot remain quiet and yet fulfill her duty. If they are not true but are just the mists in men's minds, the Church has a duty to work for understanding and accord through negotiation and conciliation.

The Church must never evade her responsibility to choose the right, to protest not only against violence but also against the use of repressive laws backed by force. If she keeps silent at the command of a government when she believes that injustice is being done, then she turns her back upon her God and the Church of that age will wither. It is not persecution which saps the strength of the Church but the tolerance of evil and the withholding of righteous action. The Church's strength may be based upon prayer and worship but her vindication is seen in her practical, outgoing concern for the people of the land.

When the Samaritan on his way from Jerusalem to Jericho found a man, robbed, battered and penniless beside the road, he may have prayed at his side, but our Lord didn't mention this. What we are told is that the Samaritan saw the man's need, that he put him on his donkey, took him to a hotel, bathed his wounds, and paid for his keep during the period of his convalescence.

The Christian Church in Africa is confronted by a nationalist uprising, but also by a great need. Through its schools, its worship, its doctrine, the Church helped to set this revolution in motion. The nationalist cause is not in itself anti-Christian; in fact, in so far as it presses for freedom for the individual, for social justice for all, without distinction of race, its principles are Christian.

In Nyasaland, the late Mr. Dunduzu Chisiza was deeply concerned because so many African nationalist leaders appeared to have left the organised Church. He pled that African leaders should depend more fully upon the Christian faith. In Tanganyika, Mr. Julius Nyerere, who is a devout Catholic, gives Christian leadership to his people. In Ghana, Dr. Roseveare fearlessly criticises godlessness amongst the nation's youth and is expelled by the government, but we have not seen the defeat of the Christian religion in Ghana. In Lagos, Prime Minister Abubakah Tafawa Balewa is a devout Muslim, and as I said goodbye to him some months ago, he said: "Pray for us, for without God's help we will not solve Nigeria's difficulties." The leaders of the nationalist cause in Africa are not godless men. In Southern Rhodesia, so many nationalists and their leaders are Christian men: Christian men who see hope in the nationalist cause, who condemn murder, the use of petrol bombs and violence against any man, black or white. Whether African or European, we should be able to come together, to work together, to live together in security and harmony. In our land the Church is today challenged to bring her leadership, her prayers, her spiritual powers, her practical action in word and deed to achieve an atonement between black and white.

Danger! Men Thinking!
The First Feetham Lecture

The University of the Witwatersrand, Johannesburg, South Africa, where Todd studied in the medical school for one year, established the Richard Feetham Memorial Lecture in 1959 to support the university's dedication to the ideals of academic freedom. While various academics have appropriately delivered this annual address, Todd was given the first of two invitations to deliver the address on August 6, 1964. The university has a history of independent thought and concern for social justice in the South African context and so Todd was considered an appropriate choice. He did not disappoint on either occasion.

Todd reframed the issue of academic freedom to the larger question of political freedom needed for a true democracy. Underlying his entire argument against racism, intimidation, and undemocratic restrictions is Todd's belief in Christian ideals and the incarnation of Christ: "Many of us believe that the most critical moment of history was posed over the minority of one, and Him crucified. At that moment the world held no hope—"What is truth?" Pilate had asked. The promise given to men is that we shall yet know the truth and that it shall set us free. I believe that truth alone can set us free so that he who finds freedom for himself and for his fellows must seek truth with clear eyes, an open mind, and a resolute heart." Even in the dark days of the 1960s Todd could see hope as he pled for change. Later in the speech he said, "I wish with all my heart that I could show you how easily the impossible will happen. I cannot, but there are two things I will say for I say them continually to myself. The first is that the impossible continually happens, and the second is that your responsibility starts with yourself." These quotes still do not do justice to this powerful speech. The text is from the Todd papers in the possession of Susan Paul.

Racing, rugby and mountain climbing are some of the hallmarks of youth. There are others, and to the list, in your country and in mine, we might add another dangerous thrill, that of thinking.

I quote from an article by a student at the University College, Salisbury: "The challenge to every student in this college lies in the fact that the guilt of all wrongful actions in Rhodesia, restriction without trial, repugnant legislation, petrol bombing, etc. rests on all those who do not actively disassociate themselves from, and work for the eradication of, a system breeding such evils. We lose our moral place in any society if we do not cherish, protect, and promote the principles on which men's most fundamental liberties rest—freedom of speech, thought, association. . . . These liberties are being infringed by all races in our country today and the University proud guardian of man's wisdom and toleration stands mutely by, a hotbed of apathy." The article from which I took that quotation was commissioned by the editor of Unicorn, the college newspaper, written by my daughter Judith, and refused for publication by the firm of printers.

There can come a time in the life of a nation when people in business begin to consider what is politic. This is one of the symptoms of a malignant disease which threatens all freedom in southern Africa today.

It was suggested that I should speak on academic freedom but the choice was kindly left to me and I decided to take a somewhat wider view. I did this because I consider that academic freedom is a flower which blooms only in a suitable climate. I doubt if we shall see it flourish again in its full beauty either in your country or in mine until widespread changes have been made in the infrastructure of our national life. While lecturers and students are deported or imprisoned without trial there can be no real academic freedom. Under such threats I am afraid many men and women will hold that there is good reason to think only such thoughts as are socially and politically acceptable.

That men are so tempted to take the less worthy line highlights the courage of those who refuse to be cowed, who are determined to think for themselves—in truth, I believe that these men and women, think for others. Mankind would long ago have stagnated, if each generation were not provided with people who are prepared to persevere in their thinking and in their working, and not to count the cost. The price sometimes is high.

And so as I read recently in a Nusas report of lecturers and students from this University and from other South African universities who today are detained because of their beliefs, I thanked God in my heart for courageous South Africans who surely are maintaining the finest traditions of your country in demonstrating a readiness to disagree and to set out upon their own spiritual and intellectual treks.

Why in the context of Southern Africa are students and lecturers and so many others detained? What is there, fundamental to the two regimes, which has as an outward manifestation the necessity to imprison? Or to deport people who have committed no crime for which they can be brought before the courts, people whose chief fault is that they think differently from the official policies of their governments?

It is thirty years since I came from New Zealand and today I consider myself an African. What I would say in favour of New Zealand, other than to mention its scenic delights and its sometimes good rugby, is that they have no security legislation of the type so well known to all of us here. Nevertheless in New Zealand there is a proportion of dissenters and besides that they actually have a Communist party which regularly nominates candidates for parliament. So far it has never been successful in getting a member elected but that happens to be the decision of the electors themselves. Why can New Zealand permit a Communist party to function? Why is Britain able to do the same? There are very good reasons. Even fire itself burns only when conditions are right. When the grass is green ranchers like me can scan the veld with pleasure and without anxiety. The little fires of the fishermen along the riverside add only to the beauty of the scene. But in Rhodesia when October comes and the grass is tinder dry, the rancher is tempted not just to imprison fire lighting campers but to shoot them on sight.

In Southern Africa there is much to suggest that it is now October and many people have smoldering fires in their hearts, deeply resentful of the circumstances which others decree shall surround their lives. But this is our home. These are our people, the Verwoerds, the Patons, the Vorsters and Mandelas, the Smiths and the Nkomos. These are men of strength who, working together could give leadership which would inspire Africa. Is there no way by which we can go forward together free of police brutality, repression and mob hysteria?

There are many bonds between our countries and your influence upon us is great, both for good and for evil. In 1953 I believed we would establish in central Africa a non-racial regime which could have given a new lead in a world where two-thirds of the people are of varying shades of brown. I had hoped that our Federation would have contributed to men's understanding of each other and especially that we would have been of help to South Africa.

We were proved not big enough—we lacked the faith to trust our fellow men. It all worked out to be a deception, a pretence of sharing power but offered to the African people in a rigid machine designed to keep political control in the hands of whites—there is nothing that embitters more surely than hypocrisy of this kind. And having betrayed ourselves we then proclaimed to the world the perfidy of Her Majesty's Government in the United Kingdom. The very hardest thing we can be called upon to do is face facts, unpleasant facts, facts before which we stand condemned. I know, for no man can stay for years in a position of power without having some regrets when he looks back on his record.

Another symptom of our malady is our common desire to cut ourselves off from the main current of world thinking. Our three great hates in Southern Rhodesia are the U.K., the U.N. and the U.S.A. and when you have rejected the United Kingdom, the United States and the United Nations there are not so many friends left to you. Why do we reject these powers? Because they all disagree with our racial outlook, because those that are free nations call upon us to join the family of democracies. We reject them all for what appear to many to be good and noble reasons. The U.S.A. has her own racial troubles, it behooves her to keep silent on ours. The immigration policy of the U.K. is misguided and will result in her becoming an effete people. We are superior to her in our understanding of these things and she should heed our warning. The Commonwealth resembles a circus and as for the United Nations Organization if we find ourselves short of cogency, we can always point to the hypocrisy of authoritarian governments pleading for democratic rights for people in other lands.

There can well be truth in some of the criticisms we make; but even the validity of our arguments will not defend our regime from the mounting determination of the world to eradicate racial discrimination.

One hundred and fifty years ago the conscience of the world turned against slavery. Those who condemned the traffic were by no means without fault. In Britain the conditions of labour for women and children were in many instances probably worse than the lot of some slaves. In our erratic social progress, and with all the faults and weaknesses of mankind we highlight certain problems and seek solutions. While we are concentrating on one evil we may be inclined to close our eyes to a thousand other injustices, especially those that are more intimate to our own national life. Whether the nations, the United Nations, including the United States and the United Kingdom, are themselves without fault is largely irrelevant. The point is that the nations of the world have decided that racial discrimination is as unacceptable today as slavery and it will have to go. It is because of the determination, so forthrightly expressed, that our countries want to have as little as possible to do with other nations.

But we cannot isolate ourselves from the influence of others and there is no denying that the history of the past three centuries has been a slow unfolding of the democratic idea. During this period, and especially during this century, we have seen some very terrible reactions against liberty but we have also seen men ready to sacrifice their lives for its promotion and its defence.

In this same century we have seen a proud procession of liberated peoples taking their place in the world of nations. Not all the entries are on the credit side of course but who is to draw up a balance sheet for progress? What do you list? The gross national product, the number of houses built and new roads made, a diminution of crime, an absence of war, and an advance in education, a rise in church membership? I hold that any such statement would be in combination of the material, the measurable, together with the intellectual and spiritual and the material would be given its full meaning only in terms of the spiritual.

World opinion is a very real power today. It is a frightening power, not only to those who disagree with it but also to those who are inclined to look to minorities for sensitive understanding of the truth. Many of us believe that the most critical moment of history was posed over a minority of one, and Him crucified. At that moment the world held no hope—"What is truth?" Pilate had asked. The promise given to men is that we shall yet know the truth and that it shall set us free. I believe that truth alone can set us free so that he who would find freedom for himself and for his fellows must seek truth with clear eyes, an open mind, and a resolute heart.

How does the majority of whites in southern Africa explain and attempt to justify its determination to maintain a position of privilege, of political, social and economic domination? By holding that there are irreconcilable differences between the races of men and by postulating that the differences between white and brown are differences of superiority and inferiority, e.g. such differences would lead, if the U.K. continues to permit coloured immigration, to the deterioration of the British people.

If this were true, and scientifically it is obsolete, then the world is doomed to decay for the figures are two to one against us. I do not believe that it is true but it is obvious that if one-third of the world's population challenged the majority along these lines the tensions would soon undermine world peace. One of the reasons why the free nations condemn our racial policies is that their continuance is a threat to the peace of the world.

But is the race myth really the whole story? We whites have led a privileged life and nothing is harder to abandon than privilege. I believe that this factor is an important one even if there are others. This is not the first country, nor is it the first time, that has seen the sort of situation which confronts us today. Always there have been select groups of people, minorities, who have believed it to be their privilege to rule their fellow men. Their attitude has provoked amongst their fellow-citizens of the same race a reaction very similar to that which we see today amongst the African people of our countries. We look back less than two centuries to the situation in Europe, we remember the Reform Laws of Britain passed not much over 100 years ago. By that time tensions had reached such a pitch that rebellion was close at hand. Our regime, our thinking is really so old-fashioned that we belong to the pre-revolution period of the eighteenth century. And we would like to repeal the 20th century and all its talk of democracy! At least we are determined to stand on our rights. No one may interfere in our internal affairs; but of course they do.

We depend upon our interdependence. We trade with each other, we share in the scientific advances of the world. New drugs, new technologies come to us from other people in other lands and cure our sicknesses. Through the radio and the press the minds of our people are in touch with world thought. Also there is world concern. It is not true to say that we in southern Africa are surrounded by enemies. Do you remember—of course you don't—but I remember that we thought rather sombrely about Adolph Hitler's mental state when he screamed: "Democracy is lined up on one side of the Marxist dictatorship and the criminals of East and West are employing the United Nations Organization"—(sorry I mean the League of Nations)—"to encircle our country and to deny us our place in the sun."

In fact there is a great measure of world concern for us. Such concern for the white people of southern Africa can be found not only in white countries but amongst the brown people of Africa. Sympathetic concern is intervention and it is the kind of intervention that we need in full measure for over southern Africa a great question mark is poised. What is to be our future? What is your thinking? The official policies of both our countries on race are unacceptable both to the world and to the vast majority of our own fellow-countrymen. And even if they were true could they stand before the onslaught of the spiritual force of the democratic urge which has been the vital phenomenon of the last three centuries? The power of the democratic idea is at least partly explained by its results. Democracy, the right to participate equally in the government of one's country, has brought higher standards of living, better educational and medical facilities, and a new stature to the personality of the people. Maybe democracy is not the only form of government which can help to attain these ends, but most people in southern Africa believe that a democratic way of life is infinitely preferable to any authoritarian regime. Men do not live by bread alone and the growth of the personality, the development of wise responsibility, the practical acceptance of the fact that men are fallible, together with the belief that our society can be improved, all are included in the democratic ideal. The battle of the 20th century is the struggle between democracy and authoritarianism, a battle for the sanctity of the person, of each citizen, because he is a human being. When we whites of southern Africa emerge from our eighteenth-century dream, on which side will we be found?

The spread of democracy in the past century has broken down the class system and the caste system. In southern Africa it could break down the race system and bring freedom to both oppressed and oppressor—for both are bound. But amongst our white people where could it get sufficient soil in which to grow? We have deceived ourselves into believing that we share already in a democracy. In fact there is nothing so grimly dead as a form which has lost its spirit. We do have democratic forms for whites. In Southern Rhodesia we have a Constitution which has been totally rejected by the African people because it offered what was proclaimed to be first steps in democracy for African citizens but which was bound by restrictions, which was based upon first and second class rolls, which was smothered in imponderables.

This is not democracy and sometimes I despair of ever seeing it established amongst our peoples of the Republic and of Rhodesia. How can we make peaceful progress towards democracy when it is illegal to use the natural methods of getting there: free association, free discussion and the right to criticise? Democracy is not a perfection, it is marching forward together, a continuing fellowship allowing for differences of opinion, providing within itself the machinery for effecting peaceful change. Democracy is not only a system of government, it is a way of life. It has grown from the deep desire of men to develop to the limit of their ability.

What do you think about it? What do you intend to do about it? I have asked myself that question a thousand times. I cannot see the way; but the ideal is clear. You have done me great honor in inviting me to speak to you. I wish with all my heart that I could show you how easily the impossible will happen. I cannot, but there are two things I will say for I say them continually to myself. The first is that the impossible continually happens, and the second is that your responsibility starts with yourself. May I quote again: "We lose our moral place in any society if we do not cherish, protect and promote the principles on which men's most fundamental liberties rest." Be free then in your thought, courageous in your speech, sympathetic in your association with others. Remember that all South Africans are your fellow-citizens and their welfare should be your deep concern. In the words of Robert Frost I call you to a one-man revolution.

1977 UN Speech

In 1977 the Special UN Committee on Decolonization (or Committee of 24) was still meeting to try to resolve the situation in Southern Rhodesia. Todd had suffered through two stretches of imprisonment or restriction by the Smith government, mostly to silence his public speaking, which presented a real problem for the whites because Todd was such an effective speaker. In June 1976 Todd was released from a five-year restriction to his Hokonui ranch and could travel and speak again. Despite being sixty-nine years old, Todd went on a speaking tour as civil war raged and the situation in Southern Rhodesia was reaching a critical stage. Todd began a lobbying effort in the United States and Britain to bring about majority rule. Jimmy Carter had just come into power as the new U.S. president in January 1977. During his tour, Todd met with Andrew Young, the U.S. ambassador to the

UN, Vice President Walter Mondale, Secretary of State Cyrus Vance, and testified before a U.S. Congressional Committee. Todd gave testimony before the Committee of 24 on June 6, 1977, at the UN Headquarters, New York City, at 3 p.m. The committee devoted an entire hearing just to Todd's testimony.[31] Todd also spoke before numerous civic and political groups during this tour—an example of which is found in the speech text following the UN speech. The atrocities that Todd narrated clearly show that the threats against his life even in his sixties were real. The speech text is from the United Nations General Assembly, *Verbatim Record of the 1078th Meeting of the Special Committee on the Situation with Regard to the Implementation of the Declaration on the Granting of Independence to Colonial Countries and Peoples*, A/AC.109/PV.1078.

Mr. Todd: The African-American Institute invited me to visit the United States to meet people who are interested in Africa and especially those who are concerned for Rhodesia.

On my release from detention in June 1976, the British Broadcasting Corporation sent a team to interview me, and I called for massive intervention by other countries, naming especially the United Kingdom and the United States of America. At that time it appeared to be unlikely that the United States would show much interest, but in September Mr. Kissinger's initiative broke the stalemate, and we are now concerned with what has happened since then and with the future.

A week before Mr. Smith declared the independence of Rhodesia his government arrested me and restricted me to my ranch for one year. However, just at that moment the British Prime Minister visited Rhodesia—a few days before the Unilateral Declaration of Independence—and, at his request, the police took me to Salisbury to meet him. I discussed the situation with Mr. Wilson and with his military adviser, who held that the logistics of a possible campaign were too difficult to overcome. Mr. Wilson then returned to the United Kingdom and stated that force would not be used if there was a rebellion. That statement may have been politically sound in the United Kingdom but it presented Mr. Smith with a blank cheque for rebellion.

As the years passed, attempts were made to find a solution and six years later the Foreign Secretary, Sir Alex Douglas Home, came to an agreement with Mr. Smith. I met the Foreign Secretary during his visit in 1971 and he told me that at each settlement attempt the United Kingdom Government had had to ease its requirements for a settlement; in other words, it had had to ask less from Mr. Smith.

The Rhodesian Government was confident that it had won the day. In February 1972 a top-line conference of the heads of the South African State Security (BOSS), the Portuguese Security (DGS) and the Rhodesian Government was convened in Salisbury to reinforce the bonds of white supremacy over the whole of southern Africa.

A month earlier than that, Lord Pearce, together with the members of his Commission, was sent by the United Kingdom Government to determine if the Home-Smith proposals were acceptable "to the people as a whole." Three months later Lord Pearce reported that the proposals were acceptable to most whites, Asians and Coloureds, but as they were not acceptable to blacks they were not therefore acceptable "to the people as a whole."

Hundreds of black leaders had by that time, 1972, spent seven years and longer in prison or detention. In January my daughter Judith, and I were also imprisoned, but five weeks later we were transferred to detention. The struggle continued, but in the past three years the intensity of the struggle and the suffering have escalated. On 5 June 1976 I was set free, but many hundreds of black citizens are still detained without trial in primitive camps or in prisons.

Following Mr. Kissinger's visit last September, Mr. Smith publicly accepted majority rule within two years. The following morning the *Washington Post* expressed world relief in the headline "Smith accepts plan for black rule." But we were all deceived, for in the fruitless months which have followed it has become clear that to Mr. Smith majority rule means a franchise which is so restricted that, while it may list 80,000 white voters, it will list only perhaps 80,001 black voters. Electoral reality in that situation would ensure a continuation of white rule. The roll should of course list the 80,000 whites and 20 times that number of black voters. So a stalemate now escalates into civil war.

Almost every African is a nationalist, but the government actively propagates the fallacy that the mass of blacks are intimidated by a few men who are Marxists and that the people wish to be protected from them by the security forces. The guerrillas are in fact the cutting edge of the nationalist movement; the guerrillas and the people are one. However, whatever the Government may say, their actions show that they do recognize that the people support the guerrillas, and in that knowledge the government pursues a policy of terror against the civilian population. Innocent people are killed, villages are destroyed, cattle are killed or confiscated.

To give the security forces unrestricted action in that campaign, an "Indemnity and Compensation Act" was passed in 1976 which gives full protection to all government employees against legal-action, civil or criminal. The Secretary of Law and Order has told police graduates "not to be squeamish in departing from the niceties of established procedures" which, he says, are more appropriate for normal times.

It is generally accepted that the conference convened in Geneva in October last was a failure, but I believe it was at least another step—and an important one—in the clarifying of the Rhodesian issue.

Since then we have had the visit to Rhodesia of Dr. Owen, the new British Foreign Secretary. His approach seems to rule out a further negotiating conference—but I may be wrong about that. In place of a conference he apparently has sent a team to discuss the possible content of a new constitution for Zimbabwe which will be drawn up by Her Majesty's Government. Dr. Owen appears to have gained the support of the Government of the United States of America. This is really why I have come to the United States, particularly to let my views be known to the Government of the United States. At one point it appeared that the United States Government might be a co-sponsor of the conference, which was a possibility not acceptable to the nationalist movement.

At first glance the new combined approach seems splendid and full of hope, but it will prove significant only to the extent that it can succeed where all other attempts so far to find a solution have failed. There seem to be only two possibilities before us. We can find a settlement, which means that, without further fighting, Mr. Smith can be forced to transfer power from the whites to the people as a whole, including the whites; or the guerrilla war will continue and increase in intensity until the gun is seen to bring the required shift of power. If the transfer of power can be made now, we can hope without too much more suffering to set up a democratic state; but if the war continues until Mr. Smith is to surrender, so much damage will have been done both to the institutions of government and to the economy that a totalitarian regime may well result.

We stand at that point in history, and my visit here is to plead for maximum support for the British initiative. However, I cannot determine how clear-sighted or how resolute the British initiative is likely to be or whether or not it is likely to succeed. But where I am ignorant I would suggest that the United States Government, in its cooperation with Britain, must be knowledgeable, and where I may doubt the effectiveness of the British plans the United States Government must determine that the programme of action will be carried through to a successful conclusion.

If Dr. Owen's plans stop at offering Mr. Smith a democratic constitution and, in the event of his refusal to comply with it, he has nothing else to suggest except that the war continue, then the United States of America might well not participate.

What is required today is a full commitment by the United Kingdom and the United States that they will use every means short of armed intervention to bring the war to an end on the basis of a transfer of power. There has been a fairly thorough examination of possible methods of exerting pressure on the Smith Government, but there has never really been a full and categorical statement by the governments which are endeavouring to establish justice in Rhodesia that the full weight of their resources will be brought to bear upon this issue.

In the meantime, the Governments of the United States of America and of Great Britain and the United Nations itself seem unable to defeat about 90,000 white adult men and women in Rhodesia who 11 years ago hijacked a country and its then 5 million people.

There is a good deal more I could say but perhaps representatives would like to get it from me by way of questions.

The Chairman: On behalf of the Committee I thank Mr. Todd for his important, informative statement. Mr. Todd has another engagement but can stay with us for a short time. I shall therefore call on any representatives who may wish to make comments on his statement or put questions to him. Before doing so, however, I wish to note the presence in our midst of the representative of the administering Power, the United Kingdom, and the representative of the liberation movement.

Mr. Jaipal (India): I should like to begin by saying: Thank God for people like Mr. Garfield Todd. I was very interested in the statement he made. I was particularly impressed by his affirmation that the guerrillas and the people are one. Such a categorical statement has not been made so far in this Committee.

I have two questions to put to Mr. Todd. First, I should like to have Mr. Todd's own assessment of the number of white people in Rhodesia who might be genuinely in favour of majority rule and the number who would be likely to stay on under the conditions of majority rule. What is his estimate of the number of people who might want to leave? My second question arises from the part of his statement in which he advocated that the United States and the United Kingdom Governments should resort to every means short of armed intervention. Would he include among those means sanctions against South Africa?

Mr. Todd: My thoughts on the first question are these. Probably some 15 per cent of the white people in the present Rhodesia are so committed to white supremacy that they could not stay. I would think there are about 10 per cent of the white people who are prepared to stand up and be counted for majority rule. With regard to the rest of the people, while at the moment they acclaim Smith, they would probably—if the change were to be made tomorrow—acclaim Nkomo, or Muzorewa, or Mugabe.

We know that a large proportion of the people want to carry on a reasonable life. They have their homes there; they would like to work there; they would like to stay there. I would think that a very high proportion of the whites would like to stay. So I believe that if the change could be made we could be left with a very high percentage of the white people—75 or 80 per cent—who would really stay.

With regard to the second question I would say this. I am an ordinary civilian. I do not have much knowledge of the inside workings of government nowadays, as I have been out of government for more than 15 years. I realize that in some ways there is one, common situation in southern Africa, because there are so many common aspects of the whole problem. On the other hand, it seems to me, from my position in the Rhodesia of today—the Zimbabwe of tomorrow—that, practically speaking, it would be a very good idea to have Namibia and Zimbabwe fixed up and set free first, and then the world could look at South Africa. I myself, selfishly, do not want to see this matter become one campaign against the whole of southern Africa. I think it will be more effective if we look at what can be done in Namibia, what can be done in Zimbabwe—clear the ground there—and then look at the needs of the people in South Africa. I do not mean to say that we should forget the people in South Africa. All I am saying is: first things first.

Mr. Diakite (Mali) (interpretation from French): First, I should like to tell Mr. Todd how happy my delegation is to see him here and to hear his opinion on the situation in Zimbabwe and get the information he has given us. My delegation noted with interest that Mr. Todd spoke of a very close relationship between the guerrillas and the people. But during his statement he spoke also of two possibilities for achieving the liberation of Zimbabwe. On the one hand, he spoke of the peaceful transfer of power to the majority. The other possibility was that if that method did not succeed, the war of national liberation would continue. That leads me to put a question.

Mr. Todd stated that if the war of national liberation continued and was victorious, independent Zimbabwe could find itself under a totalitarian regime. Of course, I am paraphrasing what he said, but I should like to have some clarification of his statement that the success of the war of national liberation could lead to the installation of a totalitarian regime.

My second question is this. We know that since the Unilateral Declaration of Independence there has existed in Southern Rhodesia a minority of whites that has been increasingly supporting the armed struggle taking place there. Could Mr. Todd give us some idea of the percentage of whites who today favour the armed struggle because of their general discouragement and Ian Smith's obstinacy?

Mr. Todd: As I understood it, the first question related to what I meant when I said that there would be a totalitarian State if the armed struggle continued and succeeded and Mr. Smith were overthrown. I think that at the present moment, a large proportion of the people within Rhodesia would like to see us go to an election and, from such an election, to choose our new government. But elections can be held and people can plead their case as political leaders only in a certain atmosphere.

If we could come to reasonable terms now, we would hope to be able to allow the various nationalist leaders of today to campaign freely for their particular parties. But if the struggle goes on for several more years, and if, as could well happen, in that time there arose an internal struggle within the nationalist armed groups themselves, which I do not at the moment foresee—though of course we cannot see what is going to happen—we could have a continuation of civil war of a more terrible kind between black and black. So what I am particularly concerned about is not so much who is coming out of this, or what particular type of government even whoever does come out of it wants. I should like to see freedom and opportunity for the people to make quite clear what is their wish and who they wish to rule over them. I hope that may answer the question, but I do not know if it will.

The other one is this. It is quite clear now, from what many of my friends tell me, that many of the young whites in Rhodesia would like this war to finish quickly because, they say, "Smith has said there will be majority rule within two years. Since, when we started this fight to stop the possibility of majority rule, Smith had already given in on the main principle, what are we dying for?" But they do not have their way. There is no poll among the armed forces to find out whether the war should stop or not.

The Chairman: Since no other member wishes to speak at this time, I shall myself now address one or two questions to Mr. Todd. In the first place, I think the latest explanation he has given concerning what he said about an authoritarian state will perhaps shed further light, because, like my colleague from Mali, I was worried by his saying that if the war should continue and the liberation movements should eventually succeed in toppling Smith by force of arms, then the danger inherent there would be the creation of an authoritarian regime. If my understanding is correct, his definition of the creation of an authoritarian regime in this context means the creation of a state without going through the normal processes as understood in the Westminster concept. Therefore, I think we do not wish to initiate a debate on the matter, but I believe my colleague from Mali raised an important point in order to allay misconceptions. I have three specific questions.

First, we know of the initiatives now under way, undertaken by the British Government as the administering power. In the light of those initiatives and of what is being said about the possibility not so much of a peaceful settlement, because quite frankly one cannot talk of a peaceful settlement in a situation in which war is going on, but rather of a negotiated settlement, how does Mr. Todd interpret those persistent acts of aggression committed by the Smith regime now against Mozambique and, before Mozambique, against Botswana, and the threats against Zambia?

The second question relates to the matter of sanctions. I think the question raised by the Ambassador of India did not originally really refer to what we should do with South Africa as such but to what we should do to South Africa as the principal violator of sanctions imposed on Rhodesia. I would ask Mr. Todd how effective sanctions have been in the context of the Rhodesian situation, and what in his opinion could be done to improve that aspect of the international contribution to the developments in Zimbabwe?

My final question is this. Since he has understandably lamented the inability of the United Nations itself to resolve the problem or at least to help the administering power to resolve the problem in Rhodesia, what other sort of measures or pressures could the international community bring to bear to assist the efforts of the Zimbabweans themselves in the present situation?

Mr. Todd: It is very difficult to be clear on the way Mr. Smith acts. I am certainly not an authority on the thinking of Mr. Smith. What one sees on all sides is desperation.

A year or so ago Mr. Smith and his Government seemed to be absolutely on top of the world. It seemed they were going to manage to come through economically. They were quite sure they could clear up the people they called terrorists. But by the beginning of last year the picture was changing very radically, and at that time they passed an Act called the Indemnity and Compensation Act, which showed how desperate they were getting, because they were at last recognizing that the people and the guerrillas were one and that, as soon as the guerrillas came over the border, they were lost among the people.

That to some extent answers the Chairman's first question, in this way. Across the border they can see the camps. They are something they can see and strike at. It is good for morale to be able to strike at something definite. Within Rhodesia, the guerrillas are so fluid that you cannot see them; they look just the same as everybody else, and they are just the same as everybody else. It was quite clear how desperate the government was getting when last year it passed that particular Act, because it gives the soldiers and all other security people a blank cheque. It is the sort of indemnity act you pass at the end of a war, sadly, because some terrible things have happened and you want to clear the matter up. This being passed in the middle of a war and being extended back retrogressively to 1972 and progressively forward, it really gives the people authority to do anything they want.

At the same time the Secretary of Law and Order encourages a passing-out parade of young policemen not to be too squeamish, not to keep to the ordinary methods and the behaviour we would expect in normal circumstances. "You will have to lose this squeamishness in the present situation." The Minister, Mr. Van Der Byl, said that, if people had anything to do with terrorists, then they could expect to suffer and be killed.

A week or two ago the General in charge of the war was exhorting the people to look at the terrorists and to make up their minds whether it was a good idea to have anything to do with them, and he suggested it was not. He seemed to think the terrorists were people who came from Mars or something, not from the villages of the people among whom they were really operating. And now, of course, that all these permissions have been given, and now that we have recognized the desperation of the government, we see terrible things happening. I will cite just one instance.

The Lutheran Church has a mission about 20 miles from my place, and there, since the very beginning of the century, they have had a very fine hospital. Eight or ten years ago they produced their first black doctor, Dr. Zhou. Now, in that area the guerrillas have been very active indeed—all through that area. And, as we have seen with other missions, when the guerrillas come into a mission they expect to get the sort of treatment missions would hand out to everybody who comes to see them, they expect to be able to get help, and they expect to be able to get medicines. We saw this situation when Bishop Lamont was sentenced to 10 years.

Recently, about four weeks ago, I think, one of those young men came through Munene mission. He roused the sisters at the hospital, and they had some singing and, I believe, some dancing and so on. Then, as the day broke, the children in the primary boarding school heard the singing and went up and shared in it and were taught some freedom songs.

If when one of the guerrillas leaves a place it is not reported that he has been there, the security forces will take very strong action and blot out people in that area or village. That is well known. So, before he left, this particular young man who two weeks later was shot at another mission station farther down, went to the doctor's house and asked to use the phone, or demanded to use the phone—after all, he was carrying a gun. He used the phone and rang up the police station about 20 miles away and announced that he was present, and then went on his way. When the security forces came they were particularly angry and accused the doctor of being the centre of guerrilla activity. They did not accept the statement that he had been helpless in this situation. Let us be quite clear. I am sure in my own mind that the doctor's inclinations would have been to help the guerrilla movement so to that extent he was guilty—if a person is guilty amongst the African people for supporting the guerrilla movement. Anyway, some days later, early in the morning, there was a knock at his door. His wife looked out of the window and said, "There are three men with rifles." He said, "Well, anyway I must go." He went out and he was executed on the doorstep, and we are told that the guerrillas executed him. Two days later when he was buried, soldiers who were on duty there were laughing at the funeral.

That is only one example of the type of event that we have in our present situation. But that is the sort of thing that drives me to do what I can to get this war brought to a conclusion. So many people, white and black, are unnecessarily losing their lives. Even more important, so very many people, thousands, half a million, have been taken from their villages and put into keeps. Hundreds of thousands of people are suffering daily because of the continuation of this terrible situation. Also, it is a fact which I think the world should be terribly concerned about, even if only with the racial aspect, that 90,000 white adults can keep 6 million black people submerged and bring the whole of the southern Africa situation into a time of crisis.

The next question concerned sanctions. There is no doubt, of course, that the critical thing is oil. It can probably be traced from Iran through South Africa. It is sold to South Africa. South Africa is quite open in its statement that it will not apply sanctions and that business will go on as usual. The guerrillas walk from place to place. They do not even use bicycles. But wherever they strike—helicopters, aeroplanes, lorries the whole power of the war in Rhodesia depends on oil. If there were a shortage of oil, Mr. Smith would come to an accommodation with the black nationalist leaders. The oil situation is absolutely critical. I know that America and Britain have been having conversations with South Africa. At a certain point Mr. Vorster may recognize that his own situation has been worsened to such an extent that, as a responsible leader of a people, he may find it in his interests to take a strong line with Smith and turn off the tap. That is what I would hope.

As far as the United Nations is concerned, I would think that moral suasion is enormously important. Of course, the moral suasion of one's friends has more strength than that of one's enemies. As far as the whites of Rhodesia are concerned, they have been taught that the United Nations is their enemy, so that what is said at the United Nations is usually received with derision. But within the United Nations there are not only white nations but black nations, that still have some call on the respect of the whites, if one wants to have their respect, in Rhodesia. There is no doubt that if we could eliminate from the minds of the white people that there is any thought on the part of any nation of coming to their support in the event of intervention from the north, then maybe that would at least bring them to a sense of reality which they seem to lack today.

Mr. Forrester (Australia): Mr. Todd has spoken on the one hand, of the great majority of whites in Rhodesia wanting to see an end to the war, and yet, on the other hand, he has given us also very graphic pictures of the way in which the whites of Rhodesia maintain particularly brutal repression. Does Mr. Todd have some reason to offer for the way in which the whites seem captive to that system of repression and is there any way in which we outside Rhodesia can assist in breaking down that system? Is there some way in which we can appeal to the whites of Rhodesia to accept the fact that majority rule has to come and that that repression cannot continue?

Mr. Todd: I have, of course, been bitterly disappointed in the white population and in the fact that they have gone along with Mr. Smith. But I am afraid that they are probably just the same as any other group of human beings of any colour who find themselves in a position of absolute power, complete power; over a large population whose exploitation gives them a standard of living almost unequalled, whereby white wages on the average are 10 times those of black wages. Such a situation should not arise. That is it. And when it does arise, well, this is what we see.

Australia is one of those places which, I believe, could have some moral power as far as Rhodesia is concerned. Australia could also—although I know it has its own problems—be prepared, if it would, to accept some of those who will find it impossible to stay. Whether Australia would like to add those to its population, of course, is another matter. But I would think that the main thing would be to let the nations of the world speak out on every occasion and tell those 90,000 whites that they must ditch Smith and hand over power from white to black. It is very simple. But while they have the guns they are as difficult to displace as any other brutal leadership would be who has all the military power.

The Chairman: I am glad that Mr. Todd mentioned one aspect in his statement which we found at our discussions in Maputo aroused a lot of interest and specific attention on the part of the liberation movements. I am referring to the example of the doctor who was obviously murdered by the Smith security forces and the attempt that was made to pin the blame on the freedom fighters. One of the subjects which much concerned the leaders of the liberation movement in Zimbabwe at our Conference in Maputo and which was discussed very vehemently was the systematic persecution of the white missionaries in Zimbabwe. I wonder whether from your own experience, Mr. Todd, and from your own knowledge of the developments in Zimbabwe, you can enlighten us more on this point. I know you have been persecuted, not so much as a missionary but also perhaps because of your own historical background, and I also know of the persecution of your daughter. We also know of the case of Bishop Lamont. I wonder how systematic is the deliberate attempt to try and intimidate the white missionaries in Zimbabwe by the Smith regime.

Mr. Todd: I think, in a situation like this, that it is not very easy to stand out against all the people among whom you have worked. Now, most white people work largely among whites. I was probably fortunate in having worked for many years entirely among blacks, so that I was not so sensitive to white criticism. Anybody who stands out on the side of the blacks, I think, is open to persecution. But what people do not seem to understand is this: I do not think of myself as being anti-white. I remember a white woman coming up to me in an office one day and saying. "Mr. Todd, I would like to ask you a question. Why aren't you on our side?" I said: "Well, actually, I thought I was on your side. If you are a person who wants her children and her grandchildren to stay happily in this country, then you should know that the policies that I am putting forward are the policies which would ensure that all the people will stay happily together. But I am afraid that you are either on Smith's side or you are irresponsible and want chaos and confusion."

I was head of a big mission school for years, and it came to the point where I saw blacks take over completely and do the job better than I had ever done it. In such a case one learns humility.

The Chairman: I want once again to thank Mr. Todd for his very informative presentation to the Committee. We have had in this Committee the opportunity to listen to representatives of the liberation movements; in fact, the year before last we also had the opportunity to listen to the leaders of the liberation movements. I think it also was valuable to have the opportunity to listen to Mr. Todd, a leader in his own right, and a person who has played and is playing an active role in developments in Zimbabwe. I think his contribution to our Committee is important, not just for the purpose of the Committee's understanding of the issues involved, but also in the light of his background and position, in a world where sometimes issues tend to be confused and where there is a lot of ignorance about what is going on in Zimbabwe. And I am particularly glad, as Ambassador Rikhi Jaipal rightly pointed out, that he clearly put the problem of the freedom fighters in its proper perspective by saying that you cannot really differentiate between the freedom fighters and the people: they are one and the same thing. That is a point which has to be made, and which, I think, needs to be emphasized, particularly in countries and places such as the location of the United Nations, where the tendency is always to over-simplify things and not really to understand the issues in their proper perspective.

So in the name of the members of the Committee and in my own name, I want to thank him very much for appearing before us, and I am sure that his information and contribution will be invaluable to the Committee's consideration of the question of Southern Rhodesia, soon to be Zimbabwe.

International Center of Indianapolis
Luncheon on Basic Issues

Unfortunately, very few recordings exist of Todd's speeches; however, the Disciples of Christ Historical Society found a recording of this speech delivered before the International Center, Indianapolis, Indiana, on June 13, 1977. I have transcribed the text and it expresses the rough form of an extemporaneous address, bearing out Todd's comment to me that many of his speeches were extempore and that he made no attempt to systematically preserve them. This speech was delivered one week after the 1977 UN speech, and it reveals many of the people he met and events in which he participated in both the United States and Britain during this crisis period in the waning years of the Smith regime. Dr. Robert Nelson, the chair of the International Center and executive secretary of the department of Africa in the division of overseas ministries of the American Disciples of Christ, had known Todd since the 1950s when Todd was prime minister. Nelson had kept the Rhodesian situation before the American Disciples.[32] Nelson made this speaking opportunity available.[33]

Chairman Dr. Nelson, ladies and gentlemen. I am told that I can speak until five past one and I know that some of you have to go back to your businesses and then I understand I'm going to be able to answer questions from those who have questions to put. Now my wife and I went out from New Zealand in 1934 from the Christian Church—which, of course, are the Churches of Christ there—to take over a little mission station in Rhodesia. We were fortunate in this way that we didn't go to a place where there were other missionaries although there had been earlier, and a great deal of work had been done. We found ourselves two quite young—twenty-six and twenty-three—young people amongst twenty thousand blacks and we established our own behavior patterns.

We hadn't been there very long when one day an old, old, old man in just a little leather apron and sandals and carrying a little axe came into the mission and he came up to me haltingly and I could see that one eye had quite withered away. And he said to me that he had come to get medicine for his eye. So I suggested that it was a good job that he had one good eye but this was a little bit old and after all he was an old man. He looked at me very straightly with his one eye and then he said, "Are you saying that it's because I'm so old that this eye is like this?" And I said, "Well I was sort of saying that." "But," he said, "This eye is exactly the same age." (Laughter) So I learned that even though you're old and illiterate you can be a little bit right.

Coming through the school in its early days was the man who is now known as the Rev. Ndabaningi Sithole, who was one of the four African leaders to assemble in Geneva last year. My wife taught him for several years and he got really all his English from my wife. And she says that he was the brightest student she ever put through the big school that we have at Dadaya where she was the headmistress for twenty years. We've had no doubt about the ability of Africans. We watched them at first in the 1930s without very much desire to make progress. Then in the '40s came a real revolution in their attitudes to education. And then having established something of a foundation of education, in the '50s the political revolution. And whites around didn't quite understand what was happening. They always think there must be some whites usually communists to effect any change in the African population. They don't realise that some of these important things are grassroots movements. But in the '50s, as I say, there was this revolution in political attitudes. In the '60s there was—the peaceful demand—for change, for sharing in the decision-making within Rhodesia. But it was all to no avail. And in the '70s we find ourselves really in the situation of a civil war which is so horrible. I have always been on the side of peace. But if you are going to work for peace you've first got to work for justice because peace must be established on justice. And where in the scriptures we're told that peacemakers are the children of God and it is interpreted as being you just haven't to cause any trouble at all—that's not a proper interpretation. It's proper exegesis in my estimation—if you've got to put foundations to peace, those foundations are the foundations of justice.

Then eventually in 1946 I was asked to stand as a Member of Parliament. I said to the then prime minister who became Lord Malvern, "Well this is silly. I'll consider standing but I really don't see that farmers and miners, a white electorate, are going to put a missionary in as their local member of Parliament." And my first big address in my constituency was on what was called in those days "native policy"—in other words what I thought should have happened vis à vis the African population, the black population in Rhodesia. I gave a long address, most of which I still agree with now—this was reasonably enlightened for its day—I thought to myself that finishes me, but it's better to be finished now. The white electorate—it didn't cause a ripple because they just thought it was Grimms' fairy tales. It had no significance. It had no basis in reality but they thought I had some other positive qualifications which would make me perhaps a reasonable Member of Parliament. And so they elected me as a Member of Parliament. And it was all right until I was prime minister and brought in the new franchise bill which immediately opened the common roll to 10,000 blacks on to that common roll that people realized what a terrible mistake they had made and in the next election they recognized that.

But it was all very sad, because the Federation of Rhodesia and Nyasland was established in 1953, and it was established on a common roll such as we had in Rhodesia. We've always had a common roll, because we got our constitution from Great Britain, and she had to show a reasonable fairness with the whole population. But the federation at one point—the government—decided that they were not going to have this because in the federation there were sixty blacks to one white. And the whites were determined, to my utter disbelief—that's how I found later it was true—they were determined to control the whole federation of the two Rhodesias and Nyasaland. This was going to be a run for white interests. So they brought up an "A" roll and a "B" roll. And later the next prime minister following me did the same in Rhodesia. The "A" roll can give and maintain white control absolutely for all time. Of course it was supposed to finish sometime in the constitution but everybody knew it would be for all time. And the black "B" roll was to bring the ultimate in frustration, which of course it did. And once those two rolls were set up in Rhodesia—and of course the federation broke up in '62—it could not be maintained on such a basis of injustice. And so when in 1959 the "A" and the "B" rolls were introduced into Rhodesia—into Rhodesian law—I saw and I am sure many Rhodesian people saw, too, that it was only a matter of time before there would be an absolute confrontation between black and white.

Well, you would have thought maybe with an electoral system like that, the whites would have been satisfied, but no. In 1965 Mr. Ian Smith and the white men who were with him decided that any remaining tie with the outside world and with Britain and the British Commonwealth—any remaining tie was dangerous. Any remaining tie with Britain threatened white rule. So having failed to get the British to agree to the constitution, which would make sure of white supremacy, came the Unilateral Declaration of Independence. And the Unilateral Declaration of Independence—of course the whites thought everything was in their hands—after that Unilateral Declaration of Independence, just before they made the announcement of the Unilateral Declaration of Independence, they used the words of the American Declaration of Independence, except they took the heart out of it. They forgot to put in that it would be a government of the people, for the people—that bit was left out.

Just before they announced their independent Rhodesia I was arrested. I was on my way to the University of Edinburgh to take part in a seminar and I think they did not want me wandering around just at that particular time. So they arrested me as I was going to the airport and put me into detention for 12 months on my ranch.

Then came several attempts to find a solution. And then in 1971 Sir Alec Douglas Home, the foreign minister from Britain, and Mr. Smith came to terms. At that time it was thought by Sir Alec Douglas Home, who said to a friend of mine in Britain, "Oh, we're going to send out a commission to investigate and see if this is acceptable to the people as a whole." Because this was one of the stipulations: that whatever had been decided must be found to be acceptable to the people as a whole. But he said, "You know, they won't have to go below the chiefs because the people have no real interest in politics." Well, that was just about as inaccurate a statement as you could make because when Africans saw that the suggested constitution would put off the day of liberation for the blacks into an uncertain future and many years ahead, there again was a reaction from the grassroots. And then it was when Judith and I were caught up in January of that year before Pearce had really got properly started on his investigation that five carloads of armed police came out to arrest two very peaceful people on my ranch and put us into prison.

Well, Pearce had surrendered in one way to the Rhodesian government, who said, "you cannot have outdoor meetings for security reasons." And Pearce in his report said, "We could not really stand up to them when they were speaking about security because we were speaking about something of which we really did not know." So Pearce agreed to have meetings in the halls, and Africans in their reserves said, "We are told if we want to meet with Pearce we've got to register at the district commissioners' office." In other words the situation was going to be hopeless.

Now in his report Pearce said that "circumstances soon impressed upon us the need to have wider meetings, and so from a certain date we had open air meetings and thousands of people came to us." He didn't give in detail the fact that those circumstances led to the death of thirteen people at the hands of the security forces when people were trying to get in to see Pearce. And when they couldn't get in, then came rioting and eventually thirteen were killed. At that point the meetings were opened. And when Pearce went back to London, he said, "the terms of the Home-Smith agreement I find are generally acceptable to whites, Asians, and coloureds, but as they are not acceptable to blacks, they are therefore not acceptable to the people as a whole."

Though Mr. Smith thought the blacks couldn't have come to this conclusion on their own and suspected that people like the Todds were stirring up trouble which is just so far from the truth. Judith and I only went to such meetings as we were actually asked to go to and went only for the purpose of explaining to the people what they wanted to know regarding the published terms of the Home-Smith agreement.

Since then, of course, things haven't gone so well. And the failure of the Smith-Home agreement and the revolution of the blacks has led to this terrible civil war. The government says or has been saying—I have been away now a fortnight and it may have changed its mind, I don't know—but it has been saying that of course the mass of blacks want peace. They are satisfied with their government. There's better conditions here. Better pay, etc. than there is in any country to the north and all this stuff. And they want to be protected against the guerrillas, the terrorists, and they are glad to see the army come out. And when we take half a million of them out of their villages and put them into concentrated areas, they rejoice because they know now they are going to be safe. They've left their cattle at home and left their chattels and their whole life is disturbed and broken up but they're glad because the government is going to protect them—which the government can't really do—so Smith says.

So while they say that, the government knows very well that it will not be able to protect them. And in 1976 it passed what is called the Indemnity and Compensation Act. Now at the end of a war governments pass Indemnity acts so there can't be a whole lot of court cases on things that happened during the war or at the beginning of a war. This indemnity act was passed in '76 and made retrospective to 1972. And it just says that no civil or criminal action may be taken against any employee of the government, security forces or anyone for doing anything which they believe is necessary in the war against terrorism or in the maintenance of public order.

And in a passing out parade of police recruits the secretary for law and order exhorted the young men not to be squeamish to depart from accepted practices because these were exceptional times and a few people extra killed at the moment would save many more deaths in the future. The minister of the army, the minister of defense at that time, Mr. van der Byl, said that if people were prepared to give hospitality to terrorists within their villages then they could expect to be killed, and they would be responsible themselves. So all sorts of terrible things were happening. For example, down at Zungudza a couple of months ago some of the guerrillas had come to the villages and of course they're welcomed wherever they go. I mean, they are the people. A guerrilla puts his rifle behind the grain bin and walks out—you can't tell him from the people because he's at home with father and mother, his brothers or his cousins.

Three or four of these guerrillas had held a meeting in this very remote place and two hundred villagers—women and children and men—had come flocking in, and they were singing and having talks and so on. The guerrillas were teaching them freedom songs and a stick of security forces—I think fifteen men—came. They had been alerted because a couple of buses had been robbed in that area. So they had been sent down and they came up quietly through the bushes. Now they approached with their automatic rifles at the ready. So when a sentry fired a warning shot, they opened up with their automatic weapons and kept firing for seven minutes. When they moved into the village there were thirty-five dead, thirty-one seriously wounded. So our army does not mind killing thirty-five innocent villagers in order to kill one freedom fighter. Now that's only one instance of so many things that are happening because we have entered a time of complete ruthlessness. It is because of the tragic situation that I at the moment find myself in England and America. I have been speaking through Britain to the heads of government and here the Americans have been very kind. I started off in a very propitious way by rushing from my plane to having two hours with Andy Young. And I think probably he has smoothed my way. I don't know. But doors have opened in Washington. Just before I left on Friday morning I had forty minutes with Mr. Mondale. And I found myself so encouraged to find Mr. Mondale absolutely in sympathy with the things that I was saying and taking a line I thought was the right one. In other words he wants to see a democracy. I said to Mr. Mondale that the African leaders want to see a democracy. And he said, "Well, get them to say it more often." He added, "The American government has made it very clear that we want a universal franchise." I said, "Well, I don't want to be told if I look in the *New York Times* on October 27 on page 4 I will see that the American government has said this. What I want to hear is that repeating it time and time again. Because unless we can get power changed from white to black we will not remove the cause of the war and we will not be able to stop this horrible time." He said America would help in any possible way.

When I was released from detention in June of last year the BBC immediately sent out a team from Britain to interview me. And I said at that time, "It is quite clear to me now that this situation has gone beyond anything we can do, so there must be outside intervention. Britain is legally responsible but Britain keeps on saying to me, "We haven't got the power. We haven't got the power." I reply by saying, "You got the will. If you had the will you could get the help you need to accomplish what has to be done." I pointed this out to Mr. Mondale and thanked him for the assurance that in every way possible, I know short of armed intervention, that the United States government would assist us.

Now I don't know whether we can stop it. I do know this: if we could stop it now we would be able to set up a democracy in Zimbabwe. But if war drags on for another three or four years we will destroy the last of the functions of government. The government itself has already destroyed the law and the economy will also be destroyed because even now at this moment all whites up to fifty years of age have got to register for military service. The economy is badly hit. You can't pull people out of their businesses—especially one-man businesses—without doing tremendous damage.

And so just to explain why I am here: I've been here in the United States to see people like Mr. Andy Young, Mr. Mondale, Mr. Cyrus Vance, the various congressmen who were very kind, very happy to see me. I appeared before Congressman Diggs's Investigative Committee and have seen so many people. And I am hoping that I may in this visit [have] made some small contribution to a coming peace in Zimbabwe.

University of Otago Graduation Speech

When Todd studied at Glen Leith Theological College in Dunedin, he also took courses in education and English at Otago University but he never completed a degree. However, over the course of his career many colleges and universities gave Todd honorary doctorates for his accomplishments: Butler University, Eureka College, Minnesota Bible College, and Milligan College. Finally, in 1979, Otago granted Todd an honorary doctorate and invited him to give the commencement address on December 7, 1979, to four hundred graduates at a packed Dunedin Town Hall. Otago University Professor R. G. Mulgan said in presenting Todd with the honorary degree, "New Zealanders may take pride that they have produced a statesman who has become an international champion of racial equality." One observer said, "The applause which followed the address showed the appreciation with which it had been heard."[34] The speech text is from the Todd papers held by Susan Paul.

Mr. Chancellor, members of council, members of staff, graduates, students of the University of Otago, ladies and gentlemen, fifty years ago I could not have imagined that I would have a part to play in a graduation ceremony of the University of Otago. You have given me great honour and I would like to offer something to you young men and women whom it is my privilege to address.

Unfortunately for me I am fifty years behind in almost any subject you could mention. The only subject in which I have kept reasonably up to date is life itself. My concern has been with people and there are certainly plenty of them. When God addressed the first couple and said "Be fruitful and multiply," he enunciated the only commandment which men and women have accepted with alacrity and obeyed with enthusiasm!

When we arrived in Rhodesia 45 years ago we found that our home was within a fairly primitive community. I had no doubts about the role we had come to play. We had come to give: we were the people who knew. We had a position of superiority. I am sure we didn't consciously acknowledge this but the fact remains. One morning an old man made his way slowly up the road to our house. He was leaning on a long stick and wore only a leather apron, his skin so tanned and wrinkled that the leather apron seemed part of his body. He had come for help. He pointed to one eye which had almost withered away. Did I have any medicine which could renew the eye? From my position of advanced knowledge and with my background of five years of First Aid, I contemplated the eye. If I had just been honest and admitted that I had no idea why the eye had withered, all would have been well. Obviously I had no medicine which could renew a withered eye and this I explained. Then I went on to explain that the reason for the deterioration of the eye was age—old age. At that point the old man seemed a little startled, drew himself up and turned his one good eye on me with a very direct stare. "You say that my eye has withered because it is old but that is not so." He pointed to his good eye. "This eye is exactly the same age."

Where I found myself far behind my primitive neighbours was in my lack of good manners. Even now I have not fully caught up but I am improving. Africans have time-consuming and elaborate behaviour patterns. I admit with shame that I am chronically short of time. I stop my car beside a person on the road and say, "Could you please tell me the way to Marabanidze?" The person, whether man or child will probably reply, "Good morning, sir." Rebuked, I relax and say "Good morning. How are you?" The reply will come, "I am well, sir and how are you?" "I am well, and could you please tell me the way to Marabanidze?"

People! Living and adventuring with people! Years ago, in Nyasaland, now Malawi, I relaxed one evening with a senior British Colonial Magistrate. He told me that it was he who had imprisoned Mr. Nehru, but what he really wanted to speak about was the common people of India. They were wonderful people to live with—just the finest and most pleasant in the world.

But he must have been wrong for only last year I sat in the Adirondacks with an athletic 87-year-old white American and listened to his stories of the days of his youth when he had been a metalworker and lived in China. He had quite lost his heart to the happy, industrious, patient, pleasant people and their delightful families. They were just the most wonderful people in the world and so one could go on.

From the University of Otago five men and women of my own tribe, and in my own lifetime, have gone from New Zealand to make their homes in China, India, the United Kingdom, Africa and Russia. A few months ago in London, I met my cousin from Moscow. I had not seen her for 50 years. She was not only in good health and looking splendid but she had with her a charming daughter and photos of her grandchildren. Louie looked none the worse for her physical labours in having to carry timber for the building of the Moscow Underground Railway, nor had her life been shattered by having to retreat from Moscow as the Germans advanced on the city. Whether working on English-Russian dictionaries or in manual labour for the state she had fulfilled her life amongst pleasant people.

All of which leads me to the conclusion that in the adventure of living, people everywhere are just the most delightful in the world and none more so than the people of New Zealand!! Sometimes however a country stagnates: the vision dims. People grow tired or self-centred and avaricious. The common good is spurned in the pursuit of power or personal gain. Tragedy strikes. In Colonial Africa the breech-loading rifle and the Maxim gun made it possible for western nations to suppress the masses of the people for many years. At the end of last century King Lobengula and his warriors, who in warfare had surpassed all neighbouring tribes, had to retreat from Bulawayo and eventually to surrender to Cecil Rhodes.

Then came 60 years of peace and from 1896 until 1959 no one in Rhodesia was killed by policeman or soldier. In that period a subjected people found themselves again. They accepted church and schools, were responsive to new ideas and lived at peace. In this exciting adventure we have shared for 45 years.

However, the combination of education, the insights and compelling power of the Christian Gospel, the world-shattering effects of the war of 1939 with its racial aspects, stimulated the ferment in the spirits of the people. Soon there came demands for equality of opportunity—for an equal say in government. So the killing began again and people were imprisoned for political activity. The next step was to make the laws harsher, then to build detention camps and fill them with people who would not be charged with offences or taken before a court of justice, but would still be imprisoned. The vision, the courage, the endeavour which might have generated a more liberal era in a united country were spent by the two races in resisting each other as they drew apart and took up new and dangerous positions in confrontation.

Racism is real and this evil expresses itself in many ways. Its horrors made a hell of Nazi Germany and the whole world shuddered under its impact. In Rhodesia a similar madness seized us whites and became government policy. Although we are fewer than 5% of the population we severed our colonial ties with Britain by the Unilateral Declaration of Independence and then we highjacked our five million protesting black fellow-citizens. We defied world opinion and declared that we had launched Rhodesia on "a thousand years of white rule." That declaration for a thousand years was made just 14 years ago and it has been overwhelmed and destroyed in seven years of bloody civil war in which probably as many as 30,000 people have lost their lives. A third of all our schools are closed and our medical services are in disarray. No mission hospital has a doctor and most are closed. A quarter of a million of our people have fled to neighbouring countries and now live destitute in refugee camps. The black population of our towns has doubled as more than a million people have left their rural homes to escape the war and have tried to find refuge with relatives or friends in the towns. Only massive military and economic aid from South Africa has enabled our government to resist the nationalist forces.

The political changes which the people demand could have come by peaceful evolution if there had been sympathetic understanding between the races. If people would understand with the head and temper their judgments and attitudes with the heart we would not go far wrong. But even pleasant people—and there are none more pleasant than the white people of Rhodesia—do not necessarily concern themselves with the reasonable needs of their neighbours and if *precedent* and *statute* and *propaganda* all combine to keep the people apart then misunderstanding and strife must result.

In 1972 I was in prison in Gatooma. My cell was slightly apart from the main prison block and it had a tiny courtyard attached. In the morning the guard would unlock my door and then I could use the courtyard which in its turn opened on to the main prison courtyard by a steel door which was locked. In this door there was a grill measuring about 8" by 6". In it there were two bars and through them I could see some of the hundreds of black prisoners as they washed their clothes and ironed them, talked together or just sat around on the concrete floor. At one point on the first day there was the sound of sweeping just outside the courtyard door and then there was quiet and a low voice asked, "Are you all right, sir?" The day passed. I was brought midday meal and then later in the afternoon the fingers of a black hand slipped quietly through the bars of the grill. No word was spoken and I placed my hand on the fingers of my unknown friend. Then the hand was withdrawn.

These slender communications must have been observed and reported for early next morning there was the noise of sawing and tapping and when eventually my cell door was unlocked and I entered the courtyard I found that the grill had been covered by a steel plate. Now my only contact with humanity was limited to three visits each day when, after much unlocking of padlocks, a black fellow-prisoner entered with a tray. He was always accompanied by a white warder, not for security but to ensure that there was no communication between us.

And just a word in passing: if you should contemplate going to prison do so in your twenties, not in your sixties for by then it is difficult to adjust. I hope that this advice will prove as irrelevant to you as some given to me a couple of years ago by a man who had just celebrated his 100th birthday. In his youth he had been an employee of Cecil John Rhodes and on one occasion had been instructed to off-load some giraffes which were on their way to a zoo in East London. They were to be stabled, fed and watered in Bulawayo for the night. "Garfield," said my friend Mr. Cooke, "if you ever have to lead a giraffe just remember that they kick sideways, not backwards."

You are graduates. In certain subjects you are on your way to becoming experts. That I accept but I suggest that your responsibilities and your opportunities lie not just with your subject but should extend across the whole spectrum of life.

Never have physical communications been so efficient. Telephones, cables, satellites, newspapers, the radio and television are at the service of the nations, but never before have the people of the world been subjected to and antagonised by such buffeting waves of propaganda. For the past fourteen years our TV and radio, which are state-controlled, have been used to divide white from black, tribe from tribe, our people from the hated British. In the past seven years of war, accepting that the first casualty in war is truth, the government security forces have been portrayed as the upholders of justice and peace while the nationalist guerrillas are named Marxist terrorists. But the truth is that these young men and women too, have left our schools and villages and have gone to fight for the freedoms which they and their fathers had sought patiently for the past thirty years and had always been denied.

Both sides commit atrocities, so terrible and nauseating that I will not attempt to describe the horrors I have both heard of and I have seen. In qualitative terms one side is as bad as the other. The security forces use napalm. The guerrillas use fire. In quantitative terms the security forces kill ten times as many as the guerrillas, on their own statements. On TV at the end of each day an official communiqué lists first the murders committed by terrorists and then comes the day's kill by security forces. Maybe it will list the deaths of thirty-two guerrillas, fifteen terrorist-collaborators, four cattle thieves. There were, of course, no investigations, no inquests, just a tidy classification of bodies into acceptable groupings: terrorists, collaborators, cattle-thieves—all people who deserve to be killed. The facts could be very different. Two months ago at Lundi, a centre which has church and school, the security forces came in with guns blazing. When the firing stopped twenty-four men, women and children from neighbouring villages lay dead and fourteen others were wounded. There was not one guerrilla amongst either the dead or the wounded.

The situation in Zimbabwe is our special tragedy and a new day will not dawn—until dividing walls are broken down and people meet with a desire to understand one another. In London two weeks ago I spent an evening with General Tongogara, head of the guerrilla forces. We talked, not of war but of elections. The following morning I spent an hour with General Peter Walls, head of the Rhodesian Security Forces. Amongst other things we spoke of the possibility of a cease-fire which could bring in a new era in which there would no longer be enemies. I asked General Walls if he had met General Tongogara. They had not met but I hope that by now that has been changed.

I suggested to the Foreign Office that their guarantee of equal time on radio and TV for all political parties did not go far enough to meet our need and in a aide-memoir I wrote, "The Governor will need technical men but more especially will he need men who know how to set up an impartial news service and who know how to conduct interviews. Radio/TV in Rhodesia is a propaganda machine and it would not lie within the capacity of the staff to change the system into one which would serve the Governor in his work of keeping the peace, building the morale of the nation, and guiding the country to free and fair elections." Radio and TV, I noted, must change radically in approach and content and should be the first and most striking evidence, seen and heard, of the arrival in Zimbabwe of a new and democratic order.

In our case the lack of adequate communication between the races has led to tragedy but I suggest that in every country, not excluding New Zealand, there is the danger that people will take up unquestioning attitudes, divisive attitudes, within trade unions, employers' organizations, even church and educational institutions, certainly in political parties and in even wider streams within the nation itself. Contacts are broken and cooperation may fail.

In our life, day by day, we can play our specialised parts but we should also cultivate an awareness of our wider responsibilities. If we accept this doctrine then, at the end of the day we may find that although we have not achieved world-fame in our profession or have blazed new trails through the stars all will not have been lost if we can say:

> "I have adventured with people,
> I have lived."

"The Speech that Says it All—in Silence"
The Second Feetham Lecture

Many times governments feared Todd's eloquence and prophetic voice and so on many occasions he was denied opportunities to speak in the 1960s and 1970s. Todd received his second invitation to deliver a Feetham lecture at the University of the Witwatersrand in Johannesburg, South Africa, in 1980. When the South African government read the advance copy of the lecture, they refused to give him a visa. Unlike many other times the ban on Todd was circumvented by other means. The students placed an empty chair on the stage at the University and had his speech published in the *Daily Rand Mail* of July 7, 1980. The speech became known by the title "The Speech that Says it All—in Silence." The speech impressively narrates a history that white South Africa feared and allowed Todd to hope, "We can fulfill the Christian ideal of being one in Christ."

It is 16 years since I last stood in the Great Hall to deliver the Richard Feetham Lecture. I can't say that it seems like yesterday: in some ways it seems more than 50 years ago. In that period of 16 years our country has been turned upside down. It has been a traumatic experience for all of us in Zimbabwe. Nevertheless there is this satisfaction, for most of our seven million people the country is at last right side up.

Where there should have been understanding between people, a recognition of the need for change in the clear light of history and of the circumstances of our time, there came confrontation. Confrontation led to civil war and a recital of the obvious cost, 27,000 people killed and an unknown number wounded and maimed, 250,000 refugees living in destitution in camps in Botswana, Mozambique and Zambia, a million people uprooted from their demolished villages and fleeing for refuge to the cities: that is just the tip of the iceberg.

A closer examination reveals a deeper hurt. Schools were destroyed and hundreds of thousands of children have lost their normal chance of getting an education. In most cases this will not be made up to them. Clinics and hospitals were closed and at the end of the war only four mission doctors remained at their posts. Prophylactic routines had to be discontinued so that malaria, measles and other diseases which had been reasonably under control before the war broke out again. Many people died and others will suffer all their lives as a result. Hundreds of white farms were abandoned and farmers who had hoped to make a good life in Zimbabwe were made bankrupt.

Within the security fences around their homes intolerable tensions and fears made life miserable and many families emigrated. The breakdown of veterinary services in the African areas made it impossible to control foot and mouth disease and anthrax. As a result one million cattle died. "Operation Turkey" was the cynical name for the official policy of limiting food supplies to the people. Only small amounts of the staple food mealie meal could be purchased at stores in towns, and all rural stores were closed. All grinding mills in the rural areas were removed by the security forces. The aim was to starve out the guerrillas. If the fighters had been 40% or even 20% of the population the policy might have been successful but as they were less than 2%, they were never seriously inconvenienced.

It was dangerous for any village to store meal but if a group of guerrillas came through an area their organisation amongst the people very quickly gathered small amounts of food from each of many villages, and their needs were met. However, the presence of armies in the rural areas put an almost intolerable strain on village life and on food supplies. In some areas even the chickens and the goats were eventually used up and following upon "Operation Turkey" we now have widespread undernourishment and disease, especially amongst children. I am quite sure that this travail was neither foreseen nor desired by Mr. Ian Smith or his friends either in Rhodesia or in the outside world.

When Mr. Smith hijacked the six million blacks in 1965 and proclaimed 1000 years of white rule he really believed he could get away with it: he did not realise that his action would inevitably lead to civil war. It has been said that people act according to what they think the facts are but they live or die in accordance with what the facts really are. Mr. Smith got his facts very wrong and eventually he was defeated by the truth, which he probably has not yet recognised.

The road from Rhodesia to Zimbabwe was long and rough and when eventually we arrived at election day and Robert Mugabe became Prime Minister, the event took the world by surprise; many quarters suffered not surprise, but deep shock. The world in general, whites and the government within Zimbabwe in particular were stunned. What had gone wrong? Two and a half million blacks had gone to the polls and only 13% had voted for the government of Bishop Muzorewa and friends. The press of the world was embarrassingly wrong; what was worse for the friends of white rule, Mr. Ian Smith and all his white advisers were wrong. The people of Rhodesia in general had shown that they were determined to rule themselves. No matter how well the whites might manage the economy, nothing less than political liberation would satisfy blacks. They were, like the whites—well, just like the whites. They desired political power and as they were 96% of the population. That meant that 96% of the power would from now on be exercised by blacks, Rhodesia had become Zimbabwe.

But how could this truth have been hidden from the West? That it is possible in this age of instant and massive communication for people to be so deceived is one of the frightening and dangerous phenomena of our age. A terse comment made just over a month ago in the report of a British Broadcasting Commission which Prime Minister Mugabe had asked to examine our TV and radio, lifts a corner of the curtain: "Because for so long programmes and editorial decisions have become subordinate to political considerations, whether Rhodesian Front or UANC and its allies, the whole broadcasting service has suffered." In fact the country was betrayed by its media, and we have now reached the point where a leading member of Mr. Smith's Rhodesia Front, Wing Commander Gaunt, claims that the whites were "deceived" by their own propaganda. The Rhodesia Front was deceived by its own propaganda and like the gullible emperor to the fairy tale it now walks naked before the world. As we moved towards elections in January of this year the results seemed obvious. The government of Bishop Muzorewa would enjoy a resounding victory.

All the important forces were working for the Bishop and what a power-bloc it was. There were the whites under Mr. Ian Smith, the government itself under Bishop Muzorewa, the police, the army and the civil service. Could such a combination fail? In our history we have never seen so much money spent on advertising and as a last magnificent effort the Bishop laid on a rally in Salisbury for his supporters. There were free drinks and food for a million people and six motor cars as prizes, if you picked up the paper with the right number on it. At the last minute the High Court banned the free motor cars. Spread throughout the country were the army, the police and the civil service, all dedicated to achieving victory for the Bishop upon whose slender shoulders had incongruously fallen the mantle of Mr. Smith. Then to make matters quite, quite certain there was Bishop Muzorewa's private army of 18,000 men, the "spear of the people." These armed men intimidated the villagers and instructed them to vote for the Bishop.

I have said that all the important forces, all the important people were working for the Bishop. To the outside world that is what it seemed to be. The really important people, however, were the 2.5 million voters, people who until that point had been without importance, people who did what they were told. On this occasion things were different and Zimbabwe must be ever grateful for the one perfect contribution which Britain made to our liberation; she really did convince the people that the voting would be secret, that the election would be a genuine performance. As a seal of integrity 500 British policemen, complete with helmets, received a great welcome from the voters. It was a splendid and imaginative gesture.

Two years ago my wife and I were not at all sure that we would live to see Zimbabwe born. There had been so many time-consuming false starts in negotiation and we lived precariously in a war-zone. Over the years we have been deeply involved with church and school, with the economics of a large ranch, in the political life of the country and with the people of our area. Except for five years in Salisbury we have lived at Dadaya for 46 years and we have been committed to the struggle for liberation. We believed that negotiation was possible and that a peaceful evolution was in the best interests of all the people.

Over the years we watched with sadness and mounting fear the hardening of attitudes and the eventual confrontation of the politically powerful white minority and the vast black majority whose determination to beat the system which had dominated Rhodesia for 90 years had become implacable. The day came when the desire of the white minority for complete freedom to run their own affairs, including the right legally to dominate the black majority, became overpowering and on November 11, 1965, Mr. Ian Smith proclaimed Unilateral Independence. The gate was broken down and Rhodesians could enter their promised land, to enjoy 1000 years of white rule. The declaration itself borrowed many sonorous phrases from the American Declaration but the foundation stone was missing. Mr. Smith's freedom was to be for whites only. We were not to have government of the people, by people, for the people, and confrontation between black and white was now a fact of life and death.

The blacks could not accept the crisis situation which Mr. Smith had precipitated. From 1972 onwards the situation for the Smith Government deteriorated though the economy kept strong until 1975. There were waves of arrests, detentions and imprisonments without trial and eventually martial law was proclaimed throughout most of the country. The media were used by government for straight propaganda and so lost all credibility. Danger lurked on every road and in every situation. Motor traffic moved in convoys, trains were blown up, and every male under 60 became eligible for military service. News bulletins nightly told the whites that they were winning the war: that the security forces were inflicting 10 times the casualties on enemy that they were suffering themselves. In fact the great majority of casualties were civilians. Right through the war years we were told that the guerrillas were terrorising the civilian population.

The facts were that the guerrillas were receiving support in every way from their brothers and sisters in the villages. That this was the fundamental truth was established beyond doubt when the election results showed that almost 90% of the people had voted for the Patriotic Front which represented the liberation armies. It was a fact that the fish swam safely in the water; the guerrillas being the fish and the village people being the life sustaining water.

As the war intensified, the Smith government decided to try a different strategy. After the Geneva Conference the Rev. Ndabaningi Sithole recognised that he had no significant following outside Rhodesia so he came to terms with Mr. Smith and returned home. By this time Mr. Smith had concluded that world recognition and the lifting of sanctions could be achieved only by white power working through a black government. The man who had proclaimed that a national minority of whites could dominate for 1000 years the great black majority, now turned from a policy of overt force to a strategy of subversion. Mr. Smith set out to erect a facade of cooperative blacks, a government of men who would sell their people's birthright for an illusion of power for themselves; he looked to Bishop Muzorewa and the Rev. Ndabaningi Sithole.

Mr. Smith told a Bulawayo audience that the criticism the world had of the proposed new constitution was that "it gives the white man too much." Said Mr. Smith: "If you vote 'no' the external terrorist alliance will be your next government." *The New York Times* commented: "The only reason Smith has felt it necessary to agree with one set of blacks . . . is because another set has mounted a steadily more effective guerrilla war against him. . . ." Our local *Sunday Mail* took a different line: "Perhaps the world will get a message from the latest and in many ways surprising development—that Rhodesians black and white, can show unity and, despite external pressures and internal problems, are doing their level best to solve their own problems to the benefit of all." I disagreed entirely and wrote: "The realities remain: no peace, no economic recovery, no lifting of sanctions, no recognition by the rest of the world will ever be achieved without genuine independence under genuine majority rule."

Then came the farcical election of March, 1979 when the army, the police and every white employer cooperated to bring every black man and woman to the polls. The promise was peace. Hundreds of thousands of voters responded willingly and joyfully but as many, if not more, went to the polls because they were forced to do so and cast their votes for men they did not want. So came the disastrous six months' rule of the puppets under Bishop Muzorewa, the man of God, now Minister of War.

Then came what Shridath Ramphal hails as the Commonwealth's finest hour; the Lusaka Conference and massive pressure upon Britain to set up the Lancaster House Conference. At the same time the Commonwealth pressed Mugabe and Nkomo to accept negotiation. Another force whose power and significance has not been fully recognised was the pressures exerted upon the whole guerrilla movement by the people themselves. When Nkomo and Mugabe went to London they were well aware of the proportions of suffering of the people. With this knowledge fed to them by 30,000 guerrillas sharing in the life of the people, the leaders were fully aware of the grave responsibility which they carried when they went to London.

From the time of Lusaka, where a united Commonwealth agreed to initiate and to participate in negotiation, to Rufaro where on April 18, the representatives of 100 nations gathered to see the flag of Zimbabwe raised in hope, we dealt in miracles. But in the years preceding Lancaster House the cost in lives, in destroyed homes, in spiritual devastation was appalling. I hope that we, the ma-Zimbabwe, will not forget the sacrifices made nor will we prove unworthy of the heroes we are to remember on August 11 and 12 of each year.

We will accept our heroes, not as demi-gods or even only those who died in battle or were executed by the state, or who died in prison, but the ordinary people of the villages who suffered most cruelly and who were killed in thousands by the security forces. Sixteen years ago in this Hall I said:

> How can we make peaceful progress towards democracy when it is illegal to use the natural methods of getting there: free association, free discussion and the right to criticise. Democracy is not a perfection, it is a marching forward together, a continuing fellowship allowing for differences of opinion and providing within itself the machinery for effecting peaceful change. Democracy is not only a system of government, it is a way of life. It has grown from the deep desire of men to develop to the limit of their ability.

As I stood here on that occasion I was despondent. Our tragedy was that peaceful evolutionary changes were being deliberately frustrated by decree. When that happens the great and irresistible forces within men and women build up to such pressure that no power, no force, no army can contain them and they burst with volcanic fury. Sixteen years ago I said:

> I cannot see the way but the ideal is clear. I wish with all my heart that I could show you how easily the impossible will happen. I cannot, but there are two things I will say. I say them continually to myself. The first is that the impossible continually happens, and the second is that your responsibility starts with yourself.

From Rhodesia to Zimbabwe is not just a cold event in history, not just the mechanics of a guerrilla war but the emergence of a nation from racial darkness into the light of hope.

Now we can dream again, we can laugh again, we can be happy together; we can sing, we can dance, we can clasp hands. We can fulfill the Christian ideal of being one in Christ.

We can set aside prohibitions, overcome inhibitions—both white and black—we have been liberated.

Of course there are dangers. Men have not changed. There will be greed and corruption and a lust for power in the new society and there are tensions because in the Lancaster House constitution our new wine has been poured into old wineskins.

We will face the new challenges and I believe we will overcome.

The Tübingen Festival Address

The Tübingen Festival is an annual arts festival held in Tübingen, Germany, and lectures addressing key social, historical, and political concerns are given. This speech was delivered May 28, 1983. It is significant for a number of reasons. Todd narrates important information about Masotsha Ndlovu (1890–1982), a leading Zimbabwean nationalist. While attention has been paid to Ndlovu's trade union and political activities,[35] Todd reveals that Ndlovu, converted by early missionaries from the New Zealand Churches of Christ, also was a preacher for the Churches of Christ, and that his activism was centered in Christianity. The speech also shows Todd's narrative abilities at its finest. His command of facts is evident: they are tightly woven into an effective story form with one of the most effective and quotable endings for any speech. The speech is also a key text for Todd's prophetic narrative rhetoric. The speech text is from a manuscript in the Todd papers held by Susan Paul.

Early this month a long Telex came to me from Germany giving a detailed analysis of the subject for this address: really a doctoral thesis on Southern Africa. The message concluded, "rather a tall order but then 45 to 60 minutes is a long time." I have had many requests for addresses but I have had to wait 75 years for anyone to suggest that I speak for an hour though some may have got it without asking! Unfortunately I would need five hours to do justice to my subject for it covers an area a third of the continent of Africa; a population of 80 million diverse peoples and a time span of a century. You may relax. You are not going to get it! What you will get is not a balanced treatise, not the subject in detail but just sketches and stories to bring you one man's reaction to his fifty years in Southern Africa—49 years, to be exact.

It is a great honour to be with you at the Tübingen Festival. You have had the temerity, perhaps the foolhardiness, to invite a "failed politician" to speak on the subject of his failure, human and political relations in southern Africa. If, in the fifties, the white electorate in Southern Rhodesia had believed with me in the sharing of political power there would not have been a civil war. In 1958, at the end of a five-year period in which some advances had been made in education, in labour conditions, in political opportunity, I stood on the brink of defeat and warned:

> The position today is disturbing and serious. On the race relations side it cannot be denied that my leadership of this Party represents to the African almost his sole symbol of hope that "partnership" is not an empty word but a genuine and honest policy held by a majority of the Europeans in this country.

Six months earlier I had addressed an appropriately-mixed audience of the "Multiracial Society" and had said, "We must work for the day when it will not be significant to a child whether he is born black or white or coloured for all will be offered equal opportunity in Southern Rhodesia." My colleagues in government were shocked both at my addressing a society which defied the colour bar and for suggesting that its aims should be the aims of government. The political axe was about to fall. Some years later Kwame Nkrumah wrote:

> This state of affairs in Southern Rhodesia was not created by the Smith regime. It is part and parcel of the settler system which no individual settler or group of settlers, however well intentioned, can overthrow. For example I have known personally for many years Mr. Garfield Todd who was one of our guests at the Ghana Independence celebrations. He is a man of the greatest goodwill and was at the time of our independence Prime Minister of Southern Rhodesia. Yet even in this position of power he was not able to do anything.

I thought, and still believe, that I did do something, several things, but Kwame Nkrumah was right, I did not succeed in laying a foundation for peaceful progress towards rule by the majority. That was what mattered and in that context smaller gains were insignificant.

In the 1930s there were only a million people in Southern Rhodesia. Today we have nearly eight million. There was no shortage of land and over vast areas of the country herds of elephant and buffalo, sable, roan, kudu and zebra roamed at will. People were still able to move to new lands as their old, unfertilised fields gave out. When we looked at the villages scattered in sunshine on hillside and plain, watched children playing and women returning from the river with buckets of water balanced on their heads, we thought that no matter how long we might live in Rhodesia nothing would change. This is the way life had been for generations, this was the way it would continue. We had much to learn for behind the deceptive sunshine there were deep shadows. Half the babies died before they were a year old, medical facilities hardly existed, schools were primitive and could cater for only a few children, men had to leave home for long periods to find work, progressive people were deeply dissatisfied with their lot.

There was peace in the sense that there was an absence of war. The war had ended with Lobengula 30 years earlier. One of the last despairing messages from the old king as he fled from defeat was "Matabele! The white men will never cease following us while we have gold in our possession for gold is what the white men prizes above all things. Collect now all my gold and carry it to the white men. Tell them they have beaten my regiments, killed my people, burnt my kraals, captured my cattle, and that I want peace." But the spirit of resistance, the desire for liberty, continued to flame in the hearts of some men and women and one was a young man named Masotsha Ndhlovu.

I knew him well for some of his people lived in the district in which we settled in 1934 and where we still have our home.

Masotsha Ndhlovu was regarded by government as a dangerous revolutionary. In the twenties he had approached the first Prime Minister, Mr. Coghlan, and asked that regulations should be changed to allow blacks to use the footpaths in the towns instead of having to walk on the roads. Masotsha was a marked man. When Archives were opened Dr. Terence Ranger found C.I.D. reports and verbatim records of speeches relating to Ndhlovu. (I use the name 'Ndhlovu' with great respect as the people would use it: a praise name.) Ndhlovu was in contact with a labour union blossoming in the arid soil of South Africa, the Industrial and Commercial Union, the ICU, and was a leading spirit in commending it to workers around Bulawayo. One weekend there had been a riot in which people were hurt and some arrested. The following week Ndhlovu called a meeting and a C.I.D. verbatim report tells of the occasion. Speaking of the riot and the suffering Ndhlovu said, "If you had all been members of the ICU you would not have fought for you would have been brothers. The missionaries have come to tell us of the way to Heaven. The ICU tells us how to live on earth; and anyway, my brothers; we are living under the British flag and that stands for peace."

At 80 years of age the Smith regime released Ndhlovu from his latest and last spell of detention. For some years he had been at Gonakudzingwa with hundreds of political leaders and as a devout Christian lay-worker he held meetings in the Camp. He would write to our boarding school at Dadaya asking for hymnbooks and Bibles. From time to time offerings would be taken up at the church service and on the plates would be not only money but socks and shirts and under-pants for Masotsha Ndhlovu and his work at Gonakudzingwa. When Ndhlovu was released he came to the school to thank us for our support. The old man, with walking-stick tapping, made his way down the aisle and entered the pulpit. As always his message was one of unity and peace. "There is plenty for everyone in our beautiful country," he said. Then, as he was about to leave, he smiled broadly, showing two rows of very white teeth. "Anyway," he concluded, "I must thank the government for they have made a young man of me. They have given me new teeth."

You may think I have spent too long on the story of Masotsha Ndhlovu but when he died last year at 90 his life had spanned sixty years of protest. Yet he was so quiet, so unassuming, that he might not have been much noticed either in life or in death. So I was surprised and delighted when it was announced that Masotsha Ndhlovu was to be given a State funeral. And so it was. On a glorious afternoon special trains brought thousands of friends from Bulawayo to join great numbers from Harare to give honour to Ndhlovu as his earthly remains were laid to rest in "Heroes' Acre." "His whole life," said the Prime Minister in an oration, "was lived for unity and peace." Then Shona-speaking Robert Mugabe stood at the open grave and gave his farewell greeting in Sindebele, "Hamba kuhle, Mdala."

That day, as bugles sounded and rifles cracked in honour of Masotsha Ndhlovu, it seemed to me that much honour came also to the Prime Minister and his government who had recognized in an old man of 90, quiet and unassuming in his ways, most humble in his life, a Hero of the Revolution.

In the thirties there was little movement amongst the people. There were churches and some schools but only the most progressive parents thought it worthwhile to educate daughters. In a little school where two girls had actually made their way to the third and top grade available I noticed that while boys were being given a lesson in Oral English the girls were left drawing oxen and huts on their slates. When I questioned this discrimination the teacher replied with great surprise at my ignorance, "But surely you realise that girls could never learn English!"

And then came the forties, the Second World War, the slogans for liberty. Amongst the forces from Rhodesia were some blacks who went overseas to defend a freedom they had never known. The world was in turmoil and overnight the attitude of the people to education entirely changed. Now they would help to build schools, they would pay school fees; they would even sell their prized cattle so that the children could be educated. Since then no mission, nor even today's government has been able to meet the demand of the people for education.

In the fifties this demand for education was maintained but it was not so noticeable because a new call became imperative—a call to share in the political life of the country. After my defeat in 1958 the Central Africa Party, Federation-wide, was formed and soon had more black members than white with myself as President and Stanlake Samkange as Vice-President. Education was the handmaiden of politics and while many blacks were still ready to work with whites, Mr. Joshua Nkomo, a friend of many years, was now moving into competition and opposition. In 1959 Ndabaningi Sithole asked me for a foreword to his book, "African Nationalism," and I wrote:

> African Nationalism has already brought a great part of the Continent under the control and government of black people but so far the countries concerned have been populated almost exclusively by people of one race. African Nationalism now clamours for the control of multiracial

countries: such as the Union of South Africa, the Federation of Rhodesia and Nyasaland and Kenya. In our multiracial world the struggle between European nationalism and African nationalism is watched with deep apprehension and with the fervent hope that the conflicting forces may yet be aligned behind a new and compelling loyalty to the country instead of to the group.

The sixties brought an end to the Federation of Rhodesia and Nyasaland. I had been a supporter of Federation for I believed that as the white electorate of Southern Rhodesia was prepared to accept incorporation they would recognize that in changing the racial structure from 1 white to 16 blacks, as it then was in Rhodesia, to 1 white to almost 60 blacks as it would be in the Federation, they would react sensibly and recognize that there could be no stability in trying to balance a great black pyramid upside-down on a white pinnacle. We would have to turn it over and place it firmly on its black base before it fell on top of us. I was wrong. I underestimated the selfishness: of my fellow whites, their blindness in that they could not see, or would not recognise, that their best interests—the only peaceful path into the future—lay in sharing political power, generously, immediately.

In 1964 Mr. Smith became Prime Minister. He was well aware that Britain would not grant independence to a minority government which was determined to maintain political control in white hands. He put the decision to the people, but only to the white people, who 10 to 1 voted in favour of independence for Rhodesia. The black nationalist leaders were detained without trial and on November 11th, 1965, Mr. Smith declared the independence of Rhodesia. He borrowed heavily from the American Declaration of Independence but omitted the soul of that document: "Governments are, instituted among men, deriving their just powers from the consent of the governed." The consent of the governed! The Nationalist leaders were in prison—and I had begun my first year of restriction to my ranch.

In 1971 Britain's Foreign and Commonwealth Secretary, Sir Alec Douglas Home, arrived in Rhodesia. I met Sir Alec and when I heard him say that each time Britain negotiated with Mr. Smith they had to make further concessions to him I knew the mission would fail, for success depended upon concessions being made to the blacks, not to the whites. The Smith-Home agreement was totally rejected by the blacks and by some of us in the white community. Increasing numbers of recruits slipped across the border to join the liberation forces—and then Portugal collapsed and the whole scene changed.

When one is tempted to give up in despair, to say stalemate has been reached and nothing further can be done, we should remember the situation as it was during the years of Federation. I visited the Central Africa Office in Whitehall in 1960 and was told by an official that a Federal Minister had stood there in front of a map of Africa and with great confidence had traced the great belt of land, the security Maginot line of white supremacy, which stretched across Africa: Mozambique, Northern Rhodesia, Angola, from Nacala in the East in unbroken line to Lobito Bay in the West. The winds of change might blow even in gale force down the continent but no force would break that white line. Only twenty years later representatives of the black governments of Mozambique, Zambia and Angola, that entirely black line of countries, that unbroken black line, stretching from Nacala in the East to Lobito Bay in the West, were meeting together with representatives of the people's governments of Botswana, Lesotho, Malawi, Swaziland, Tanzania and Zimbabwe listening to His Excellency Comrade Samora Machel, President of the People's Republic of Mozambique declare:

> Attending this Conference are nine countries which in their economic backwardness still feel the effects of colonial domination. . . . The programmes that will be analysed at this Conference are daring, they are programmes aimed at making a break with underdevelopment in southern Africa.

And who had gathered with these countries, with the Kingdom of Swaziland, the benevolent dictatorship of Malawi, the Socialist countries of the Southern Africa Development Coordination Conference? A large number of the North group, amongst whom I list a selection: representatives of the Kingdom of Sweden, the Kingdom of the Netherlands, the Kingdom of Norway, the United Kingdom, the Federal Republic of Yugoslavia, the Federal Republic of Germany, the Republic of Italy, the German Democratic Republic. And who was sitting with this mixture of East and West, this politically mixed selection of countries? The capitalist giant of the west, the United States of America. Here was Willy Brandt's North-South programme stirring, promising. Maybe Willy Brandt should have been present to say again,

> The new governments of the world need not only economic solutions, they need ideas to inspire them, hopes to encourage them. They need a belief in man, in human dignity, in basic human rights: a belief in the value of justice, freedom, peace, mutual respect, in love and generosity, in reason rather than force.

In 1976, with the assistance of Mozambique and Zambia together with the other front line states, the war of liberation was intensified. A total of about 27,000 people died in the struggle: so many of them peaceful people from the villages. There is no time to tell of the war itself. What is of importance today is the Prime Minister's policy of reconciliation at work in a liberated country.

However it was not the democracies of the West who armed the liberation forces: it was China and the eastern States of Europe. The West, after the liberation forces had cleared the way for the establishment of democracy, came generously to our aid. During the struggle itself the West was best represented by the World Council of Churches and the Catholic Church who gave liberally and helped with medicines, education and in the sustenance of thousands of women and children left without support when husbands and brothers were detained by the Smith government. The regular monthly cheques to cover basic food will not be forgotten. To desperate people they were a lifeline.

Nor will we forget the assistance given by many governments and universities around the world to those of our young men and women who were able to leave Rhodesia and receive valuable training in countries both East and West. Even during the war some of the great aid agencies such as your Protestant Central Agency for Development Aid and its Catholic counterpart, the famous Bread for the World fund and other groups faithfully worked with us preparing for the new day which was bound to dawn. At the height of the war the Protestant Agency of the German Churches agreed to help our school at Dadaya to raise its enrollment from 400 to 800 and by the time the war ended a million dollars had been committed to this project.

I wish there was time to tell you of the new day that has dawned in Zimbabwe; of schools and clinics, roads and equipment, of the re-settlement programme and the Cooperatives, of the new fellowship between the peoples of white and black serving Zimbabwe together even up to Cabinet level. I admit that many whites have left, leaving us the poorer. Some in high office whom we accepted and trusted have deliberately betrayed the State. With their knowledge and position some have taken part in sabotage, the blowing up of Zanu party headquarters, the destruction of a large section of our small air force, the mighty explosion at Nkomo Barracks and other sabotage that was not as spectacular. Some, former Rhodesians have been killed by our security forces as they attempted to return over the South African border loaded with explosives for sabotage.

What of South Africa? Of one thing we may be certain. South Africa, great and powerful as she is, fears the rise of black people because the philosophy of the nation is based on the premise that whites are a superior people and have a status and a destiny ordained by God. Some people believe that white South Africans are different and evil. They are neither different nor are they especially evil. After the Second World War thousands of immigrants came to Rhodesia from Great Britain. Most came from a liberal background but many of them quickly succumbed to privilege, cheap servants, enjoying and rationalising their exercise of power. People are basically much alike. Give privilege and power and soon you will hardly distinguish a Briton or a German from a South African. I think Mr. Mugabe's experience since he became Prime Minister would make him go further and agree that blacks are as susceptible to the corruption of power as whites. Power and privilege are but two sides of one coin. South Africa should be the concern, not the enemy, of people of goodwill. Fears are expressed about the horror of what will happen "when trouble starts down south." But the conflict has already begun. Even in military terms every white home is under siege. Husbands, fathers, sons are all under military command. All serve in one way or another. All suffer the disruption of family life today and this will inexorably increase. John Kennedy said, "Peace and liberty walk together," but there is neither peace nor liberty in South Africa today.

Thirty years ago I sat one day with Dr. Hendrik Verwoerd, architect of apartheid and at that time Minister of Native Affairs. He spoke of the God-given status and responsibility of the Afrikaner people, of the nation set aside in these last days, given its own language ready to do God's will. The race so ordained by God must be kept pure, he said, and went on to talk of plans for the future; of the development of the Homelands, of factories on the white side of the borders, of the workforce coming each day to work and returning to the black areas in the evening.

Thirty years later it seems to me that the policy is little different. There are now ten Homelands covering 14% of the area of South Africa. All nineteen million blacks should either be living in that small area, or at least be registered there, given their local citizenship but deprived of their South African status. 70% of the people confined to 14% of the land! As the proportion of blacks steadily rises while that of whites falls it is estimated that by the year 2000 whites will have dropped to 14% of the population while blacks by then will be 75%. The passage of time makes the maintenance of a policy of white supremacy futile but Mr. Botha carries on. If Pretoria seems full of blacks in the daytime they can be sent home at 5 p.m. to a nearby Homeland so that the city can be "white by night."

South Africa is a world-problem. Continuing and careful study should be mounted by a specialist committee of the United Nations. If the welfare of 4 and 1/2 million whites is not of sufficient concern, the anguish and misfortune of 20 million captive blacks is certainly a world responsibility.

However the Southern African Development Coordination Conference is not primarily concerned either with the situation within South Africa or with how its great majority can be liberated. The Conference spends little time speaking about such matters for it faces economic problems so vast as to threaten the very existence of its members. Two hundred years ago when the American colonies came together Benjamin Franklin remarked, "We must indeed all hang together, or, most assuredly, we shall all hang separately." The nine countries of SADCC must also assuredly work together or, most assuredly, they will founder one by one.

One of their major obstacles is South Africa whose influence and deliberately aggressive policy continually threaten their stability. The continuing delay over Namibia negates security in Southern Africa and the presence of South African Forces in Angola is a reproach to the civilised world. The United States of America does not hesitate to slash its sugar quota for Nicaragua from 58,000 tons to 6,000 tons annually in order to exert political influence, but its attitude to South African military adventures in southern Africa appears to be passive if not benignly permissive.

It is understandable that South Africa greatly fears what is happening around her for the emergence of black rule in contiguous countries is a challenge to the validity of her own philosophy. South Africa did everything in her power to assist the Portuguese to maintain their rule in Mozambique and Angola; she armed the Smith regime and sent her troops as far north as the Victoria Falls. Planes, helicopters, tanks and guns were sent north to help maintain white Rhodesia and all the petrol required was made available through the services of not unwilling petrol companies, British, French and American. The Portuguese have departed and the Smith Government has fallen but South Africa does not give up. Now she supports rebel groups in Mozambique, Angola and Zimbabwe.

South Africa has an area of 470,000 square miles and a population of 27 million. The SADCC countries cover twice as much land and their population is nearly 60 million. A clear and concise description of SADCC was given by the Chairman, President Q. K. J. Masire of Botswana at the 1982 Summit:

> Our determination to seek a peaceful, non-racial and prosperous region in which our people can have hope for the future develops naturally into

a commitment to work together. It was out of this solidarity that SADCC was born. It was not conceived as a platform for rhetoric nor a plaything for those who desire a larger canvas on which to experiment with their patent solutions for Africa's problems. Rather, SADCC has grown out of a common awareness of common interests. Its immediate objectives are well defined and limited. SADCC exists only to the extent that the member states breathe life into its common programmes and projects. It does not have an autonomous existence, separate from the priorities of the member states.

In my personal life I suppose I have been of an independent spirit and I have always been reluctant to seek help so I react adversely to people or nations holding a begging-bowl. However, when I consider what is at stake in southern Africa, when I observe the poverty of the people and set that against both the potential of the people themselves and the resources of the area, all my qualms evaporate and I would emphasise that here in southern Africa is a vital focal point at which the North/South policy should be planted, where it should germinate and flourish. Such growth in this area would be a positive and healthy counter against apartheid, but the main consideration of course is the need of 60 million people. I quote from the North/South report,

> For low-income countries . . . the over-riding priority is rapid growth. Equal shares of poverty do not necessarily imply a progression to equal shares of wealth. For this, both the mobilisation of domestic resources and an increased flow of external resources are critical.

For a body to be healthy, all its parts must be healthy. If the world is to become healthy and safe then the welfare of all countries must be our concern. The North/South Report raises my hopes. In it, in its economic wisdom, I sense a deeper wisdom, maybe the first tender shoots of a world morality.

But SADCC plans for development have been cruelly interrupted by the catastrophe of widespread drought, by the immediate need to divert resources to the saving of lives of both people and livestock. Grain imports required will exceed one and a half million tons. Transport, distribution, the search for and the provision of water will cost hundreds of millions of dollars. Today's crisis underlines the urgency of SADCC planning of longer-term measures in seed breeding, water-management, soil-conservation and forestry so as to increase security of access to water and to reduce vulnerability to drought.

An hour is such a short time! But there is one matter I must mention or you might think that I am trying to evade a difficult issue. Three years ago Zimbabwe captured world headlines as we celebrated our independence. Sharing our joy and to our assistance in the Zimcord Conference came many well-disposed countries from both East and West. This year some press reports have been extremely critical of us. We ourselves have had reason for distress but not for dismay as we faced serious trouble and much suffering in Matabeleland. Matabeleland lies in the south and shares a common boundary with South Africa. Across that border, after independence, fled some thousands of political malcontents both black and white: men ready to turn against the Mugabe Government if opportunity and support became available. Within our country were others, similarly disaffected. These dissidents, many of them ex-army and without work, others people just unwilling to accept the people's choice of a Mugabe Government, have robbed buses and stores, assaulted and killed innocent people. Limited areas of the country were destabilised and the government was faced with insurrection.

The security of the government itself was not threatened for it has the support of the vast majority of the people. The first task of government is to maintain law and order and to do this it has the right to use all measures at its disposal, including such force as may be required to restore peace and order to a community. In such action it has the support and protection of the law.

Foreign Press reporters were not the first people to alert government to the need to bring some units of the army to heel. There is no department of government more susceptible to the danger of becoming a government within a government than is the army, especially in a time of crisis. Individual citizens, representatives of churches, politicians were readily received by Ministers and by the Prime Minister himself as they reported incidents in which they believed that the army had used unnecessary force and also incidents in which individual soldiers had committed crimes. Government did not evade the issue and the Prime Minister himself as they reported incidents in which they believed that the army had used unnecessary force and also incidents in which individual soldiers had committed crimes. Government did not evade the issue and the Prime Minister himself gave an assurance that allegations would be examined, the situation considered, and that soldiers involved in criminal actions would be apprehended and brought to trial. These assurances have been honoured and the situation rapidly improved. Curfews have been lifted, communications have been restored and the Prime Minister has visited the troubled areas to meet and address the people. He has been given an enthusiastic welcome by tens of thousands of people. When we speak of human rights in relation to Zimbabwe there is one thing which should always be remembered. Many of our leaders, including the Prime Minister himself, suffered long years of imprisonment in their quest for justice and liberty and their crusade was not a selfish one. The struggle was for the country and the people. I do not wish to make our situation seem better than it is. In Matabeleland innocent people suffered and there was great distress, not only of the people but of the government also. It is significant that the Prime Minister sought out the leaders of the churches and spoke to them at length. He said,

> Accordingly, the struggle against political bandits and their collaborators will continue unabated until every corner of Matabeleland has been rid of every dissident element. If we are at one with the Church on this matter, as indeed we are at one with the majority of the nation, then at least we will feel united in the spirit to create true justice and peace.

I count myself fortunate to be a citizen of Zimbabwe. I am so fortunate to be able to look back over almost fifty years in Africa. As a young man I saw visions and as an old man I can dream dreams. I am upheld in my hope for the future of my country for I know that there is a host of young women and young men in Zimbabwe today whose vision is of a country where liberty and peace walk hand in hand. And as for me . . . I would a thousand times rather be a Senator in a free Zimbabwe than be Prime Minister of the Self-governing Colony of Southern Rhodesia.

Keynote Speech at the Celebration of Joshua Nkomo's 72nd Birthday and 40th Wedding Anniversary

This speech was delivered in Bulawayo, Zimbabwe, on September 30, 1989. Todd was invited to give the after dinner speech at the celebration. The speech is extensively analyzed in chapter 6, "Todd's Narrative Rhetoric: The Preacher of Democratic Virtues." The speech is an important part of Todd's prophetic narrative rhetoric where he narrates the meaning of Zimbabwe's liberation for democracy in Africa. The speech also gives more information about the early African nationalist Masotsha Ndlovu. The text is from the Judith Todd file located in the Terrance Ranger papers, Rhodes House, Bodleian Library, Oxford University.

This is a great occasion for Father and Mother Zimbabwe! and for me, for I am glad to have an opportunity to express my admiration for a man who has sacrificed so much for Zimbabwe: for us all. Also you are likely to gather from what I say tonight that Nkomo has had a greater influence on my life in Zimbabwe than any other man, which will surprise him as greatly as it no doubt, surprises everyone else. You will judge for yourselves as we go along. I don't really know Mrs. Nkomo except through the warm tributes paid to her by her husband, but he should know! As I read those tributes it occurs to me that Nkomo's wife and my wife are peas from the same pod. Nkomo dedicated his Book to "My wife ma Fuyana, who stood by me through it all." If I were ever to write a book it would have a similar dedication.

When I arrived from New Zealand 55 years ago I knew even less than I do today and I remember asking a boy to tell me his Mother's name. You can guess what he replied and so I learned that in African culture a Mother's name is not to be mentioned lightly. In our culture it is slightly different. Anyway I have to admit that we had been married for 54 years and then I had to inspan assistance from the Prime Minister of New Zealand, the Prime Minister of Zimbabwe and the kind co-operation of her Majesty the Queen to make my wife a Lady: Lady Grace.

As I look around this splendid gathering I am reminded of Desmond Lardner-Burke. In 1965 he wrote to command me not to leave Hokonui Ranch for twelve months because he believed that I had actively associated myself with members of Zapu. He admitted that his belief was founded on information which he was unable to divulge because of the confidential nature of its sources. I was furious and thought I would ask the opinion of my lawyer—until I remembered that my lawyer, was named Desmond Lardner-Burke. But now, here I am, unrepentant, still associating with enemies of Rhodesia but who are now friends of Zimbabwe . . . people, of—Zimbabwe.

I count myself fortunate to have lived to see the miracles that have happened in Zimbabwe. Of course we have all suffered in some way but Joshua Nkomo and his wife have especially suffered. They have had pain, disappointments, long periods of separation from each other over far too many years.

Some day a film should be made of the life of Joshua and then it would be possible to put into perspective the efforts and sacrifices of other men and women, some very notable ones who are with us tonight; all honour to you! The struggle continues and Joshua Nkomo has played leading man for forty years. Looking at the changes that Nkomo has lived through a filmwriter might entitle the film "From Amabhetshu to dinner jacket."

The years of my glory as Prime Minister stretched from 1953 to 1958 and Dr. Nkomo was not impressed with my performance. He was in good company! Kwame Nkrumah wrote in his "Africa File" that I was a friend and that he had invited me to the Independence Celebrations in 1957 but, he said, "If Mr. Garfield Todd, during the five years he was Prime Minister could not change, in any significant respect, the racial nature of the Colony, how can anyone seriously imagine it can be changed by any group of settlers?" And Dr. Nkrumah was right: it had to take a civil war to drag Rhodesia to Zimbabwe.

By 1958 Dr. Nkomo and Garfield Todd had not worked together but we had met and talked. At the 1958 Congress of the United Rhodesia Party when I lost my leadership, one of the reasons given was that I was a security risk: to be specific, "Todd had talked with Joshua Nkomo without the presence of the Chief Native Commissioner."

I was out, but people loyal to the cause established the Central Africa Party with Stanlake Samkange as my Deputy. In 1960 I went to London with an appointment to meet the Commonwealth Secretary, Lord Home. Joshua Nkomo was also in London and he came to my hotel one morning. I told him of my appointment with Lord Home and gave him the statement I had prepared for the British Government. Nkomo read the Statement and said that if I would add a recommendation that the United Kingdom should suspend the Constitution of Rhodesia and call a Conference of representatives of the people, he would be glad to give his support in, of course, what would be my political suicide. Anyway I thought it was a good idea and I suggested that he should accompany me to the Foreign Office. I thought that Lord Home would be glad to have the opportunity to meet the leader of the African people, especially at a time when relations between the Rhodesian Government and the African people had sunk to a dangerous low. I was wrong again. The secretary went to tell Lord Home of my nice idea but after quite a long time he returned to say that the Commonwealth Secretary thought so badly of it that he had cancelled my appointment. We left our prepared statement, just for luck, and went on our way to call a Press Conference. Apparently Lord Home read the statement almost immediately for we were "pursued" in an effort to persuade us not to issue it. The reaction of the whites in Rhodesia was so antagonistic that I was advised not to fly to Salisbury so I landed at the Victoria Falls where my wife collected me by car. But even my friends in the Central African Party thought I had gone too far so I resigned. That was the end of formal politics for me and I moved across to the informal sector with the Nkomos, the Msikas, the Dumbutshenas, etc.

The Todd Family Christmas, 1914 [young boy in the middle is Garfield Todd]

The Todd Family, 1932 in New Zealand [center: Thomas Todd, Garfield's father; to his left are Grace and Garfield Todd]

Garfield, Alycene and Grace Todd

Emory Ross and Grace Todd [Garfield climbing the windmill]

Todd with Emory Ross, Disciples of Christ missionary to the Congo and President of the Albert Schweitzer Society, 1953

Garfield and Grace Todd as Prime Minister and First Lady, 1954

Todd Receiving Honorary Doctorate at Butler University, 1955

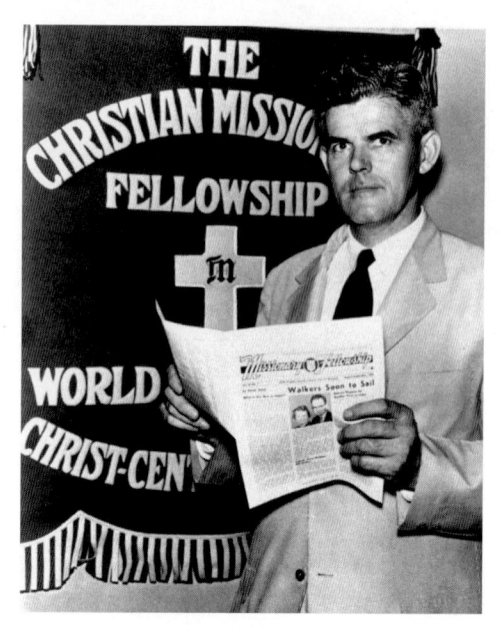

Todd at World Convention in Toronto, 1955

Todd Giving a Radio Interview on NBC, 1955

Todd and Basil Holt in South Africa, 1957

Todd Giving a Speech in New York City, 1955

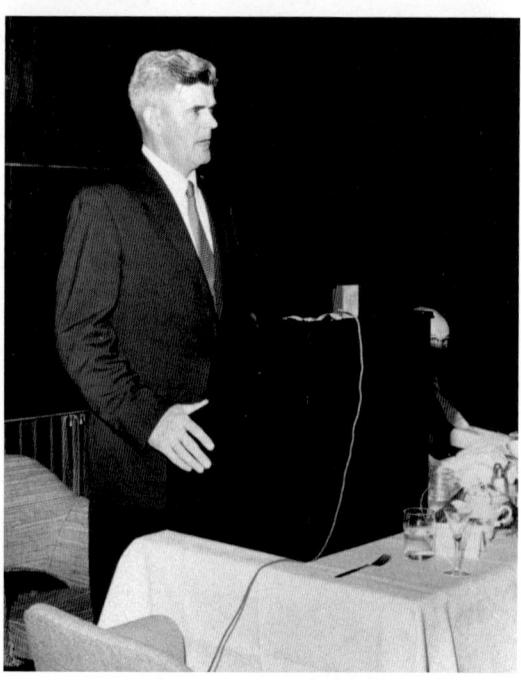

Todd Family at Church in Indianapolis, Indiana, 1955

Todd as a Member of Parliament

Todd on Safari, 1956

Joshua Nkomo, Leader of the African National Congress

Todd as Nkomo Advisor at 1976 Geneva Talks

Celebrating Release from Detention in London, 1976
[from l to r: Johnny Acton, Grace Todd, Richard Acton, Garfield Todd, Judith Todd]

Todd Speaking at a Discussion about Africa at Yale University, 1976

Garfield Todd, 1980

Grace Todd

Garfield and Grace Todd at Garfield's Eightieth Birthday, 1988

Garfield Todd Talking

Garfield Todd in Action

In March 1962 Joshua Nkomo went to New York to address the Committee of 24 at the United Nations. He was accompanied by Ndabaningi Sithole and linked up with Willie Musarurwa who was studying there. Nkomo asked Willie to cable me and ask that I come to New York and I arrived two days later. The point at issue was the rejection by Great Britain of any responsibility for Rhodesia. The U.K. held that all responsibility for government had passed from London to Salisbury. After our representations the Committee voted 23 to 1 against the British stand and you, Dr. Nkomo, later said that it followed from that Resolution that Britain agreed to resume her role as Colonial Power over Rhodesia and undertook to de-colonise it. What Joshua Nkomo does not know about that visit to New York I will now tell him and you. When I arrived in the city I rang my friend Hugh Foot, the British Representative at the United Nations. He told me that Joshua Nkomo and Ndabaningi Sithole were coming to see him at his home that evening. "We are going to talk about the 1961 Constitution," said the Ambassador. "I think it is a very good effort, don't you," he asked? I replied that I thought the Constitution a disaster. "Oh, my God," he said, "can I come round and see you?" I said that I would come to his house immediately if he wanted to talk about it. He welcomed me and took me to his study where we talked. It was not long before Nkomo and Sithole arrived at the front door but Hugh Foot said he would get Sylvia, his wife, to take them upstairs and look after them till he was ready. So, eventually I left and went on my way. Later, Dr. Nkomo wrote "Sir Hugh told me that he would soon have to resign in protest against the instructions he was receiving from London." A few months later the Ambassador did resign.

Soon came Gonakudzingwa and in the first years the Camp was a hive of industry, of political discussions and planning and of vibrant influence. I had the privilege of visiting a number of times but then came harsh regulations, visitors were forbidden and you, Dr. Nkomo, had to endure the long years of complete separation from your wife and family. There is a paragraph in the history of Gonakudzingwa that I would like to mention.

Masotsha Ndhlovu, whose remains lie at Heroes' Acre, was a detainee at Gonakudzingwa. Ndhlovu belonged to the Church at Dadaya and he would write to the School for supplies of Bibles and Hymn books and any other help we could give. This was the man who so many years before had approached Prime Minister Coughlan with the request that Africans should be allowed to walk on the footpaths instead of being forced to walk on the roads. When we were asked for help we would take up a special offering. The plates would be passed along the pews and the scholars would load them, not only with money but also with articles of clothing: socks, under-pants, handkerchiefs etc. When

Ndhlovu was eventually freed he made his way to Dadaya to thank the school for its help. It was Sunday and he was invited to come up to the pulpit. He was now a frail old man tapping his way with his stick down the long aisle to the platform. He thanked the scholars for their help and told them that theirs was a wonderful and bountiful country with room for everyone. "There should be no antagonism between black and white and anyway," he said with a wide smile showing a set of white artificial teeth, "the Government has now made a young man of me!"

Masotsha Ndhlovu was one of the earliest and most honourable of our fighters for peace and democracy. In his old age he could so easily have been overlooked. He owned nothing. He was modest. He fought injustice with a quiet resolution and with a deep faith in God and in his fellow men. I feel a great debt of gratitude to President Mugabe for determining that this humble and patient old man should be buried at Heroes' Acre. I will not forget the sight of Robert Mugabe standing at the open grave saying his last message, "Hamba gahle, 'Mdala.'"

Another of my happy memories is of a recent experience. I had been burned through my own carelessness, but that did not lessen the pain. Those marvelous nurses at the Mater Dei Hospital had just levered me into a bath when a Sister came rushing in to say, "The President and Dr. Nkomo have come to see Sir Garfield." I looked up and said, "There is just one chair. Get another and bring them in!" Well, they got me out and into bed and in came my visitors. I was so glad to see the President but delighted that Mugabe and Nkomo had come together to see me, together again. Of course when they had departed the Matron came: I think it was to thank me for my accident which had brought such important visitors to her hospital: a visit which had brought excitement and happiness to nurses and patients.

Well I could go on and on, but I am a disciplined man and I will stop soon. I wanted to be sure that I would not have to stand directly in front of Nkomo when I was speaking this evening, for in 1980 I was in such a position at a meeting in Zvishavane where I had been invited to speak. I apparently had got carried away and was waxing either too eloquent or too ideological for I became suddenly aware that I was being hammered on my calves by a ceremonial stick! Of course that is an incident I have long forgotten!

There are certain experiences which Nkomo and I have shared: knowledge gained through the blessing of a good marriage and this evening we celebrate not only 72 years of Nkomo's life but also its best 40 years, the years of marriage. Mrs. Nkomo once said of her husband, "When he is with people he makes them feel they are as good as anyone else." So that is the way they feel about each other. Now, being my usual diffident and humble self I would not venture to give advice, but I can give an assurance from the vantage point of my 57 years with Lady Grace. Joshua and ma Fuyana, the next 17 years will be the best, so go along with the prayers and best wishes of us all.

Concluding Sermon

REFLECTIONS ON FIFTY-FOUR YEARS OF SERVICE

In November 1988 Todd spoke for the final time to a World Convention of Churches of Christ. Appropriately he spoke in his native country of New Zealand among his brothers and sisters of his religious heritage. The speech has an overview of his entire career giving many details of his courageous stand against Ian Smith that involved among many things his imprisonment. While his beloved Zimbabwe has not remained a place of reconciliation as he had hoped, the ideals Todd articulates in this speech and elsewhere in this volume remain as truthful standards for his adopted country, Africa, and all persons interested in making this a better world in which to live. The text is reproduced from the *Christian Standard*, May 7, 1989.

In 1934, Grace at twenty-three, and I at twenty-five, went to represent our churches at Dadaya Mission in Southern Rhodesia. Our missionaries first went in 1906. All had made their contribution; some had given their lives.

1934 was in the middle of the world depression. Lack of funds and other circumstances led to Grace and I being the only whites in the Dadaya area for thirteen years. We lived amongst more than 20,000 people and worked in the twenty or more churches and schools which had already been established within a thirty-mile radius of the head station. We also had in our care about ten churches and a few schools at Mashoko, some 150 miles distant.

In 1956 the Mashoko work was handed over to the American churches under the leadership of Dr. Dennis Pruett and John Pemberton. That was an act in line with God's will and is testified to by the splendid hospital, churches, and schools which now flourish at Mashoko.

We stayed and worked at Dadaya for twenty years and we look back on that period as being happy and fulfilling. Grace taught and wrote lesson material which was soon in use in all the schools in the country, while I worked with the churches and schools in the villages.

During that period we lived in primitive surroundings with neither clinic nor hospital in the area. Malaria, burned babies, tooth extractions, difficult births, assaults—all brought people seeking help which we gave beyond our knowledge or ability! With preaching, teaching, building, and the setting up of agricultural demonstration plots, our days were full, our consciences were clear. This was the missionary work we had been sent to do.

In 1946 our white neighbors suggested that I stand for parliament. This was followed by an invitation from the Prime Minister, Sir Godfrey Huggins (later Lord Malvern). Grace and I doubted if this would be in line with our work as Christian missionaries, but we did recognize the great need of whites to learn more about the African people amongst whom they lived and to learn to respect them. We thought that maybe I could play a part.

We had lived amongst the people in sickness and in health, in birth and death, through witchcraft and murder, in the happiness of church gatherings, weddings, in the joy of flourishing churches and the challenge of overcrowded schools. It is all recorded in a thousand stories written month by month to the churches and Bible schools in New Zealand.

Of course there was a serious difference of opinion amongst our church members in New Zealand when I eventually did stand and was elected to parliament. I expected that, so I dropped my mission stipend of £400 a year and we lived on my parliamentary allowance for the following seven years until I became Prime Minister. During that period we still carried on our work at Dadaya, though for about sixteen weeks a year I had to attend sessions of parliament in Salisbury.

The first twenty-year period closed when I was chosen as Prime Minister of Southern Rhodesia. I liked being Prime Minister and was hoping for twenty years of office as my predecessor had enjoyed! However, the electorate had had more than enough of me by the time five years had passed!

Things in general were going well and the economy was healthy, but my concern for African advancement, on which I believed white security was based, was neither accepted nor understood. Statements such as this (which was reproduced earlier this month in the *Herald*) were totally rejected:

> 25 Years Ago: Mr. R. S. Garfield Todd, former Prime Minister of Southern Rhodesia, said in Salisbury yesterday that the chapter of Southern Rhodesia was closing and the chapter on Zimbabwe was opening. And he added, "The problem of the whites is to find a way of closing the old chapter with dignity and open the new one with hope."

During that first period we believed that we were doing God's will. But how does one recognize God's will? You try to do your work in an atmosphere of prayer—not maybe the careful disciplined daily worship which I know friends of mine faithfully observe, but as Christians—whether missionaries, cattle ranchers, or politicians—seeking guidance.

In the 1970s, events caught up on us. In November, 1971, I spoke at the local university and compared the decline of the morality of our government "to the rise of Nazism" and the authorities decided to act. On January 18, 1972, my daughter Judith and I arrived home to find five carloads of armed police, including a policewoman, at our home. Judith and I slept in separate prisons that night while Grace was denied knowledge of where we were being taken or what charges we might face.

On the following day when the last contingent of police departed, after searching house and offices and collecting more than 10,000 documents and letters, Grace asked when the papers would be returned. The reply was, "Only those papers which will be required to substantiate charges against your husband and your daughter will be held and the rest will be returned."

"In that case," Grace replied, "all the papers will be returned." Eventually it was so. No charges were levied against us.

But when I was unlocked from my solitary cell on the morning of January 19, 1972, I really wondered if I could be in harmony with God's will. My cell opened onto a tiny, walled enclosure which was separated from the main compound by a solid steel door. In the door was a peephole about eight inches by six inches with two bars. I could look out on the activities of hundreds of black prisoners; I was the only white one.

Later in the morning there was the sound of sweeping outside the door and then a voice whispered, "Are you all right, Sir?" Later still a black hand rested on the ledge of the peephole and I placed my hand over it. I believe this is called solidarity! On the second morning, before my cell door had been unlocked, I heard the sounds of cutting and hammering. When I was later allowed out and into the enclosure I discovered that a steel plate had been bolted over the peephole, so now I was quite on my own! I have always thought that the act of closing that tiny area of communication was symptomatic of our basic problem—a determination to prohibit understanding between black and white.

My daughter, Judith, and I were just two individuals in a mass movement, but we were white. That meant special concern, even special treatment in prison. From America, from the countries of the Commonwealth, from Scandinavia, came protests against our imprisonment. And so, after five weeks, our home at Hokonui, in the middle of a 17,000-acre ranch, was designated a "protected area." Notices were placed warning people to keep out, a white policeman put on guard duty, and we were brought back home. No letters, no visitors, no telephoning, and a limit of 800 metres to our walking from the house!

Nevertheless Grace was free to come and go—"always a respectable person," she held! But a few people in the five years of my detention were able to get permits from the police to visit us. One of these was Bishop Haine from Gwelo who brought me a message from Rome. In New Zealand, just last month, a Catholic paper reported,

> Memories of a special gesture by Pope Paul were recalled by a former Prime Minister of Rhodesia, New Zealand-born Sir Garfield Todd. Sir Garfield was held in detention for five and a half years before Rhodesia moved to independence as Zimbabwe. The Pope, on learning of the detention of the Churches of Christ missionary, asked a Rhodesian bishop visiting Rome to pass on a medal and a message of blessing to him. The medal and message had been passed from one bishop to another and eventually were able to be delivered to the detained Sir Garfield.

The civil war was long and brutal and cost 40,000 lives. Dadaya Mission and Hokonui Ranch were at times a center of warfare. But in 1979 peace was negotiated successfully at Lancaster House in London. Robert Mugabe announced a policy of reconciliation, not a Nuremberg trial, and we have experienced eight years of healing instead of a period of vengeance.

"It is time that people who in the past denigrated you, should now see you honored," said Mr. Mugabe when he asked that I accept a seat in the Senate. "Rise, Sir Garfield," said Her Majesty the queen, at a private investiture in Buckingham Palace in 1986. With me were Grace and Judith and Mr. Lange, the Prime Minister of New Zealand.

As I have said, in the first half of our service in Africa we didn't question the validity of the life we lived, but in the second half we were racked by doubt. Could the horrors of civil war, of opposition to the government of the day, be justified? It was clear that much that was done by both sides in the conflict should not be supported by Christians, black or white. Many questions are left unanswered, but in Zimbabwe today we live in an atmosphere of reconciliation and of hope. Grace and I emerge from our fifty-four years' service thanking God for His blessings and His mercy.

NOTES

Introduction

1 Dickson A. Mungazi, *The Last British Liberals in Africa: Michael Blundell and Garfield Todd* (Westport: Praeger, 1999); Ruth Weiss, *Sir Garfield Todd and the Making of Zimbabwe* (London: British Academic Press, 1999); Ian Hancock, *White Liberals, Moderates and Radicals in Rhodesia 1953–1980* (New York: St. Martin's, 1984); Michael O. West, "Ndabaningi Sithole, Garfield Todd and the Dadaya School Strike of 1947," *Journal of Southern African Studies* 18 (1992): 297–316; David Chanaiwa, "The Premiership of Garfield Todd in Rhodesia: Racial Partnership Versus Colonial Interests," *Journal of Southern African Affairs* 1 (1976): 83–94; *Hokonui Todd*, prod. Alison Landon and Richard Driver, dir. Richard Driver, 47 min., Limehurst Films, 1990.

2 Mungazi, *British Liberals*, 175.

3 Weiss, *Garfield Todd*, 217.

4 Miles Hudson, *Triumph or Tragedy: Rhodesia to Zimbabwe* (London: H. Hamilton, 1981), 32.

5 "'Fraternal Workers' Return to Zambia: Mission Interviews Chester and Angela Woodhall," *Mission*, January 1976, 133.

6 Hardwicke Holderness, *Lost Chance: Southern Rhodesia 1945–58* (Harare: Zimbabwe Publishing House, 1985), 134.

7 *Sunday Mail*, quoted in the *New Zealand Christian*, October 1946, 8.

8 Jesse Bader, "Emory Ross Comments on Congo Visit," *Christian-Evangelist*, November 17, 1954, 13.

9 Most of the information in the next three paragraphs are from Michael W. Casey, "Todd, Sir Garfield (1908–2002) and Lady Grace (1911–2001)," in *The Encyclopedia of the Stone-Campbell Movement: Christian Churches, Churches of Christ and the Christian Church (Disciples of Christ)*, ed. Paul Blowers, Anthony Dunnavant, and Douglas Foster (Grand Rapids: Eerdmans, 2005), 743–44, and Graeme S. Mount, "Todd, Reginald Stephen Garfield," in *Historical Dictionary of the British Empire*, vol. 2 (Westport: Greenwood Press, 1996), 1099–1101.

10 Chris Ashton, "Watching to See How It is Done . . . This Time," *Illustrated Life Rhodesia*, May 25, 1978, clipping in DCM Africa file, Disciples of Christ Historical Society, Nashville, Tennessee.

11 Graham Boynton, *Last Days in Cloud Cuckooland: Dispatches from White Africa* (New York: Random House, 1997), 76.

12 "Todd, Hon. Sir (Reginald Stephen) Garfield," *The International Who's Who 1994–95*, 58th edn. (London: Europa Publications, 1994), 1551.

13 C. F. Hallencreutz, "A Council in Crossfire: ZCC 1964–1980," in *Church and State in Zimbabwe*, ed. Carl F. Hallencreutz and Ambrose M. Moyo (Gweru, Zimbabwe: Mambo, 1988), 54, 71–72, 89, 92–94, 103n29, 105n121, 111nn277, 278, 281, 282.

14 Cornel West, *Democracy Matters: Winning the Fight against Imperialism* (New York: Penguin, 2004), 15.

15 West, *Democracy Matters*, 16.

16 West, *Democracy Matters*, 16–17.

17 West, *Democracy Matters*, 17–18.

18 James Darsey, *The Prophetic Tradition and Radical Rhetoric in America* (New York: New York University Press, 1997), 20.

19 West, *Democracy Matters*, 163.

20 West, *Democracy Matters*, 19.

21 Darsey, *Prophetic Tradition*.

22 West, *Democracy Matters*, 210.

23 Wayne Booth, *The Rhetoric of Rhetoric: The Quest for Effective Communication* (Oxford: Blackwell, 2004), 107–47.

24 Jim A. Kuypers, *The Art of Rhetorical Criticism* (Boston: Pearson Educational, 2005), 9.

25 Martin J. Medhurst, "Afterword: The Ways of Rhetoric," in *Beyond the Rhetorical Presidency*, ed. Martin J. Medhurst (College Station: Texas A&M University Press, 1996), 223–24.

26 Thomas M. Conley, *Rhetoric in the European Tradition* (New York: Longman, 1990), 17.

27 Isocrates, *Antidosis*, in *Isocrates*, vol. 1., ed. G. P. Gould, trans. George Norlin, Loeb Classical Library 209 (Cambridge, Mass.: Harvard University Press, 1945), 254.

28 *De Oratore* I.viii.31–32.

29 George Kennedy, ed. and trans., *Aristotle on Rhetoric: A Theory of Civic Discourse* (Oxford: Oxford University Press, 1991). On deliberative rhetoric see book 1, chs. 4–8.

30 West, *Democracy Matters*, 73.

31 West, *Democracy Matters*, 73–74.

32 West, *Democracy Matters*, 74.

33 David Buttrick hints at this analogy/definition but does not fully develop it in his homiletics. David Buttrick, "Preaching to the Faith of America," in *Communication and Change in American Religious History*, ed. Leonard I. Sweet (Grand Rapids: Eerdmans, 1993), 301.

34 Also see Michael W. Casey, "'Come Let us Reason Together': The Heritage of the Churches of Christ as a Source for Rhetorical Invention," *Rhetoric & Public Affairs* 7 (2004): 487–98. The name for the tradition can be confusing. Sometimes Disciples of Christ is preferred and in other places Churches of Christ. Chapter 1 will explain the confusion over the name.

Chapter 1: Democratic Disciples

1 Hans Rollman, "Sir Garfield Todd: 'White Hero of Zimbabwe,'" *Telegram* (St. John, New Foundland), February 24, 2002, A10.

2 Robert L. Friedly, "Garfield Todd the Prophet Who Can't Be Silenced," *Disciple*, September 4, 1977, 2.

3 Garfield Todd, e-mail to the author, February 16, 2001. On James A. Garfield's religious background, see William C. Ringenberg, "Religious Thought and Practice of James A. Garfield," in *The Stone-Campbell Movement: An International Religious Tradition*, ed. Michael W. Casey and Douglas A. Foster (Knoxville: University of Tennessee Press, 2002), 219–33; W. W. Wasson, *James A. Garfield: His Religion and Education* (Nashville: Tennessee Book Co., 1952). This is a revision of Wasson's dissertation under Sidney Mead at the University of Chicago. Also see Jerry Bryant Rushford, "Political Disciple: The Relationship between James A. Garfield and the Disciples of Christ" (Ph.D. diss., University of California at Santa Barbara, 1977).

4 Garfield Todd, e-mail to the author, February 16, 2001. The biography Todd read was a hagiography written soon after Garfield's assassination. See William M. Thayer, *From Log Cabin to the White House: Life of James A. Garfield, boyhood, youth, manhood, assassination, death, funeral* (New York: John B. Alden, 1885).

5 Grace Todd to Guy Clutton-Brock, September 21, 1991, in Guy Clutton-Brock correspondence, Terrance Ranger papers, Rhodes House, Bodleian Library, Oxford University.

6 The various names for the tradition are very confusing to outsiders. At the beginning of the movement led by Alexander Campbell and Barton Stone the names "Disciples of Christ," "Christian Church," and "Church of Christ" were interchangeable throughout the nineteenth century. Often the name "Restoration Movement" was used in the nineteenth century as well. In the United States conservatives began to prefer the name "Church of Christ" or "Churches of Christ" while moderates and liberals preferred "Disciples of Christ" or "Christian Church." In the twentieth century the moderates and liberals divided, with the moderates preferring "Christian Churches and Churches of Christ" and liberals preferring "Disciples of Christ (Christian Church)." Some American moderates refer to their churches as the "independent Christian Church." To add to the confusion, in Britain, New Zealand, and Australia the name "Church of Christ" was the preferred name for the entire movement. When American Christians from the conservative groups immigrated to those countries a person would find "Churches of Christ" along a large theological spectrum who share a theological heritage but who will not recognize each other as fellow Christians. Hopefully the context of my usage of the different terms will be clear in the rest of the book. I will identify Todd's fellowship as the New Zealand Churches of Christ which have the closest affinity with the twentieth-century Disciples of Christ in the United States. However, Todd also had significant connection with the moderates or the independent Christian Churches in the United States as well.

7 Alexis de Tocqueville, *Democracy in America*, trans. G. Lawrence, in *Great Books of the Western World*, vol. 44 (Chicago: Encyclopedia Britannica, 1990), 28.

8 Arthur Schlesinger, "The Age of Alexander Campbell," in *The Sage of Bethany: A Pioneer in Broadcloth*, ed. Perry Gresham (St. Louis: Bethany, 1960), 25–44, and Nathan Hatch, *The Democratization of American Christianity* (New Haven: Yale University Press, 1989), 71–73, 75. Also see William Moorhouse, "The Restoration Movement: The Rhetoric of Jacksonian Restorationism in a Frontier Religion" (Ph.D. diss., Indiana University, 1968).

9 Schlesinger, "Age of Campbell," 26.

10 Schlesinger, "Age of Campbell," 33.

11 Robert Richardson, *Memoirs of Alexander Campbell*, vol. 1 (Philadelphia: J. B. Lippincott, 1868), 465–66.

12 Paul Blowers, "Liberty," in *The Encyclopedia of the Stone-Campbell Movement*, ed. Douglas A. Foster, Paul M. Blowers, Anthony Dunnavant, and D. Newell Williams (Grand Rapids: Eerdmans, 2004), 476.

13 Quoted by James Egbert, *Alexander Campbell and Christian Liberty* (St. Louis: Christian Publishing, 1909), 73–74.

14 Schlesinger, "Age of Campbell," 40. Also see Hatch, *Democratization*, 163, and Robert Frederick West, *Alexander Campbell and Natural Religion* (New Haven: Yale University Press, 1948), 7–28.

15 A Berean, "On the Rights of Laymen—No. 1," *Christian Baptist*, January 29, 1826, 209. Campbell published this article in his serial because he agreed with its sentiment.

16 Harold L. Lunger, *The Political Ethics of Alexander Campbell* (St. Louis: Bethany, 1954), 77.

17 Campbell, quoted by D. Ray Lindley, *Apostle of Freedom* (St. Louis: Bethany, 1957), 90–91.

18 Campbell, quoted by Lunger, *Political Ethics*, 88.

19 Campbell, quoted by Lunger, *Political Ethics*, 91.

20 Lunger, *Political Ethics*, 167.

21 Michael W. Casey, "Mastered by the Word: Print Culture, Modernization, and the Priesthood of All Readers in the Churches of Christ," in *Restoring the First-Century Church in the Twenty-First Century: Essays on the Stone-Campbell Restoration Movement*, ed. Warren Lewis and Hans Rollman (Eugene: Wipf and Stock, 2005), 311–22.

22 Campbell, quoted by Schlesinger, "Age of Campbell," 41.

23 Campbell, quoted by Lunger, *Political Ethics*, 168.

24 Lunger, "Education in a Republic," in *Political Ethics*, 167–78; Thomas Olbricht, "Alexander Campbell as an Educator," in *Lectures in Honor of Alexander Campbell Bicentennial*, ed. James M. Seale (Nashville: Disciples of Christ Historical Society, 1988), 79–100; John Morrison, "Alexander Campbell and Moral Education," (Ph.D. diss., Stanford University, 1967), and Thomas L. Smith, "The 'Amelioration of Society': Alexander Campbell and Education Reform in Antebellum America" (Ph.D. diss., University of Tennessee, 1990).

25 Alexander Campbell, "On Common Schools," in *Popular Lectures and Addresses* (1861; repr., Rosemead: Old Paths Book Club, n.d.), 255.

26 John L. Morrison, *Alexander Campbell: Educating the Moral Person* (n.p, 1991), 190.

27 Perry Gresham, "Alexander Campbell—Schoolmaster," in *The Sage of Bethany: A Pioneer in Broadcloth*, ed. Perry Gresham (St. Louis: Bethany, 1960), 20–22.

28 The literature on Campbell's philosophy and grounding in the British Empiricist and Scottish Enlightenment is vast. See my own work: Michael W. Casey, *The Battle Over Hermeneutics in the Stone-Campbell Movement, 1800–1870* (Lewiston: Edwin Mellen, 1998); Michael W. Casey, "From British Ciceronianism to American Baconianism:

Alexander Campbell as a Case Study of a Shift in Rhetorical Theory," *Southern Communication Journal* 66 (2001): 151–66; and Carisse Mickey Berryhill, "Alexander Campbell's Natural Rhetoric of Evangelism," *Restoration Quarterly* 30 (1988): 111–24.

29 The literature on nineteenth-century American reform movements is vast. Ronald G. Walters, *American Reformers: 1815–1860*, rev. ed. (New York: Hill and Wang, 1997) is one of the best. For an excellent older source see Alice Felt Tyler, *Freedom's Ferment: Phases of American Social History from the Colonial Period to the Outbreaks of the Civil War* (New York: Harper and Row, 1944). On the Disciples of Christ and the various reformist impulses, see David Edwin Harrell Jr., *Quest for a Christian America: The Disciples of Christ and American Society to 1866*, 2nd ed. (Tuscaloosa: University of Alabama Press, 2003).

30 Alexander Campbell, "Abolitionism," *Millennial Harbinger*, June 1836, 282–83.

31 Michael W. Casey, "'Come Let us Reason Together,'" *Rhetoric & Public Affairs* 7 (2004): 493. Also see Michael W. Casey and Douglas A. Foster, "The Renaissance of Stone-Campbell Studies: An Assessment and Directions," in *The Stone-Campbell Movement*, Casey and Foster, 1–65.

32 Robert O. Fife, "Alexander Campbell and the Christian Church in the Slavery Controversy" (Ph.D. diss., University of Indiana, 1960), and Earl Eugene Eminhizer, "The Abolitionists among the Disciples of Christ" (Th.D. diss., School of Theology at Claremont, 1968).

33 "Hon. Lloyd George in St. Louis," *Christian-Evangelist*, October 25, 1923, 1383.

34 Peter Ackers, "West End Chapel, Back Street Bethel: Labour and Capital in the Wigan Churches of Christ c. 1845–1945," in *The Stone-Campbell Movement*, Casey and Foster, 398–432, and Peter Ackers, "The Churches of Christ as a Labour Sect," *Dictionary of Labour Biography*, vol. 10 (London: Macmillan, 2000), 199–205. For the best history of the British Churches of Christ, see David M. Thompson, *Let Sects and Parties Fall: A Short History of the Association of Churches of Christ in Great Britain and Ireland* (Birmingham, UK: Berean, 1980).

35 Lloyd Bitzer, "Religious and Scientific Foundations of 18th-Century Theories of Rhetoric," the Van Zelst Lecture in Communication, May 11, 1995 (pub. Evanston: Northwestern University, 1996), 8.

36 George Campbell, *The Philosophy of Rhetoric* (1850; repr., Carbondale: Southern Illinois University Press, 1963), 71–94.

37 Alexander Campbell, *Christian System* (1835; repr., Nashville: Gospel Advocate, 1974), 260.

38 Casey, "Ciceronian," 163.

39 West, *Democracy Matters*, 91. Again, see my *Rhetoric & Public Affairs* article, "Come," and my essay with Doug Foster, "Renaissance," where I list many reformers produced from the Campbell tradition.

40 Peter A. Verkruyse, *Prophet, Pastor, and Patriarch: The Rhetorical Leadership of Alexander Campbell* (Tuscaloosa; University of Alabama Press, 2005), 153.

41 Perry Gresham, "Garfield Todd of Zimbabwe: A Mission and a Victory," *Disciple*, September 7, 1980, 11.

Chapter 2: The Democratic Missionary

1 Boynton, *Cloud Cuckooland*, 56.
2 Boynton, *Cloud Cuckooland*, 58.
3 Boynton, *Cloud Cuckooland*, 58.
4 Boynton, *Cloud Cuckooland*, 58.

5 Unfortunately, no critical history of the New Zealand Churches of Christ exists. The numbers of churches and members as well as much of the history of the Restoration Movement in New Zealand is sketchy and sometimes contradictory. The best source is Lyndsay Jacobs, "The Movement in New Zealand," in *The Encyclopedia of the Stone-Campbell Movement*, Foster et al., 563–66. I have supplemented the story of the New Zealand Churches with other primary and secondary sources which are cited in the footnotes.

6 Peter Ackers, "West End Chapel," 410–11. Also see Louis Billington, "The Churches of Christ in Britain: A Study in Nineteenth-Century Sectarianism," in *The Stone-Campbell Movement*, Casey and Foster, 367–97, and David M. Thompson, *Let Parties and Sects Fall*.

7 Murray J. Savage, *Haddon of Glen Leith: An Ecumenical Pilgrimage* (Dunedin: Associated Churches of Christ in New Zealand, 1970), 37, and Ron O'Grady, "Garfield Todd: Missionary, Prime Minister, Prophet," *Press* (Christchurch, New Zealand), October 7, 1967, 5.

8 Jacobs, "New Zealand," 564–65.

9 Winfred Ernest Garrison and Alfred T. DeGroot, *The Disciples of Christ: A History* (St. Louis: Christian Board of Education, 1948), 459, and A. L. Haddon, "Churches of Christ in New Zealand," *Christian Standard*, 1945, 707–8.

10 Associated Churches of Christ in New Zealand, *Handbook 1978–79*, [NZ]: Associated Churches of Christ [1979], 30, and Jacobs, "New Zealand," 566. This means that the 1979 handbook statistics are inflated because they include all the members of the "uniting congregations" from other traditions.

11 Weiss, *Garfield Todd*, 5.

12 R. S. Garfield Todd, *Christian Unity, Christ's Prayer* (Grahamstown: Rhodes University, 1955), 8, and "Todd," *New Zealand Christian*, November 18, 1929, 12.

13 *A Short History of the Churches of Christ in Invercargill, 1858–1979* (n.p., n.d.), 13.

14 Alexander Campbell, "School and Colleges—No. 2," *Millennial Harbinger*, March 1850, 172.

15 Alexander Campbell, *Christian System* (Nashville: Gospel Advocate, 1974), 96.

16 Michael W. Casey, "'Come Let us Reason Together.'"

17 Todd, *Christian Unity*, 14.

18 R. S. Garfield Todd, "From a Former Student," *New Zealand Christian*, January 20, 1962, 5.

19 Savage, *Haddon of Glen Leith*, 52.

20 Savage, *Haddon of Glen Leith*, 43.

21 Associated Churches of Christ, *Yearbook 1931–1932* [NZ]: Associated Churches of Christ [1932], 6; Associated Churches of Christ, *Yearbook 1929–1930* [NZ]: Associated Churches of Christ [1930], 8; Associated Churches of Christ, *Yearbook 1930–1931* [NZ]: Associated Churches of Christ [1931], 9.

22 John Rigg, *Elocution and Public Speaking (lessons in)* (Christchurch: Andrews, Baty, 1921), ii.

23 Rigg, *Elocution and Public Speaking*, 149.

24 Rigg, *Elocution and Public Speaking*, 156.

25 Rigg, *Elocution and Public Speaking*, 156–57.

26 Rigg, *Elocution and Public Speaking*, 157.

27 Rigg, *Elocution and Public Speaking*, 158.

28 Weiss, *Garfield Todd*, 6–8.

29 *Hokonui Todd*.

30 On Todd's relation to Wright, see Garfield Todd, letter to the author, April 10, 2001.

31 Murray J. Savage, *Achievement: 50 Years of Missionary Witness in Southern Rhodesia* (Wellington: A. H. & A. W. Reed, 1949), 21–24; 29, 33, 49, 78, 104, 83–84, and Weiss, *Garfield Todd*, 11–12.

32 Murray J. Savage, *Forward into Freedom: Associated Churches of Christ in New Zealand Missionary Outreach, 1949–1979* (n.p., n.d.), 12.

33 Savage, *Achievement*, 104.

34 Garfield Todd, "Annual Report, Dadaya and Mashoko Year 1935," *New Zealand Christian*, March 1936, 4.

35 Garfield Todd, "Our Work in South Africa," *New Zealand Christian*, March 1938, 8.

36 Weiss, *Garfield Todd*, 25–27.

37 Garfield Todd, "Our Work in South Africa," *New Zealand Christian*, March 1938, 8, and Savage, *Achievement*, 85–89.

38 Savage, *Achievement*, 85–89, 104, and *Hokonui Todd*.

39 Garfield Todd, "Our Work in South Africa," *New Zealand Christian*, January 1945, 6.

40 Weiss, *Garfield Todd*, 28.

41 Garfield Todd, "Our Work in South Africa," *New Zealand Christian*, March 1941, 15.

42 Garfield Todd, "Our Work in South Africa," *New Zealand Christian*, October 1941, 7–8, and Garfield Todd, "Our Work in South Africa," *New Zealand Christian*, November 1941, 9.

43 Garfield Todd, "Our Work in South Africa," *New Zealand Christian*, May 1944, 7.

44 *New Zealand Christian*, September 1944.

45 Garfield Todd, "Our Work in South Africa," *New Zealand Christian*, October 1944, 7.

46 Garfield Todd, "Our Work in South Africa," *New Zealand Christian*, June 1945, 5.

47 Savage, *Achievement*, 85–89, 104, and *Hokonui Todd*.

48 Garfield Todd, "Our Work in South Africa," *New Zealand Christian*, February 1944, 6.

49 "Statement by Mrs. Todd in No. 7 Letter," *New Zealand Christian*, September 1944.

50 Garfield Todd, "Our Work in South Africa," *New Zealand Christian*, November 1940, 12.

51 *New Zealand Christian*, November 11, 1940, 12.

52 J. Grace Todd, "Our Work in South Africa," *New Zealand Christian*, November 1944, 20; Garfield Todd, "Our Work in South Africa," *New Zealand Christian*, May 1944, 7; Garfield Todd, "Our Work in South Africa," *New Zealand Christian*, May 1946, 9, and Michael O. West, "Ndabaningi Sithole, Garfield Todd and the Dadaya School Strike of 1947," *Journal of Southern African Studies* 18 (1992): 301.

53 Garfield Todd, *War Time Report, Foreign Mission Union Associated Churches of Christ in N.Z. Bulletin No. 9, Supplement to the "New Zealand Christian" 11th May, 1944*.

54 J. Grace Todd, "Our Work in South Africa," *New Zealand Christian*, November 1944, 20.

55 *Bantu Mirror*, March 11, 1944, as quoted by West, 300.

56 Manikidza Nyoni, "Bible School Letter," *New Zealand Christian*, July 1945, 10.

57 West, "Garfield Todd," 301.

58 West, "Garfield Todd," 301–2, 316, and "Ndabiningi Sithole," http://nda-baningi-sithole.biography.ms/ (accessed July 14, 2006).

Chapter 3: Moving Toward Democracy

1 Professor Solomon M. Nkiwane, e-mail to Judith Todd, January 4, 2004. I thank both Judith Todd and Professor Nkiwane for a copy of this e-mail and for permission to quote from it.

2 Nkiwane to Judith Todd.

3 Martin J. Medhurst, "Afterword: The Ways of Rhetoric," in *Beyond the Rhetorical Presidency*, 219, 220, 222–24.

4 Medhurst, "Afterword," 223.

5 L. H. Gann and M. Gelfand, *Huggins of Rhodesia: The Man and Country* (London: Allen and Unwin, 1964), 67. A. W. Ladbrook, "Report from Rhodesia," *New Zealand Christian*, June 1952, 5.

6 Garfield Todd, "Our Work in South Africa," *New Zealand Christian*, August 1935, 8.

7 Garfield Todd, "Our Work in South Africa," *New Zealand Christian*, November 1938, 6; Garfield Todd, "Our Work in South Africa," *New Zealand Christian*, October 1939, 12; and Garfield Todd, "Our Work in South Africa," *New Zealand Christian*, April 1941, 11.

8 Gann and Gelfand, *Huggins of Rhodesia*, 67, 163.

9 Gann and Gelfand, *Huggins of Rhodesia*, 106, 128, 158. The liberalism of Davies and probably Danziger must be seen in their proper context. Davies still wanted a segregated society where whites remained in control. See Carol Summers, *From Civilization to Segregation: Social Ideals and Social Control in Southern Rhodesia, 1890–1934* (Athens: Ohio University Press, 1994), 255.

10 Garfield Todd, "Our Work in South Africa," *New Zealand Christian*, August 1941, 7.

11 Garfield Todd, "Our Work in South Africa," *New Zealand Christian*, October 1942, 5.

NOTES TO PP. 42–46

12 Garfield Todd, "Our Work in South Africa," *New Zealand Christian*, August 1944, 10.

13 Garfield Todd, "Our Work in South Africa," *New Zealand Christian*, September 1939, 10.

14 Garfield Todd, "Our Work in South Africa," *New Zealand Christian*, September 1938, 10.

15 Garfield Todd, "Our Work in South Africa," *New Zealand Christian*, March 1943, 6.

16 Garfield Todd, "Our Work in South Africa," *New Zealand Christian*, April 1944, 7.

17 Garfield Todd, *War-Time Report, Foreign Mission Union Associated Churches of Christ in N.Z. Bulletin No. 9, Supplement to the "New Zealand Christian" 11th May, 1944.*

18 Quoted by Weiss, *Garfield Todd*, 44–45.

19 Garfield Todd, "Our Work in South Africa," *New Zealand Christian*, April 1945, 8, and R. S. Garfield Todd, letter to Prime Minister Godfrey Huggins, April 15, 1945, Sir Garfield Todd papers, Bulawayo, Zimbabwe.

20 Gann and Gelfand, *Huggins of Rhodesia*, 157, 189–90.

21 Garfield Todd, "Our Work in South Africa," *New Zealand Christian*, June 1946, 8.

22 Summers, *From Civilization to Segregation*, 226–92, and Gann and Gelfand, *Huggins of Rhodesia*, 99–101.

23 Southern Rhodesia Parliament, *Debates of the Legislative Assembly*, May 28, 1947, 1183.

24 Gann and Gelfand, *Huggins of Rhodesia*, 126–32.

25 Robert Blake, *A History of Rhodesia* (New York: Alfred A. Knopf, 1978), 238.

26 Southern Rhodesia Parliament, *Debates of the Legislative Assembly*, May 28, 1947, 1183.

27 Southern Rhodesia Parliament, *Debates of the Legislative Assembly*, February 8, 1951, 3280.

28 Garfield Todd, "Our Work in South Africa," *New Zealand Christian*, June 1946, 8.

29 "'Native Standard Should Rise' Says Rev. Garfield Todd," *African Weekly*, March 27, 1946, 1.

30 Garfield Todd, "Our Work in South Africa," *New Zealand Christian*, July 1946, 7.

31 "An All Party Basis," *Rhodesia Herald*, April 12, 1946, 8.

32 Gann and Gelfand, *Huggins of Rhodesia*, 191.

33 Weiss, *Garfield Todd*, 43.

34 Weiss, *Garfield Todd*, 54.

35 Weiss, *Garfield Todd*, 52.

36 Blake, *History*, 286.

37 Weiss, *Garfield Todd*, 52.

38 Garfield Todd, e-mail to the author, June 17, 2002. Much has been written on ghostwriting in the U.S. presidency. See Kurt Ritter and Martin J. Medhurst, eds., *Presidential Speechwriting: From the New Deal to the Reagan Revolution and Beyond* (College Station: Texas A&M University Press, 2003).

39 J. Grace Todd, "Mrs. Todd's Letter," *New Zealand Christian*, August 1946, 10.

40 Pauline Horn, Margaret Leniston, and Pauline Lewis, "The Maiden Speeches of New Zealand Women Members of Parliament," *Political Science* 35 (1983): 232.

41 Horn, Leniston, and Lewis, "Maiden Speeches of New Zealand," 232. Also see Diane Dees, "Bernadette Devin's Maiden Speech: A Rhetoric of Sacrifice," *Southern Speech Communication Journal* 38 (1973): 326–39, for an example where tradition was not followed. On maiden speeches in Southern Rhodesia, see "Maiden Speeches," *Rhodesia Herald*, June 7, 1946, 14.

42 "All night rush job: How Hansard is Prepared and Printed each day," *Rhodesia Herald* June 23, 1956, 8. Printed speeches were "substantially a verbatim account for every word spoken. Shorthand writers took notes which were dictated to typists. Speakers were allowed a week to correct copies of their speeches, but they could not alter the sense of what was said. Only changes in grammatical errors and "obvious errors in reporting" were permitted. After a week the speeches were sent to be included in the final bound copy.

43 Southern Rhodesia Parliament, *Debates of the Legislative Assembly*, June 4, 1946, 154.

44 Southern Rhodesia Parliament, *Debates of the Legislative Assembly*, June 4, 1946, 154.

45 Southern Rhodesia Parliament, *Debates of the Legislative Assembly*, June 4, 1946, 153.

46 Southern Rhodesia Parliament, *Debates of the Legislative Assembly*, June 4, 1946, 154.

47 Edwin Black, *Rhetorical Criticism: A Study in Method* (Madison: University of Wisconsin Press, 1978), 35.

48 David Chanaiwa ("The Premiership of Garfield Todd in Rhodesia: Racial Partnership Versus Colonial Interests," *Journal of Southern African Affairs* 1 [1976]: 83–94) argues that Todd was not a liberal but simply followed the same path as Huggins and other paternalistic whites. Bowman also sees Todd's liberal premiership as a last chance for African-European cooperation as more legend than factual or a reading back into Todd's paternalistic policies his later liberalism and activities. See Larry M. Bowman, *Politics in Rhodesia: White Power in an African State* (Cambridge: Harvard University Press, 1973), 32. Hancock takes a moderate position that Todd ignored or repressed African Nationalist agitation until 1957 when his claims "to be a visionary and liberal" actually began. See Ian Hancock, *White Liberals*, 61. The documentary *Hokonui Todd* takes the position that Todd was a consistent liberal as a politician and prime minister. I am not sure that any exact date can be established for any conversion over to liberalism. "Liberalism" in Rhodesia was a relative term that many different people could embrace. My view is more evolutionary. By taking Todd's rhetoric seriously the seeds of his radical views were present even in New Zealand. He was a paternalist who truly believed in the gradualist ideas of civilization and training Africans, so it was not a mere political ploy with Todd and that made all the difference. His true radicalism did not emerge until after he was out of office but his contradictory liberalism was there all along.

49 " 'Native Standard Should Rise' Says Rev. Garfield Todd," *African Weekly*, March 27, 1946, 1.

50 "Plea for Better Education for Africans," *African Weekly*, June 12, 1946, 1.

51 "The African Teacher," *African Weekly*, August 7, 1946, 4.

52 "African Teachers' Association," *African Weekly*, July 17, 1946, 1.

53 Holderness, *Lost Chance*, 50.

54 Southern Rhodesia Parliament, *Debates of the Legislative Assembly*, June 23, 1952, 2677.

55 Southern Rhodesia Parliament, *Debates of the Legislative Assembly*, May 22, 1947, 1183.

56 Southern Rhodesia Parliament, *Debates of the Legislative Assembly*, February 8, 1951, 3282.

57 Southern Rhodesia Parliament, *Debates of the Legislative Assembly*, May 22, 1947, 1184.

58 Southern Rhodesia Parliament, *Debates of the Legislative Assembly*, February 8, 1951, 3282.

59 "Africa's Hope Put Up to Christians," *New York Times*, September 5, 1955, 12.

60 Southern Rhodesia Parliament, *Debates of the Legislative Assembly*, October 18, 1949, 2685–86.

61 Undated newspaper clipping, Welensky Papers, Box 676, Folder 4, fol. 51, Rhodes House, Bodleian Library, Oxford University.

62 Southern Rhodesia Parliament, *Debates of the Legislative Assembly*, November 24, 1948, 258.

63 Southern Rhodesia Parliament, *Debates of the Legislative Assembly*, July 22, 1946, 1577.

64 Southern Rhodesia Parliament, *Debates of the Legislative Assembly*, July 22, 1946, 1576.

65 Southern Rhodesia Parliament, Debates of the Legislative Assembly, May 3, 1949, 129.

66 Southern Rhodesia Parliament, Debates of the Legislative Assembly, May 3, 1949, 129.

67 Summers, *From Civilization to Segregation*, 75.

68 Summers, *From Civilization to Segregation*, 81–103.

69 Summers, *From Civilization to Segregation*, 226–93.

70 Southern Rhodesia Parliament, *Debates of the Legislative Assembly*, February 8, 1951, 3281.

71 Southern Rhodesia Parliament, *Debates of the Legislative Assembly*, February 12, 1952, 4156.

72 Southern Rhodesia Parliament, *Debates of the Legislative Assembly*, February 8, 1951, 3281.

73 Southern Rhodesia Parliament, *Debates of the Legislative Assembly*, February 8, 1951, 3281–82.

74 R. S. Garfield Todd, "Conference Sermon," *New Zealand Christian*, May 20, 1950, 4.

75 Southern Rhodesia Parliament, *Debates of the Legislative Assembly*, August 14, 1957, 916.

76 Southern Rhodesia Parliament, *Debates of the Legislative Assembly*, May 21, 1947, 1008.

77 Southern Rhodesia Parliament, *Debates of the Legislative Assembly*, June 29, 1949, 2171.

78 Southern Rhodesia Parliament, *Debates of the Legislative Assembly*, March 20, 1952, 90–91.

79 Southern Rhodesia Parliament, *Debates of the Legislative Assembly*, July 11, 1946, 1280.

80 Southern Rhodesia Parliament, *Debates of the Legislative Assembly*, July 11, 1946, 1280.

81 Southern Rhodesia Parliament, *Debates of the Legislative Assembly*, July 11, 1946, 1280.

82 Southern Rhodesia Parliament, *Debates of the Legislative Assembly*, June 18, 1946, 575–76 and 585–87; July 10, 1946, 1217–19; July 11, 1946, 1277–85; May 31,1948, 536–37; October 18, 1949, 2684–92; March 20, 1952, 90–92; May 23, 1952, 1291–99; April 27, 1953, 294–96; August 10, 1954, 1347; March 27, 1956, 2429–35; and July 20, 1956, 318–26.

83 Southern Rhodesia Parliament, *Debates of the Legislative Assembly*, October 23, 1946, 2041–44.

84 Southern Rhodesia Parliament, *Debates of the Legislative Assembly*, July 11, 1946, 1277–85.

85 This is true of many, if not most of his speeches on African education. For a specific example see the last speech cited above in note 78, and Southern Rhodesia Parliament, *Debates of the Legislative Assembly*, July 20, 1956, 325–26.

86 Southern Rhodesia Parliament, *Debates of the Legislative Assembly*, May 28, 1952, 1540–43.

87 Weiss, *Garfield Todd*, 71, 72; and Blake, *History*, 288.

88 Southern Rhodesia Parliament, *Debates of the Legislative Assembly*, July 15, 1955, 852.

89 Thomas W. Benson, "Desktop Demos: New Communication Strategies and the Future of the Rhetorical Presidency," in *Beyond the Rhetorical*, 51.

90 Blake, *History*, 309.

91 Southern Rhodesia Parliament, *Debates of the Legislative Assembly*, May 3, 1957, 1421–22.

92 Southern Rhodesia Parliament, *Debates of the Legislative Assembly*, July 15, 1955, 854.

93 Southern Rhodesia Parliament, *Debates of the Legislative Assembly*, July 15, 1955, 855–56.

94 One of the speeches, the 1956 Congress Address by the prime minister, is published in this volume. See the background to the text, pp. 208–09.

95 Weiss, *Garfield Todd*, 107.

96 "Disciple Missionary Is Prime Minister," *Christian-Evangelist*, September 9, 1953, 870; Basil Holt, "A Disciple Becomes Premier," *Christian-Evangelist*, October 28, 1953, 1034–35; A. C. Watters, "Disciples Missionary Becomes Prime Minister," *World*

Call, December 1953, 26; and "A Missionary Statesman," *Christian-Evangelist*, October 12, 1955, 996.

97 Lorraine and Lyndsay Jacobs, "World Convention of the Churches of Christ," in *Encyclopedia of the Stone-Campbell Movement*, 785–86.

98 "Mr. Todd Arrives in Washington For Talks," *Rhodesia Herald*, August 10, 1955, 8; "Mr. Todd Discusses U.S. Aid," *Rhodesia Herald*, August 14, 1955, 1; "U.S. Told of Progress in S.R.," *Rhodesia Herald*, August 16, 1955, 15; "Mr. Todd's Busy Time on U.S. Visit," *Rhodesia Herald*, August 17, 1958, 8; "Christian Missions Helped Rhodesians To Proper Place," *Rhodesia Herald*, August 19, 1955, 1; "Commonwealth Aid to Federation Suggested," *Rhodesia Herald*, August 24, 1955, 1; "Mr. Todd Tells Americans About the Position of Rhodesian Africans," *Rhodesia Herald*, September 2, 1955, 1; "Mr. Todd Kept Busy in America," *Rhodesia Herald*, September 3, 1955, 1; "Mr. Todd Broadcasts," *Rhodesia Herald*, September 7, 1955, 1; "No Definite Offers from America," *Rhodesia Herald*, September 8, 1955, 1; and "Mr. Todd Impressed by His American Visit," *Rhodesia Herald*, September 19, 1955, 1, 4. On U.S. press coverage see *New York Times*, July 23, 1955, 3; *New York Times*, September 4, 1955, 19; and *New York Times*, September 5, 1955, 12.

99 Todd, "Our Timeless Missionary Mandate," sermon text published in this volume.

100 "A Missionary-Statesman," *Christian-Evangelist*, October 12, 1955, 996.

101 "U.S. Told of Progress in S.R.," *Rhodesia Herald*, August 16, 1955, 17.

102 "Federation, Colonialism and Race in Central Africa," The Georgetown University Forum, August 14, 1955, transcript in Garfield Todd papers, AC 91-70, Disciples of Christ Historical Society, Nashville, Tenn.

103 Morris Kaplan, "South Rhodesia Shuns Race Bias," *New York Times*, September 4, 1955, 19.

104 "Mr. G. Van Eeden's Appraisal of Todd," *Chronicle*, November 8, 1955, newspaper clipping, Welensky Papers, Box 676, Folder 4, fol. 11, Rhodes House, Bodleian Library, Oxford University.

105 "The Naïve Mr. Todd Should Go On Another World Tour," *Rhodesia Herald*, March 17, 1959, 9.

106 Weiss, *Garfield Todd*, 5, and "Mr. Todd Discusses Aid," *Rhodesia Herald*, August 13, 1955, 1.

107 Weiss, *Garfield Todd*, 84.

108 Southern Rhodesia Parliament, *Debates of the Legislative Assembly*, August 10, 1954, 1347.

109 "Rhodesia to Push Negro Education," *New York Times*, March 16, 1956, 10.

110 Weiss, *Garfield Todd*, 81–83.

111 Weiss, *Garfield Todd*, 94.

112 Southern Rhodesia Parliament, *Debates of the Legislative Assembly*, October 5, 1956, 970.

113 Bengt Sundkler and Christopher Steed, *A History of the Church in Africa* (Cambridge: Cambridge University Press, 2000), 800.

114 "Southern Rhodesia: Who's Civilized?" *Time*, July 8, 1957, 18. No text exists for the Interracial speech. The quotes that follow are from the sources listed in the following footnotes.

115 Garfield Todd, "Tübingen Festival Address," speech published in this volume, pp. 325–26. Todd quotes this part of the speech in his Tübingen address.

116 Holderness, *Lost Chance*, 195–97; Hancock, *White Liberals*, 65.

117 "The Chips are Down," *Rhodesia Herald*, June 17, 1957, 8.

118 "Vote Plan Gets Approval of Africans," *Rhodesia Herald*, June 24, 1957, 1.

119 "Todd Commended in 'Brave Franchise Stand,'" *Rhodesia Herald*, June 18, 1957, 9.

120 "More than Distressed," *Rhodesia Herald*, June 18, 1957, 9, and E. J. H. Leighton, letter to editor, *Rhodesia Herald*, June 24, 1957, 5.

121 "Todd Commended in 'Brave Franchise Stand,'" *Rhodesia Herald*, June 18, 1957, 9.

122 Hancock, *White Liberals*, 65.

123 Southern Rhodesia Parliament, *Debates of the Legislative Assembly*, July 25, 1957, 374–76.

124 Southern Rhodesia Parliament, *Debates of the Legislative Assembly*, July 25, 1957, 376.

125 Southern Rhodesia Parliament, *Debates of the Legislative Assembly*, April 30, 1957, 1246.

126 Southern Rhodesia Parliament, *Debates of the Legislative Assembly*, April 30, 1957, 1247.

127 Southern Rhodesia Parliament, *Debates of the Legislative Assembly*, April 30, 1957, 1251.

128 Quoted by Blake, *History*, 315.

129 Quoted by Blake, *History*, 316.

130 Quoted by Blake, *History*, 316.

131 Southern Rhodesia Parliament, *Debates of the Legislative Assembly*, November 14, 1951, 3338.

132 Southern Rhodesia Parliament, *Debates of the Legislative Assembly*, August 9, 1956, 811.

133 Quoted by Weiss, *Garfield Todd*, 98.

134 Weiss, *Garfield Todd*, 99.

135 "Premier Makes his Position on Integration Clear," *African Weekly*, December 4, 1951, 1.

136 "Central Africa: Who's Liberal?" *Time*, January 27, 1958, 29.

137 Weiss, *Garfield Todd*, 115.

138 "Through a Glass Darkly," *Central African Examiner*, February 15, 1958, 8. The *Central African Examiner* printed a summary of Todd's responses based on the notes he used during the speech. See February 15, 1958, 7.

139 Reprint from the *African Daily News*, February 10, 1958 in Garfield Todd papers, AC 91-70, Disciples of Christ Historical Society, Nashville, Tenn.

140 "Hatty's Plan to Prevent the Colony being in the Dark," newspaper clipping in DCM Africa, Disciples of Christ Historical Society, Nashville, Tenn.

141 Ian Smith, *Bitter Harvest: The Great Betrayal* (London: Blake, 2001), 35.

142 Blake, *History*, 300.

143 "People of Rhodesia Divided According to Skin Color," *African Weekly*, February 27, 1957, 1.

144 "Discrimination, Part II," *African Parade*, December 1956, 17, in Garfield Todd biographical file, Disciples of Christ Historical Society, Nashville, Tenn..

145 Reprint from the *African Daily News*, February 10, 1958.

146 "Removal of Todd Distresses S.R. Africans: Non-Committal on Whitehead," reprint from the *African Daily News*, February 10, 1958.

147 Nathan Shamuyarira, *Crisis in Rhodesia*, quoted by Blake, *History*, 312-13.

148 Quoted by Blake, *History*, 312.

149 "Removal of Todd Distresses S.R. Africans: Non-Committal on Whitehead," reprint from the *African Daily News*, February 10, 1958, in Garfield Todd papers, AC 91-70, Disciples of Christ Historical Society.

150 F. S. Joelson, "Matters of Moment," *East Africa and Rhodesia*, January 16, 1958, 634, and F. S. Joelson, "Matters of Moment," *East Africa and Rhodesia*, February 6, 1958, 723.

151 Quoted by *East Africa and Rhodesia*, February 6, 1958, 727.

152 Quoted by *East Africa and Rhodesia*, February 13, 1958, 753.

153 Quoted by *East Africa and Rhodesia*, February 13, 1958, 753, and *East Africa and Rhodesia*, January 23, 1958, 670-71.

154 Hancock, *White Liberals*, 74-75.

Chapter 4: Todd the Prophetic

1 Peter Stiff, *See You in November* (Alberton: Galago, 1985), 185-86.

2 Stiff, *See You in November*, 187.

3 There was at least one failed attempt to assassinate Todd by Smith's government; see Boynton, *Cloud Cuckooland*, 180, and Weiss, *Garfield Todd*, 198.

4 Darsey, *Prophetic Tradition*, 31.

5 Darsey, *Prophetic Tradition*, 49.

6 Darsey, *Prophetic Tradition*, 16.

7 R. S. Garfield Todd, Interview with Chris Laidlaw, "Ideas—Sir Garfield Todd," Radio New Zealand, Wellington, March 24, 2002.

8 Darsey, *Prophetic Tradition*, 20.

9 "Ideas—Sir Garfield Todd."

10 Darsey, *Prophetic Tradition*, 22.

11 Darsey, *Prophetic Tradition*, 23.

12 Darsey, *Prophetic Tradition*, 75.

13 Weiss, *Garfield Todd*, 131.

14 "Todd Backs Government: Abhors Colour Bar," *Rhodesia Herald*, March 10, 1959, 1.

15 "Todd Backs Government: Abhors Colour Bar," *Rhodesia Herald*, March 10, 1959, 1.

16 "Our Own Policies Responsible for Present Troubles," *Rhodesia Herald*, March 12, 1959, 13. On the whites' reaction, see E. V. G. Cresswell-George, "The Naïve Mr. Todd Should Go On Another World Tour," *Rhodesia Herald*, March 17, 1959, 9; Anne Parker, "Todd Policy Would Lead to a Mulatto Country," *Rhodesia Herald*, March 13, 1959, 11.

17 Clipping of the *Sunday Mail*, March 15, 1959, in the Roy Welensky Papers, Box 676, Folder 4, fol. 44, Rhodes House, Bodleian Library, Oxford University.

18 "7,000 Africans Travel by Car, Cycle and on Foot to Hear Todd," *African Daily News*, March 17, 1959, 1.

19 "True Partnership in Months, Not Years—Todd," *Rhodesia Herald*, March 17, 1959, 2.

20 Weiss, *Garfield Todd*, 131.

21 "7,000 Africans," 2.

22 "Woman Heckler Gave Most Trouble," *African Daily News*, March 17, 1959, 1.

23 "7,000 Africans," 1.

24 "7,000 Africans," 1.

25 "True Partnership."

26 "Star-Billing for Mr. Todd," *Rhodesia Herald*, March 18, 1959, 14.

27 "Todd Says Federation Must be Kept Together," *African Daily News*, March 11, 1959, 1.

28 "Star-Billing for Mr. Todd," *Rhodesia Herald*, March 18, 1959, 14.

29 "Garfield Todd on Situation in Nyasaland," *Bantu Mirror*, September 19, 1959, 11.

30 "Todd Says Partnership is still a Car which Does not Go," *African Daily News*, November 9, 1959, 1.

31 Darsey, *Prophetic Tradition*, 85–86.

32 West, *Democracy Matters*, 163.

33 Terrance Ranger, *Are We Not Also Men? The Samkange Family & African Politics in Zimbabwe 1920–64* (London: James Currey, 1995), 175, 178–89, 182–88.

34 Garfield Todd, "Africa: Britain Must Intervene in Crisis," *Scotsman*, August 6, 1960, newspaper clipping, DCM Africa files, Disciples of Christ Historical Society.

35 Ranger, *Are We Not Also Men?*, 189–90; Weiss, *Garfield Todd*, 140–41; and J. R. T. Wood, *The Welensky Papers: A History of the Federation of Rhodesia and Nyasaland* (Durban: Graham, 1983), 802.

36 Enoch Dumbutshena, Paul Mushonga, Joshua Nkomo, and Garfield Todd, "Letter delivered to Secretary of State for Commonwealth Relations 26th July 1960," in Welensky Papers, Box 676, Folder 4, fol. 54, Rhodes House, Bodleian Library, Oxford University. The entire letter is published in this volume.

37 Welensky Papers, Box 676, Folder 4, fol. 55, Rhodes House, Bodleian Library, Oxford University.

38 Ranger, *Are We Not Also Men?*, 190.

39 "Todd Said to be Political Prophet," *African Daily News*, August 10, 1960, 3.

40 M'Takati, "Todd—A Figure of Outstanding Courage," *African Daily News*, May 5, 1964, 7.

41 Wood, *Welensky Papers*, 802.

42 Weiss, *Garfield Todd*, 143.

43 "Todd Condemned by MPs after UK attack," newspaper clipping, *Evening Standard*, July 27, 1960, in Welensky Papers, Box 676, Folder 4, fol. 57, Rhodes House, Bodleian Library, Oxford University.

44 "I'm no Traitor, I am a Patriot," newspaper clipping, *Evening Standard*, July 28, 1960, in Welensky Papers, Box 676, Folder 4, fol. 60, Rhodes House, Bodleian Library, Oxford University.

45 "Todd Quits Politics—'I Have Failed after 14 Years,'" *Rhodesia Herald*, September 3, 1960, 1.

46 "Todd Launches New Africa Party in Come-Back," *Rhodesia Herald*, August 1, 1961, newspaper clipping, Welensky Papers, Box 512, Folder 4, fol. 1, Rhodes House, Bodleian Library, Oxford University, and "Majority Should Rule, New African Party Declares," *African Daily News*, August 1, 1961, Welensky Papers, Box 512, Folder 4, fol. 2, Rhodes House, Bodleian Library, Oxford University.

47 "Garfield Todd—Rhodesia's Prisoner," *The Australian Christian*, February 7, 1976, 36.

48 "Todd Dubbed 'White Rhodesia's Most Rejected White Man,'" *Christian*, September 22, 1968, clipping, R. S. G. Todd file, AC 91–70, Disciples of Christ Historical Society.

49 Darsey, *Prophetic Tradition*, 51.

50 Darsey, *Prophetic Tradition*, 57.

51 "Garfield Todd Stresses Church's Role in Africa," *World Call*, May 1960, 4.

52 Todd, "After Independence, What?"

53 West, *Democracy Matters*, 18.

54 Todd, "After Independence, What?"

55 Todd, "After Independence, What?"

56 Todd, "After Independence, What?"

57 Todd, "After Independence, What?"

58 Todd, "After Independence, What?"

59 Garfield Todd to Emory Ross, in Garfield Todd Papers, AC 91–70, Disciple of Christ Historical Society, Nashville, Tennessee.

60 M'Takati, "Todd—A Figure of Outstanding Courage."

61 United Nations General Assembly, *Special Committee On The Situation With Regard To The Implementation Of The Declaration On The Granting Of Independence To Colonial Countries And Peoples Verbatim Record Of The Two Hundredth and Forty-Ninth Meeting*, A/AC.109/PV.249.

62 See the next chapter, "The 'Horrible Speech': Todd's Effort to End White Supremacy," where this speech is analyzed.

63 "S.R. Situation 'Intolerable' Says Todd," *African Daily News*, July 23, 1962, 1; *African Daily News*, July 28, 1962, 1; and *African Daily News*, August 4, 1962, 7.

64 "Fur Hat Fashion Spreads to Todd," *African Daily News*, September 3, 1962, 3.

65 "Todd Wants Butler to Meet Nkomo," *African Daily News*, May 18, 1962, 3.

66 West, *Democracy Matters*, 145.

67 Garfield Todd, "The Local Congregation in an Ecumenical World," in W. B. Blakemore, ed., *The Challenge of Christian Unity: The William Henry Hoover Lectures on Christian Unity for 1961* (St. Louis: Bethany, 1963), 104.

68 R. S. Garfield Todd, "Can Christianity Survive In Africa?" speech, Federal Broadcasting Corporation, Salisbury, Southern Rhodesia, January 2, 1963.

69 Darsey, *Prophetic Tradition*, 202.

70 Bowman, *Politics in Rhodesia*, 153.

71 "Todd Tells Whites to Get Relations with Blacks Right," *African Daily News*, April 11, 1962, 3.

72 "Todd Warns of SR Strife," *African Daily News*, August 14, 1963, 1.

73 "Southern Rhodesia: Black and White," *Time*, May 11, 1964, 48.

74 "Southern Rhodesia: Black and White," *Time*, May 11, 1964, 47.

75 "Todd SR Whites' Saviour—Kaunda," *African Daily News*, April 27, 1964, 1.

76 Todd, "Danger! Men Thinking!"

77 Todd, "Danger! Men Thinking!"

78 Todd, "Danger! Men Thinking!"

79 Todd, "Danger! Men Thinking!"

80 "DC Bans a Todd Rally," *African Daily News*, August 19, 1964, 1.

81 Bowman, *Politics in Africa*, 70.

82 Lawrence Fellows, "Rhodesia Balks Mediation Plan," *New York Times*, October 19, 1965, 1; Lawrence Fellows, "Rhodesia Sends Britain a Plea," *New York Times*, October 21, 1965, 4; and Weiss, *Garfield Todd*, 161–62.

83 "Rhodesia Warns Against Apartheid," *New York Times*, July 29, 1967, 13.

84 Weiss, *Garfield Todd*, 175–89.

85 "United States Policy Toward Rhodesia," *Hearing Before the Subcommittee on Africa of the Committee on International Relations House of Representative, Ninety-Fifth Congress, First Session, June 9, 1977* (U.S. Government Printing Office, 1978), 62–72.

86 United Nations General Assembly, *Verbatim Record of the 1078th Meeting of the Special Committee on the Situation with Regard to the Implementation of the declaration on the Granting of Independence to Colonial Countries and Peoples* A/AC.109/PV.1078. This text is reproduced in this book.

87 For example, see Garfield Todd, "Speech before International Center of Indianapolis," July 13, 1977. This text is reproduced in this book.

88 "International Center speech."

89 Darsey, *Prophetic Tradition*, 20.

90 Darsey, *Prophetic Tradition*, 20.

91 "The Speech that says it all—in Silence," *Rand Daily Mail* (Johannesberg), July 25, 1980, newspaper clipping in possession of author. I thank Sir Garfield Todd for supplying a copy of the newspaper clipping.

92 *Hokonui Todd*.

93 Weiss, *Garfield Todd*, 220.

94 Shelia Rule, "From a Gift of Earth, Many Dreams to Till," *New York Times International*, March 19, 1988, 4.

95 Jane Flanagan, "Ex-Premier Vows That Mugabe Will Not Stop Him Claiming His Vote," *The Sunday Telegraph* (London), February 17, 2002, 32.

96 Darsey, *Prophetic Tradition*, 202.

Chapter 5: The "Horrible Speech"

1 Todd tells the story publicly for the first time in his speech to celebrate Joshua Nkomo's seventy-second birthday and fortieth wedding anniversary, published in this volume.

2 Weiss, *Garfield Todd*, 150.

3 Garfield Todd, e-mail to the author, January 23, 2001.

4 Sir Roy Welensky, *Welensky's 4000 Days: The Life and Death of the Federation of Rhodesia and Nyasaland* (London: Collins, 1964), 373.

5 Welensky, *Welensky's 4000 Days*, 298.

6 *African Daily News*, January 8, 1962, 8.

7 Welensky, *Welensky's 4000 Days*, 310.

8 *Yearbook of the United Nations 1962* (New York: Columbia University Press, 1964), 57.

9 "U.N. Probe into Status of Southern Rhodesia Starts," *African Daily News*, March 7, 1962, 1.

10 Joshua Nkomo, *Nkomo: The Story of My Life* (Harare: Sapes Books, 2001), 103. Secret Memo to Julian Greenfield, June 26, 1962, Welensky Papers, Box 620, Folder 1, fol. 46, Rhodes House, Bodleian Library, Oxford University.

11 *Yearbook 1962*, 419–28.

12 Weiss, *Garfield Todd*, 150.

13 Kenneth Burke, *Permanence and Change: An Anatomy of Purpose* (Indianapolis: Bobbs-Merrill, 1965), 80–81.

14 Burke, *Permanence and Change*, 74.

15 Burke, *Permanence and Change*, 7.

16 Burke, *Permanence and Change*, 119. Also see Martha Solomon, "Ideology as Rhetorical Constraint: The Anarchist Agitation of "Red Emma" Goldman," *Quarterly Journal of Speech* 84 (1988): 184–200, and Thomas Rosteck and Michael Leff, "Piety, Propriety and Perspective: An Interpretation and Application of Key Terms in Kenneth Burke's Permanence and Change," *Western Journal of Speech Communication* 53 (1989): 327–41.

17 Chaim Perleman and L. Olbrechts-Tyteca, *The New Rhetoric: A Treatise on Argumentation* (Notre Dame: University of Notre Dame Press, 1969), 20.

18 "Praise for Todd," *African Daily News*, March 27, 1962, 1.

19 Patrick Keatley, "Sir Garfield Todd," *The Guardian*, October 14, 2002, 20.

20 "Mr. Todd Attacks S.R. Government," *East Africa and Rhodesia*, March 29, 1962, 741.

21 "PM Attacks Rhodesians who Give 'False Evidence' at UN," *Chronicle*, March 21, 1962, 11, and "Letters to the Editor," *Chronicle*, March 26, 1962, 2.

22 West, *Democracy Matters*, 16.
23 West, *Democracy Matters*, 114.

Chapter 6: Todd's Narrative Rhetoric

1 Terrance O. Ranger, "The Service of Celebration of The Lives of Garfield and Grace Todd, February 13, 2003: Report to the Organising Committee and to the Executive Committee of the Britain Zimbabwe Society," March 30, 2003, unpublished letter in possession of the author. I would like to thank Professor Terrance Ranger for providing me a copy of the report.

2 Cornel West, *Prophetic Fragments: Illuminations of the Crisis in American Religion and Culture* (Grand Rapids: Eerdmans, 1988), xi.

3 For Aristotle on epideictic rhetoric, see George Kennedy, *Aristotle on Rhetoric*, 78–87.

4 G. D. Munro, "Otago Doctorate Honours Garfield Todd," *New Zealand Christian*, February 1980, 1, and Garfield Todd, "Otago University Graduation speech," in Garfield Todd papers held by Susan Paul, Haddington, East Lothian, Scotland. I thank Susan Paul for making a copy of the text available to me.

5 "The Speech that Says it all—in Silence," *Daily Rand Mail* of July 7, 1980, in newspaper clipping from Garfield Todd to the author.

6 Garfield Todd, "Tübingen Festival: Address to be delivered Saturday May 28, 1983," in Garfield Todd papers held by Susan Paul, Haddington, East Lothian, Scotland. I thank Susan Paul for making a copy of the text available to me.

7 *Christian Standard*, May 7, 1989.

8 Garfield Todd, "Dinner in Bulawayo: September 30, 1989: To Celebrate Dr. Joshua Nkomo's 72nd Birthday and 40th Wedding Anniversary," speech text, Terrance Ranger Papers, Rhode House Library, Oxford University, Oxford, England.

9 Richard M. Weaver, "Language is Sermonic," in *Language is Sermonic: Richard M. Weaver on the Nature of Rhetoric*, ed. Richard L. Johnssesen, Rennard Strickland, and Ralph T. Eubanks (Baton Rouge: Louisiana State University Press, 1970), 225.

10 Garfield Todd, "Conference Sermon," *New Zealand Christian*, May 1950, 1.

11 Thomas G. Long, *The Witness of Preaching* (Louisville: Westminster/John Knox, 1989), 158–60.

12 Fred Craddock, *Preaching* (Nashville: Abingdon, 1985), 204.

13 Kathleen Jamieson, *Eloquence in an Electronic Age: The Transformation of Political Speechmaking* (New York: Oxford University Press, 1988).

14 Many observers have pointed out this shift in preaching that parallels what Jamieson articulates for political speaking. For example, see David Buttrick, *A Captive Voice: The Liberation of Preaching* (Louisville: Westminster/John Knox, 1994), and Fred Craddock, *As One Without Authority: Essays on Inductive Preaching* (Enid: Phillips University Press, 1971).

15 Marshall McLuhan, *Understanding Media: The Extensions of Man*, 2nd ed. (New York: Signet, 1964); Neil Postman, *Amusing Ourselves to Death: Public Discourse in the Age of Show Business* (New York: Viking Penguin, 1985); and Walter J. Ong, *Orality and Literacy: The Technologizing of the Word* (London: Routledge, 1982).

16 Judith Todd, e-mail to the author, November 11, 2005. Judith Todd said that her father read McLuhan and "was fascinated by the world of communications." He "never was without a radio."

17 Garfield Todd, *Christian Unity*, 5.

18 Todd, "Local Congregation," 97.

19 "The Speech that Says it all—in Silence."

20 Karlyn Kohrs Campbell and Kathleen Hall Jamieson, "Form and Genre Criticism: An Introduction," in *Form and Genre: Shaping Rhetorical Action*, ed. Karlyn Kohrs Campbell and Kathleen Hall Jamieson (Falls Church: Speech Communication Association, n.d.), 9.

21 Todd, "Tübingen."

22 Todd, "Nkomo."

23 Todd, "Tübingen."

24 Todd, "Nkomo."

25 Todd, "Reflections."

26 Todd, "Tübingen."

27 Todd, "Reflections." Also see Todd telling this story in *Hokonui Todd*.

28 Todd, "Tübingen."

29 Todd, "Nkomo."

30 Todd, "Reflections."

31 Walter Fisher, *Human Communication as Narration: Toward a Philosophy of Reason, Value, and Action* (Columbia: University of South Carolina Press, 1987), 111.

32 Celeste M. Walls, "You Ain't Just Whistling Dixie: How Carol Mosley-Braun Used Rhetorical Status to Change Jesse Helm's Tune," *Western Journal of Communication* 68 (2004): 343–64; Suzanne K. Daughton, "The Fine Texture of Enactment: Iconicity as Empowerment in Angela Grimke's Pennsylvania Hall Address," *Women's Studies in Communication* 18 (1995): 19–25; Richard W. Leeman, *African-American Orator: A Bio-Critical Source Book* (Westport: Greenwood Press, 1996); and Shirley W. Logan, *We Are Coming: The Persuasive Discourse of 19th Century Black Women* (Carbondale: Southern Illinois University Press, 1999).

33 Todd, "Tübingen,"

34 Todd, "Tübingen,"

35 Todd, "Tübingen,"

36 Todd, "Nkomo."

37 Todd, "Nkomo."

38 Weiss, *Garfield Todd*, 217–18.

39 Todd, "Nkomo."

40 Fisher, *Human Communication as Narration*, 47.

41 Graeme Mount, Sir Garfield Todd, interview by Graeme Mount, Harare, Zimbabwe, June 14, 1990. I would like to thank Professor Mount for sharing his transcription of the interview with Todd.

42 Fisher, *Human Communication as Narration*, 95.

43 Here I am answering one of Fisher's questions about good reasons: "Are the values the message offers those that, in the estimation of the critic, constitute the ideal basis for human conduct?"

44 Fisher, *Human Communication as Narration*, 187.

45 West, *Prophetic Fragments*, xi.
46 George Stroop, *The Promise of Narrative Theology* (London: SCM Press, 1984), 133.
47 Stroop, *Narrative Theology*, 133.
48 Stroop, *Narrative Theology*, 133.
49 Stroop, *Narrative Theology*, 133.
50 Fisher, *Human Communication as Narration*, 119.
51 Fisher, *Human Communication as Narration*, 121.

Conclusion

1 Ranger, "Service of Celebration."
2 Quoted by Michael Hyde, "Introduction: Rhetorically, We Dwell," in *The Ethos of Rhetoric*, ed. Michael J. Hyde (Columbia: University of South Carolina Press, 2004), xiv–xv.
3 Hyde, "Rhetorically, We Dwell," xv.
4 Rollman, "'White Hero of Zimbabwe'"; Flanagan, "Ex-Premier Vows"; and Ann M. Simmons, "Fear Clouds Zimbabwe Election," *Los Angeles Times*, February 20, 2002, A3.
5 Rollman, "'White Hero of Zimbabwe.'" In a further irony, Noyse Dube, the polling agent in Bulawayo who kept Todd from voting, was a former student and headmaster at Dadaya Mission. Todd had married Dube's parents. See "Sir Garfield Todd Fails to Vote," *Daily News*, March 12, 2002, Lexis-Nexis database. See Dube as the Dadaya headmaster in *Hokonui Todd* in the scene where Todd spoke before the Dadaya students at the local church.
6 Ranger, "Service of Celebration."

Sermons and Speech Texts

1 Weiss, *Garfield Todd*, 64.
2 Savage, *Forward into Freedom*, 16.
3 Todd is quoting "Prayer," a poem by Georgian poet John Drinkwater (1882–1937).
4 Gertrude Shoemaker, "Disciples in Africa Hold Convention," *World Call*, December 1954, 44, and Savage, *Achievement*, 24.
5 Basil Holt, "Disciples Taking Greater Part in Work of Missions of Southern Africa," *Christian-Evangelist*, April 13, 1955, 16.
6 "Southern Rhodesian Disciple Honored," *Christian-Evangelist*, December 1, 1954, 1205, and R. S. Garfield Todd, "The Unfinished Task of Christian Missions in Southern Africa," *Southern African Sentinel*, November 1954, 198.
7 *Hokonui Todd*.
8 Todd, *Christian Unity*, 2, and "Disunity 'Shameful': Disciple Prime Minister Gives Annual Peter Ainlsey Lecture," *World Call*, September 1955, 42.
9 Basil Holt, "R. S. Garfield Todd, Ainsley Lecturer," *Christian-Evangelist*, July 13, 1955, 684.

10 William Robinson (1888–1963) was a leader in the British Churches of Christ serving as the principal of Overdale College in Birmingham and editor of the journals *Christian Quarterly* and *Christian Advocate*. He was a leading ecumenical theologian and activist representing the British Churches of Christ in the World Conferences on Faith and Order at Geneva (1920), Lausanne (1927), and Edinburgh (1937). He also was a Churches of Christ representative in the World Council of Churches meetings at Amsterdam (1948) and Evanston (1954). See James Gray, *W.R.: The Man and His Work* (Birmingham, U.K.: Berean, 1978), and Anthony Calvert, "The Published Works of William Robinson: An Interpretative, Annotated Bibliography of a Catholic Evangelical" (M.A. thesis, University of Birmingham, 1984).

11 *Christian-Evangelist*, September 14, 1955, 903, and "A Missionary-Statesman," *Christian-Evangelist*, October 12, 1955, 996.

12 "Editorial," *Christian Standard*, February 13, 1972, 123.

13 "U.P. Candidate on Native Affairs," *Rhodesia Herald*, March 21, 1946, 7.

14 "The Native Standard Should Rise," *Bantu Mirror*, March 20, 1946, 1.

15 "U.P. Candidate."

16 "The Native Standard Should Rise," *Bantu Mirror*, March 20, 1946, 1.

17 Dr. Olive Robertson was a right-wing politician known in Southern Rhodesia whose speeches were often extreme and later to be proven false but were still given wide media coverage. Sir Garfield Todd, e-mail to the author, April 24, 2002.

18 Holderness, *Lost Chance*, 172.

19 Weiss, *Garfield Todd*, 106.

20 Hancock, *White Liberals*, 65.

21 Holderness, *Lost Chance*, 197.

22 Hancock, *White Liberals*, 65–67, and Weiss, *Garfield Todd*, 106–7.

23 Hancock, *White Liberals*, 62.

24 Holderness, *Lost Chance*, 186. Also see Weiss, *Garfield Todd*, 101–4.

25 Holderness, *Lost Chance*, 186.

26 Holderness, *Lost Chance*, 187.

27 Quoted by Weiss, *Garfield Todd*, 98.

28 Quoted by Weiss, *Garfield Todd*, 99.

29 Sir Garfield Todd, letter to the author, April 10, 2001.

30 Garfield Todd, letter to Susan Paul, April 8, 2001.

31 "Former Premier Calls for Full UK, US Commitment," *UN Chronicle*, July 1977, 25.

32 Robert G. Nelson, "Justice in Rhodesia is a Christian Concern," *World Call*, May 1972, 24–25, 37.

33 International Center speech, tape recording, Disciples of Christ Historical Society. Nelson's introduction is on the recording and is not transcribed in this volume.

34 G. D. Munro, "Otago Doctorate Honours Garfield Todd," *New Zealand Christian*, February 1980, 1.

35 Pathisa Nyathi, *Masotsha Ndlovu: In Search of Freedom* (Harare: Longman Zimbabwe, 1998), and Terrance Ranger, *The African Voice in Southern Rhodesia 1898–1930* (Evanston: Northwestern University Press, 1970), 156–69, 182–84.

BIBLIOGRAPHY

Books

Ackers, Peter. "The Churches of Christ as a Labour Sect." *Dictionary of Labour Biography*. Vol. 10. London: Macmillan, 2000, 199–205.

———. "West End Chapel, Back Street Bethel: Labour and Capital in the Wigan Churches of Christ c. 1845–1945." In *The Stone-Campbell Movement: An International Religious Tradition*, edited by Michael W. Casey and Douglas A. Foster, 398–432. Knoxville: University of Tennessee Press, 2002.

Benson, Thomas W. "Desktop Demos: New Communication Strategies and the Future of the Rhetorical Presidency." In *Beyond the Rhetorical Presidency*, edited by Martin J. Medhurst, 50–74. College Station: Texas A&M University Press, 1996.

Berryhill, Carisse Mickey. "Alexander Campbell's Natural Rhetoric of Evangelism." *Restoration Quarterly* 30 (1988): 111–24.

Billington, Louis. "The Churches of Christ in Britain: A Study in Nineteenth-Century Sectarianism." In *The Stone-Campbell Movement*, 367–97.

Bitzer, Lloyd. *Religious and Scientific Foundations of 18th-Century Theories of Rhetoric*. The Van Zelst Lecture in Communication. Evanston: Northwestern University, 1996.

Black, Edwin. *Rhetorical Criticism: A Study in Method*. Madison: University of Wisconsin Press, 1978.

Blake, Robert. *A History of Rhodesia*. New York: Alfred A. Knopf, 1978.

Blowers, Paul. "Liberty." In *The Encyclopedia of the Stone-Campbell Movement: Christian Churches, Churches of Christ and the Christian Church* (Disciples of Christ), edited by Douglas A. Foster, Paul M. Blowers, Anthony Dunnavant, and D. Newell Williams, 476. Grand Rapids: Eerdmans, 2004.

Booth, Wayne. *The Rhetoric of Rhetoric: The Quest for Effective Communication*. Oxford: Blackwell, 2004.

Bowman, Larry M. *Politics in Rhodesia: White Power in an African State*. Cambridge: Harvard University Press, 1973.
Boynton, Graham. *Last Days in Cloud Cuckooland: Dispatches from White Africa*. New York: Random House, 1997.
Burke, Kenneth. *Permanence and Change: An Anatomy of Purpose*. Indianapolis: Bobbs-Merrill, 1965.
Buttrick, David. *A Captive Voice: The Liberation of Preaching*. Louisville: Westminster/John Knox, 1994.
———. "Preaching to the Faith of America." In *Communication and Change in Religious History*, edited by Leonard I. Sweet, 301–19. Grand Rapids: Eerdmans, 1993.
Campbell, Alexander. *Christian System*. 1835. Repr., Nashville: Gospel Advocate, 1974.
———. *Popular Lectures and Addresses*. 1861. Repr., Rosemead: Old Paths Book Club, n.d.
Campbell, George. *The Philosophy of Rhetoric*. 1850. Reprint, Carbondale: Southern Illinois University Press, 1963.
Campbell, Karlyn Kohrs and Kathleen Hall Jamieson. "Form and Genre Criticism: An Introduction." In *Form and Genre: Shaping Rhetorical Action*, edited by Karlyn Kohrs Campbell and Kathleen Hall Jamieson, 9–32. Falls Church: Speech Communication Association, n.d.
Casey, Michael W. *The Battle over Hermeneutics in the Stone-Campbell Movement, 1800–1870*. Lewiston: Edwin Mellen, 1998.
———. "'Come Let us Reason Together': The Heritage of the Churches of Christ as a Source for Rhetorical Invention." *Rhetoric & Public Affairs* 7 (2004): 487–98.
———. "From British Ciceronianism to American Baconianism: Alexander Campbell as a Case Study of a Shift in Rhetorical Theory." *Southern Communication Journal* 66 (2001): 151–66.
———. "Mastered by the Word: Print Culture, Modernization, and the Priesthood of All Readers in the Churches of Christ." In *Restoring the First-Century Church in the Twenty-First Century: Essays on the Stone-Campbell Restoration Movement*, edited by Warren Lewis and Hans Rollman, 311–22. Eugene: Wipf and Stock, 2005.
———. "Todd, Sir Garfield (1908–2002) and Lady Grace (1911–2001)." In *Encyclopedia of the Stone-Campbell Movement*, 743–44.
Casey, Michael W., and Douglas A. Foster. "The Renaissance of Stone-Campbell Studies: An Assessment and Directions." In *The Stone-Campbell Movement*, 1–65.

Chanaiwa, David. "The Premiership of Garfield Todd in Rhodesia: Racial Partnership versus Colonial Interests." *Journal of Southern African Affairs* (1976): 83–94.
Cicero. *De Oratore*. Books I–II. Edited by G. P. Gould. Translated by E. W. Sutton and H. Rackham. Loeb Classical Library 348. Cambridge: Harvard University Press, 1976.
Conley, Thomas M. *Rhetoric in the European Tradition*. New York: Longman, 1990.
Craddock, Fred. *As One Without Authority: Essays on Inductive Preaching*. Enid: Phillips University Press, 1971.
———. *Preaching*. Nashville: Abingdon, 1985.
Darsey, James. *The Prophetic Tradition and Radical Rhetoric in America*. New York: New York University Press, 1997.
Daughton, S. "The Fine Texture of Enactment: Iconicity as Empowerment in Angela Grimke's Pennsylvania Hall Address." *Women's Studies in Communication* 18 (1995): 19–25.
DCM Africa file. Disciples of Christ Historical Society. Nashville.
de Tocqueville, Alexis. *Democracy in America*. Translated by G. Lawrence. *Great Books of the Western World*. Vol. 44. Chicago: Encyclopedia Britannica, 1990.
Dees, Diane. "Bernadette Devin's Maiden Speech: A Rhetoric of Sacrifice." *Southern Speech Communication Journal* 38 (1973): 326–39.
Egbert, James. *Alexander Campbell and Christian Liberty*. St. Louis: Christian Publishing, 1909.
Eminhizer, Earl Eugene. "The Abolitionists among the Disciples of Christ." Th.D. diss., School of Theology at Claremont, 1968.
Fife, Robert O. "Alexander Campbell and the Christian Church in the Slavery Controversy." Ph.D. diss., University of Indiana, 1960.
Fisher, Walter. *Human Communication as Narration: Toward a Philosophy of Reason, Value, and Action*. Columbia: University of South Carolina Press, 1987.
Flanagan, Jane. "Ex-Premier Vows That Mugabe Will Not Stop Him Claiming His Vote." *The Sunday Telegraph* (London), February 17, 2002, 32.
"'Fraternal Workers' Return to Zambia: Mission Interviews Chester and Angela Woodhall." *Mission*, January 1976, 133–36.
Friedly, Robert L. "Garfield Todd the Prophet Who Can't Be Silenced." *Disciple*, September 1977, 2–4.
Gann, L. H., and M. Gelfand. *Huggins of Rhodesia: The Man and Country*. London: Allen and Unwin, 1964.

Garrison, Winfred Ernest, and Alfred T. DeGroot. *The Disciples of Christ: A History*. St. Louis: Christian Board of Education, 1948.

Gresham, Perry. "Alexander Campbell—Schoolmaster." In *The Sage of Bethany: A Pioneer in Broadcloth*, edited by Perry Gresham, 20–22. St. Louis: Bethany, 1960.

———. "Garfield Todd of Zimbabwe: A Mission and a Victory." *Disciple*, September 1980, 11.

Hallencreutz, C. F. "A Council in Crossfire: ZCC 1964–1980." In *Church and State in Zimbabwe*, edited by Carl F. Hallencreutz and Ambrose M. Moyo. Gweru, Zimbabwe: Mambo, 1988.

Hancock, Ian. *White Liberals, Moderates and Radicals in Rhodesia 1953–1980*. New York: St. Martin's, 1984.

Harrell, David Edwin Jr. *Quest for a Christian America: The Disciples of Christ and American Society to 1866*. 2nd edition. Tuscaloosa: University of Alabama Press, 2003.

Hatch, Nathan. *The Democratization of American Christianity*. New Haven: Yale University Press, 1989.

Holderness, Hardwicke. *Lost Chance: Southern Rhodesia 1945–58*. Harare: Zimbabwe Publishing House, 1985.

Hokonui Todd. Produced by Alison Landan and Richard Driver. Directed by Richard Driver. 47 min. Linehurst Films, 1990. Videocassette.

Horn, Pauline, Margaret Leniston, and Pauline Lewis, "The Maiden Speeches of New Zealand Women Members of Parliament." *Political Science* 35 (1983): 229–66.

Hudson, Miles. *Triumph or Tragedy Rhodesia to Zimbabwe*. London: H. Hamilton, 1981.

Hyde, Michael. "Introduction: Rhetorically, We Dwell." In *The Ethos of Rhetoric*, edited by Michael J. Hyde, xii–xxviii. Columbia: University of South Carolina Press, 2004.

Isocrates. *Antidosis*. In *Isocrates*, Vol. 1. Edited by G. P. Gould. Translated by George Norlin. Loeb Classical Library 209. Cambridge: Harvard University Press, 1945.

Jacobs, Lorraine, and Lyndsay Jacobs. "World Convention of the Churches of Christ." In *The Encyclopedia of the Stone-Campbell Movement*, 785–86.

Jacobs, Lyndsay. "The Movement in New Zealand." In *The Encyclopedia of the Stone-Campbell Movement*, 563–66.

Jamieson, Kathleen. *Eloquence in an Electronic Age: The Transformation of Political Speechmaking*. New York: Oxford University Press, 1988.

Kennedy, George. *Aristotle on Rhetoric: A Theory of Civic Discourse*. Oxford: Oxford University Press, 1991.

Kuypers, Jim A. *The Art of Rhetorical Criticism*. Boston: Pearson Education, 2005.

Leeman, Richard W. *African-American Orator: A Bio-Critical Source Book*. Westport: Greenwood Press, 1996.

Lindley, D. Ray. *Apostle of Freedom*. St. Louis: Bethany, 1957.

Logan, S. W. *We Are Coming: The Persuasive Discourse of 19th Century Black Women*. Carbondale: Southern Illinois Press, 1999.

Long, Thomas G. *The Witness of Preaching*. Louisville: Westminster/John Knox, 1989.

Lunger, Harold L. *The Political Ethics of Alexander Campbell*. St. Louis: Bethany, 1954.

McLuhan, Marshall. *Understanding Media: The Extensions of Man*, 2nd edition. New York: Signet, 1964.

Medhurst, Martin J. "Afterword: The Ways of Rhetoric." In *Beyond the Rhetorical Presidency*, 218–26.

Moorhouse, Jerry Bryant. "The Restoration Movement: The Rhetoric of Jacksonian Restorationism in a Frontier Religion." Ph.D. diss., Indiana University, 1968.

Mount, Graeme S. Interview with Sir Garfield Todd, Prime Minister of Southern Rhodesia, 1953–1958, Harare, Zimbabwe, June 14, 1990.

———. "Todd, Reginald Stephen Garfield." in *Historical Dictionary of the British Empire*. Vol. 2, 1099–1101. Westport: Greenwood Press, 1996.

Morrison, John L. *Alexander Campbell: Educating the Moral Person*. N.p., 1991.

———. "Alexander Campbell and Moral Education." Ph.D. diss., Stanford University, 1967.

Mungazi, Dickson A. *The Last British Liberals in Africa: Michael Blundell and Garfield Todd*. Westport: Praeger, 1999.

"Ndabiningi Sithole." http://ndabaningi-sithole.biography.ms/

Nkomo, Joshua. *Nkomo: The Story of My Life*. Harare: Sapes Books, 2001.

Nyathi, Pathisa. *Masotsha Ndlovu: In Search of Freedom*. Harare: Longman Zimbabwe, 1998.

O'Grady, Ron. "Garfield Todd: Missionary, Prime Minister, Prophet." *Press* [Christchurch, NZ], October 7, 1967, 5.

Olbricht, Thomas H. "Alexander Campbell as an Educator." In *Lectures in Honor of Alexander Campbell Bicentennial*, edited by James M. Seale, 79–100. Nashville: Disciples of Christ Historical Society, 1988.

Ong, Walter J. *Orality and Literacy: The Technologizing of the Word*. London: Routledge, 1982.
Perleman, Chaim, and L. Olbrechts-Tyteca. *The New Rhetoric: A Treatise on Argumentation*. Notre Dame: University of Notre Dame Press, 1969.
Postman, Neil. *Amusing Ourselves to Death: Public Discourse in the Age of Show Business*. New York: Viking Penguin, 1985.
Ranger, Terrance. *The African Voice in Southern Rhodesia 1898–1930*. Evanston: Northwestern University Press, 1970.
———. *Are We Not Also Men? The Samkange Family & African Politics in Zimbabwe 1920–64*. London: James Currey, 1995.
Richardson, Robert. *Memoirs of Alexander Campbell*. Philadelphia: J. B. Lippincott, 1868.
Rigg, John. *Elocution and Public Speaking (lessons in)*. Christchurch: Andrews, Baty, and Co., 1921.
Ringenberg, William C. "Religious Thought and Practice of James A. Garfield." In *The Stone-Campbell Movement*, 219–33.
Ritter, Kurt, and Martin J. Medhurst, eds. *Presidential Speechwriting: From the New Deal to the Reagan Revolution and Beyond*. College Station: Texas A&M University Press, 2003.
Rollman, Hans. "Sir Garfield Todd: 'White Hero of Zimbabwe.'" *Telegram* [St. John, New Foundland, Canada], February 24, 2002, A10.
Rosteck, Thomas, and Michael Leff. "Piety, Propriety and Perspective: An Interpretation and Application of Key Terms in Kenneth Burke's Permanence and Change." *Western Journal of Speech Communication* 53 (1989): 327–41.
Rushford, Jerry Bryant. "Political Disciple: The Relationship between James A. Garfield and the Disciples of Christ." Ph.D. diss., University of California at Santa Barbara, 1977.
Savage, Murray J. *Achievement: 50 Years of Missionary Witness in Southern Rhodesia*. Wellington: A. H. & A. W. Reed, 1949.
———. *Forward into Freedom: Associated Churches of Christ in New Zealand Missionary Outreach, 1949–1979*. N.p, n.d. A copy at the Disciples of Christ Historical Society, Nashville, Tenn.
———. *Haddon of Glen Leith: An Ecumenical Pilgrimage*. Dunedin: Associated Churches of Christ in New Zealand, 1970.
Schlesinger, Arthur. "The Age of Alexander Campbell." In *The Sage of Bethany*, 25–44.
A Short History of the Churches of Christ in Invercargill, 1858–1979. N.p., n.d. A copy at the Alexander Turnbull Library, Wellington, New Zealand.

Smith, Ian. *Bitter Harvest: The Great Betrayal*. London: Blake, 2001.

Smith, Thomas L. "The 'Amelioration of Society': Alexander Campbell and Education Reform in Antebellum America." Ph.D. diss., University of Tennessee, 1990.

Solomon, Martha. "Ideology as Rhetorical Constraint: The Anarchist Agitation of 'Red Emma' Goldman." *Quarterly Journal of Speech* 84 (1988): 184–200.

Southern Rhodesia Parliament, *Debates of the Legislative Assembly*, 1946–1958.

Stiff, Peter. *See You in November*. Alberton: Galago, 1985.

Stroop, George. *The Promise of Narrative Theology*. London: SCM Press, 1984.

Summers, Carol. *From Civilization to Segregation: Social Ideals and Social Control in Southern Rhodesia, 1890–1934*. Athens: Ohio University Press, 1994.

Sundkler, Bengt, and Christopher Steed. *A History of the Church in Africa*. Cambridge: Cambridge University Press, 2000.

Thayer, William M. *From Log Cabin to the White House: Life of James A. Garfield, boyhood, youth, manhood, assassination, death, funeral*. New York, 1885.

Thompson, David M. *Let Sects and Parties Fall: A Short History of the Association of Churches of Christ in Great Britain and Ireland*. Birmingham, UK: Berean, 1980.

"Todd, Hon. Sir (Reginald Stephen) Garfield." in *The International Who's Who 1994–95*. London: Europa Publications, 1994, 1551.

Todd, R. S. Garfield. *Christian Unity, Christ's Prayer*. Grahamstown: Rhodes University, 1955.

———. "The Local Congregation in an Ecumenical World." In *The Challenge of Christian Unity: The William Henry Hoover Lectures on Christian Unity for 1961*, edited by W. B. Blakemore. St. Louis: Bethany, 1963, 97–109.

Tyler, Alice Felt. *Freedom's Ferment: Phases of American Social History from the Colonial Period to the Outbreaks of the Civil War*. New York: Harper and Row, 1944.

United Nations General Assembly. *Special Committee on the Situation with Regard to the Implementation of the Declaration on the Granting of Independence to Colonial Countries and Peoples Verbatim Record of the Two Hundredth and Forty-Ninth Meeting*. A/AC.109/PV.249.

———. *Special Committee on the Situation with Regard to the Implementation of the Declaration on the Granting of Independence to Colonial Countries and Peoples Verbatim Record of the Sixteenth Meeting*. A/AC.109/PV.18.

———. *Special Committee on the Situation with Regard to the Implementation of the Declaration on the Granting of Independence to Colonial Countries and Peoples Verbatim Record of the Sixteenth Meeting*. A/AC.109/PV.17

———. *Verbatim Record of the 1078th Meeting of the Special Committee on the Situation with Regard to the Implementation of the declaration on the Granting of Independence to Colonial Countries and Peoples.* A/AC.109/PV.1078.

Verkruyse, Peter A. *Prophet, Pastor, and Patriarch: The Rhetorical Leadership of Alexander Campbell.* Tuscaloosa: University of Alabama Press, 2005.

Walls, Celeste M. "You Ain't Just Whistling Dixie: How Carol Mosley-Braun Used Rhetorical Status to Change Jesse Helm's Tune." *Western Journal of Communication* 68 (2004): 343–64.

Walters, Ronald G. *American Reformers: 1815–1860.* Rev. ed. New York: Hill and Wang, 1997.

Wasson, W. W. *James A. Garfield: His Religion and Education.* Nashville: Tennessee Book Co., 1952.

Weaver, Richard M. "Language Is Sermonic." In *Language Is Sermonic: Richard M. Weaver on the Nature of Rhetoric,* edited by Richard L. Johnessen, Rennard Strickland, and Ralph T. Eubanks. Baton Rouge: Louisiana State University Press, 1970, 202–25.

Weiss, Ruth. *Sir Garfield Todd and the Making of Zimbabwe.* London: British Academic Press, 1999.

Welensky, Sir Roy. *Welensky's 4000 Days: The Life and Death of the Federation of Rhodesia and Nyasaland.* London: Collins, 1964.

West, Cornel. *Democracy Matters: Winning the Fight against Imperialism.* New York: Penguin, 2004.

———. *Prophetic Fragments: Illuminations of the Crisis in American Religion and Culture.* Grand Rapids: Eerdmans, 1988.

West, Michael O. "Ndabaningi Sithole, Garfield Todd and the Dadaya School Strike of 1947." *Journal of Southern African Studies* 18 (1992): 297–316.

West, Robert Frederick. *Alexander Campbell and Natural Religion.* New Haven: Yale University Press, 1948.

Wood, J. R. T. *The Welensky Papers: A History of the Federation of Rhodesia and Nyasaland.* Durban: Graham, 1983.

Yearbook of the United Nations 1962. New York: Columbia University Press, 1964.

Newspapers and Journals

African Daily News (Harare, Zimbabwe)
African Weekly (Harare, Zimbabwe)
Australian Christian

Bantu Mirror (Bulawayo, Zimbabwe)
Central African Examiner
Christian Baptist
Christian-Evangelist
Christian Standard
Chronicle (Bulawayo, Zimbabwe)
East Africa and Rhodesia (London)
Guardian (Manchester, England)
Millennial Harbinger
The New York Times
New Zealand Christian
Press (Christchurch, New Zealand)
Rhodesia Herald (Harare, Zimbabwe)
Southern African Sentinel
Telegram (St. John, New Foundland)
Time
UN Chronicle
World Call

Archival Materials

Ranger, Terrance. Papers. Rhodes House. Bodleian Library. Oxford University.
Todd, R. S. Garfield. Biographical file. Disciples of Christ Historical Society. Nashville.
———. Papers. AC 91-70. Disciples of Christ Historical Society. Nashville.
———. Papers. Bulawayo, Zimbabwe.
Welensky, Sir Roy. Papers. Rhodes House. Bodleian Library. Oxford University.

INDEX

Ackers, Peter, 26, 351n34, 352n32
Aderman, E. P., 29
African Daily News, 60, 66
African National Congress (ANC), 61, 63–64, 72, 106, 238, 241–42, 248, 298
African nationalists, African nationalism, 78, 80–81, 87, 91, 94, 106, 198, 200, 207, 217, 282–83, 285, 286, 295, 299, 328
African Parade, 65
African Teachers' Association of Southern Rhodesia, 49
African Weekly, 48, 65
Afrikaners, 83, 256
Ainslie, Peter, 145
American Revolution, 77
Apartheid, 83, 85, 332
Aristotle, 9, 12, 102
Athenaeum Hall, 72
Atlantic Charter, 36
Australian Churches of Christ, 171

Baconianism, 20, 27–28, 29, 30
Banda, Hastings, 72
baptism, 156
BBC, 57
Benson, Thomas, 56, 358n89
Berryhill, Carisse M., 351n28
Bethany College, 20
Billington, Louis, 352n6
Bitzer Lloyd, 22, 351n35
Black, Edwin, 48, 356n47

Blair, Tony, 101
Blake, Robert, 65, 355n25, 355n36, 357n87, 357n90, 360nn128–30, 361n142, 361nn147–48
Blowers, Paul, 350n12
Booth, Wayne, 8, 348n23
Bowman, Larry, 81, 356n48, 364n70, 364n81
Boynton, Graham, 347n11, 352nn1–4, 361n3
Brandt, Willy, 330
Bread for the World Fund, 331
Britain-Zimbabwe Society, 117
British Churches of Christ, 21–22, 26–27, 136; democratic *ethos*, 22
British empiricists, 77
Bruggemann, Walter, 86
Bulawayo, 30, 75, 336
Burke, Kenneth, 9, 12, 91, 94, 97, 99, 365nn13–16
Buttrick, David, 366n14
Buttrick, George, 348n33

Calvert, Anthony, 369n10
Campbell, Alexander, 16, 27–28, 149; *Christian System*, 27–28; democratic spirit, 16–24; and universal suffrage, 18; support for universal education, 19; support for the Bill of Rights, 18
Campbell, George, 22, 351n36
Campbell, Karlyn Kohrs, 105, 367n20

382 INDEX

Campbell, Thomas, 16, 149–50
Carrington, Lord, 101
Carter, Jimmy, 86, 293
Casey, Michael W., 117, 347n9, 348n34, 349n3, 350n21, 350n28, 351n28, 351n31, 351nn38–39, 352n6, 352n16
Central Africa Party (CAP), 74, 76, 328, 338
Central African Federation, 3, 55, 62, 73, 92, 94, 198–216, 242, 245–47, 258
Central Intelligence Organization (Southern Rhodesia), 69
Chainaiwa, David, 347n1, 353n29, 356n48
Christ, 83, 139–40, 146–48, 150, 152–55, 157–59, 163, 166–67, 174–77, 287, 290
Cicero, 9–10, 117, 348n28
Civil Rights Movement, 78
civilization, 52–54, 141, 169, 181, 198, 204, 209
Clutton-Brock, Guy, 241–42
colonialism, 169, 248, 253
Communism, 143, 173, 225
community, 114–15
Confederate Party, 56
Conley, Thomas, 8, 348n27
Coughlin, Sir Charles, 110, 229, 327, 340
Craddock, Fred, 104, 366n12, 366n14
Criminal Investigation Department, 110, 327

Dadaya Mission, 3, 25, 31–7, 86, 110–11, 157, 161–65
Daily Rand Mail, 87, 103, 318
Daily Telegraph, 66
Danziger, Max, 41, 354n9

Darsey, James, 6, 7, 70, 74, 77, 81, 86, 99, 117, 348n18, 348n21, 361nn4–6, 361n8, 361nn10–12, 362n31, 363nn49–50, 364n69, 364nn89–90, 365n96
Daughton, Suzzanne, 367n32
Davies, Harry H., 41
de Tocqueville, Alexis, 16, 349n7
debate, 30
Declaration of Independence, 77
Dees, Diane, 356n41
DeGroot, Alfred T., 352n9
democracy and reason, 79
Diefenbaker, John, 4, 15, 58
Disciples of Christ, 136, 144, 149–50, 156; democratic *ethos*, 11, 13, 15–24, 33, 37, 105; education, 16, 34; impulse to reform society, 16; optimistic and pragmatic outlook, 20; priesthood of all believers, 16–7, 33–34, 81–82; reasonable approach to religion, 20, 27–28; right of individual to think for oneself, 16–17; role of rhetoric, 16
Dominion Party, 60
Dulles, John Foster, 4, 58

East Africa and Rhodesia, 66
egalitarianism, 77
Egbert, James, 350n13
Elizabeth II (queen), 1, 101, 109, 123, 327, 346
elocution, 29
Emerson, Ralph Waldo, 10, 120
Eminhizer, Earl Eugene, 351n32
enactment, 12
ethics, 146

faculty psychology, 22
Field, Winston, 82, 242
Fife, Robert O., 351n32

INDEX

Fisher, Walter, 12, 109, 113–15, 119, 367n31, 367n40, 367n42, 367n44, 368nn50–51
Foot, Hugh, 91, 339
Foster, Douglas, 349n3, 350n12, 351n31
Franklin, Benjamin, 333
Friedly, Robert, 349n2

Gadamer, Hans-Georg, 114
Gann, L. H., 354n5, 354nn8–9, 355n24, 355n32
Garfield, James A., 3, 15, 21, 27, 117, 349n3
Garrison, Winfred E., 352n9
Gelfand, M., 354n5, 354nn8–9, 355n24, 355n32
Ghana, 107
Ghoko, 43
Glen Leith Theological College, 4, 26, 28
Gonkudzingwa, 110, 327–28
Good Samaritan, 139–40
Graham, Billy, 153
Gray, James, 369n10
Great Britain, 79, 91, 97–98, 112
Greek democratic tradition, 6, 119
Greenfield, Julian, 64
Gregory the Great, 152
Gresham, Perry, 24

Habermas, Jürgen 114
Haddon, A. L., 4, 28, 146, 352n9, 352nn19–20
Hadfield, F. L., 31, 40
Hallencreutz, Carl F., 348n13
Hancock, Ian, 67, 227, 347n1, 356n48, 360n116, 360n122, 361n154, 369n154, 369n20, 369nn22–23
Harare (Salisbury), 72, 75, 80, 96
Harrell, David E. Jr., 351n29

Hatch, Nathan, 16, 350n13
Hayden, E. V., 171
Hebrew prophets, 70, 77, 117
Heroes' Acre, 110–11, 328, 340
Hitler, 42
Hokonui ranch, 85, 293, 346, 337
Hokonui Todd, 347n1, 353n29, 353n38, 356n48, 358n47, 364n92, 368n7
Holderness, Hardwicke, 2, 49, 62, 101, 227, 347n6, 357n53, 360n116, 369n18, 369n21, 369nn24–26
Holt, Basil, 136, 145
Home, Lord Alec Douglas, 76, 85, 260, 266, 294, 308–9, 329, 338
homiletics, 29
Horn, Pauline, 356nn40–41
Hudson, Miles, 2, 347n4
Huggins, Godfrey, 3, 41, 43–45, 47, 49, 55, 93, 96, 198–99, 208, 231–32, 265–66, 307, 344
Hyde, Michael, 120, 367nn2–3

Industrial and Commercial Union (ICU), 110
Interracial Association of Southern Rhodesia, 60, 217
Invercargill, 127
Invercargill Church of Christ, 27
Iona Community, 145
Isocrates, 8, 9, 117, 120, 348n28

Jackson, Thomas, 26
Jacksonian America, 16
Jacobs, Lorraine, 359n97
Jacobs, Lyndsay, 351n5, 352n8, 352n10, 359n97
James, William, 77
Jamieson, Kathleen, 104–5, 366n13, 367n20
Jardine, George, 22

Jefferson, Thomas, 77, 249
Jeffersonian Republicanism, 78
Jevon, William Stanley, 29
Jewish prophetic tradition, 6, 7
Joelson, F. S., 66
Johannesburg, 43, 136, 318

Kaunda, Kenneth, 80, 83
Kennedy Edward, 4
Kennedy, George, 348n29, 366n3
Kennedy, John, 332
kenosis, 110
King, Martin Luther Jr., 119
Kuypers, Jim, 8, 348n24

Laidlaw, Chris, 70
Lakoff, George, 10
Lancaster House accords, 108, 323, 348
Lord's Supper, 156
Lardner Burke, Desmond, 109, 337
Leeman, Richard, 367n32
Leff, Michael, 365n16
Lenniston, Margaret, 356nn40–41
Lewis, Pauline, 356nn40–41
Lindley, D. Ray, 350n17
Livingstone, David, 153
Lloyd-George, David, 21
Lobengula, King, 106, 110, 326
Logan, Shirley, 367n32
logic, 29
London Times, 66
Long, Thomas, 104, 366n11
Lunger, Harold L., 350n16, 350nn18–20, 350nn23–24

MacLeod, George, 145
Malawi (Nyasaland), 72, 92, 136, 214, 216, 257
Manchester Guardian, 66
Maori, 25

Maripe, K. T. T., 66
Mashoko, 343
Masire Q. K. J., 333
McLuhan, Marshall, 104, 366nn15–16
Medhurst, Martin J., 8, 348n25, 354nn3–4, 355n38
memory, 114–15
Mondale, Walter, 86, 294, 311
Moorhouse, William, 349n8
Morrison, John, 350n24, 350n26
Mount, Graeme, 347n9, 367n41
Movement for Democratic Change (MDC), 39
Mugabe, Robert, 37, 39, 71, 87, 89, 102, 108–9, 111–13, 121, 319, 332, 346
Mulgan, R. G., 102
Mungazi, Dickson, 2, 347n1n2
Muzorewa, Abel, 37, 320–23

Nairobi, 153
narrative coherence, 113, 115
narrative fidelity, 113–15
narrative paradigm, 12, 119
National Democratic Party (NDP), 75–6, 79, 92–93
Nazism, 42–43
Ndhlovu (Ndlovu), Masotsha, 110–11, 113, 324, 326–28, 336, 339–40
Nelson, Robert, 306
New Africa Party, 76
New Statesman, 66
New York City, 91
New York Times, The, 50, 322
New Zealand Christian, 26, 127
New Zealand Churches of Christ, 2–3, 22, 25–27, 30–31, 41–42, 44, 77, 118, 127, 136, 150, 324, 352n5

Nkiwane, Solomon, 39, 354nn1–2
Nkomo, Joshua, 4, 37, 62–63, 69, 76, 80–81, 83, 91–93, 106, 111–13, 238, 241, 260–62, 265–67, 269, 274, 276–79, 328, 337–41, 365n10
Nkrumah, Kwane, 107, 253, 326, 338
Nyandoro, George, 63, 238, 241–42
Nyathi, Pathisa, 369n35
Nyerere, Julius, 248, 286

O'Grady, Ron, 352n7
Oamaru, 30, 127
Olbricht, Thomas, 350n24
Ong, Walter, 366n15
Osborn, S. H., 29
Otago University, 102, 312

paideia, 7–8, 23–24, 120
parrhesia, 6, 9–10, 98
Paul, 78, 147, 152, 174
Paul VI (pope), 1
Pearce Commission, 85
Pearce, Lord, 85, 295, 309
Pemberton, John, 343
Perelman, Chaim, 95, 365n17
perspective by incongruity, 91, 94–98, 119
Peter Ainsley Memorial Lecture, 145
phronesis (practical wisdom), 12–13, 115
Pilate, 83
Plato, 6, 8–9
Postman, Neil, 104, 366n15
preaching, 22
preaching, narrative, 104
presidential rhetoric, 3, 56–59, 118
prophetic speech, 98–99
Prosser, Hugh, 15
Protestant Central Agency for Development Aid, 331
Pruett, Dennis, 343

Quintilian, 10

racism, 34, 42–43, 49, 72–73, 78, 82–83, 94, 121, 315
Ramphal, Shrideth, 323
Ranger, Terrance, 101, 110, 117, 327, 336, 349n5, 362n35, 362n38, 363n33, 366n1, 368n1, 368n6, 369n35
Reid, Thomas, 22
Restoration Movement, 150
restoration of New Testament Christianity (primitive Christianity), 17, 28, 105, 145–46, 154–5
rhetoric, 8; builds democracy 8, 13, 22–24; civic tradition 8, 9, 117, 120; epideictic rhetoric, 102–3; improves civic life 8; narrative rhetoric 12; prophetic rhetorical tradition 9, 119; reasonable rhetoric 28–30; Scottish rhetoric 22–23; as street smarts 10
rhetorical presidency, 3
Rhodes, Cecil, 60, 96
Rhodesia Herald, 45, 60, 74
Rhodesia National Affairs Association, 49
Rhodesian Front, 73, 82, 85, 320
Richards, I. A., 74
Richardson, Robert, 350n11
Rigg, John, *Elocution and Public Speaking (lessons in)*, 29–30, 353nn22–27
Ringenberg, William C., 349n3
Ritter, Kurt, 355n38
Robertson, Olive, 369n17
Robinson, William, 154, 368n10
Rollman, Hans, 348n1, 368nn4–5
Ross, Emory, 3, 79
Rosteck, Thomas, 365n16
Rushford, Jerry, 349n3

sacraments, 156

386

INDEX

Samkange, Stanlake, 60, 328
Sankange, Sketchly, 75
Savage, Murray, 31, 352n7, 352nn19–20, 353nn31–33, 353n38, 353n47, 368n2
Schlesinger, Arthur Jr., 16, 349n8, 350nn9–10, 350n14, 350n22
Schweitzer, Albert, 3
Scottish Common Sense Philosophy, 20, 27–30, 77
Shabani, 45
Sheriff, John, 30–1
Sithole, Ndabinigi, 35–37, 62, 91, 106, 164, 306, 322, 339; *African Nationalism*, 26, 328
Smith, Ian, 1, 7, 36, 59–60, 65, 71, 82–83, 85–86, 98, 105, 107, 109–10, 113, 295–96, 300–1, 303–4, 319, 321–22, 329, 343, 361n141
Smith, Thomas L., 350n24
Smith-Home agreement, 107, 329
Socrates, 6
Solomon, Martha, 365n16
sophists, 6
South Africa, 84, 136, 255–56, 318, 332–33
South Africans, 83
Southern Africa Development Coordination Conference, 330, 333–34
Southern African Sentinel, 137
Southern Rhodesia Debates of the Legislative Assembly, 46, 123
Southern Rhodesia Missionary Conference, 34, 42
Southern Rhodesia Trade Union Congress, 66
Spectator, 66
St. Francis of Assisi, 153
St. Martin-in-the-Fields, 101, 117
Stark, Glen, 41
Steed, Christopher, 60, 359n113

Stiff, Peter, 361nn1–2
Stroop, George, 14–5, 367n46, 368nn47–49
Subcommittee on Africa of the Committee on International Relations in the House of Representatives, 86
Sumbwanyame, Zeko, 33
Summers, Carol, 52, 354n9, 357nn67–69
Sunday Mail, 3, 322
Sundkler, Bengt, 359n113

Takavarisha, William, 76
Tanzania, 248
Thayer, William, 349n4
theology, postliberal, 104
Thompson, David M., 351n34, 352n6
Thomson, Lord, 122
Time, 82
Todd, Edith (Garfield's mother), 15
Todd, Edith (Garfield's sister), 41
Todd, Garfield: and African suffrage, 49–50, 52–53, 60, 62; African support for Todd, 65–67; appealed to British tradition, 51; birth, 15; Christian political philosophy, 50–51, 53–54; as Christ persona, 66, 76, 79, 106–8; and democratic *ethos*, 33, 35, 81, 121; as democratic missionary, 11, 25, 31–37; as democratic politician, 11, 48; democracy, 84; denied visa by South Africa, 87; detention, 85, 109, 293–95, 308, 311; and education, 32, 55, 184–86, 197–99; enactment, use of, 109–10; *ethos*, 7, 11, 65–67, 79–80, 106, 110, 119, 120; ghostwriting, 46–47; honorary doctorates 312–18; identification with Africans, 80–81; as

impious evangelist, 94–98; liberalism, 59–63; as MP, 49; as Moses persona, 66, 69, 87–88, 118; as narrator, 109–10; 1955 speaking tour, 15, 57–59; as noble rhetor, 103; ouster as prime minister, 64–67, 71; place of reason, 11, 28–29, 31–32, 46–48, 64, 67, 88, 115, 120, 248; as politician, 6; preacher for democracy, 12, 101–15, 120; press coverage, 48, 57–59; as prime minister, 39, 49, 55–67; prophet, 6, 11, 12, 115, 118–19; prophetic call, 75–76, 112, 121, 165; prophetic *ethos*, 70–71, 74–75, 82, 88, 112, 119–20; prophetic *logos*, 70–71, 83, 87–88, 119; prophetic optimism, 108; prophetic *pathos*, 70–71, 74, 80, 88, 119; prophetic rhetoric, 108; race relations, 54, 58; rhetorical leadership, 56–59; sacred and secular united, 35; as senator of Zimbabwe, 87; speeches banned, 84–85; support for Africans, 47–48, 56, 58, 61; support for economic development, 54, 183–97; stripped of citizenship, 122; training in public speaking, 29–30; University of Rhodesia, 107, 345; use of narrative, 103–15, 324–25

Todd's speeches: Africa Trades Union Congress speech (1962), 80; "After Independence, What? Political Imperatives," Wellesley College speech (1960), 78–79, 247–60; "Christian Unity Christ's Prayer" (1955), 145–56, "Can Christianity Survive in Africa?" (1963), 81, 282–87; "The Church Knows No Boundaries," Edinburgh World Convention speech (1960), 165–71; Conference Sermon (1950), 127–36; Congress address (1956), 208–26; First Campaign speech (1946), 45, 181–86; "Danger! Men Thinking," First Feetham Lecture (1964), 82–83, 286–93; Franchise speech (1957), 217–26; Immorality debate speech (1957), 227–38; International Center, Indianapolis, Indiana, speech (1977), 305–12; Interracial Association speech (1957), 60, 217; Letter to Lord Home (1960), 76, 260–62; Maiden speech (1946), 46–48, 186–98; "My World Its Need," Adelaide World Convention speech (1970), 171–77; 1962 sermon at Harare, 80; 1962 UN speech, 80, 91–99, 119, 262–81, 339; 1964 UN speech, 82–83, 98; 1967 speech at Sinoia (1967), 85; 1977 UN speech, 86, 293–315; Nkomo Celebration speech (1989), 103, 106, 108–9,111–14, 336–41; "Our Timeless Missionary Mandate," Toronto World Convention speech (1955), 58, 156–65; "Reflections on Fifty-Four Years of Service," Auckland World Convention speech (1988), 103, 107, 109, 343–46; "Reply to the Toast 'Southern Rhodesia'" (1957), 63, 238–42; speech defending premiership (1958), 64; speech on Federation (1952), 198–208; speech at Harare (1989), 87; "The Speech that Says It All—In Silence," Second Feetham lecture (1980), 84, 87, 103, 105, 318–24; speeches at Athenaeum Hall (1959), 72–74, 245; Statement against the 'colour bar' (1959), 245–47; Tübingen Festival speech (1983), 103, 106, 108, 110–11, 324–36; "Unfinished Task of Christian Missions in Southern Africa" (1954) 136–45; University of Otago graduation speech (1979), 102–3, 312–18

Todd, Grace, 3–4, 30–31, 34, 35, 79, 109, 121, 337, 343–46, 349n5; developed Dadaya Mission curriculum, 5, 32, 41

Todd, Judith, 4, 85, 107, 117, 137, 345

Todd, Thomas, 15, 27

Treaty of Waitangi, 25

Tredgold, Sir Robert (Federal chief justice), 97, 217, 279

Tyler, Alice Felt, 351n29

UN General Assembly, 93

UN Special Committee on Colonialism, 93

Unilateral Declaration of Independence (UDI), 85, 98, 107, 294, 308, 315, 321, 329

United Federal Party, 72

United Independence Party, 97

United Party, 43–44

United Rhodesia Party, 55, 61, 208, 210–11, 214, 216, 227

United States, 79, 98

unity, Christian, 104–5, 145, 148–49, 154, 159

University of the Witwatersrand, 43, 87, 103, 286, 318

Vance, Cyrus, 86, 294

Verkruyse, Peter, 24, 351n40

Verwoerd, Hendrik, 332

Victoria, Queen, 117

Wallis, James, 26

Walls, Celeste, 367n32

Walters, Ronald G., 351n29

Wasson, W.W., 349n3

Weaver, Richard, 102–3, 366n9

Weiss, Ruth, 2, 57, 91, 347n1n2, 352n11, 353n28, 353n36, 353n40, 354n18, 355nn33–35, 355n37, 357nn110–11, 358n87, 358n95, 359nn106–7, 360nn133–34, 360n137, 361n3, 362n13, 362n20, 362n35, 363n42, 364n84, 364n93, 365n2, 365n12, 368n1, 369n19, 369n22

Welensky, Roy, 92, 94, 209, 215–17

Wellesley College, 248

West, Cornel, 5–7, 9–10, 74–75, 78, 81, 98–99, 102, 114, 119, 348nn14–17, 348nn19–20, 348n22, 348nn30–32, 351n39, 362n31, 363nn49–50, 364n69, 365nn22–23, 366n2, 367n45

West, Michael, 347n1, 354n52, 354nn57–58

West, Robert Frederick, 17, 350n14

Whigs, 77

white liberals, 49

white Rhodesians, 81, 83, 94, 97, 98, 115, 338

Wood, J. R. T., 362n35, 363n41

Woodhall, Chester, 2

World Convention of Churches of Christ, 57, 156, 165, 171, 343

World Council of Churches, 154, 331

Wright, John Inglis, 30

Young, Andrew, 86, 293

Zambia (Northern Rhodesia), 83, 92, 98, 257

ZANU (PF), 39, 89, 122
ZANU, 112
ZAPU, 76, 93, 112–13

Zimbabwe African National Union (ZANU), 36, 112
Zimbabwe Christian Council, 5